Communicating
With QuarkXPress

Integrating Principles of Design
and Techniques of Layout

Claudia Cuddy

Rowan University

KENDALL/HUNT PUBLISHING COMPANY
4050 Westmark Drive   Dubuque, Iowa 52002

Developmental Editor: *Billee Jo Hefel*
Senior Prepress Editor: *Angela Shaffer*
Literary Editor: *Sandy Haney*
Copyeditor: *Cristin Kastner*
Page Layout and Design: *Claudia Cuddy*
Front Cover Design: *Alexis Andriano*
Back Cover Design and Copy: *Chris Lukach*
Icons and Art Consultant: *Kari Palmieri*
Clipart Designers for CD: *Larry Gilbert, Sonny Johnson, Regina Marmon, Kari Palmieri*
Quest Terms Editor: *Anya Cronin*; Assistant: *Andrea Pujat*
Technical Production Consultant: *Adam Szyfman*
Permissions Editor: *Renae Heacock*
Permissions Coordinator: *Terri Walsh*
Publisher Representative: *Greg DeRosa*
Proofreaders: *Stephanie Zultanky, Chris Lukach, Sandy Haney, Diane Caldwell,*
       Kathryn Quigley, Katie Brownlow, Shannon Soldano

Communicating with QuarkXPress

QuarkXPress is a registered trademark of Quark, Inc.
Adobe Illustrator and Adobe Photoshop are trademarks of Adobe Systems Incorporated.
Clipart used from Art Explosion, Nova Development Corporation, Calabasas, CA; DeskGallery Image Catalog
by Zedcor, Inc. (ArtToday.com, Inc.); and Microsoft Office, Microsoft Corporation.
Microsoft Word and PowerPoint are registered trademarks of Microsoft Corporation.
SnapZPro is a registered trademark of Ambrosia Software, Inc.
ProScale is a registered trademark of Gluon, Inc.
Any other product and company names mentioned may be the trademarks of their respective owners.

Colophon

Body type: 10.5/13.5 New Century Schoolbook
Directions: 10/13 New Century Schoolbook
Heads: 20-point Franklin Gothic Heavy
Subheads: 15-point Franklin Gothic Condensed
Captions: 9/11 ITC Stone Sans, Stone Sans Bold
Sidebars: 9.5/14 ITC Stone Sans
Columns: widths – 11p, 29p6

Layout by author on PowerMac G4
in QuarkXPress 5.0.
Scans on Microtek ScanMaker 5900 with
ScanWizard.
Photos and art adjusted in Photoshop.
SnapZPro used for screen captures.
ProScale by Gluon used for scaling
sample publications.

086.22544
C964

To

my father,
who taught me to value perfection;

my mother,
who thinks I'm perfect; and

my husband,
who knows I'm not and loves me anyway.

Contents

Contents

Preface

If there's a book you really want to read but it hasn't been written yet, then you must write it.

Toni Morrison (author)

When I learned last year that the book my students normally use would not be reprinted in time for my September classes, I panicked. Then I realized the time had come: I could write the book that hadn't been written yet — one that combined design, page layout, editorial work and QuarkXPress.

The know-how and how-to

No matter what your QuarkXPress skill level is, this book should give you new insights and skills. I have discovered that it is best to show students how to do something basic using basic skills, and then as they are capable and willing, show them more advanced ways to move ahead.

By the end of this book, students will understand the underlying principles governing the publication field and know how (and why) to follow these guidelines in their own work. They will be confident in producing professional-level publications on their own, using QuarkXPress or transferring those skills to another layout program.

Communicating my classroom experience

My years of teaching created a course that could not be found in any one book — a course where students, regardless of experience or knowledge in any of the communication fields, could learn the basics well enough to find a job in the field. This book is that course in writing. It is my hope that my years of experience in professional publications and as a professor of this subject will help you in *Communicating with QuarkXPress*, whether you use my book as a teacher or student, experienced or inexperienced.

The first edition

Ivan Turgenev said, "If we wait for the moment when everything, absolutely everything, is ready, we shall never begin." In this complex and ever-changing world of publication layout, a book can never truly be finished. Thus, I have written this book knowing that a second edition will follow. I ask that as you read this book, please send me comments, suggestions or ideas for the next edition via my Web site, **www.claudiacuddy.com**. *Have a quintessential quest!*

Claudia M Cuddy

About the author

Claudia Cuddy has worked in publications since she was 12, when she put together her first newspaper for her sixth grade class, using a manual typewriter and paste — before computers or photocopy machines. As managing editor of nursing publications for 23 years, she took the journals and books from hand pasteup to layout on QuarkXPress. Her passion for page layout and editing carried over to her collegiate teaching, where she delights in passing on her tricks of the trade to future Quark gurus.

For specifics, check out **www.claudiacuddy.com**

Thanks

This is my first authored book. Please indulge me this page of thank-yous!

Thanks...

to all my students over the years for your suggestions, enthusiasm, support, camaraderie and spirit. This book has been written for you and because of you.

To live and work daily with an "attitude of gratitude" turns a job into a joyful adventure — one that led to this book. Many people shared that adventure with me. My heartfelt appreciation goes to:

- Kelley Desmond Lieberman, Amy Bogdanoff, Blake Taylor, Paul Petrella and Buck Williams for introducing me to the Mac and QuarkXPress.

- Karla Guido, who first suggested putting our course into a book, and Judy Harch who shared her own first-time book publishing wisdom with me.

- John Chard, Len Stevens, Don Bagin and Anthony Jannetti, who gave me many communication and publication experiences. This book is the culmination of all those experiences.

- Jean Hernandez, Jack Bryant, Darin Peters and Todd Lockhart for sharing their love of art and lending technical support over the years.

- Kathleen Stevens for recruiting me and Toni Libro for believing in me.

- Rowan President Donald Farish for his vision and support, Carl Hausman for his wise advice, Tom Kloskey for his Mac enthusiasm, Larry Litwin for his camaraderie, Diane Ferraina, Esther Mummert and Janice Rowan for their encouragement, George Reinfeld and Phil Sidotti for their continual approbation, Wynn Norman for naming the book, Sparky Beschen for keeping the book at her desk for people to borrow, Diane Penrod for late-night mentoring e-mails, Tony Fulginiti for turning over *PRomo* to me, Suzanne FitzGerald and Sue Verrico for cheering me on and Kathryn Quigley for making me laugh.

- Morgan Johnson, Kamali Brooks, Dan Reigel, Craig Stratton, Michele Gordemer, Michelle Perez, Nicole Patzer, Jen Roycroft, Joe Checkler, Paul Dice, Kim Tweed, Brian Hunter, Mark Marmur, Dan O'Neill, Zachary Bush, Paul Terruso, Jan Powers, Maureen Reilly, Joe Ogden, Sándra Lee Burlile, Jackie Devine, Gary Baker, Jacob Farbman, Kerry Caspare, Brian Salvatore, Courtney Eitel, Yolanda Colón, Diane Stafford and Tara Bennett for helping me see through students' eyes.

- Diane Caldwell for sharing numerous teaching techniques.

- Chris Lukach for his unwavering support and honesty along with his editing, writing and design expertise.

- Stephanie Zultanky for her astute proofreading and design "eye" and for reminding me how to stay playful at work.

- Cristin Kastner for being a perspicacious editor, sharing her fascination with words, crusading on my behalf and bailing me out of last-minute situations.

- Kari Palmieri for her creative artwork throughout the book, Alexis Andriano for the cover design and Jen Riggio for her "apple-bet" and last-minute help.

- Larry Gilbert, Regina Marmon and Sonny Johnson for their art expertise and Adam Szyfman for his computer expertise.

- Anya Cronin and Andrea Pujat for their word-smithing on the Quest Terms.

- Laura Albert and Carol DeSimine for testing the book in their classes.

- Terri Walsh, who enthusiastically pitched in at the end to bring it all together.

- Sandy Haney, my daughter, for her remarkable rewriting, editing, and overall support, and Jason Haney, the best son-in-law, for his Web site expertise.

- John, my son, who gave me his opinions from a college student's viewpoint.

- Fred, my husband, who put up with cereal for dinner, piles of papers and messy rooms for a very, very long time.

- Finally and foremost, the One who makes all things possible, the source of my ability, joy, peace and love.

Contributors

The author thanks all those who contributed their publications, photos or writing. May your work serve as an inspiration to other students who start their Quark quest.

Contributors

Page

211. Fig. 16-4. Used with permission from College of Communication, Rowan University, Glassboro, NJ

211. Fig. 16-5. Reprinted from *Profiles and Perspectives*, 2003, Vol. 8, No. 1, with permission of the publisher, Anthony J. Jannetti, Inc., East Holly Avenue Box 56, Pitman, NJ 08071-0056. Phone 856-256-2300

211. Fig. 16-5. Used with permission from *Home Connections*, Fred Hutchinson Plumbing, Heating, Cooling, Cherry Hill, NJ

212. Fig. 16-6. Used with permission from *Communication Briefings,* copyright 2003 by Briefings Publishing Group, 1101 King Street, Suite 110, Alexandria, VA 22314, Phone 800-722-9221, www.combriefings.com

212. Fig. 16-6. Used with permission from *The Editorial Eye*, copyright 2003 by EEI Press, a division of EEI Communications, 66 Canal Center Plaza, Suite 200, Alexandria, VA 22314-5507, 703-683-0683, www.eeicommunications.com/eye/

212. Fig. 16-6. Used with permission from Jay Nelson, *Design Tools Monthly*. 400 Kiowa, Suite 100, Boulder, CO 80303, 303-543-8400, www.design-tools.com

213. Fig. 16-7. Used with permission from *PRomo*, Rowan University Public Relations Student Society of America

213. Fig. 16-7. Used with permission from *NAON News*, copyright 2002 by National Association of Ortho-paedic Nurses, 401 North Michigan Ave., Suite 2400, Chicago, IL 60611

213. Fig. 16-8. Used with permission from *Touch of Class,* Morgan Johnson, Editor

213. Fig. 16-8. Courtesy of Andrew Garguilo, Sr.

214. Fig. 16-9. Used with permission from Public Interest GRFX, 1334 Walnut St., 6th Fl., Phila.,PA 19107

218. Fig. 16-12. Used with permission from *PRomo*, Rowan University Public Relations Student Society of America

Page

218. Fig. 16-13. Reprinted from *Profiles and Perspectives*, 2003, Vol. 8, No. 1, with permission of the publisher, Anthony J. Jannetti, Inc., East Holly Avenue Box 56, Pitman, NJ 08071-0056. Phone 856-256-2300

219. Fig. 16-14. Used with permission from East Greenwich Township Board of Education, Mickleton, NJ

220. Fig. 16-15. Used with permission from National Schools Public Relations Association, 15948 Derwood Road, Rockville, MD 20855

220. Fig. 16-16. Used with permission from *ITECH News*, Eileen Stutzbach, Instructional Technology Specialist, Rowan University, Glassboro, NJ

220. Fig. 16-17. Used with permission from *NAON News*, copyright 2002 by National Association of Orthopaedic Nurses, 401 North Michigan Avenue, Suite 2400, Chicago, IL 60611

220. Fig. 16-18. Used with permission from Logan Township Board of Education, 10 School Lane, Swedesboro, NJ 08059

220. Fig. 16-19. Artwork by Elaine Finn

235. *Quark Quandary* breakdown idea by Paul Dice

252. Fig. 16-21. Thomas Quinn

255. Fig. 17-2. Jessica Haviland

256. Fig. 17-3. Jean Nevius

257. Fig. 17-4. Stephanie Zultanky & Jamie Schron

258. Fig. 17-5. Kari Palmieri

266. Fig. 17-9. Michelle Ulrich

267. Fig. 17-10. Daniel Reigel

295-296. Clipart by Larry Gilbert.

297-298. Clipart by Regina Marmon.

299-302. Clipart by Sonny Johnson.

303. Clipart by Kari Palmieri.

All figures not listed on these two pages originated from the author.

Thanks to Jay Nelson (editor) for contributing 12 issues of *Design Tools Monthly* newsletter for our accompanying CD. **www.design-tools.com**

How to use this book

Chapters are divided into various sections with headings, sometimes with symbols. In addition, symbols designate sidebar information (information runnning down the left side of the page).

Chapter sections

On title page of each chapter

 Quest Objectives   objectives of chapter

 Quest Skills   new skills you will learn in this chapter

 Quest Terms   vocabulary words to learn

At end of each chapter

 Quick Quiz   questions to highlight some main points of the chapter

 Out of the Quandary   assignments to do outside of class — not usually on the computer

 Quantum Leap   something for the more advanced or extremely interested student

 Quark Quest   specific instructions for working through an activity in QuarkXPress

Sidebar icons

 Quicktip   a tip about QuarkXPress that will make your life easier

 Qool Fact   a piece of information that I'm dying to tell you

CD An accompanying CD contains assignments, templates, clipart and a year's worth of *Design Tools Monthly* newsletter (courtesy of Jay Nelson, Editor).

Web The author's Web site provides additional instructional material, writing and editing tips, more Quark tips and many other features. Check it from time to time: **www.claudiacuddy.com**

Mechanics of classroom

Be prepared

Being prepared is one of the most important factors for success in this course. Come in, sit down, get your computer up and running and put in your disk. Open QuarkXPress. Of course you will have done the required reading and have your sketch, if applicable, in front of you.

Restart

If the computer is on when you arrive, restart it. Click on the desktop and then go to the top menu bar (**Special → Restart**) [**Windows: Start → Shutdown→ Restart**]. This gives you a fresh start each class. Put your disk in and open up QuarkXPress as per the instructor's directions. See Chapter 3 to learn how to name a disk.

Frozen computer

A common problem of malfunctioning is the power cord coming out of the monitor or computer. When it seems as if your computer or mouse is frozen, or if the monitor is black, first check all the cords. If that didn't solve the problem, try restarting (**Special → Restart**) [**Windows: Start → Shutdown→ Restart**].

Your disk doesn't show up

Restart the computer and most likely the disk will appear (**Special → Restart**) [**Windows: Start → Shutdown→ Restart**].

Screen says "File not found"

Restart the computer and most likely the file will appear (**Special → Restart**) [**Windows: Start → Shutdown→ Restart**]. Or try opening QuarkXPress and then opening your file (**File → Open**).

Put it in perspective

Would you let 6–10 people drive your car each day? Of course not! Just think how much abuse the car would take. But each day, several students use the same computers in a computer lab. You may become frustrated with the mechanical problems of computers in a classroom, but try to be patient.

And finally, the turnoff

When wanting the attention of the whole class, the instructor may tell you to turn off your monitor. This way you are not tempted to play on the Internet while the instructor is demonstrating a technique or giving instructions.

AP Style?

The overall writing style of this book is Associated Press (AP), but you may find occasional deviations from the rules. For example, in figure captions and exercises, I used numerals for measurements or numbers of items: 3 inches, 4 picas, 1 column, 5 columns. Also, I used *copyediting* as one word rather than two (*American Heritage Dictionary*).

An author of a publication has the "style license" to tailor a particular style — however, consistency throughout is the goal.

If you find inconsistencies in the style of this book, please e-mail the author through the Web site: **www.claudiacuddy.com**

What people say about the book

The rough draft of this book was used in classes during the 2002-2003 school year.

I have found *Communicating with QuarkXPress* to be a valuable tool in my classroom. I have referenced the information on layout and design techniques, typography and communication concepts many times in my lessons. I also found that the exercises are informative and adaptable, even if you are using other design software!

Marty Bouchard, Communications Technology Teacher
Washington Township High School, Sewell, NJ

"Come to the edge," he said.
They said, "We are afraid."

"Come to the edge," he said.
They came.
He pushed them.
They flew.

Guillaume Apollinaire
French poet

Since 1994, I have been interested in desktop publishing and exclusively used Microsoft Publisher. Now I realize what QuarkXPress offers. Claudia Cuddy's book has helped me tremendously in converting to QuarkXPress, the program the publishing industry uses in today's business world.

Diane Stafford, Graduate Student

Not only am I Mac-illiterate, but half the time I feel as if I'm computer illiterate as well. However, Professor Cuddy managed to write this textbook without any of the over-complicating jargon, and even I could follow. It's so easy to apply these concepts when they are in plain English. This text turns Quark and page layout from an obstacle into a fun and easy solution.

Jill Karatz, Student

Since I'm not very artistic, I was a little apprehensive about taking a layout class. Cuddy's book guided me through the steps of layout at a beginner's pace. I learned key elements that would help make even the least artistic person a master of design. Now I can create impressive and professional marketing materials at my job.

Jamie Schron, Student

This book, peppered with Professor Cuddy's teaching style, has revolutionized my thinking about publications, public relations and the communications world. Creativity is never hindered. In the words of Professor Cuddy, "If you can think it, Quark can do it. You just have to find out how."

Jaclyn Devine, Student

I see this text as creatively filling the gap that is quickly dissolving between writing — expository, creative and journalistic — and visual communication. As a teacher and writer and a former editor and typographer, I am interested in the practical applications and cultural implications of visual design and its increasing role in communications studies. Cuddy has designed a course — and now created a text — that addresses and synthesizes the conceptual and mechanical aspects of these topics in a way that is accessible to students from various disciplines. In this course, students learn not only how to design a document that "speaks" effectively to an audience and how to work within Quark to create such documents, but how to "read" the visual stimuli that hit them every day.

Laura Albert, Instructor, Publication Layout and Design
Rowan University and Richard Stockton State College

1 Start the Quest

Only the curious will learn and only the resolute over-come the obstacles to learning. The quest quotient has always excited me more than the intelligence quotient.

Eugene S. Wilson
(Dean of Admissions, Amherst College)

Quest Objectives

- Identify which traits you have and which traits you would like to develop to be successful working in QuarkXPress and publications.

- Explain the inverse relationship between interest level and importance of design.

- List the questions you need to ask before you start a project.

Quest Terms

chunks of information   page layout

Cuddy's seesaw   plan

desktop publishers   sketch

graphic design   thumbnails

Who does page layout?

With PCs or Macs for almost every office employee, people are expected to produce publications without formal layout or design experience. From secretary to administrative assistant, from school physical trainers to nurses, employees are asked to design patient education materials, information sheets for customers and in-house newsletters. All of these employees are potential *desktop publishers* — producers of publications from computer programs. The question is, "Will they produce haphazard publications or publications that follow accepted guidelines for layout?"

Is page layout for you?

Although some people would rather work on *page layout* in QuarkXPress than do anything else, it may not be for everyone. The good news is that you don't have to be gifted in art to create effective page layout. Listed below are some of the characteristics that make a person successful in page layout:

- patience
- creativity
- flexibility
- attention to detail
- good planning skills
- organizational skills
- multitasking ability
- a "good eye" for design
- persistence in practice
- ability to meet deadlines
- ability to deal with stress
- knowledge of your audience
- ability to be a constructive critic
- willingness to keep irregular hours
- ability to take constructive criticism
- skills in QuarkXPress and Adobe Photoshop
- up-to-date knowledge of the publishing industry

Of course, you don't have to have all those characteristics, but during this semester, focus on a few you want to enhance. Take it one step at a time as you learn some basics of page layout and design, incorporating the QuarkXPress program.

True Confession

The making of a desktop publisher

"I remember when I was around 10 years old, I never played house. I played magazine.

"There were two versions. In the first one, I would be the boss, and I would make my friends cut pictures out of magazines and write captions and articles. I was in charge of layout, gluing pictures and articles to construction paper and designing the cover the same way.

"In the second version — again, with me as the boss — my friends and I would draw pictures (or trace coloring books) that kids could color in. I attached the pages together and sold the "books" to my neighbors for a penny a page, with the pitch that it's cheaper than buying their kids coloring books."

Cristin

Are there jobs out there?

You'll be amazed at how desktop publishing skills cross over into many other fields. When you are looking in the want ads for internships or jobs, these are some of the key words to look for:

- advertising
- artist
- communications
- computer
- copy editor
- designer
- desktop publisher
- editor
- editorial field
- graphic design(er)
- Macintosh
- layout
- marketing
- page layout
- pagination
- printing
- publishing: book, magazine
- public relations
- QuarkXPress
- writer

What is graphic design?

Good *graphic design* results when type and visuals on the page complement each other to present the message clearly. Arranging the type and elements on the page is called *page layout*. Although design's main job is to present the message, it can also be used to portray an image or an identity.

Design or content? Which is more important?

It's a catch-22. Without worthwhile content in a publication, great graphic design is wasted. The design might attract readers, but then they are disappointed in the message.

On the other hand, well-written, informative content can go unnoticed if the graphic design fails to attract the readers.

One student offered this analogy: The design-content relationship is like an ice cream sundae. The ice cream is the critical element in the sundae, just like the content is critical for delivering your message. It's the whipped cream and hot fudge, however, that make the sundae delicious, just as the design enhances the content, making your publication more attractive and your message more powerful.

Cuddy's seesaw

Put importance of design on one seat of the seesaw and interest level on another. Let's play seesaw with this (Cuddy's seesaw – Figure 1-1). As the reader's interest level goes up, importance of graphic design goes down. For example, parents of school-aged children will most likely read a school newsletter, even if it is poorly designed, because they are interested in the content. They don't care much about the design because their interest is high.

However, as the reader's interest level goes down, the importance of graphic design goes up. For example, a single adult not involved in school events receives the latest school newsletter. How will the newsletter catch that person's attention? The importance of graphic design goes up because that person has a low interest level in the school newsletter.

Let's look at another example using a CD cover. Someone loves The Dave Matthews Band and has all their CDs. The person goes to the store to buy the group's latest CD. It doesn't matter if the cover is badly designed; the person doesn't care about the look of the cover. Interest is high — importance of graphic design is low.

On the other hand, someone who likes a wide variety of music goes to the store to make a purchase in no particular genre. The CD cover that catches this person's eye will win. Interest is low (in a particular CD), so importance of graphic design is high.

Quicktip

If interest is low, the importance of design is high.

If interest is high, the importance of graphic design is lower.

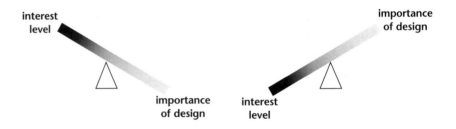

interest level

importance of design

importance of design

interest level

Figure 1-1. Cuddy's seesaw.
First assess interest level and then consider design.

The relevance of the seesaw: Form follows function

What does this have to do with you and your publications? Foremost, each publication needs to be designed with its audience(s) in mind. Decide the function, and then let form follow that decision. If the publication reaches senior citizens, choose larger type. If the publication reaches busy mothers or busy executives, present the copy in short segments (*chunks of information*). Help readers get the most out of your publication in the limited amount of time they have.

Starting a project

As you begin a layout project, you need to ask certain questions:

1. Who is the audience?

2. What is the message? And the purpose?

3. What kind of publication will I produce? Will it be a newsletter, a flier, an ad, a brochure? How will it be distributed?

4. What is the timeline for the project?

5. What is my budget? Is this black and white, spot color or four-color process?

Then more questions arise as planning begins.

6. What other publications has our company produced in the past that will affect this one? For example, does a certain logo appear on every page? What colors represent our company?

7. Who will do each task? Am I chief editor, layout person and proofreader? Do I have help? Who is writing the copy? Who signs off on the final proof?

The competition

It's necessary to look at the competition. Will your publication be noticed before theirs? Will it be more memorable? For example, perhaps several campus service clubs are collecting money for charities. How are they advertising? What can you do differently?

You will have other questions to answer as you prepare your publication for printing, but we will deal with them later. *Refer to Chapter 8 (Communication Concepts) for both writing and layout considerations to meet the needs of your audience.*

The plan

After you answer the questions about your proposed publication, write a *plan* to guide your project. A plan not only answers the questions but keeps you focused on your audience and purpose. Figure 1-2 presents a sample plan for a brochure. You will be asked to write a plan for at least one of your projects.

The sketch

With the plan in mind, do a rough pencil *sketch* first. Never try to design at the computer without a pencil sketch in front of you. Sketches will be required with most of your assignments. Some students like to compose *thumbnails*, which are small mockups of the page (Figure 1-3). Other students like to sketch in full size.

Quicktip

To start a project, consider:

1. Audience

2. Message

3. Kind of publication

4. Timeline

5. Budget

6. Connection to company

7. Who does what

A novice can follow a few simple guidelines to make publications look professional.

Laughter is the Best Medicine

Brochure for Organ Donor Awareness Day

I. Statement of purpose

The national PRSSA's (Public Relations Student Society of America) annual project promotes organ donations. Therefore, Rowan's chapter is holding a one-day event called "Organ Donor Awareness Day." Getting the word out to our college and local communities makes a difference in attendance at the event. This brochure will announce the day, present a schedule and inform people about organ donation.

II. Audience and distribution

The audience for this brochure will be Rowan University students and local community members. The brochure will be sent to all faculty through interoffice mail and placed in strategic locations on campus and in a few places in the community (post office, municipal building, Wawa).

III. Key points and benefits

a. What is Organ Donor Awareness Day?

b. Organ Donation Facts

c. What you can do to help

d. The day's schedule

e. List of sponsors and contributors

IV. Format

8½ x 11 three-panel brochure, white cardstock

Ink: black only

V. My Timeline

a. Plan submitted to client — April 1

b. Copy written by me and approved by client — April 5

c. Rough sketch — April 7

d. Computer draft approved by client — April 12

e. Completed brochure to duplicating center/printer — April 13

f. Ready to distribute — April 15

VI. Division of duties

a. Writing and layout – Jamie and Steph

b. Proofreading – Steph

c. Final approval – Melissa (president)

d. Pickup and distribution around campus – Jackie

Figure 1-2. Sample plan for a brochure. See Chapter 17 (Brochure) for more information on this.

Qool Fact

Thumbnail sketches

The name *thumbnails* arose because designers made their sketches about the size of a thumbnail, thus fitting dozens of various sketches on one page.

Although people still call them thumbnails, most of the time the sketches will be larger than the size of a thumb. Four to a page is a common size.

QuarkXPress has an option for thumbnails under "View" on the menu. Take a look. You can see a multipage document all at once. These are not sketches — they are the actual pages in very small format.

Figure 1-3. Thumbnail sketches of a flier. See the finished flier on page 25. You can also call these "rough sketches."

Quick Quiz

1. What traits of a desktop publisher do you think are most important?

2. Explain Cuddy's seesaw and give a real-life example.

3. What are seven questions to ask before you start a project? Which is the most important question and why?

4. Why is a sketch of a design necessary?

Out of the Quandary

1. Self-survey

Do a self-survey using the desktop publisher traits. Check off the traits you already possess. Circle the traits you would like to improve.

☐ patience   ☐ attention to detail

☐ creativity   ☐ good planning skills

☐ flexibility   ☐ organizational skills

☐ multitasking ability   ☐ a "good eye" for design

☐ persistence in practice   ☐ ability to meet deadlines

☐ ability to deal with stress   ☐ knowledge of your audience

☐ ability to be a constructive critic

☐ willingness to keep irregular hours

☐ ability to take constructive criticism

☐ skills in QuarkXPress and Photoshop

☐ up-to-date knowledge of the publishing industry

2. Interview

Interview a designer or editor who does page layout. Write up the interview, and later in the semester, use it for your magazine article layout assignment.

3. See-saw examples

Draw the two see-saws. Next to or under each one, give an example of an audience and a publication that would apply to it.

Mac's Apple-bet

 A   Select all

 B   Frame (border)

 C   Copy

 D   Duplicate

 E   Get photo/Get text

 F   Find/Change

 G   Group

 H   Hyphenation

 I   Invisibles

 J   Jump to page

 K   Kill

 L   Check spelling

 M   Modify

 N   New document/
     New folder

 O   Open

 P   Print

 Q   Quit

 R   Rulers

 S   Save

 T   Text runaround

 U   Ungroup

 V   Paste

 W   Close

 X   Cut (delete)

 Y   Preferences

 Z   Undo (zap it back!)

 0   Fit in window

 1   Actual size

Quantum Leap

Ideas File

Start an *ideas file*, also called a *clip file* or an *inspiration file*. Buy an expanding file and label the categories on the file tabs. The brown kind of file that stands on its own works the best for long-term growth. You might want to write on a Post-it™ note or on the piece itself the reason you like this publication and then attach the note to the item. Otherwise, years later you will have no idea why you saved it.

Some of the categories you can include are listed below:

fliers

small black and white ads
   (¼ page, ⅓ page)

letterheads

business cards

newsletters

brochures

pullquote examples

menus

bill stuffers

direct mail packages

booklets

invitations

convention programs

full-page ads

magazine articles

magazine covers

programs (dinners, shows)

workshop fliers

calendars

surveys

coupons

postcards

fax cover sheets

catalogs

tipsheets

résumés

annual reports

logo ideas

really bad examples

great color ideas

good newspaper page

good layout of photos

clip art examples

2 Design Principles

I am enough of an artist to draw freely upon my imagination. Imagination is more important than knowledge. Knowledge is limited. Imagination encircles the world.

Albert Einstein

Quest Objectives

- List three ways to achieve contrast.
- Identify aligned items on a page.
- Explain the principle of proximity.
- Describe a way to achieve repetition on one page and on multipage documents.
- Relate dominance to the other principles.
- Draw the eye direction theories.
- Explain the rule of thirds.
- Define the K.I.S.S. guideline.
- Describe a balanced page.

Quest Terms

alignment of items	K.I.S.S.
backward-6	point of entry
balance	proximity
contrast	reading Z
dominance	repetition
emphasis	rule of three
eye direction	upper half prominence
floating heads	upper third rule
gray page	visual connection

A well-designed page is attractive and easy to read. In addition, it emphasizes the important points. Design principles help us communicate our message. Although there are many design principles, the five introduced in this chapter are contrast, alignment, proximity, repetition and dominance. All are closely related, but all do not have to be incorporated in the same layout. Other guidelines for communicating effectively through design are included as well.

Contrast

Can you imagine every day being the same? Without contrast in routine or location, you'd live a dull life. The same goes for publications. *Contrast* adds zip to a page by changes in size, color or shape of page elements.

Contrast by size

Varying the size of items creates contrast on a page. When you want to create contrast, don't tiptoe — take that giant step. Make an element VERY different. Give your most important story the largest headline. Make a picture very large. Make your dominant element stand out. Figures 2-1 and 2-2 show contrast by size.

Figure 2-1. Contrast by size.

Kevin sketched several ideas for his business cards. The left example has some contrast in type size, but it just didn't have the *oomph!* he was looking for. He rearranged items and wound up with the strong size contrast on the right.

Figure 2-2.
The all-text small ad (left) uses very slight contrast in type for the head. Notice the differences in the larger ad. Stephanie made good use of size and color contrast in two different ways.

Size contrast
- head in large letters
- bullets are larger than first version

Color contrast
- head is in white type in black box (reverse)
- white space around solid black character
- larger bullets add touch of black to typed list
- bold words at bottom

Graduate school, anyone?

Learn:
- Helpful hints for taking the GREs
- How to select the best program for you
- What grad schools are looking for in applicants
- If grad school is right for you

The discussion begins Thursday, 10/17, at 6:30 in Bozorth Auditorium. Don't miss it!

Graduate school, anyone?

Lambda Pi Eta presents a night of grad school questions and answers with Communication Professor Dan Schowalter!

Learn:
- *Helpful hints for taking the GREs*
- *How to select the best program for you*
- *What grad schools are looking for in applicants*
- *If grad school is right for you*

The discussion begins Thursday, 10/17 at 6:30 in Bozorth Auditorium.
Don't miss it!

Contrast by color

Color gives contrast to a page. However, if you can't afford the luxury of color, you can create contrast with black and white. Use shades of black for boxed copy, drop shadows, rules (lines) and bigger, bolder type for heads and subheads (Figure 2-3). Create some white space, which is the strongest contrast to black (Figure 2-4). Pictures or framed, boxed copy add contrast to the overall layout.

 Figure 2-3. Giving color to a gray page.

This page is dull. It appears "gray" because there is not much contrast.

"Color" is achieved by the large, bold nameplate running up the left side, as well as the shaded apple, the shaded boxed copy and lots of breathing space (white space) around all the copy and heads.

Qool Fact

A *gray page* is one that is text-intensive (full of body copy). When you add strong contrast, you have now added "color," even though you are still working in black and white.

Figure 2-4.
Contrast by color in a small ad.
Patti's small ad is the epitome of contrast — solid black with white type and images. These white items are referred to as *reverse type* or a *reverse image.*

Contrast by shape

Sometimes an irregularly shaped item adds contrast to the page. A silhouetted photo serving as a corner border to a page might work. With Quark's text capabilities, you can run the text around an irregularly shaped item and create an interesting effect. As in all cases, use moderation with this technique. Figures 2-5 and 2-6 show contrast by shape.

Figure 2-5.
Contrast by shape.

The girl doing exercises adds contrast in four ways:
• solid black silhouette
• irregular shape
• white space created around it
• text wrapped around it (this would be contrast by alignment)

The shaded box adds contrast to the page and balances well with the girl.

Using vertical and horizontal shapes together creates contrast.

Quicktip

Two tests for contrast

1. Hold the page at arm's length. Squint at your page. Strong elements should be visible while some others fade away.

If *every element* disappears, you don't have enough contrast.

If *no elements* disappear, you don't have enough contrast.

In other words, something has to disappear!

2. Turn the page upside down to view contrast.

Some elements should stand out by their shape, size or color. Holding the page upside down lets you focus on the overall look — you should see the elements (and contrast). You won't get distracted by reading the copy and the heads.

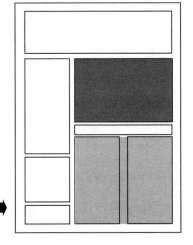

Figure 2-6.
Contrast by shape.

This newsletter has three vertical columns of type. The photo is horizontal and pulled across two columns to add shape contrast.

Figure 2-7. Same newsletter as Figure 2-6 but formatted with boxes so you can examine the contrasting shapes.

Alignment

A visual *alignment of items* creates a connection between them, thus leading to unity on the page. Examine Figure 2-7 (on the previous page) to see how items align along the top, bottom, left and right. Along with item alignment, consider type alignment (Figures 2-8 and 2-9). Does the edge of the type align left, right, both sides (justified) or on the center? Many publications favor left aligned heads. Sometimes a short caption can align against the side of the photo, even if it means right alignment. During this course, experiment with alignment of type and items.

This ad was created by an engineering graduate student, Fred, who designed this clutch knob for guitars. He is currently marketing this product. With some minor alignment adjustments, Fred wound up with the ad on the far right. (His e-mail is real.)

Figure 2-8. Overall alignment of items and type. The ad on the left centers everything (dotted line). The ad on the right uses a left alignment (dotted line) and a right alignment (dotted line).

Type is **centered** over itself. The thick rule is arbitrarily placed on the card.

The rule now is aligned at the top of the camera lens. Copy is **left aligned** and also aligns under the left point of the rule.

The rule is aligned at the top of the camera lens. Copy is **right aligned** and also aligns under the right point of the rule. The camera is also larger to give it more emphasis on the card.

Figure 2-9. Three different alignments of type on business cards.

It is often difficult to understand the alignment principle regarding items on the page (Figure 2-10). Look at the flier on the left. Items are not aligned across the top or along the sides. However, in the flier on the right, Jessica now has aligned these items (follow dotted lines):

across the top: the gray box with the tip of the wing
down left side: black box with all the text and the line
down right side: eagle's tail feathers with light gray box

She has now created a *visual connection* between the items by using alignment. Good alignment may seem subtle, but its impact is mighty!

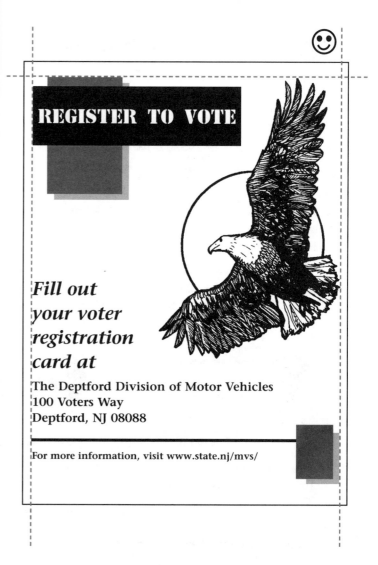

Figure 2-10.
Alignment can be accomplished by moving text boxes and choosing type alignments to follow an invisible line (the dotted line). *Left:* alignment not adhered to. *Right:* alignment changes the connectivity. Proximity is also improved in the example to the right. (Read about proximity in the next few pages.)

Alignment of subheads in a magazine article

Current designers are using left alignment for the first paragraph after a head or subhead. It makes sense and looks much better — read the captions inside Figures 2-11 and 2-12.

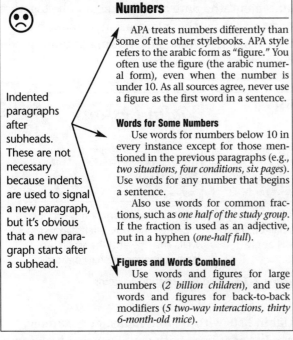

Indented paragraphs after subheads. These are not necessary because indents are used to signal a new paragraph, but it's obvious that a new paragraph starts after a subhead.

Numbers

APA treats numbers differently than some of the other stylebooks. APA style refers to the arabic form as "figure." You often use the figure (the arabic numeral form), even when the number is under 10. As all sources agree, never use a figure as the first word in a sentence.

Words for Some Numbers

Use words for numbers below 10 in every instance except for those mentioned in the previous paragraphs (e.g., *two situations, four conditions, six pages*). Use words for any number that begins a sentence.

Also use words for common fractions, such as *one half of the study group*. If the fraction is used as an adjective, put in a hyphen (*one-half full*).

Figures and Words Combined

Use words and figures for large numbers (*2 billion children*), and use words and figures for back-to-back modifiers (*5 two-way interactions, thirty 6-month-old mice*).

Numbers

APA treats numbers differently than some of the other stylebooks. APA style refers to the arabic form as "figure." You often use the figure (the arabic numeral form), even when the number is under 10. As all sources agree, never use a figure as the first word in a sentence.

Words for Some Numbers

Use words for numbers below 10 in every instance except for those mentioned in the previous paragraphs (e.g., *two situations, four conditions, six pages*). Use words for any number that begins a sentence.

Also use words for common fractions, such as *one half of the study group*. If the fraction is used as an adjective, put in a hyphen (*one-half full*).

Figures and Words Combined

Use words and figures for large numbers (*2 billion children*), and use words and figures for back-to-back modifiers (*5 two-way interactions, thirty 6-month-old mice*).

No indented paragraphs after subheads. Paragraphs are left aligned.

Subsequent paragraphs would be indented.

Notice the neat, clean look of total left alignment.

Figure 2-11. Both above examples have left-aligned subheads, but they differ in the first paragraphs under the subheads.

The editor chose centered subheads and indented the first paragraphs. The subheads are actually centered over the entire column, but they look centered over the first line. Because the first line is indented, the heads do not look centered — they look slightly off.

Numbers

APA treats numbers differently than some of the other stylebooks. APA style refers to the arabic form as "figure." You often use the figure (the arabic numeral form), even when the number is under 10. As all sources agree, never use a figure as the first word in a sentence.

Words for Some Numbers

Use words for numbers below 10 in every instance except for those mentioned in the previous paragraphs (e.g., *two situations, four conditions, six pages*). Use words for any number that begins a sentence.

Also use words for common fractions, such as *one half of the study group*. If the fraction is used as an adjective, put in a hyphen (*one-half full*).

Figures and Words Combined

Use words and figures for large numbers (*2 billion children*), and use words and figures for back-to-back modifiers (*5 two-way interactions, thirty 6-month-old mice*).

Numbers

APA treats numbers differently than some of the other stylebooks. APA style refers to the arabic form as "figure." You often use the figure (the arabic numeral form), even when the number is under 10. As all sources agree, never use a figure as the first word in a sentence.

Words for Some Numbers

Use words for numbers below 10 in every instance except for those mentioned in the previous paragraphs (e.g., *two situations, four conditions, six pages*). Use words for any number that begins a sentence.

Also use words for common fractions, such as *one half of the study group*. If the fraction is used as an adjective, put in a hyphen (*one-half full*).

Figures and Words Combined

Use words and figures for large numbers (*2 billion children*), and use words and figures for back-to-back modifiers (*5 two-way interactions, thirty 6-month-old mice*).

Solve the off-centered look by left aligning first paragraphs after subheads (no indent).

Paragraphs after the first paragraph are indented so the reader knows where a new paragraph starts.

Figure 2-12. Both above examples have centered subheads, but they differ in the first paragraphs under the subheads.

Proximity

Proximity means closeness. Think in terms of *chunks of information* as you place similar items together. For example, your address and phone number should be together on a business card (Figure 2-13). For an event announcement, the date and time should be together. Don't make the reader search for the information — make the information jump out! When designing ads, be sure to place product information near the picture of the product.

Rob used proximity, alignment and size contrast to create a better business card (right example).

Rob's information is all over the place. Yes, it's just a small business card, but guidelines still apply.

Now all his information is grouped together. All copy is left aligned as well. The title and the violin are larger, creating better contrast.

Figure 2-13. Proximity relating to items.

Proximity is essential in lists with related items. For example, Figure 2-14A shows a list of officers with equal spacing between all items. If you group the items into chunks, title and name become a chunk, as shown in Figure 2-14B.

Qool Fact

Follow the principle of proximity in these scenarios:

1. placing related items on a page
2. listing names and titles (and positions, addresses, etc.)
3. using bulleted lists (use space above each unit)
4. placing a subhead near its copy

Co-Presidents
Diane Caldwell
Laura Hausman

VP/Secretary
Lara Ulrich

Treasurer
Shannon Stecher

Open House Chair
Michelle Ulrich

Initiation Chair
Stephanie Tofani

Public Relations Chair
Kerry Caspare

Each unit consists of the name and position.

Co-Presidents
Diane Caldwell
Laura Hausman

VP/Secretary
Lara Ulrich

Treasurer
Shannon Stecher

Open House Chair
Michelle Ulrich

Initiation Chair
Stephanie Tofani

Public Relations Chair
Kerry Caspare

A Equal space between every-thing. No sense of unity. At least the positions are bold for some contrast.

B Proximity is achieved. Title and name go together as a chunk.

Figure 2-14. Proximity relating to lists.

You can achieve proximity with bulleted lists by adding space between each of the units. In QuarkXPress, the setting for this is called "space before" (**Style → Formats → Space before**). Figure 2-15 shows a bulleted list without space (left) and with space (right).

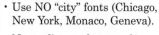

- Use NO "city" fonts (Chicago, New York, Monaco, Geneva).
- Never distort photos unless you have a super reason.
- Always check spelling.
- Save your document at least every 5 minutes.
- Always make a backup copy.

Notice how all the items run together in this list. Units aren't clear.

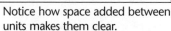

- Use NO "city" fonts (Chicago, New York, Monaco, Geneva).
- Never distort photos unless you have a super reason.
- Always check spelling.
- Save your document at least every 5 minutes.
- Always make a backup copy.

Notice how space added between units makes them clear.

Figure 2-15. Proximity related to bulleted lists.

Subheads in a publication also require adherence to the principle of proximity. Subheads should be close to the copy they describe. More space needs to be *above* the subhead than below it (Figure 2-16).

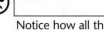

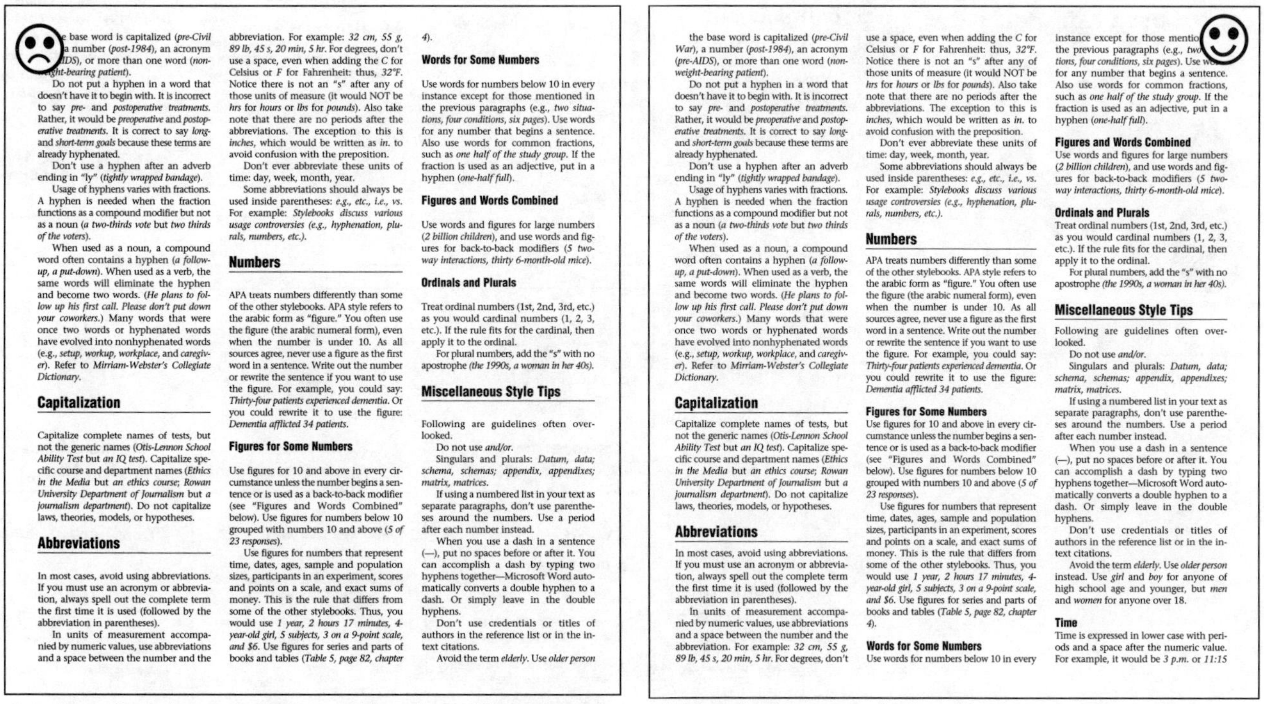

the base word is capitalized (*pre-Civil* a number (*post-1984*), an acronym *AIDS*), or more than one word (*non-weight-bearing patient*).

Do not put a hyphen in a word that doesn't have it to begin with. It is incorrect to say *pre-* and *postoperative treatments*. Rather, it would be *preoperative and postoperative treatments*. It is correct to say *long-* and *short-term goals* because these terms are already hyphenated.

Don't use a hyphen after an adverb ending in "ly" (*tightly wrapped bandage*).

Usage of hyphens varies with fractions. A hyphen is needed when the fraction functions as a compound modifier but not as a noun (*a two-thirds vote* but *two thirds of the voters*).

When used as a noun, a compound word often contains a hyphen (*a follow-up, a put-down*). When used as a verb, the same words will eliminate the hyphen and become two words. Write out the number or rewrite the sentence if you want to use the figure. For example, you could say: *Thirty-four patients experienced dementia.* Or you could rewrite it to use the figure: *Dementia afflicted 34 patients.*

Capitalization

Capitalize complete names of tests, but not the generic names (*Otis-Lennon School Ability Test* but *an IQ test*). Capitalize specific course and department names (*Ethics in the Media* but *an ethics course; Rowan University Department of Journalism* but *a journalism department*). Do not capitalize laws, theories, models, or hypotheses.

Abbreviations

In most cases, avoid using abbreviations. If you must use an acronym or abbreviation, always spell out the complete term the first time it is used (followed by the abbreviation in parentheses).

In units of measurement accompanied by numeric values, use abbreviations and a space between the number and the

abbreviation. For example: *32 cm, 55 g, 89 lb, 45 s, 20 min, 5 hr*. For degrees, don't use a space, even when adding the C for Celsius or F for Fahrenheit: thus, *32°F*. Notice there is not an "s" after any of those units of measure (it would NOT be *hrs* for *hours* or *lbs* for *pounds*). Also take note that there are no periods after the abbreviations. The exception to this is *inches*, which would be written as *in.* to avoid confusion with the preposition.

Don't ever abbreviate these units of time: day, week, month, year.

Some abbreviations should always be used inside parentheses (*e.g., etc., i.e., vs.* For example: *Stylebooks discuss various usage controversies (e.g., hyphenation, plurals, numbers, etc.).*

Numbers

APA treats numbers differently than some of the other stylebooks. APA style refers to the arabic form as "figure." You often use the figure (the arabic numeral form), even when the number is under 10. As all sources agree, never use a figure as the first word in a sentence. Write out the number or rewrite the sentence if you want to use the figure. For example, you could say: *Thirty-four patients experienced dementia.* Or you could rewrite it to use the figure: *Dementia afflicted 34 patients.*

Figures for Some Numbers

Use figures for 10 and above in every circumstance unless the number begins a sentence or is used as a back-to-back modifier (see "Figures and Words Combined" below). Use figures for numbers below 10 grouped with numbers 10 and above (*5 of 23 responses*).

Use figures for numbers that represent time, dates, ages, sample and population sizes, participants in an experiment, scores and points on a scale, and exact sums of money. This is the rule that differs from some of the other stylebooks. Thus, you would use *1 year, 2 hours 17 minutes, 4-year-old girl, 5 subjects, 3 on a 9-point scale, and $6.* Use figures for series and parts of books and tables (*Table 5, page 82, chapter

4*).

Words for Some Numbers

Use words for numbers below 10 in every instance except for those mentioned in the previous paragraphs (e.g., *two situations, four conditions, six pages*). Use words for any number that begins a sentence. Also use words for common fractions, such as *one half of the study group*. If the fraction is used as an adjective, put in a hyphen (*one-half full*).

Figures and Words Combined

Use words and figures for large numbers (*2 billion children*), and use words and figures for back-to-back modifiers (*5 two-way interactions, thirty 6-month-old mice*).

Ordinals and Plurals

Treat ordinal numbers (1st, 2nd, 3rd, etc.) as you would cardinal numbers (1, 2, 3, etc.). If the rule fits for the cardinal, then apply it to the ordinal.

For plural numbers, add the "s" with no apostrophe (*the 1990s, a woman in her 40s*).

Miscellaneous Style Tips

Following are guidelines often overlooked.

Do not use *and/or*.

Singulars and plurals: *Datum, data; schema, schemas; appendix, appendixes; matrix, matrices*.

If using a numbered list in your text as separate paragraphs, don't use parentheses around the numbers. Use a period after each number instead.

When you use a dash in a sentence (—), put no spaces before or after it. You can accomplish a dash by typing two hyphens together—Microsoft Word automatically converts a double hyphen to a dash. Or simply leave in the double hyphens.

Don't use credentials or titles of authors in the reference list or in the in-text citations.

Avoid the term *elderly*. Use *older person*

Equal spacing above and below subheads. Subheads are not close to the body copy they describe. These are called *floating heads* because they float in the middle, between blocks of copy.

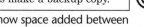

the base word is capitalized (*pre-Civil War*), a number (*post-1984*), an acronym (*pre-AIDS*), or more than one word (*non-weight-bearing patient*).

Do not put a hyphen in a word that doesn't have it to begin with. It is incorrect to say *pre-* and *postoperative treatments*. Rather, it would be *preoperative and postoperative treatments*. It is correct to say *long-* and *short-term goals* because these terms are already hyphenated.

Don't use a hyphen after an adverb ending in "ly" (*tightly wrapped bandage*).

Usage of hyphens varies with fractions. A hyphen is needed when the fraction functions as a compound modifier but not as a noun (*a two-thirds vote* but *two thirds of the voters*).

When used as a noun, a compound word often contains a hyphen (*a follow-up, a put-down*). When used as a verb, the same words will eliminate the hyphen and become two words. (*He plans to follow up his first call. Please don't put down your coworkers.*) Many words that were once two words or hyphenated words have evolved into nonhyphenated words (e.g., *setup, workup, workplace, and caregiver*). Refer to Mirriam-Webster's Collegiate Dictionary.

Capitalization

Capitalize complete names of tests, but not the generic names (*Otis-Lennon School Ability Test* but *an IQ test*). Capitalize specific course and department names (*Ethics in the Media* but *an ethics course; Rowan University Department of Journalism* but *a journalism department*). Do not capitalize laws, theories, models, or hypotheses.

Abbreviations

In most cases, avoid using abbreviations. If you must use an acronym or abbreviation, always spell out the complete term the first time it is used (followed by the abbreviation in parentheses).

In units of measurement accompanied by numeric values, use abbreviations and a space between the number and the abbreviation. For example: *32 cm, 55 g, 89 lb, 45 s, 20 min, 5 hr*. For degrees, don't

use a space, even when adding the C for Celsius or F for Fahrenheit: thus, *32°F*. Notice there is not an "s" after any of those units of measure (it would NOT be *hrs* for *hours* or *lbs* for *pounds*). Also take note that there are no periods after the abbreviations. The exception to this is *inches*, which would be written as *in.* to avoid confusion with the preposition.

Don't ever abbreviate these units of time: day, week, month, year.

Some abbreviations should always be used inside parentheses (*e.g., etc., i.e., vs.* For example: *Stylebooks discuss various usage controversies (e.g., hyphenation, plurals, numbers, etc.).*

Numbers

APA treats numbers differently than some of the other stylebooks. APA style refers to the arabic form as "figure." You often use the figure (the arabic numeral form), even when the number is under 10. As all sources agree, never use a figure as the first word in a sentence. Write out the number or rewrite the sentence if you want to use the figure. For example, you could say: *Thirty-four patients experienced dementia.* Or you could rewrite it to use the figure: *Dementia afflicted 34 patients.*

Figures for Some Numbers

Use figures for 10 and above in every circumstance unless the number begins a sentence or is used as a back-to-back modifier (see "Figures and Words Combined" below). Use figures for numbers below 10 grouped with numbers 10 and above (*5 of 23 responses*).

Use figures for numbers that represent time, dates, ages, sample and population sizes, participants in an experiment, scores and points on a scale, and exact sums of money. This is the rule that differs from some of the other stylebooks. Thus, you would use *1 year, 2 hours 17 minutes, 4-year-old girl, 5 subjects, 3 on a 9-point scale, and $6.* Use figures for series and parts of books and tables (*Table 5, page 82, chapter 4*).

Words for Some Numbers

Use words for numbers below 10 in every

instance except for those mentioned in the previous paragraphs (e.g., *two situations, four conditions, six pages*). Use words for any number that begins a sentence. Also use words for common fractions, such as *one half of the study group*. If the fraction is used as an adjective, put in a hyphen (*one-half full*).

Figures and Words Combined

Use words and figures for large numbers (*2 billion children*), and use words and figures for back-to-back modifiers (*5 two-way interactions, thirty 6-month-old mice*).

Ordinals and Plurals

Treat ordinal numbers (1st, 2nd, 3rd, etc.) as you would cardinal numbers (1, 2, 3, etc.). If the rule fits for the cardinal, then apply it to the ordinal.

For plural numbers, add the "s" with no apostrophe (*the 1990s, a woman in her 40s*).

Miscellaneous Style Tips

Following are guidelines often overlooked.

Do not use *and/or*.

Singulars and plurals: *Datum, data; schema, schemas; appendix, appendixes; matrix, matrices*.

If using a numbered list in your text as separate paragraphs, don't use parentheses around the numbers. Use a period after each number instead.

When you use a dash in a sentence (—), put no spaces before or after it. You can accomplish a dash by typing two hyphens together—Microsoft Word automatically converts a double hyphen to a dash. Or simply leave in the double hyphens.

Don't use credentials or titles of authors in the reference list or in the in-text citations.

Avoid the term *elderly*. Use *older person* instead. Use *girl* and *boy* for anyone of high school age and younger, but *men* and *women* for anyone over 18.

Time

Time is expressed in lower case with periods and a space after the numeric value. For example, it would be *3 p.m.* or *11:15*

Subheads sit on top of related body copy. This is the way it should be.

Figure 2-16. Applying the principle of proximity to subheads.

Repetition

To create a sense of consistency in a document, repeat certain elements. For example, headers or footers would be repeated on every page. Type would be consistent: all body copy the same font, all heads the same font but most likely different from body copy. The same logo or symbol might be used throughout (Figure 2-17). Achieve *repetition* also through use of color or rules on each page.

Repetition occurs from page to page and also from issue to issue. People get used to something (e.g., nameplate of newsletter, logo, colors), and the publication gets its brand identity. Thus readers gain instant recognition of the publication.

Tereze made the blood drop by using picture boxes to make the shapes. She overlapped the shapes, applied "no runaround," and grouped them. She also colored them red.

Figure 2-17. Example of repetition in a brochure.

This is a three-panel brochure. The dotted lines are drawn to show you where it folds. Notice the use of the blood drop throughout. Also, the American Red Cross logo and tagline are repeated.

Cover panel is far right panel. (Imagine this being folded.)

Inside panels all show at the same time when you open the brochure. It is important to align items well for a consistent look. The blood drops, heads, lines under heads and first line of copy in each panel align across the page.

Rowan University is holding its annual Blood Drive!!

🩸 When: December 17, 2003
🩸 Where: Student Center Pit
🩸 Time: 12:00p.m. - 4:00p.m.
🩸 Cookies and juice will be given after donations!

✚ American Red Cross
Together, we can save a life

Contacts

🩸 Phone # : 1-800-GIVE LIFE
🩸 Web site : www.givelife.com
🩸 Or stop by the Rowan University student center and stop by the information desk.

✚ American Red Cross
Together, we can save a life

Save a Life Today!!

Each year, millions of Americans take time to save a life. So please take an hour out of your day and donate blood.

✚ American Red Cross
Together, we can save a life

Requirements For Donating Blood

🩸 Over the age of 17
🩸 Over 110 lb
🩸 Healthy
🩸 Have not given blood within the last year
🩸 No tattoos or piercings within the last year
🩸 To find out more go to www.givelife.org

Reasons To Give Blood

🩸 You will save lives
🩸 I think that is reason enough, don't you?!!!!

✚ American Red Cross
Together, we can save a life

Myths About Giving Blood

🩸 **Enough people donate blood so I don't have to** (not true — we never have enough blood; millions of people go into the emergency in need of blood each day).

🩸 **I do not have time to donate** (it takes only an hour out of your day, and you are back to your regular life).

🩸 **I can get a disease from the needles** (each needle is completely sterile, individually wrapped, and changed after every use).

Repetition of elements in all your publications creates a brand identity and breeds familiarity (Figure 2-18).

Letterhead

Business card

Repetitive elements

Figure 2-18.
Repetition from publication to publication.

Jeff carried his theme of balloons from project to project.

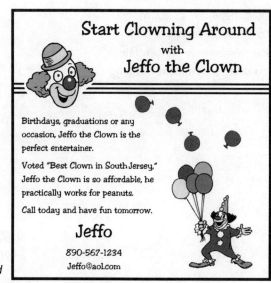

Small ad

Look back at Jessica's flier on page 14. Notice the use of two box-and-drop-shadow units as effective repetition elements.

Dominance

Dominance and contrast are closely related. The dominant element will be in strong contrast to the other elements on the page. The dominant element will most likely be the eye-catcher. Some people call it *emphasis*. Make it stand out by its size or its boldness. This is usually the item that creates the *point of entry* on the page — the reader's eye is drawn to that point first. It could be a big, bold headline or it could be a large photo or a spot of color. Figures 2-19 and 2-20 present examples of dominance.

Qool Fact

Robin Williams is one of the most well-known authors on page layout, design and typography. Her book, *The Non-Designer's Design Book*, goes into more detail on contrast, repetition, alignment and proximity. Her style is whimsical and enjoyable. It's a good book to add to your bookshelf.

In this book, I have added **dominance** as a principle in its own right. I have found that "newbies" in layout tend to produce better ads and fliers when they concentrate on using a dominant element.

Figure 2-19. This flier uses Jack's picture to achieve dominance. The picture was isolated from its original background using the block tool and its variations in Adobe Photoshop. The headline is typed on an arc (see page 90).

Figure 2-20. The Australian map is the dominant element on Amanda's newsletter. What contrast elements can you identify?

Figure 2-21. Flawed example

Proximity not achieved

Violin lessons are given by Rob Bradshaw, but how do we contact him? Notice the contact information at the bottom. And "Violin lessons" for whom? A shaded hexagonal box separates the answer from the title.

Alignment

It is hard to find a visual connection between items on the page.

Contrast not effective

Notice the number of shapes on the page: a rectangle around the main head, a hexagon, a drop-shadowed circle, type in an arc and a violin shape.

No dominance

What is our dominant element? Elements compete.

Three fonts are used. Three is not overdoing it, but two would be better on such a simple page.

Rob's PR degree paid off for him — he started a business giving violin lessons and does his own advertising and publications. This is his actual contact information.

Figure 2-22. Improved example

Changes in this example

- Elements closer together to achieve proximity.
- Eliminated circle and book and made the violin the dominant graphic.
- Limited to two fonts: Old English and Times New Roman.
- Changed the "for beginners" from curved to straight.

Proximity

On this one, "Violin lessons for beginners" is close together. Contact information is all together at bottom.

Alignment

The three blocks of text line up along the left. Imagine a dotted line from the "V" in Violin to the "Affordable" to the name and address. There is right alignment of "s" in "Lessons," top of violin and phone information.

Contrast

The title in Old English font is distinctively contrasting, as is the size of the violin. The thick, black rules add contrast as well.

Dominance

The violin becomes an item of strong contrast and dominates the page.

Repetition

Repetition doesn't play a part in this flier except for the use of the Times New Roman font throughout.

The changes created the *reading Z* (see next page). Overall, this example is easier on the eye than the first one. The point of entry is the Old English title, and from there you follow the violin to the contact information.

More about attracting readers

Eye Direction

Several theories explain *eye direction* (Figure 2-21). One of the simplest is the Z pattern, also called the *"reading Z."* The eye is drawn to the upper left quadrant and follows a Z pattern across the page. Ad designers sometimes design their page with the Z pattern to guide the reader.

Another theory is the *backward-6*. The eye is drawn to the point of entry and then slides down in the backward-6 direction.

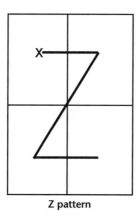 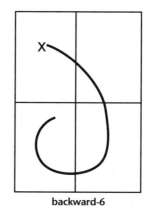

Z pattern   backward-6

Figure 2-23.
Eye direction theories.

"X" is the point of entry on a page. The upper left quadrant is the place the eye likes to gravitate toward. However, if a dominant element is placed elsewhere, then the point of entry would become that dominant element.

Keep eye directon in mind especially when designing ads. A reader needs to be led through the layout to arrive at the "call for action." Layout should not be a haphazard plan. Examine the two ads on the next page for eye direction (Figures 2-25 and 2-26).

In addition to helping effectiveness in ad design, eye direction is studied by newspaper paginators (people who do the page layout of the newspaper). It's a daily challenge for newspapers to place their items on the pages to attract the most readership.

Upper Third Rule

The *upper third rule* states that the top third of a page (or layout area) carries the most weight in attracting the reader. Thus, the most important story is placed in the upper third in a newspaper or newsletter page. In ad design, a large, bold head at the top of an ad draws readers. Some people favor the upper half instead, and call it *upper half prominence.*

Another thought on design is to design in thirds, both vertically and horizontally. Check out the Web sites listed in the back of the book for more information on this design technique.

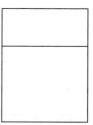

Figure 2-24.
The upper third of the page is the best place for key elements of your design.

Eye Direction Examples

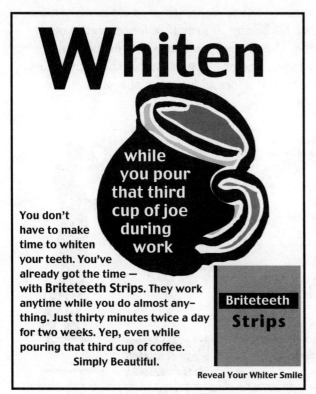

Figure 2-25.
Erin chose the Z pattern of eye direction, and she claimed contrast as the governing design principle. The large "Whiten" grabs your eye. Then as you follow the Z, you wind up at the product information. Many full-page ads are designed this way.

Figure 2-26.
Amanda chose the backward-6 pattern as she crafted this intricate small ad. She emphasized contrast as her main design principle, which is found in the heavy black and white bottom graphic, the flying dragon and the gray company name.

Some designers call it symmetric and asymmetric balance rather than formal and informal.

Balance

Balance can be formal or informal. In *formal balance,* items mirror each other, top to bottom or left to right. It's good for more serious publications, but it is a bit boring. *Informal balance,* on the other hand, is more dynamic. The elements on each side of the imaginary center line differ in weight, size or placement. But the sum of their characteristics equals that of a formal layout of the same items (Figures 2-27 and 2-28).

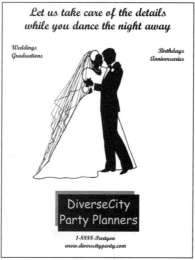

Figure 2-27. Formal balance. Draw an imaginary line through the center and each side is equal. Maryfrances thought it lacked something, so she experimented and wound up with the one on the right.

Figure 2-28. Informal balance. Proportion of graphic has changed and shape of text box at top has changed. Page still balances fairly well, but not symmetrically.

76 Design Styles

Elizabeth Adler, in her book *Print that Works*, lists 76 words to describe design styles. In the early stages of your planning, describing your publication with these kinds of words will help you make better decisions in colors, fonts and overall layout.

Contemporary	Foreign	Dignified	Masculine	Silhouette	Urban
Baroque	Modern	Lavish	Elegant	Professional	Imaginative
Arty	Business-like	French	Chic	Nautical	Floral
Comic book	Powerful	Classic	1990s	Authoritative	Graceful
African	Art Nouveau	Dynamic	Colorful	Rococo	1950s
Clean	Hard-edge	Architectural	Simple	Rustic	Japanese
1920s	Distinctive	Abstract	Realistic	Southwest	Turn-of the-century
Composite	Traditional	Decorative	Patriotic	Feminine	Futuristic
Slick	Strong	Design-y	Provincial	Art Deco	Refined
Clever	Understated	Sophisticated	Innovative	Romantic	Gothic
Creative	Old fashioned	Muted	California	Detailed	New Wave
Sketchy	1940s	Rich	Bold	Regal	Scholarly
	Folksy		Geometric	1960s	Lighthearted

K.I.S.S.

To sum it up, blending the five principles and other research findings should lead you to a graphic piece that is appealing to the eye and simple enough to give the message. We don't want clutter — aim for simplicity. Don't put irrelevant items on the page — everything needs a purpose and a connection to the message and the audience. *Keep It Simple, Student.*

Figure 2-29. Using the K.I.S.S. guideline.
Stephanie made this simple flier to put up around campus to attract people to Organ Donor Awareness Day. The attraction was Joe Conklin, a popular local comedian at WMMR radio in Philadelphia.

Discuss this flier in relation to the five design principles discussed in this chapter. Also consider eye direction, upper third rule, rule of three, simplicity and balance.

Qool Fact

The *rule of three* says that people connect things in groups of three. For example:

• red, white and blue

• executive, legislative and judicial

• earth, sea and sky

• ear, nose and throat

• Father, Son and Holy Spirit

• bat, ball and glove

• bacon, lettuce and tomato

When writing, it is best to keep your items to three if you want people to remember them. In publications, the rule of three applies to these three elements:

head, copy and **graphic.**

The past and the present
    and the future.
Faith and hope and charity,
The heart and the brain and
    the body
Give you three.
That's a magic number.
                    Bob Dorough
                    Schoolhouse Rock

Quicktip

One way to remember the five design principles is to make up an acronym. Mine is **RAP CD**:

Repetition
Alignment
Proximity
Contrast
Dominance

Qool Fact

All the words I can think of relating to design principles or design concepts (more than one word may refer to the same principle)

Alignment
Balance
Color
Consistency
Contrast
Direction
Distribution
Dominance
Emphasis
Eye direction
Formal/informal
Harmony
Line
Patterns
Positive/negative space
Prominence
Proportion
Proximity
Relevance
Repetition
Restraint
Rhythm
Shape
Simplicity
Symmetric/Asymmetric
Texture
Unity

Quick Quiz

1. What are three ways to achieve contrast?

2. What is the purpose of aligning items on the page?

3. Why is proximity essential for clear communication?

4. What does repetition accomplish in a bimonthly magazine?

5. How do you achieve dominance?

6. Sketch one eye direction theory.

7. What implications does the upper third rule have to layout?

8. What other items can you add to the rule of three?

9. What is formal vs. informal balance?

Out of the Quandary

1. Design Principles

Find ads, newsletters, magazine pages or newspaper pages that portray the five design principles: **contrast, alignment, proximity, repetition and dominance**. You can use one publication for more than one principle or use five different examples.

Staple, tape or glue a small piece of paper to the publication that explains in a sentence or two what principle you are showing. Or write directly on the publication if there is space. Another option is to mount the publication on another piece of paper.

Attach all the pages together by staple or paper clip.

2. Direction

Find a publication that clearly portrays eye direction in a Z-pattern or backward-6 pattern.

3. Evaluation

Evaluate the flier on page 25 in terms of the design principles and other related layout techniques.

Quantum Leap

Find an ad that violates a design principle and should be improved. Explain how it could be improved.

3 Construct the Page

An ounce of prevention is worth a pound of cure.
Benjamin Franklin

Quest Objectives

- Define grid, margin, column and gutter.
- Identify three-column, four-column and five-column formats.

Quest Skills

- Name a disk.
- Create a new folder.
- Set up a new document.
- Save a document.
- Pull out grids.

- Show and hide guides.
- Close document and program.
- Eject disk.
- Find a missing file.

Quest Terms

column
copybreaker
dialog box
free-floating boxes
grid
gutter
margin

Microsoft Word
1–2–2 pattern
page orientation
page setup
Sherlock
zip disk

When you open a document in QuarkXPress, you must make choices regarding page size and the grids on the page (Figure 3-1). These include grids that designate margins, columns and gutters. These make up the framework and boundaries of the page.

Decisions to make when opening a new document
- Page size
- Orientation: portrait (vertical) or landscape (horizontal)
- Margins: top, bottom, left, right
- Number of columns
- Gutter width
- Facing pages (NO)
- Automatic text box (NO)

Quicktip

Show or Hide Guides

If gridlines are not showing, go to **View → Show guides**. Or hit the **F7** key.

To hide grids, do the same.

Work with grids ON. Then hide them to see your work as it would look if it printed.

Jingle to remember this:

F7 takes you to heaven. (And you can see your beautiful work.)

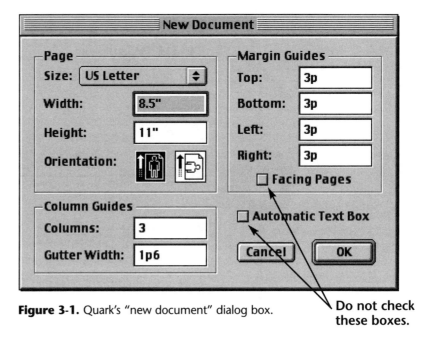

Figure 3-1. Quark's "new document" dialog box.   Do not check these boxes.

Grids

Grids are lines that divide the page into segments. You can see them on the computer but they don't print. Margin and column lines (blue) on the screen are considered grid lines. You can also draw additional gridlines (green) for placement of specific items. These grids are grabbed by your cursor from the top ruler or side ruler and dragged down or across the page.

Grids give the page guidelines or constraints, and they create a sense of consistency. Pictures might stretch from one column grid to the other, not crossing the gutter, or perhaps cross over two full columns and include the gutter. But the edges of the picture should still line up on the column grids.

Margins

Quicktip

For a professional page, set margins slightly larger at the top and bottom.
For example,
    top = 5 picas
    bottom = 5 picas
    left and right = 4 picas

This book has margins of
    top = 7 picas
    bottom = 5 picas
    outside margins = 4 picas
    inside margins = 5 picas

The header and footer go past the margin, but the distance of 3 picas is still respected.

Qool Fact

Before personal computers, space between columns was called an "alley," while "gutter" was reserved for the margins toward the binding of the book. In QuarkXPress, the book binding part is referred to as the inside margins while the outside margins refer to the edges of the pages. Clarify your terms if you are working with a commercial printer.

The *margins* are the outer edges of the page. Set margins at 3 picas (½ inch) unless otherwise instructed. (All printers and photocopiers respect ½ inch so you won't lose anything.)

A wide margin makes the page look "lighter," while a narrower margin makes a page look "darker" because more area is covered in text. Margins allow space for the document to be bound, and they also allow a reader to easily hold the page.

Nothing on the page should go past the margins unless you purposely extend the item past the margins or "bleed" it off the page.

Columns

The number of columns depends on what you are creating. Common choices are one, two and three columns. As you become more experienced, you might choose four or five for more creativity.

Columns are the actual vertical spaces within which you place your text boxes. Wider columns (such as one wide column on a page) can make reading difficult since the reader's eyes can get lost looking for the next line. Very narrow columns can create too much shifting of the eyes, which is also not conducive to good readability.

Type size goes hand in hand with column width (size choice is covered in the chapter on type). Figures 3-3 to 3-7 all delineate column variety.

Gutters

Today's computer use of *gutter* means the space between the columns. The gutter width depends on the number of columns and the width of the page.

If you use three columns on an 8½-inch-wide page, choose 1p6 (1 pica 6 points) or .2 inches for the gutter width. Two columns call for a wider gutter (2 picas or .25 inches), while four or five columns can be assigned 1 pica or .14 inch, a narrower gutter.

Additional information

In the page setup dialog box in Quark:

- Do **NOT** check the box named "facing pages."
- Do **NOT** check the box named "automatic text box." Because you can exert total control over your type and layout in QuarkXPress, never choose anything that says "automatic."

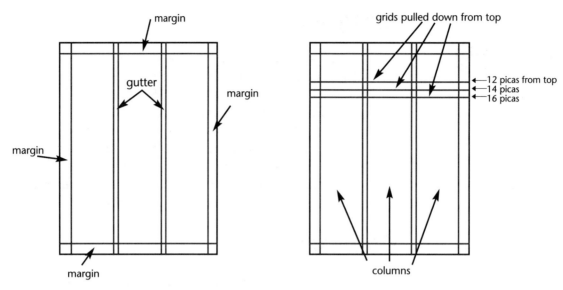

Figure 3-2. Page setup of 3 columns showing margins, gutters and grids.

Figure 3-3.
Examples of 2-column-grid format.

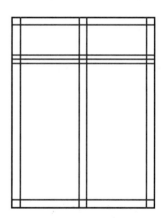

Two-column formats restrict variety in design, although they can provide a readable look. Using *copybreakers* (pictures, subheads, rules, pullquotes) is very important for 2-column formats.

Three-column-grid formats encourage variety in design
and have a high level of readability. We will be working
in a 3-column format for newsletters in this course.

These three examples use the 2-1 format. The first two columns work together, while the single column is the loner, running down the side of the right page.

Figure 3-4. All five of these Quark Quandary layouts are examples of the 3-column-grid format.

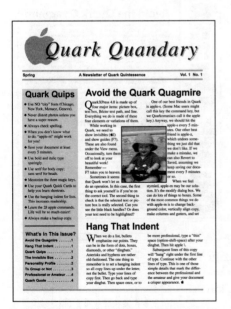

These two examples use the 1–2 format. The left column acts as a single column, while articles fill the right two columns.

Figure 3-5. This layout mimics the one to its left. It shows the 1-2 pattern more clearly than you can see in the other one.

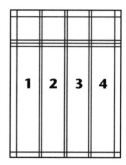

Figure 3-6. Four-column grid in a 2–2 pattern. The left one shows the gridlines. The right one is the same newsletter without the x's across the columns.

Typed copy is formatted in single columns but the articles stretch across two columns. Heads stretch across two columns to encompass their articles. The X's show the columns that work together with articles.

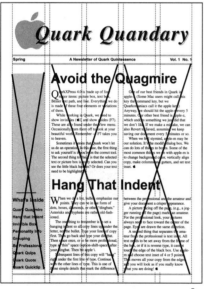

A

B

C

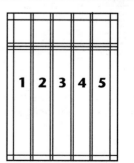

Figure 3-7. Five-column grid. Example A shows how the columns form the 1-2-2 pattern or a 1-4 pattern. If you consider the body copy, the 1-2-2 pattern fits. If you consider the number of columns the heads encompass, you might call this a 1-4 pattern. Naming it isn't so important; what's important is staying in the grids. In example B, the left column is used as a shaded box with the table of contents, while on C, the nameplate runs up the side as a column.

Quick Quiz

1. Why is it important to base your page layout on a grid?

2. How do margins change the "color" of a page?

3. What are the five decisions you need to make when opening a new document?

4. What is the purpose of a gutter?

5. What is the relationship between width of columns and width of gutters?

Quicktip

On a page of more than one column, the edges of text boxes and picture boxes should touch a vertical grid. Don't *free-float* boxes across grids unless you are experienced.

What's a zip disk?

A *zip disk* holds 100 megabytes (MB), whereas a floppy disk holds 1.3 MB. They go into different slots in the computer. Most Macs don't have built-in floppy drives anymore. However, many of them have zip drives. The 250 MB drive will accept both 100 and 250 disks, but the 100 MB drive takes only 100. Carefully check which zip drive your computer has and then buy the correct zip disk.

If your computer has a USB port, you might want to use another kind of storage device, named *keychain drive, flash drive* and *pocket drive.* These little gadgets plug into a USB slot in the computer or on the keyboard, depending on how many megabytes they hold.

Out of the Quandary

Find layout grids

Find publications that have various numbers of columns. Notice the size of the type in each. Notice ease or difficulty of reading. Do the artists respect the grids? Can you see a grid — a plan for the layout, or does it look haphazard? Are all the pages the same or does the artist use different plans on different pages? Begin collecting newsletters with grid patterns you like.

Quantum Leap

Get rid of all grids at once

Try this after you have gone through the Quark Quest exercise.

Sometimes you have many grids on a page and you want to remove them all.

The edge (top or left or both) of the page you are working on needs to be tucked under the ruler.

Hold down option key. Click twice on the top ruler. All vertical green grids should disappear.

Hold down option key. Click twice on the side ruler. All horizontal green grids should disappear.

No disk?

If you don't have a disk yet, save to the common folder on the hard drive if there is one. If you can't save at all without a disk, do the assignment anyway. Then pick up steps 1 and 2 next class.

Figure 3-8.
New folder menu.

Mac users: Under **File,** choose **New**. Then just lift your fingers off the mouse, and a new document setup box will appear.

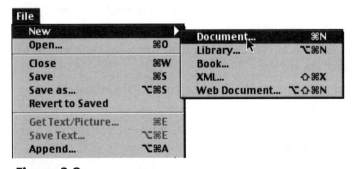

Figure 3-9.
New document menu. Or key command ⌘ **N.**

Quark Quest

Name the disk

☐ 1. Write your name on the disk or storage device in pen.

☐ 2. Then insert it into the appropriate computer slot.

☐ 3. For Mac users: Click on the icon of the disk and hit **Return**. The words will now be highlighted. *Windows users:* click on the disk, then click on the words.

☐ 4. Type your name to name the disk. You don't have to delete the old words. Just type over them.

Create a new folder

☐ 5. Open your disk by clicking on it two times.

☐ 6. *Mac users:* Under the **File** menu, choose **New → Folder** (Figure 3-8). *Windows users:* When disk is open, right click in box. A menu pops up. Click **New folder**.

☐ 7. Click on the icon of the folder and hit **Return**.

☐ 8. Name the folder *Practice*.

☐ 9. You can now close the folder's window by clicking once in the upper left box (Mac) or in the upper right box (Windows).

Open a new document (Construct the page)

☐ 10. Open QuarkXPress. Your teacher will show you how to do this.

☐ 11. Be sure you have the toolbar and the measurements bar showing. (Under **View → Show tools, Show measurements**.)

☐ 12. Under **File**, choose **New**. Slide over to **Document** (Figure 3-9). You can also use a key command: ⌘ **N.**

> *Make the following choices:*
> **Page size:** 9" x 6"
> **Orientation:** landscape
> **Margin guides:**
> top and bottom: 3p (3 picas = .5 inch)
> left and right 4p
> **Columns:** 2
> **Gutter width:** 2p (.333 inch)
> Click "**OK**" and open the document.

Chapter 4 goes into detail with points and picas. For now, just know that:
6 picas = 1 inch   12 points = 1 pica

Save the document

☐ 13. Save your document. **File → Save**. Or click ⌘ **S**. Name it *First document.qxd* and navigate to the folder on your disk. Pay attention to where you put it. Click on **Save** (Figure 3-10).

Quicktip

The default color for highlighting is light blue. Anytime you see blue words, they are calling you to "Type on me!" (Try to break the habit of deleting and then typing.)

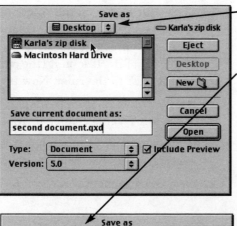

Figure 3-10. Navigate to the desktop. Choose Karla's zip disk (of course you will choose YOUR zip disk). Then navigate through your folders until you have the one you want at the top – Practice folder.

If you don't pay attention to where you saved it, you will think you lost it, but don't worry. Your instructor can help you find it by using the "Find" under the File menu. (See Quicktip.)

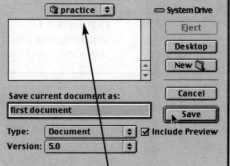

Click on this until you get the folder you want.

Quicktip

Lost a document?

There's a good chance you saved it in some folder somewhere on the disk or even on the hard drive.

To find it:

1. Click on desktop.
2. ⌘ **F** or **File → Find**.
3. *Sherlock* dialog box shows. Type part or all of the name of your file.
4. Click on the magnifying glass and Sherlock will show you where that file is.
5. Click twice on it to open the file. Then "Save As" to the folder you want it in.

Dialog box: small pop-up box that has options to choose or blanks to fill in.

Naming the document

Mac users can name the document anything they want, up to 31 characters. Windows users can use up to 27 characters. **HOWEVER,** because QuarkXPress is a cross-platform program, which means it is used on Macs and Windows, we will be using the Windows extension of **.qxd** to allow our files to open on either platform.

If you use only Mac, feel free to leave off the extension. You can always add it later if you want to open the file on a PC.

Close the document

☐ 14. Click in the LEFT top corner of the window (Mac) or right corner (Windows).

Repeat the exercise

☐ 15. Now open another document, but this time choose:

8½ x 11 vertical

3 picas all margins

3 columns

1p6 gutter (.25 inch)

☐ 16. Save the document as *Second document.qxd* in the Practice folder.

☐ 17. Use this document for the next exercise.

Grab a grid

Green is the default color for grids on a Mac. Windows users will see black grids on their computers.

☐ 18. Be sure rulers are showing on top and bottom of document. If they are not, go to **View → Show rulers.** Also be sure measurements bar is showing (Figure 3-11). If it is not, go to **View → Show measurements**.

☐ 19. Click your cursor on the ruler and hold down your finger. The cursor becomes a crosshair (Figure 3-12). Now drag down the page and a green guideline (gridline) will come with the mouse. To get rid of it, click on it (the cursor can't be on a text box) and drag it back to the ruler. Now try one from the side ruler.

☐ 20. Drag a guideline from the top to 16p. Use the measurements bar to see the Y value change to 16p. Now try 25p.

☐ 21. Drag guidelines from the left ruler to 19p and 29p. Again, use the measurements bar. Now get rid of them.

☐ 22. Save the document.

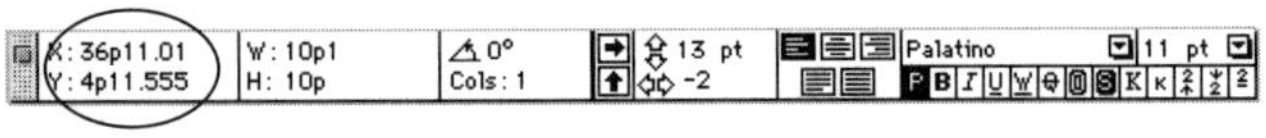

The cursor becomes a crosshair.

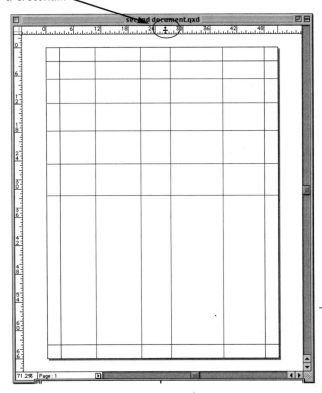

Figure 3-11.
Measurements bar (a palette). When you are pulling grids, watch the x and y scales to get to your desired position.

Show or hide guides

☐ 23. To hide or show guides, you can go to **View → Hide/show guides** or simply click **F7**.

Work with the guides ON. Hide them temporarily just to see your beautiful work! Today's task will show just a blank page, but later you will love the look of this. It can be compared to the print preview you will get in some printing dialog boxes.

Figure 3-12.
To grab a grid, put your cursor in the ruler. Click down and the cursor turns into a different symbol. Drag the gridline to where you want it. Watch the x or y scale on the measurements palette until the value you want shows up. Then let go of the mouse.

F7 takes you to heaven! (You can see your beautiful work.)

Grids off the page?

If you want the grids to go across a two-page spread, click your mouse in the ruler *outside the edge of page.* This is above the pasteboard area.

Usually you will grab a grid within the confines of the page.

Close the document

☐ 24. Mac users: **File → Close** *or* click in upper left corner.
Windows users: **File → Close** *or* click in upper right corner.

Close (or exit) a program

☐ 25. Mac users: **File → Quit** *or* ⌘**Q**. Windows users: **File → Exit**.

Delete file

Mac users:

☐ 26. Click on the file or folder you want to delete and hold down the mouse.

☐ 27. Drag the file to the trash can on your desktop. The trash can should blacken. If it doesn't, move the icon around on the trash can until it does blacken.

☐ 28. Then go to **Special → Empty trash**.

☐ 29. If you do not empty the trash, the file stays on your disk — in trash status!

Windows users:

☐ 30. Right click and choose **Delete** on the menu *or* left click and hit **Delete** on the keyboard.

Eject disk

☐ 31. Close out any open windows.

☐ 32. *Mac users:* Drag the disk to the trash can. It will pop out of the computer. *Windows users:* From the file menu, eject the disk. If you are using a portable zip drive, push the button on the drive. If for some reason the disk won't eject, shut down the computer. To do this, click on the desktop. Go to **Special → Shutdown**. Then start the computer again. The disk should eject on its own. (Restart doesn't always work, but shutting down and starting up does.)

Save or save as?

Save as makes another copy of the file. It can be useful when we want to make a copy with some variations or save a file to another folder or another disk. In most cases, use **Save**. When you **Save as**, your first copy goes away (to wherever you saved it in the first place), and you are now working on the **Saved as** version. It can get very confusing.

If you keep getting the **Save as** choice when you simply **Save**, it's because you're working in a higher version of Quark, but the original was saved in a lower version. Save it up to the higher version (option is under the box where you name the document).

The full working QuarkXPress screen

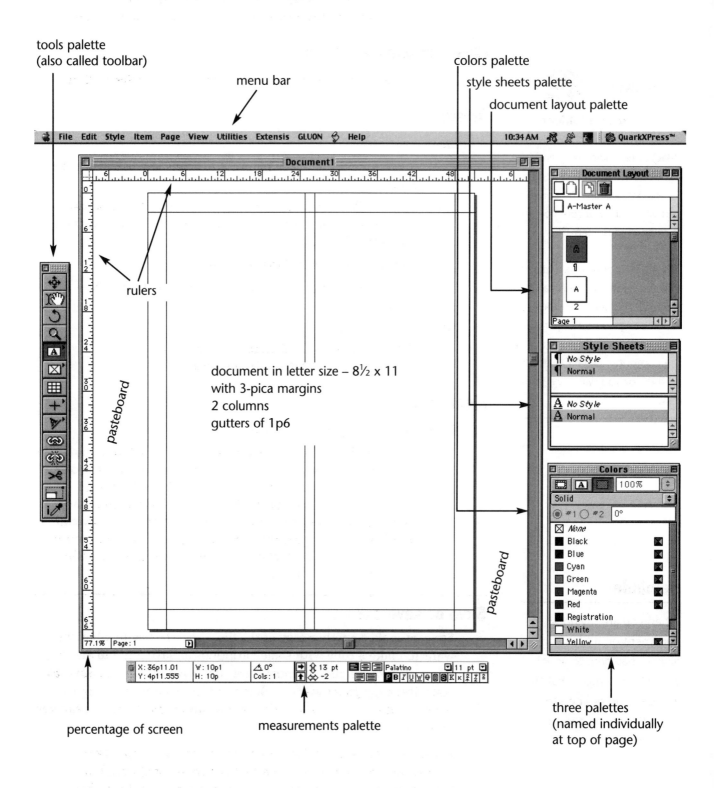

tools palette
(also called toolbar)

menu bar

colors palette

style sheets palette

document layout palette

rulers

pasteboard

document in letter size – 8½ x 11
with 3-pica margins
2 columns
gutters of 1p6

pasteboard

percentage of screen

measurements palette

three palettes
(named individually
at top of page)

Simplified screen for one-page documents

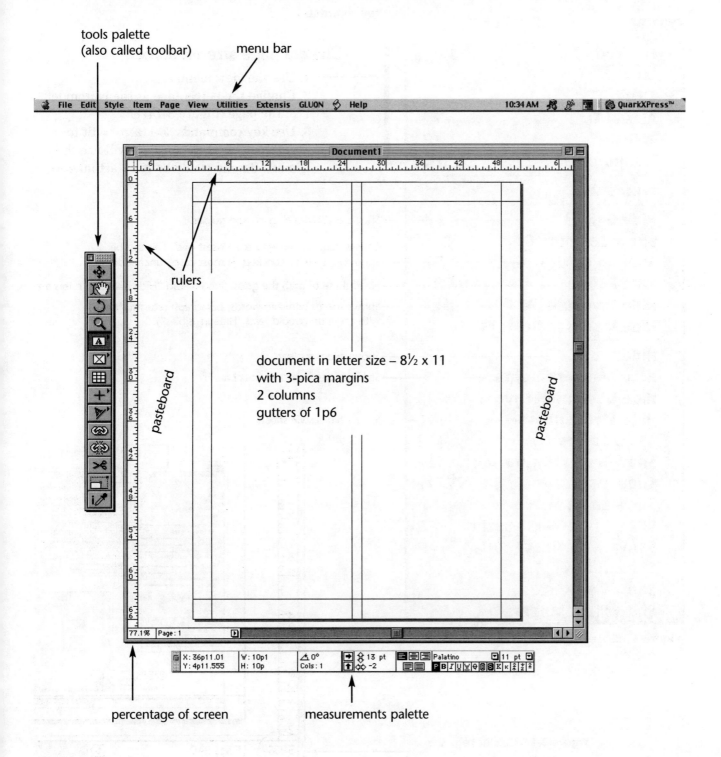

tools palette (also called toolbar)

menu bar

rulers

Pasteboard

document in letter size – 8½ x 11
with 3-pica margins
2 columns
gutters of 1p6

Pasteboard

percentage of screen

measurements palette

View Menu

The View Menu lets you VIEW things (Figure 3-13). So when you want to SEE something, choose the View menu. Or use the appropriate key command.

View	
Fit in Window	⌘0
50%	
75%	
Actual Size	⌘1
200%	
Thumbnails	⇧F6
Windows	▶
Hide Guides	F7
Show Baseline Grid	⌥F7
Snap to Guides	⇧F7
Hide Rulers	⌘R
Hide Invisibles	⌘I
Hide Visual Indicators	
Hide Tools	F8
Hide Measurements	F9
Hide Document Layout	F10
Hide Style Sheets	F11
Show Colors	F12
Show Trap Information	⌥F12
Show Lists	⌥F11
Show Layers	
Show Profile Information	
Show Hyperlinks	
Show Index	
Show Sequences	
Show Placeholders	

Figure 3-13. View menu.

Change page size on screen

1. Use the view menu *or*
2. Change the percentage at the bottom left of the page (Figure 3-14) *or*
3. Use key commands. ⌘0 (zero) = fit to screen. This is the one you will use the most. Second would be ⌘1 = actual size.

— Shows and hides all grids and guides.

Causes items to move to the closest grid. This can be annoying, so if it's checked, in most cases, uncheck it.

— Need these to grab the grids. Should read "Hide Rulers" if rulers are on.

— Shows spaces between words, paragraph returns. Work with these on (would read "Hide Invisibles").

— Shows/hides toolbar.

— Shows/hides measurements bar.

— Shows/hides style sheets.

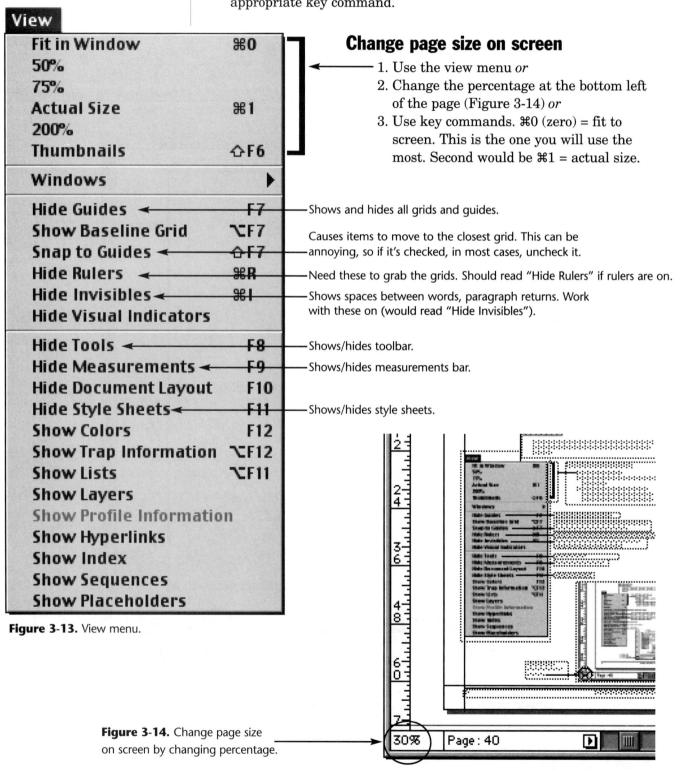

Figure 3-14. Change page size on screen by changing percentage.

4 Type

I strongly feel it is our obligation — every one of us who uses the computer to create text on a page — to uphold the highest possible level of typographic quality in this changing world.

Robin Williams
The Mac Is Not a Typewriter

Quest Objectives

- Identify the four type classes.
- Name the four alignment choices and the uses for each.
- List some of the type styles on the measurements bar.
- Describe the anatomy of a letter.
- Interpret type specs.
- Calculate points and picas.
- Distinguish between leading, tracking and word spacing.
- List several typographic "rules of thumb" for increased readability.

Quest Skills

- Draw a text box.
- Move a box.
- Rotate a box.
- Cut and paste text.
- Size a text box.
- Duplicate a box.
- Type text in a box.
- Color text.
- Manipulate text by using the measurements bar: size, font, alignment, style, tracking, leading.

Quest Terms

absolute leading	display type	sans serif
alignment	font	script or cursive
all caps	leading	serif
ascender	letterspacing	tracking
auto leading	lowercase	type specs
baseline	marquee	type styles
city fonts	monospaced	typesetting mode
classes of type	novelty	uppercase
configuration	picas	word spacing
counter	points	x-height
descender	reverse type	

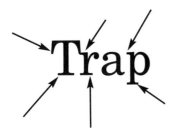

Figure 4-1.
All arrows point to serifs.

Classes of type

Although *type* can be classified into many *classes* (groups), we will divide them into just four classes: serif, sans serif, script and novelty. *Fonts* tend to have characteristics that give them their own "personality." Choose your font carefully based on the tone of the publication and its intended audience.

Serif

Serif fonts have the little strokes or "feet" on them. These tend to help guide your eye from letter to letter, resulting in better readability. It's also cultural: Americans learn to read in a serif font. Additionally, the serifs create more differentiation between letters than sans serif. Hence, use serif for body copy.

The samples below are all typed in 10 point, but notice how different they look in size. This is because their x-heights and counter spaces differ, as we will learn later.

Times and Times New Roman are the most versatile.

Times and Times New Roman look very much alike.

Stone Serif is a large, modern serif font.

Bookman is also a big type.

Palatino looks friendly yet professional.

Cooper Black is strong and good for heads.

New Century Schoolbook is easy to read.

Minion is similar to Times, but a bit more stylish.

Examples of serif fonts

Sans Serif

Sans is French for without: *sans serif* means "without serifs." Sans serif type is clean and crisp. Use sans serif for headlines and perhaps captions. For contrast, use sans serif for copy set in boxes, especially if the box is shaded. If the type is white (reverse type) and the box is dark, definitely use sans serif and make it bold. We are seeing a trend toward more sans serif in body copy, but for this course, let's stay with serif for body copy, sans serif for heads.

Helvetica is very popular.

Helvetica Narrow is a variation of Helvetica.

Arial is a little smaller than Helvetica.

This word is typed in Helvetica; the rest of the sentence is typed in Arial.

Avant Garde has a modern look.

Stone Sans is a modern sans serif font.

Charcoal shows strength.

Eurose is high-tech.

Examples of sans serif fonts

Script

Individual letters usually appear attached in *script* — also called *cursive*. Although beautiful, script is difficult to read in large blocks of copy. Limit its use to invitations, thank-you notes or perhaps an occasional headline.

Most letters are connected in Signature, Mariah, ScriptMTBold, Swing and Brush Script. Invitation and Zapf Chancery look connected, but they aren't.

Examples of script fonts

Novelty

This is our favorite group! It includes all those fonts that do not fall in the other three categories. The essential point to remember when using a *novelty* font is to match the font to the tone of the publication. For example, you wouldn't choose Nadianne for a Superbowl party invitation; instead, you might choose Subway or Tubular — something stronger and tougher. You could use Transistor for a publication with a futuristic tone. Stagecoach has the Wild West flavor. And so on.

Bavand	Nadianne	Stagecoach
BAZOOKA	GASLIGHT	Franciscan
STENCIL	Jester	Textile
MACHINE	Tubular	Calligrapher
TRANSISTOR	Subway	Old English
Klang	Stylus	Comic Sans

Examples of novelty fonts

Goals of type

Body copy

Type for body copy has two goals: to be "invisible" and to convey its message. This means the font should not get in the way of the message — a reader should not even notice the type. Body type's job is to present the message legibly so it gets read by its intended audience.

Heads

Type for heads, on the other hand, should be noticeable because it is much larger and bolder. Its two goals are to attract attention (opposite of body copy) and to convey its message — thus, clarity of font is essential.

Points and picas

In layout, we usually use *points* and *picas* for measuring. One inch equals 6 picas. Each pica equals 12 points. Therefore, one inch equals 72 points (6 x 12 = 72).

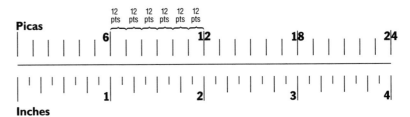

Figure 4-2.
Comparison of picas and inches.

What measures what?

Points
- font size
- thickness of rules (lines)
- leading (space between lines of type)
- text inset

Picas (& points)
- column width
- column depth
- picture boxes
- text boxes
- length of rules
- gutters
- paragraph indents

Inches
- page size (e.g., 8½ x 11)
- story lengths (newspapers)

Picas and points are combined in some of the measurements. For example, perhaps the columns are 13 picas wide. Gutters could be 1 pica, 6 points. Font size might be 11 points.

How to express points and picas

To designate points and picas in Quark, we use a "p" either before or after the number, respectively. For example:

8 points = p8   *the p goes before the number*

13 picas = 13p   *the p goes after the number*

1 pica, 6 points = 1p6   *Note that the "p" is shared between the numbers. This would be 1.5 picas in our base-10 number system.*

Equivalency list of common designations

Some common designations for gutters, paragraph indents and margins:

1p = .17 inch (.1666 rounded off, also 1/6 inch)
1p2 = .2 inch (.194 rounded off)
1p6 = .25 inch
2p = .3 inch (.3333 rounded off, also 1/3 inch)
3p = .5 inch

I informally surveyed dozens of printers, publishers and editors and found a split verdict: some are adamant in using picas and others exclusively use inches.

Which do you use as your default setting — picas or inches? The author would like feedback on this issue for future editions. Send feedback to **www.claudiacuddy.com**.

An editor who is marking up copy might designate points like this: 12'. It would obviously not mean "feet" in this context.

Quicktip

When the item is measured in points all the time, Quark uses "pt" as the abbreviation. But when the measurement could be picas OR points (or both) Quark uses "p."

Some of the values in QuarkXPress automatically default to picas or points. For example, for size of type, typing in the number automatically tells the computer it's in points because type size is always measured in points. For most other values, designate the "p" before or after the number you type to distinguish points and picas.

Set your preferences

If the preferences of your document are set in inches, change them to picas, unless your instructor prefers to leave them in inches.

Step 1

Quark 5: Edit → Preferences → Preferences (again)

Quark 4: Edit → Preferences → Document

Step 2

Measurements → Picas → OK

Figure 4-3.
Preferences menus to set the measurements default to picas.

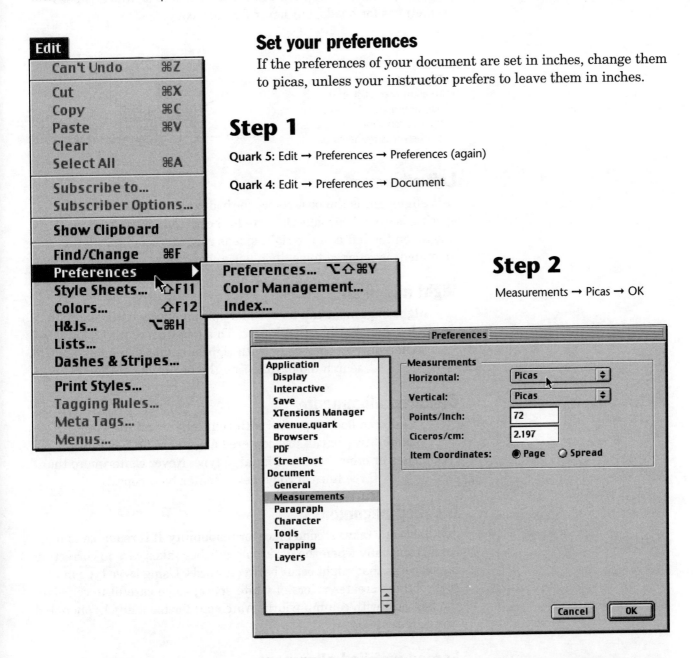

> **Don't miss this tip!** If you have a document open when you set any preferences, those choices will apply to only that document. If you have no document open and you set preferences, those choices will apply to all subsequent documents.

Horizontal alignment of type

In most of your typesetting, you will use one of four choices of horizontal alignment: *left*, *right*, *centered* or *justified*. The fifth one on the Quark measurements bar is *force justified*, which is used sometimes for heads, but never for body copy.

Figure 4-4.
To align text, click in the paragraph and then click on the desired alignment pattern on the measurements bar.

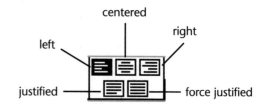

Left alignment

Left alignment is the best choice for body copy because word spacing is even. This gets the vote for best readability. All lines line up on the left and the right side is ragged. Sometimes left alignment is referred to as flush left, ragged right.

Right alignment

Right alignment can be used for special effects with a caption, a label or possibly a pullquote. This ties with centered for worst readability in body copy. With right alignment, readers have to search too hard to find the beginning of the next line.

Centered alignment

Centered body copy ties with right alignment for worst readability. You can use centered alignment for headlines, pullquotes or other items set in large type. Never center more than three lines of copy: never center body copy.

Justified alignment

Justified copy takes second place for readability. It is readable in most cases, especially when the desktop publisher takes care in correcting large spaces that might occur between words. Using large type in narrow columns creates rivers of white space, so be careful to correlate the font size with column width. Watch out for too many hyphenated words, too.

Forced justified alignment

The fifth choice is not used with body copy. This setting forces the line to stretch from left to right, even if there are only a few words on the line.   Don't   use   it   for   body   copy.

Type styles

Type styles include plain, bold, italic, underline, strike-through, outline, shadow, capitals, small capitals, superscript, subscript and superior. For school and home purposes, you may use the Quark measurements bar to stylize your font. However, for a piece that will be commercially printed, choose the "pure" font style. This means you would select a font such as "Stone Serif Italic" or "Minion Bold" from the font list — one that is already in italics if you wanted italics or already in bold if you need bold.

Italic print is read more slowly than nonitalic. Shadow, outline and underline styles of type interfere with the reader's ability to recognize shapes of words. Therefore, the best style choice in most cases is plain. Use the other styles sparingly.

Limit yourself to two or three fonts for one publication. Some people use several choices from a type family and thus give the appearance of more fonts and contrast (Figure 4-5). Styles in the family might include italic, semibold, semibold italic, bold, bold italic, condensed, ultra and so on.

Figure 4-5.
Garamond family of type.

Garamond
Garamond Bold Condensed
Garamond Bold Condensed Italic
Garamond Book
Garamond Book Condensed
Garamond Book Condensed Italic
Garamond Book Italic
Garamond Light Condensed
Garamond Light Condensed Italic
Garamond Ultra
Garamond Ultra Condensed
Garamond Ultra Condensed Italic
Garamond Ultra Italic

Why should you use a "pure" font in professional publications?

High-end printers do not pick up the stylizing messages. For example, the printer will read Garamond Bold Condensed or Garamond Book Italic as a pure font. However, if you stylize Garamond by hand on the measurements bar, the printer sees "Garamond," but it does not recognize that you made it bold or italic. Therefore, if your publication will be professionally printed, use only the pure fonts.

Quark measurements bar

Quicktip

Use the Quark measurements bar to do everything to type except color it.

To color type, choose **Color** under the **Style** menu at the top.

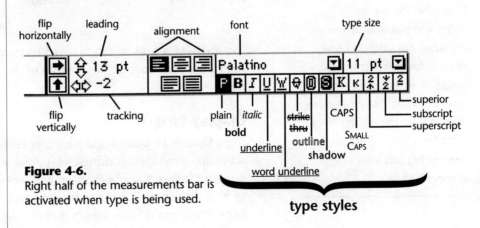

Figure 4-6.
Right half of the measurements bar is activated when type is being used.

Anatomy of a letter

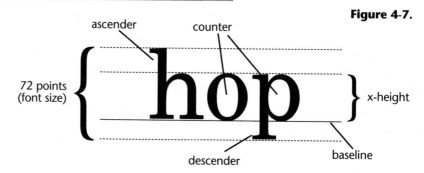

Figure 4-7.

Letters have five main components: x-height, ascender, descender, counter (some people call this bowl) and baseline (Figure 4-7).

baseline – the base of the lowercase letters sit on this line.

x-height – the height of an "x" in that font; also, the height of any other letters without their ascenders or descenders.

ascender – the part of the letter that extends above the x-height.

descender – the part of the letter that descends below the baseline.

counter – the inside white space of a letter. White space is opposite or *counter* to black (consider clockwise vs. *counter*clockwise).

Type size

Because fonts of the same size can vary in x-heights, some fonts appear bigger than others. Notice the difference in the x-heights and capital E of the fonts in Figure 4-8, all set in 24 point.

Figure 4-8.

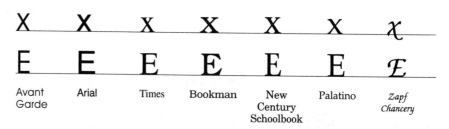

Avant Garde | Arial | Times | Bookman | New Century Schoolbook | Palatino | *Zapf Chancery*

Type size of a font is determined by measuring in points from the top of the ascender to the bottom of the descender (see sidebar on page 50).

Display type

Type that is 16 points and above is referred to as *display type*. These sizes are used for headlines. Heads should be bold and at least 2 points larger than body copy, but some type experts call for heads to be as much as 1.5 times bigger than body copy. Thus, 11-point body copy would have heads measuring from 13 to 17 points.

Quicktip

Two other factors that determine size of headline are *importance of story* and *how many columns across* the story covers. If a story goes across three columns, make the head fit the total width. If the story is the lead story, make the head as big and bold as space allows.

7 points
8 points
9 points
10 points
12 points
14 points
18 points

24 points

30 points

36 points

48 points

60 points

72 points

Figure 4-9. Type sizes in Times New Roman.

Type specs

Type specs (specifications) describe the font, size, leading, column width, alignment and any other directions. (An extra direction might be the color of the type.) Specs for this paragraph are expressed like this:

10.5/13.5 x 26   New Century Schoolbook Left al.

- 10.5-point type with 3 points of leading, expressed as 13.5 on the measurements bar (see section on Leading, page 50)
- 26-pica column width
- New Century Schoolbook is the font (if you need italic or bold, add that)
- Left al. is left aligned, ragged right

Leading

The space between lines of type is called *leading* (pronounced "ledding"). The name comes from the days when printers used lead type and put a thin strip of plain lead between the lines of type to create space. Some of your word processing programs call this "line spacing," but keeping with tradition, publishing programs refer to it by its original name.

Measured in points, leading is usually 1 or 2 points for most body copy. Instead of typing in 1 or 2 points on the Quark measurements bar, you will add 1 or 2 to the size of the type to get the leading. For example, if you are using 11-point type with 2 points leading, leading would be designated as 13 (11 + 2 = 13).

Use more leading for copy that is set in sans serif or heavier fonts. If the font size is less than 9 points, increase the leading. If longer lines of print are used, also increase leading. This helps readers find the next line more easily.

Always designate a number for leading. DO NOT use "auto" on the measurements bar.

Scenario:
Pretend this font is 11' (point) and we are using 2' leading.

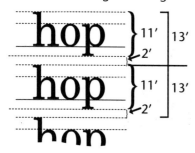

Figure 4-11.
Understanding derivation of 11/13:
11 point type, 2 point leading.

Figure 4-10.
Leading on the measurements bar.

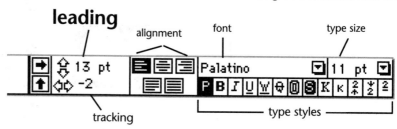

When we do a list, bullets emphasize our points. They can be in the form of dots, boxes, diamonds, or other "dingbats." Asterisks and hyphens are rather old-fashioned. The one thing to remember is to set a hanging indent, so all copy lines up under the letter, not the bullet. Type	When we do a list, bullets emphasize our points. They can be in the form of dots, boxes, diamonds, or other "dingbats." Asterisks and hyphens are rather old-fashioned. The one thing to remember is to set a hanging indent, so all copy lines up under the	When we do a list, bullets emphasize our points. They can be in the form of dots, boxes, diamonds, or other "dingbats." Asterisks and hyphens are rather old-fashioned. The one thing to remember is to set a hanging indent, so all	When we do a list, bullets emphasize our points. They can be in the form of dots, boxes, diamonds, or other "dingbats." Asterisks and hyphens are rather old-fashioned. The one thing to remember is to set a hanging indent, so all
10-point type 9-point leading	10-point type 10-point leading	10-point type 11-point leading	10-point type 12-point leading
Negative leading. Ascenders touch descenders.	0 leading. Ascenders touch descenders.	1 point of leading. This one is a little better than the other two.	2 points leading. This one looks the best.

Figure 4-12. Various leading values.

Quicktip

Left, right, left!

You can remember the position of leading and type size on the measurements bar by thinking, "Leading is on the LEFT."

Notice also the direction of the gray arrows. Leading is vertical space, so the arrows go up and down.

Type size is designated on the RIGHT of the bar. The RIGHT type size helps readability. Think, "RIGHT type size."

leading (left)   type size (right)

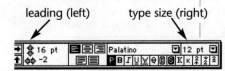

"Less leading for the heading"

What happens when you use auto leading?

Auto leading is the automatic leading setting in QuarkXPress. It will automatically adjust for the largest point size in your paragraph. Therefore, if you use auto leading, your lines may be unevenly leaded. To avoid this, manually type a number 1 or 2 points larger than your type size in the leading spot on the measurements bar.

Auto leading Notice the difference in leading because of the large bold words. Type is 9 point; large type is 15.	Si meliora dies, ut vina, poemata reddit, scire velim, chartis pretium quotus arroget annus. scriptor abhinc annos centum qui decidit, inter perfectos veteresque referri debet an inter vilis atque novos? Excludat iurgia finis, **"Est vetus atque probus,** centum qui perficit annos." Quid, qui deperiit minor uno mense vel anno, inter quos referendus erit? Veteresne poetas, an quos et…
13-point leading Same type sizes as above. Notice the consistent leading. This is *absolute leading*.	Si meliora dies, ut vina, poemata reddit, scire velim, chartis pretium quotus arroget annus. scriptor abhinc annos centum qui decidit, inter perfectos veteresque referri debet an inter vilis atque novos? Excludat iurgia finis, **"Est vetus atque probus,** centum qui perficit annos." Quid, qui deperiit minor uno mense vel anno, inter quos referendus erit? Veteresne poetas, an quos et…

Figure 4-13. Auto leading (top) and absolute leading (bottom).

Headlines and leading

Large headlines often look better with less leading. Although body copy calls for 1–2 points leading, large heads can be set solid (e.g., 36/36) or even negative (36/34). Both heads below are 18-point Franklin Gothic Heavy, but they have different leadings. Notice how the bottom one appears to be more of a unit than the top one.

University president announces construction of parking garage
18/20 or 2 points leading

University president announces construction of parking garage
18/18 or no leading (set solid)

Tracking

Tracking is the space between letters. Some word processing programs call it *letterspacing*. Notice the gray arrows that point left and right on the measurements bar. Default tracking on QuarkXPress is 0. Use -2 or -3 for most body copy. If you need to tighten the tracking, try -4 or -5, but stop there. DO NOT use positive tracking (1, 2, etc.).

DO NOT click on the arrows on the measurements bar — each click makes 10 points of tracking! Manually type in your tracking choice.

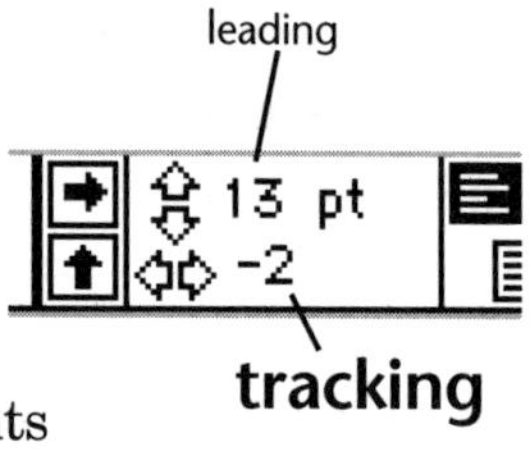

leading

tracking

Figure 4-14.
Tracking on the bar.

-10 tracking (too tight)	–2 tracking (**good choice**)	10 tracking (too much)
When we do a list, bullets emphasize our points. They can be in the form of dots, boxes, diamonds, or other "dingbats." Asterisks and hyphens are rather old-fashioned. The one thing to remember is to set a hanging indent, so all copy lines up under the letter, not the bullet. Type your ding-	When we do a list, bullets empha-size our points. They can be in the form of dots, boxes, diamonds, or other "dingbats." Asterisks and hyphens are rather old-fashioned. The one thing to remember is to set a hanging indent, so all copy lines up under the letter, not the	When we do a list, bullets emphasize our points. They can be in the form of dots, boxes, diamonds, or other "dingbats." Asterisks and hyphens are rather old-fash-ioned. The one thing to remember is to set a hanging

Figure 4-15. Set tracking at -2 or -3 for best results.

No city fonts!

Most computer fonts have a built-in *kerning* between pairs of letters to make them fit together. This is called *typesetting mode*. *City fonts* such as New York, Chicago, Geneva and Monaco look as if they had been produced on a typewriter. They are *monospaced*, which means that every letter occupies the same lateral space, whether it's an "m" or an "i." The city fonts were necessary for the dot matrix printers in earlier days. However, each city font has a counterpart that was designed in *typesetting* mode rather than monospacing (New York = Times; Chicago = Charcoal; Geneva = Helvetica; Monaco = possibly Myriad). Compare the following two paragraphs in Figure 4-16. The city font (New York) is too loose.

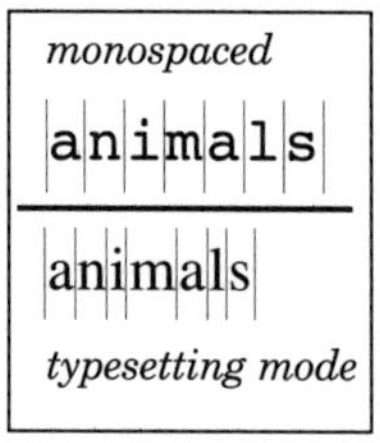

monospaced

animals

animals

typesetting mode

When we do a list, bullets emphasize our points. They can be in the form of dots, boxes, diamonds, or other "dingbats." Asterisks and hyphens are rather old-fash-	When we do a list, bullets emphasize our points. They can be in the form of dots, boxes, diamonds, or other "ding-bats." Asterisks and hyphens are rather old-fashioned. The one thing to remember is to set a hanging indent,
City font: New York, 9 point	Better choice: Times, 9 point

Figure 4-16
Comparison of city font (monospaced) to its counterpart (typesetting mode).

Qool Fact

So what is kerning?

The *kern* was actually a little notch in the side of a metal letter (slug) in the old metal-type days. It joined to the next slug to make the letters fit together in a close way.

Kerning is almost like tracking, but it concerns *pairs* of letters such as fi, WA, Ty, To, ox, (there are about 80 pairs). Most fonts have the kerning built into them by the computer program, so don't worry about it. *Tracking* is what we will be working with.

Word spacing

Word spacing is the space between each word. Justified columns create uneven word spacing, whereas left alignment produces even word spacing. Even (equal) word spacing helps readers recognize word groups, thus increasing readability. Figure 4-17 is set in 14-point type. Although exaggerated in this example, the word spacing differences are obvious between justified and left alignments.

Quicktip

Avoid
- large type in a narrow column
  OR
- small type in a wide column

When we do a list, bullets emphasize our points. They can be in the form of dots, boxes, diamonds, or other "dingbats." Asterisks and hyphens are rather old-fashioned. The one thing to remember is to set a hanging indent, so all copy lines up under the letter, not the bullet.	When we do a list, bullets emphasize our points. They can be in the form of dots, boxes, diamonds, or other "dingbats." Asterisks and hyphens are rather old-fashioned. The one thing to remember is to set a hanging indent, so all copy lines up under the letter, not the bullet.
Justified alignment can create uneven word spacing. Notice the wide word spacing.	Left alignment (not justified) eliminates the large word spacings. We still used large type, but the ragged right (left alignment) solves the problem.

Figure 4-17. Exaggerated example of word spacing.

Qool Fact

A man who would letter-space lowercase would steal sheep. (body copy)

Frederick Goudy
(great American type designer)

In the early 1900s one of the worst crimes in America was to steal someone's sheep. Goudy is trying to emphasize the "crime" it is to add spacing (tracking) between letters of body copy, which he calls "lowercase."

Quark's default is 0. A setting of -2 works nicely, and when tightening up, try -3, -4 or -5. Do not go the other way, past 0, into the positive numbers.

EXCEPTION: You may use positive tracking between "all caps" style of heads (which you will hardly use). A very large head in all caps might even use up to +40 tracking!

Readability factors

All caps

When you learned to read, you learned with capitals (*uppercase*) combined with small letters (*lowercase*). You learned "sight words" by their *configuration* — their shape was imprinted on your brain (Figure 4-18). A glance produces instant recognition. When you capitalize those words, the instant recognition disappears, and you have to decipher the message letter by letter. Therefore, avoid using all capital letters because words in all caps have no word-shape.

Furthermore, reading speed slows down. Figure 4-19 shows you the difficulty of reading in *all caps*.

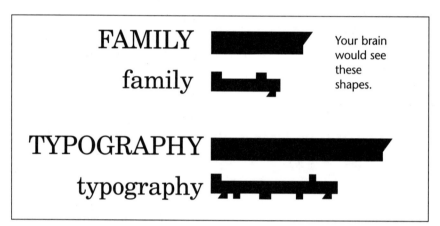

Figure 4-18. Configurations of the uppercase words show no distinction. Uppercase letters are referred to as *block letters* because their shapes form blocks. On the other hand, the versions with lowercase letters create word shapes that are more easily identifiable by the reader.

WHEN WE DO A LIST, BULLETS EMPHASIZE OUR POINTS. THEY CAN BE IN THE FORM OF DOTS, BOXES, DIAMONDS, OR OTHER "DINGBATS." ASTERISKS AND HYPHENS ARE RATHER OLD-FASHIONED. THE ONE THING TO REMEMBER IS TO SET A HANGING INDENT, SO ALL COPY LINES UP UNDER THE LETTER, NOT THE

When we do a list, bullets emphasize our points. They can be in the form of dots, boxes, diamonds, or other "dingbats." Asterisks and hyphens are rather old-fashioned. The one thing to remember is to set a hanging indent, so all copy lines up under the letter, not the bullet. Type your dingbat and space once.

Figure 4-19. Reading speed is slowed down by all caps.

Qool Fact

In earlier days (up until the 1970s) printers used metal type. These were small individual letters, made backward so that they would print forward (like a rubber stamp). A type composer had to line up each letter to make the words and sentences. These little "slugs" of letters were kept in cases of drawers.

Various kinds of cases were manufactured, but with one popular brand of cases, the capital letters were stored in the upper case of drawers while the small letters were stored in the lower case of drawers. Thus we get the terms uppercase and lowercase letters.

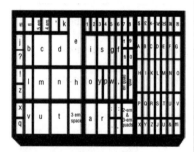

Figure 4-20.
Printer's drawer where slugs were stored. Several drawers made up the "printer's case." This one is called the "California job case."

This is an actual California job case drawer given to me by a friend who had been a printer for 50 years. Today people buy these at flea markets, fill the compartments with knick-knacks and hang them on walls.

Reverse

Reverse type is light type (usually white) on a dark background. We used to call it a *knock-out*, since ink is actually *knocked out* of the solid piece to leave white letters (white ink is not used). For best legibility, reverse copy should be in limited amounts, in sans serif, bold type and sufficient leading. Serif type's little feet often disappear into the ink (Figure 4-21). If you do use a serif font, make it larger than 10 point.

If you use a shaded box for a reverse, the background should be at least 40%. A solid color (100%) gives the strongest contrast.

Too many publications today are printing ad copy and large sections of body copy in reverse despite numerous studies that say readability is hindered. Once again, think of the seesaw: if interest is high, the audience will most likely read it anyway. But to gain the most readers, follow the guidelines.

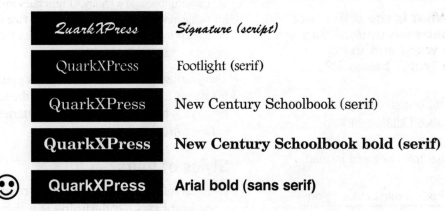

Quicktip

Use reverse type for very small blocks of copy.

It is called reverse type because it is the reverse of the usual white background with black ink.

Figure 4-21. The most effective type in a reverse is the last one, a BOLD sans serif font. The one above it isn't too bad, but the serifs create some loss of clarity. All examples are set in 12-point type with 0 tracking.

Fonts

Use serif for body copy, sans serif for heads.

You may notice many people are using sans serif for body copy, but until you get more experienced, stick with the rules of thumb.

Limit yourself to two fonts for a publication.

Remember when you seek contrast, be VERY different in font usage. Don't choose two serif fonts or two sans serif fonts. They are too similar.

Type is the "wind beneath the wings" of the message.

Type size

Choose 10-point, 11-point or 12-point fonts for body copy in most cases. Occasionally, 9 might be used, such as with Stone Serif, which is quite large because of its large counter space and high x-height.

Quicktip

Use two fonts per publication: one serif for body copy, one sans serif for heads.

What is the difference between underlining a word and using a "rule" below it?

This is underlining. Notice it cuts off all descenders (gjpqy). Don't use this. Use *italics* or **bold** instead.

This is a rule below. (gjpqy)

It is drawn by hand, using the orthogonal tool on the toolbar. Do not use the diagonal tool — your straight line can easily get tilted. The orthogonal was made for drawing perfect vertical or horizontal lines.

Notice there is a little bit of space between the bottom of the words and the rule. It does NOT cut off descenders.

use this tool →
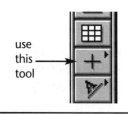

Column width (line length)

For 10-, 11- and 12-point type, about 10–12 words per line is comforting to the eye. This equals a column about 18–24 picas (3–4 inches) wide. The general rule is to double the point size of the type and set the column in that number of picas or smaller. For example, if you use 10-point type, column width would be no more than 20 picas.

Dan Daring became a QuarkXPress guru by living out his name, and he doesn't quaver in the face of new technology! When questions arise, he queries the *Communicating with QuarkXPress* book. (8/10 x 14)

Dan Daring became a QuarkXPress guru by living out his name, and he doesn't quaver in the face of new technology! When questions arise, he queries the *Communicating with QuarkXPress* book. (9/11 x 17)

Dan Daring became a QuarkXPress guru by living out his name, and he doesn't quaver in the face of new technology! When questions arise, he queries the *Communicating with QuarkXPress* book. (10/12 x 19)

Dan Daring became a QuarkXPress guru by living out his name, and he doesn't quaver in the face of new technology! When questions arise, he queries the *Communicating with QuarkXPress* book. (11/13 x 21)

Figure 4-22. Type size determines optimal column width.

Styles of fonts

Overuse of bold or italic hinders readability. Use them only when you want emphasis. Underlining is a thing of the past from typewriter days. However, you can put a rule under type — in Quark, use the orthogonal line tool (see sidebar). The tool looks like a big plus sign.

Paragraphs too long

This is in the editorial realm, but sometimes you are doing both jobs: editorial and layout. Make new paragraphs when they look too long. On a 3-column page, about 8 to 15 lines of type are easy for the reader to digest without a "breath." The "breath" comes when they move to the new paragraph, taking that breath at the indent!

Indents too big or too little

Indents can hinder readability. Recommended sizes are about 1p2 (about .2 inch) for a 3-column page and for about 1p6 (.25 inch) for a 2-column page.

One last thought

If you think your body copy is not readable, change it. Go with your instinct.

Why does this book use 3-point leading?

Type for this book is set in font size 10.5 points with 13.5 leading (3 points actual leading).

A reasonable line length (column width) is two times the point size in picas. Therefore, the best column width would be 21 picas (2 x 10.5). Then you would make your leading 2 points larger than the font size.

However, because of the book's layout plan, the column width is wider than the "two times the point size" rule. The actual typed area in width is 27p5.

Therefore, to compensate for any loss of readability from longer lines of type, we added leading. We use 3 points. The lines have enough space between them for your eye to move comfortably from the end of one line to the beginning of the next line without losing your place.

Quick Quiz

1. Which items are measured by points and which items are measured by picas?
2. Name the four classes of type and give one use for each.
3. Draw the anatomy of a letter and label its parts.
4. What are five factors that affect readability?
5. Interpret: 11/13 x 20 Times New Roman Italic.
6. Name the four alignment choices and the use for each.
7. What is the difference between stylizing a font and using a pure font style?

Quantum Leap

Tracking by keyboard command

Earlier in the chapter, the keyboard shortcut for changing type size was presented. Those who like keyboard commands will take ownership of this one as well.

1. Highlight the paragraph you want to tighten or loosen.
2. Hold down the 3 magic keys (⌘ ⌥ ⇧).
3. Use] to tighten tracking, one point each time. Use [to loosen.

⌘ ⌥ ⇧ [will tighten tracking by 1 point each time.

⌘ ⌥ ⇧] will loosen tracking by 1 point each time.

Symbol Refresher

Mac Users
⌘ = command (⌘)
⌥ = option
⇧ = shift

Windows Users
⌘ = control
⌥ = alternate
⇧ = shift

Out of the Quandary

* Find the folder named **Assignments** on your CD. The Chapter 4 folder contains a PDF of page 59 for you to use for this part of the assignment.

1. Finding Type Examples

Follow the directions on page 59. You may photocopy the page, create your own page or get it from the CD.*

2. Points and Picas Equations

Convert the following. Use the "p" before or after the number.

2" = _____ (picas)

4" x 5" box = _____ x _____ (picas)

4p = _____ (points)

2p8 = _____ (points)

p45 = _____ (picas and points)

.5p = _____ (points)

3. Type Personalities

On your computer, find fonts with personalities to fit 10 of the phrases below. You can type them in Word or any other program if you don't have easy after-class access to QuarkXPress. Type the phrase and then apply the font choice. Next to the phrase, type the name of the font you used.

Example:
Little girls' tea party (Nadianne)

1. Welcome to the Chinese Buffet
2. Wanted: Billy the Kid
3. Wedding Nuptials tomorrow
4. St. Paul's Cathedral in London
5. When the cows come home
6. February is the love month
7. Who's in charge here?
8. Monks in a monastery
9. Fashion show in Paris
10. Latest in technology
11. The New York Times
12. I learned it in Kindergarten
13. Monday night football

Finding Type Examples (Out of the Quandary, continued)

Name_____Class_____

From a magazine or newspaper, find examples of each item listed below. Cut them out and attach them to this paper, using rubber cement, a glue stick or tape. **Be neat**.

Classes of Type – Find **TWO** examples of each.

Serif

Sans serif

Script

Novelty

Type Sizes – Find **ONE** example of each. (Use the examples in this chapter to help you gauge size.)

7-point type   12-point type

36-point type   60-point type

Other

Find an example of reverse type. Label it as good or bad and explain your decision.

To show toolbar:
View → Show tools
or hit **F6** key.

text box

To use picas, change preferences (page 45).

Quark Quest

Practice with the Quark Measurements Bar

☐ 1. Create a folder called *Quark Bar*.

☐ 2. Open a new document 8½ x 11. Margins 6p (1 inch), 1 column. Gutters don't matter because the page is 1 column.

☐ 3. Name it *Quarkbar.qxd* and save into Quark Bar folder.

Make a text box

☐ 4. Click on the text box tool (box with **A** in it). Click on your document. Hold down the mouse and drag the mouse at a diagonal. Let go. You will have made a text box. Make a few boxes.

☐ 5. Now make a text box 20 picas wide, 30 picas high. Use the measurements bar to see the dimensions. You can also type in the measurements to get them exact.
Type 20p next to **W** and 30p next to **H**. Then hit **Return**.

Move an item

☐ 6. Click on the item tool. Then click on the center of the box. Now drag the box around the page. You are **moving** the text box. Now move it to align with the left side and top margin gridlines.

Highlight and resize an item

☐ 7. Click off the text box. Now click on the text box. Notice the little black **handle**s that appear on the sides and corners of the box. In this mode, the box is called **highlighted**.

☐ 8. Click on one of the side handles. Your crossbar shape will turn into a finger. Pull out the black handle. Push it back in. This is called **resizing the box**.

Type, cut and paste. Use the content tool for the next steps.

☐ 9. Click on the content tool. Now click in the text box. You will see a cursor.

☐ 10. Type a sentence.

☐ 11. Drag the cursor across the sentence to highlight it, like you would do in a word processing program.
Copy it (⌘ **C** or, using the menu, **Edit → Copy**).

☐ 12. Paste it about 6 times so you have some copy to work with. (⌘**V** or **Edit → Paste**).

Use item tool to move.

Item = **I**ce
Content = **C**ream
To remember the tools, in order, think "ice cream."

Use content tool to type.

Quicktip

Size a box using handles

Grab the black handles on the SIDE of the box and drag in or out to make smaller or bigger.

Do not use the corners because you lose control of both dimensions.

Quicktip

Don't miss this!

Often, to make an operation work, you have to hit the **Return** key (Mac) or the **Enter** key (Windows).

Quicktip

Shortcut to highlighting

Put cursor on text.

1 click = cursor blinks

2 clicks = highlight word

3 clicks = highlight sentence

4 clicks = highlight paragraph

5 clicks = highlight document

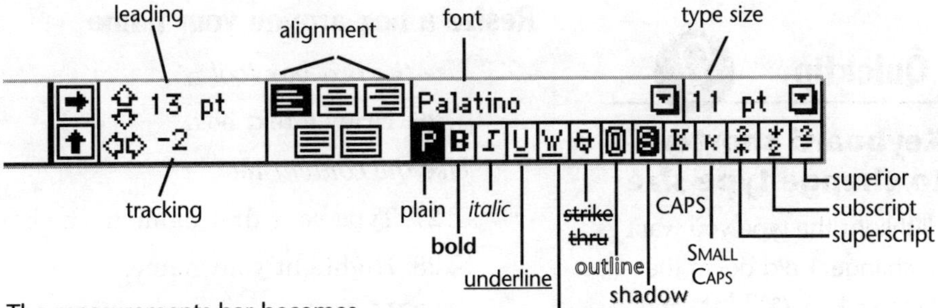

The measurements bar becomes activated when text box is highlighted.

(Diagram labels: leading, alignment, font, type size, tracking, plain, italic, bold, underline, word underline, strike thru, outline, shadow, CAPS, SMALL CAPS, superior, subscript, superscript)

Set type according to specs

☐ 13. Highlight all of it. Make it these specs (specifications): Palatino, 11/13 (that's 11-point type, 13-point leading) Tracking: -2.

☐ 14. Save your document: ⌘**S** or, using the menu, **Edit → Save**.

Apply tracking and leading

☐ 15. Highlight all of it. Make the **tracking** -30. The letters will look jumbled up on top of each other. Undo: ⌘**Z** or **Edit → Undo**.

☐ 16. Now make the **tracking** a high positive number, like 25. The letters will be far apart. **Undo**.

☐ 17. Make the **leading** a larger number. You will see lots of space between lines.

☐ 18. Make the **leading** a smaller number. It should be tighter.

☐ 19. Now make the **leading** a negative number. It will look jumbled.

☐ 20. Revert to saved. **File → Revert to saved**.

Apply various styles

☐ 21. Highlight a line or two. Go through the styles and see what happens. For example, apply **B** for **bold** Then apply **P** for **plain** to get it back to normal. Apply **I** for *italic*, then apply **P** again to get it back to normal. Try all the style choices.

Apply color

☐ 22. Highlight a line or two. From the menu, choose **Style → Color**. Slide the mouse over and pick a color.

Apply alignment

☐ 23. Select all. (That is equivalent to highlighting all of the copy). Click anywhere in the copy and use ⌘**A** or **Edit → Select all**.

☐ 24. Try the various alignments by clicking on each choice on the measurements bar.

Delete text

☐ 25. Delete typed copy by highlighting unwanted text and using the **Delete** key on the Mac, or the **Backspace** key on Windows.

Quicktip

Keyboard shortcut to change type size

Highlight the type you want to change. Hold down the 3 magic keys (⌘ ⌥ ⇧) and use the greater and less than signs to make type size go up and down. (< = smaller; > = larger)

Thus,

⌘ ⌥ ⇧> makes type
      1 point larger.

⌘ ⌥ ⇧< makes type
      1 point smaller.

Mac Users
⌘ = command (⬛)
⌥ = option
⇧ = shift

Windows Users
⌘ = control
⌥ = alternate
⇧ = shift

Wiindows extensions

qxd
qx = QuarkXPress
d = Document

qxt
qx = QuarkXPress
t = Template

qxl
qx = QuarkXPress
l = Library

Remember, ⌘ means *control* in Windows, *command* (apple) in Mac.

Resize a box around your name

Use the text box tool.

☐ 26. Draw a text box.

Use the content tool.

☐ 27. Type your first name in the box.

☐ 28. Highlight your name.

☐ 29. Make your name Arial, 24 point, bold. Use the shortcut in the sidebar if you want.
Center it.
Color it.

☐ 30. Drag the handles in to tighten the box around your name.

Duplicate a box

Use the item tool.

☐ 31. Highlight the box.

☐ 32. Duplicate the box (⌘D) or **Item → Duplicate**.

☐ 33. Use the item tool to move the box around the page.

Notice when you're on the item tool and moving a box that only the left side of the measurements bar is active.

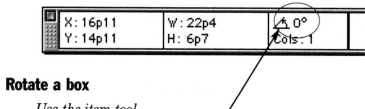

Rotate a box

Use the item tool.

Use the angle on the measurements bar to rotate a box.

☐ 34. Highlight a box.

☐ 35. Type in a value of 25°.

☐ 36. Repeat on another box.

Kill a box or line (delete an item)

Use either content or item tool.

☐ 37. Highlight item.

☐ 38. ⌘**K**.

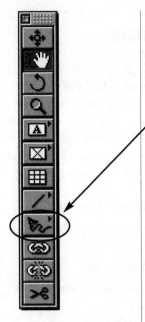

More type activities

Type on a text path

☐ 1. Choose the text path tool. Try all three: straight, diagonal and curved.

☐ 2. Draw the path.

☐ 3. Then type on the path (be sure content tool is selected).

☐ 4. To select the type to change its font, highlight the path so its black handles show. To highlight the path, draw a marquee around the path (see sidebar).

☐ 5. Then Select All (⌘A) or **Edit → Select all**. That will highlight all the type.

Move a text path

☐ 6. Use item tool. Draw a marquee around path to highlight it.

☐ 7. Move the item tool onto the typed line until the tool looks like its toolbar icon: the crossbars. It might look as if it is not on the item. That's okay. Just move the tool and the item follows. (You can't use the arrow or the pointing finger to move an entire item.)

Play with type

☐ 8. Draw a text box and type a few words in it.

☐ 9. Highlight the type. Use the black arrows on the measurements bar to flip the type horizontally and vertically.

☐ 10. Go into the modify box (⌘M). Experiment with text angle and text skew. Hit **Apply** to see the result. Then either cancel or hit **OK**.

☐ 11. Now type a text path. Go into the modify box (⌘M) and you will see some new options. Try each of those and apply to see your results. Try text alignment as well to see the type become centered or below the line. Then either cancel or hit **OK**.

What is a marquee? (mar-key)

Think of the moving neon lights of a signboard over the entrance of a theater. That's a marquee.

When you create a marquee in Quark, you get a dashed line. It disappears when you unclick the mouse. It is not permanent like a text box.

To make the marquee:
Use the item tool. Click, hold down and draw a box around the items you want included in the marquee. Let go of the mouse. Those items will now be highlighted, or activated.

Mac Users
⌘ = command (🍎)
⌥ = option
⇧ = shift

Windows Users
⌘ = control
⌥ = alternate
⇧ = shift

Tools Palette

(aka toolbar)

To show toolbar:
View → Show tools or **F6** key

Best two toolbar tricks

1 *Keep the tool*

If you want to stay on a tool (boxes, lines or linking) for repeated use, hold down the ⌥ key (Mac – option; Windows – alternate) and select the tool. Then release the ⌥ key. You can draw lines and boxes all over the place. You can also link dozens of columns.

2 *Sticky tools (the three-click switch)*

When you are switching back and forth between the item and the content tools:

1. Click on the tool you want.
2. Click on some blank space somewhere on the page.
3. Click on the page item you want.

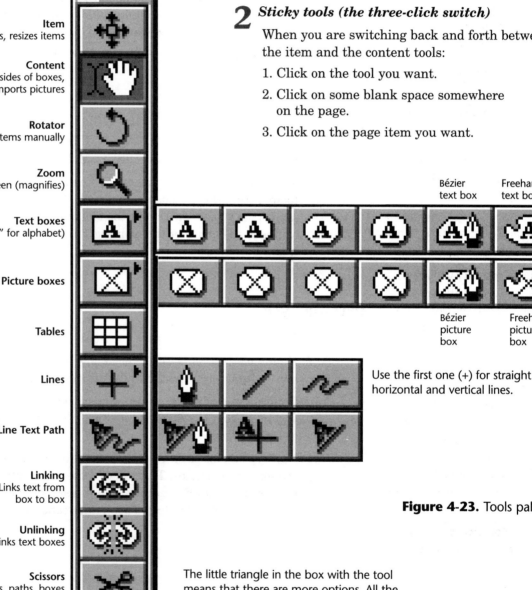

Item
Selects, moves, resizes items

Content
Works with the insides of boxes, inputs text, imports pictures

Rotator
rotates items manually

Zoom
Enlarges screen (magnifies)

Text boxes
("A" for alphabet)

Bézier text box   Freehand text box

Picture boxes

Bézier picture box   Freehand picture box

Tables

Lines

Use the first one (+) for straight horizontal and vertical lines.

Line Text Path

Linking
Links text from box to box

Unlinking
Unlinks text boxes

Scissors
Cuts lines, paths, boxes

Figure 4-23. Tools palette.

The little triangle in the box with the tool means that there are more options. All the options are shown in this figure.

5 Page Anatomy

Graphical excellence is that which gives to the viewer the greatest number of ideas in the shortest time with the least ink in the smallest space.

Edward R. Tufte
(Information-design Expert)

Quest Objectives

- Identify the elements of page anatomy.
- Describe four common headline styles.
- Explain ways a subhead produces better readability.
- Construct four different captions for photos.
- Distinguish header from headline.
- Give an example of a sidebar to accompany a national story.
- List four aspects of an effective pullquote.
- Define bulleted list, byline and jumpline.
- List four design enhancers.
- Describe characteristics of a successful logo.

Quest Terms

bleed	drop cap	sidebars
body copy	drop shadow	sink
bullet	end sign	standing head
bullet lists	footers	subheads
bylines	headers	summary deck
callout	headlines	text
captions	jumphead	text inset
chunking	jumpline	upstyle
credit line	logo	white space
dingbat	pullquotes	
downstyle	rule	

All the type on a page is referred to as *text*. Type that makes up the main content copy is called *body copy* or *body text*. The other text includes headlines, subheads, summary decks, pullquotes, headers and footers, captions, sidebars, jumplines and bylines. All these elements together make up the page anatomy, along with the framework of the page — grids, margins, columns and gutters (discussed in Chapter 3). Add visuals like logos, photos, clipart, frames and rules, and you have a complete page layout.

This chapter explains most of the elements of general page layout. Slight differences exist in terminology of magazine, newspaper and newsletter layout, but the elements fulfill the same purposes.

Headlines

Headlines attract readers to the story. Sans serif type works well for heads, but you can also use serif in the same font as the body copy as long as it's bigger and bolder.

Short heads work well — one to three lines of type. They are usually written in a subject-verb format in the present tense. Left-aligned heads have the best readability, but some editors favor centered heads for a more formal look.

Downstyle is a good choice (first letter capitalized, all others lowercase). Uppercase and lowercase combined is also a common choice for heads (capitalize the first letter of each word except for prepositions and articles). This style is referred to as *upstyle*.

Put more space above a head than below it. This makes the head and body copy look as if they belong together. Otherwise, you wind up with floating heads (see page 17).

Examine the various styles of heads in Figure 5-1 on page 67.

Summary decks

The *summary deck* is a sentence (or two) below the headline that introduces the story (Figure 5-2). Often set in italics, the type is smaller than the headline. Sometimes it is referred to as a lead-in because it leads the reader into the body copy. Some magazines run a few decks before the story begins, often reducing type size in each subsequent deck.

Heads... Headers... Headlines...

Headlines can be called heads, but NEVER headers. Headers are something different, as you will learn in this chapter.

Three ways to capitalize heads

In order of preference:

Downstyle
 Preschoolers plan walkout

Upstyle
 Preschoolers Plan Walkout

All caps
 PRESCHOOLERS PLAN WALKOUT

Students protest boring textbooks

Students picketed the university bookstore Tuesday to protest dull textbooks as professors held classes anyway.

Students say they have had enough. They have asked professors to consider finding more interesting textbooks. When 20 pages of straight text have no subheads or copybreakers, students claim they fall asleep and can't get their reading done.

summary deck

Figure 5-2
Summary deck.

Journalism students win six awards **in the national college newspaper competition**	**Left aligned** *downstyle* (first word is first-letter uppercase, all others lowercase)
Journalism Students Win Six Awards **in the National College Newspaper Competition**	*upstyle* (all major words are first-letter uppercase)
Students complain about **crowded parking lots** **and long walks**	**Centered** Do not center more than three lines of type.
Letters to editor **Confidence in Public Schools** **at an All-time High** *This one acts as a standing head that appears regularly in a publication.*	*Students Protest* **Seniors Required to Take** **Exit Writing Sample** *This one serves to give more information.*	**Kicker** word or phrase that leads into the headline; smaller, contrasting font; often has rule under it
Victory! **Toby Tennis demolishes every challenger**	**Hammer** like a kicker, but larger than the headline

Judge Rules Against Students **Students appeal case** **of inadequate parking** Two hundred students came out Wednesday to protest the lack of parking and the volumes of *3/4 box*	Judge rules against students **Students appeal case** **of inadequate parking** Two hundred students came out Wednesday to protest the lack of parking and the volumes of tick- *hood*	Judge Rules Against Students **Students appeal case of** **inadequate parking** Two hundred students came out Wednesday to protest the lack of parking and the volumes of tickets *cap*	**3/4 box, hood, cap**

Blood **drive** **breaks** **record**	An all-time record of 847 students donated blood at the annual blood drive sponsored by Rowan's junior class. As they stood in line on Tuesday in the 94° weather, many students shared emotional reasons for donating. Others said they did it for the free cookies and juice. Another group of 15 sophomores from a fitness class stood with their professor. The professor thought it would be a good learning experience for them. Junior students advertised the event, arranged for the bloodmobile setup and carried out the daily activities. More than 50 staff members participated in the drive as well, both in giving blood and in helping with moral sup-	**Sidesaddle heads** heads to the side, can be left or right aligned

Figure 5-1. Headline styles.

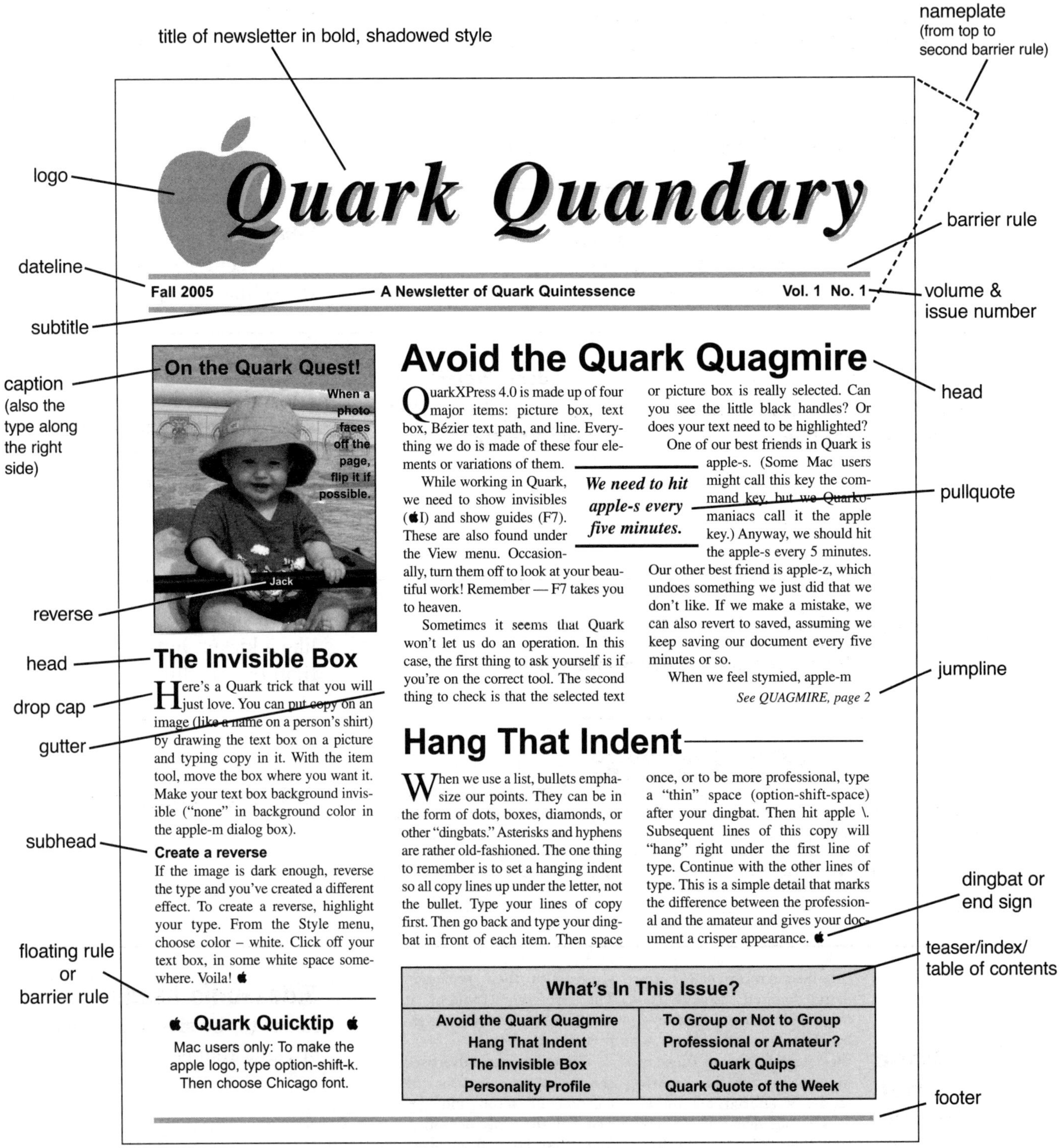
title of newsletter in bold, shadowed style
nameplate
(from top to second barrier rule)
logo
barrier rule
dateline
volume & issue number
subtitle
caption (also the type along the right side)
head
pullquote
reverse
head
jumpline
drop cap
gutter
subhead
dingbat or end sign
floating rule or barrier rule
teaser/index/ table of contents
footer

Quark Quandary

Fall 2005 — A Newsletter of Quark Quintessence — Vol. 1 No. 1

On the Quark Quest!

When a photo faces off the page, flip it if possible.

Jack

The Invisible Box

Here's a Quark trick that you will just love. You can put copy on an image (like a name on a person's shirt) by drawing the text box on a picture and typing copy in it. With the item tool, move the box where you want it. Make your text box background invisible ("none" in background color in the apple-m dialog box).

Create a reverse

If the image is dark enough, reverse the type and you've created a different effect. To create a reverse, highlight your type. From the Style menu, choose color – white. Click off your text box, in some white space somewhere. Voila!

Quark Quicktip

Mac users only: To make the apple logo, type option-shift-k. Then choose Chicago font.

Avoid the Quark Quagmire

QuarkXPress 4.0 is made up of four major items: picture box, text box, Bézier text path, and line. Everything we do is made of these four elements or variations of them.

While working in Quark, we need to show invisibles (I) and show guides (F7). These are also found under the View menu. Occasionally, turn them off to look at your beautiful work! Remember — F7 takes you to heaven.

Sometimes it seems that Quark won't let us do an operation. In this case, the first thing to ask yourself is if you're on the correct tool. The second thing to check is that the selected text or picture box is really selected. Can you see the little black handles? Or does your text need to be highlighted?

One of our best friends in Quark is apple-s. (Some Mac users might call this key the command key, but we Quarkomaniacs call it the apple key.) Anyway, we should hit the apple-s every 5 minutes. Our other best friend is apple-z, which undoes something we just did that we don't like. If we make a mistake, we can also revert to saved, assuming we keep saving our document every five minutes or so.

We need to hit apple-s every five minutes.

When we feel stymied, apple-m

See QUAGMIRE, page 2

Hang That Indent

When we use a list, bullets emphasize our points. They can be in the form of dots, boxes, diamonds, or other "dingbats." Asterisks and hyphens are rather old-fashioned. The one thing to remember is to set a hanging indent so all copy lines up under the letter, not the bullet. Type your lines of copy first. Then go back and type your dingbat in front of each item. Then space once, or to be more professional, type a "thin" space (option-shift-space) after your dingbat. Then hit apple \. Subsequent lines of this copy will "hang" right under the first line of type. Continue with the other lines of type. This is a simple detail that marks the difference between the professional and the amateur and gives your document a crisper appearance.

What's In This Issue?

Avoid the Quark Quagmire	To Group or Not to Group
Hang That Indent	Professional or Amateur?
The Invisible Box	Quark Quips
Personality Profile	Quark Quote of the Week

Figure 5-3. Anatomy of a newsletter page. This is the *Quark Quandary*, which will be a project much later in the course. The main page elements are labeled here along with several other graphic devices such as rules and drop caps.

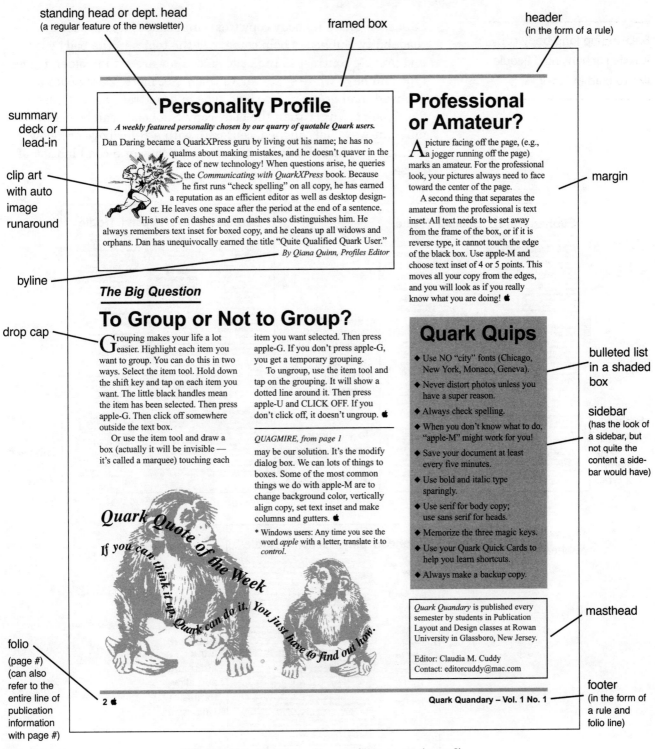

standing head or dept. head
(a regular feature of the newsletter)

framed box

header
(in the form of a rule)

summary
deck or
lead-in

clip art
with auto
image
runaround

byline

drop cap

folio
(page #)
(can also
refer to the
entire line of
publication
information
with page #)

margin

bulleted list
in a shaded
box

sidebar
(has the look of
a sidebar, but
not quite the
content a side-
bar would have)

masthead

footer
(in the form of
a rule and
folio line)

Personality Profile

A weekly featured personality chosen by our quarry of quotable Quark users.

Dan Daring became a QuarkXPress guru by living out his name; he has no qualms about making mistakes, and he doesn't quaver in the face of new technology! When questions arise, he queries the *Communicating with QuarkXPress* book. Because he first runs "check spelling" on all copy, he has earned a reputation as an efficient editor as well as desktop design-er. He leaves one space after the period at the end of a sentence. His use of en dashes and em dashes also distinguishes him. He always remembers text inset for boxed copy, and he cleans up all widows and orphans. Dan has unequivocally earned the title "Quite Qualified Quark User."

— *By Qiana Quinn, Profiles Editor*

The Big Question

To Group or Not to Group?

Grouping makes your life a lot easier. Highlight each item you want to group. You can do this in two ways. Select the item tool. Hold down the shift key and tap on each item you want. The little black handles mean the item has been selected. Then press apple-G. Then click off somewhere outside the text box.

Or use the item tool and draw a box (actually it will be invisible — it's called a marquee) touching each item you want selected. Then press apple-G. If you don't press apple-G, you get a temporary grouping.

To ungroup, use the item tool and tap on the grouping. It will show a dotted line around it. Then press apple-U and CLICK OFF. If you don't click off, it doesn't ungroup. ⌘

QUAGMIRE, from page 1

may be our solution. It's the modify dialog box. We can lots of things to boxes. Some of the most common things we do with apple-M are to change background color, vertically align copy, set text inset and make columns and gutters. ⌘

* Windows users: Any time you see the word *apple* with a letter, translate it to *control*.

Quark Quote of the Week
If you can think it up, Quark can do it. You just have to find out how.

Professional or Amateur?

A picture facing off the page, (e.g., a jogger running off the page) marks an amateur. For the professional look, your pictures always need to face toward the center of the page.

A second thing that separates the amateur from the professional is text inset. All text needs to be set away from the frame of the box, or if it is reverse type, it cannot touch the edge of the black box. Use apple-M and choose text inset of 4 or 5 points. This moves all your copy from the edges, and you will look as if you really know what you are doing! ⌘

Quark Quips

◆ Use NO "city" fonts (Chicago, New York, Monaco, Geneva).
◆ Never distort photos unless you have a super reason.
◆ Always check spelling.
◆ When you don't know what to do, "apple-M" might work for you!
◆ Save your document at least every five minutes.
◆ Use bold and italic type sparingly.
◆ Use serif for body copy; use sans serif for heads.
◆ Memorize the three magic keys.
◆ Use your Quark Quick Cards to help you learn shortcuts.
◆ Always make a backup copy.

Quark Quandary is published every semester by students in Publication Layout and Design classes at Rowan University in Glassboro, New Jersey.

Editor: Claudia M. Cuddy
Contact: editorcuddy@mac.com

2 ⌘

Quark Quandary – Vol. 1 No. 1

Figure 5-3. Anatomy of a newsletter page (page 2).

Subheads

Breaking up long body copy is called "chunking." People like to read in "chunks."

Subheads break up body copy (text) into small bites for better readability. Subheads help categorize the topics in the body copy and provide contrast to the page since they are set in bolder, bigger type and have white space above them. Set more space *above* a subhead than *below* it. Use bold type in a contrasting font, about 2 or 3 points larger than the body copy. Subheads can be set in different ways: left aligned, centered, with a rule above or below, sitting on a shaded rule, next to the body copy or a combination of these.

A

Subhead plays second fiddle

Si meliora dies, ut vina, poemata reddit, scire velim,
chartis pretium quotus arroget annus. scriptor abhinc
annos centum qui decidit,
inter perfectos veteresque
referri debet an inter vilis
atque novos? Excludat iurgia finis, "Est vetus atque
probus, centum qui perficit
annos." Quid, qui deperiit
minor uno mense vel anno,
inter quos referendus erit?
Veteresne poetas, an quos et
praesens et postera respuat
aetas?

Headline gets
top spot

"Iste quidem veteres inter
ponetur honeste, qui vel
mense brevi vel toto est
iunior anno." Utor permisso,
caudaeque pilos ut equinae
paulatim vello unum, demo
etiam unum, dum cadat
elusus ratione ruentis
acervi, qui redit in fastos et
virtutem aestimat annis
miraturque nihil nisi quod
Libitina sacravit.
    Ennius et sapines et for-
tis et alter Homerus, ut critici dicunt, leviter curare
videtur, quo promissa
cadant et somnia
Pythagorea. Naevius in
manibus non est et men-
tibus haeret paene recens?
Adeo sanctum est vetus
omne poema. ambigitur
quotiens, uter utro sit prior,
aufert Pacuvius docti
famam senis Accius alti, dicitur Afrani toga convenisse

Menandro, Plautus ad
exemplar Siculi properare
Epicharmi, vincere
Caecilius gravitate,
Terentius arte.

Jailed for
copybreaking

Hos edisci et hos arto stipata theatro spectat Roma
potens; habet hos numer-
atque poetas ad nostrum
tempus Livi scriptoris ab
aevo.
    Interdum volgus recta
videt, est ubi peccat. Si veteres ita miratur laudatque
poetas, ut nihil anteferat,
nihil illis comparet, errat. Si
quaedam nimis antique, si
peraque dure dicere credit
eos, ignave multa fatetur, et
sapit et mecum facit et Iova
iudicat aequo.
    Non equidem insector
delendave carmina Livi esse
reor, memini quae plagosum
mihi parvo Orbilium
dictare; sed emendata videri
pulchraque et exactis minimum distantia miror. Inter
quae verbum emicuit si
forte decorum, et si versus
paulo concinnior unus et
alter, iniuste totum ducit
venditque poema.

Photo overpowers
subhead

Interdum volgus recta videt,
est ubi peccat. Si veteres ita
miratur laudatque poetas,
ut nihil anteferat, nihil illis
comparet, errat. Si quaedam
nimis antique, si peraque

dure dicere credit eos,
ignave multa fatetur, et
sapit et mecum facit et Iova
iudicat aequo.
    Non equidem insector
delendave carmina Livi esse
reor, memini quae plagosum
mihi parvo Orbilium
dictare; sed emendata videri
pulchraque et exactis minimum distantia miror. Inter
quae verbum emicuit si
forte decorum, et si versus
paulo concinnior unus et
alter, iniuste totum ducit
venditque poema.

Subhead wants
space

Indignor quicquam repre-
hendi, non quia crasse compositum illepedeve putetur,
sed quia nuper, nec veniam
antiquis, sed honorem et
praemia posci. Recte necne
crocum floresque peram-
bulet Attae fabula si
dubitem, clament periisse
pudorem cuncti paene
patres, ea cum reprehen-
dere coner, quae gravis
Aesopus, quae doctus
Roscius egit; vel quia nil
recta, nisi quod placuit sibi,
ducunt, vel quia turpe
putant parere minoribus, et
quae imberbes didicere
senes.
    Quod si tam Graecis
novitas invisa fuisset quam
nobis, quid nunc esset
vetus? Aut quid haberet
quod legeret tereretque vir-
itim.
    Ut primum positis nugari

B

Subhead plays second fiddle

Si meliora dies, ut vina, poemata reddit, scire velim,
chartis pretium quotus arroget annus. scriptor abhinc
annos centum qui decidit,
inter perfectos veteresque
referri debet an inter vilis
atque novos? Excludat iurgia finis, "Est vetus atque
probus, centum qui perficit
annos." Quid, qui deperiit
minor uno mense vel anno,
inter quos referendus erit?
Veteresne poetas, an quos et
postera resuat poema.

Headline gets
top spot

"Iste quidem veteres inter
ponetur honeste, qui vel
mense brevi vel toto est
iunior anno." Utor permisso,
caudaeque pilos ut equinae
paulatim vello unum, demo
etiam unum, dum cadat
elusus ratione ruentis
acervi, qui redit in fastos et
virtutem aestimat annis
miraturque nihil nisi quod
Libitina sacravit.
    Ennius et sapines et for-
tis et alter Homerus, ut critici dicunt, leviter curare
videtur, quo promissa
cadant et somnia
Pythagorea. Naevius in
manibus non est et men-
tibus haeret paene recens?
Adeo sanctum est vetus
omne poema. ambigitur
quotiens, uter utro sit prior,
aufert Pacuvius docti
famam senis Accius alti, dicitur Afrani toga convenisse

Menandro, Plautus ad hunc
exemplar Siculi properare
Epicharmi, vincere exactis
Caecilius gravitate, totum
Terentius arte.

Jailed for
copybreaking

Hos edisci et hos arto stipata theatro spectat Roma
potens; habet hos numer-
atque poetas ad nostrum
tempus Livi scriptoris ab
aevo. Interdum volgus recta
videt, est ubi peccat.
    Si veteres ita miratur
laudatque poetas, ut nihil
anteferat, nihil illis comparet, errat. Si quaedam
nimis antique, si peraque
dure dicere credit eos, errat
ignave multa fatetur, et
sapit et mecum facit et Iova
iudicat aequo.

Photo overpowers
subhead

Non equidem insector delendave carmina Livi esse
reor, memini quae plagosum mihi
parvo Orbilium dictare; sed
emendata videri pulchraque
et exactis minimum distantia miror. Inter quae verbum emicuit si forte decorum, et si versus paulo
concinnior unus et alter,
iniuste totum ducit ven-
ditque poema.
    Interdum volgus recta
videt, est ubi peccat. Si veteres ita miratur laudatque
poetas, ut nihil anteferat,

nihil illis comparet, errat. Si
quaedam nimis antique, si
peraque dure dicere credit
eos, ignave multa fatetur, et
sapit et mecum facit et Iova
iudicat aequo.
    Non equidem insector
delendave carmina Livi esse
reor, memini quae plagosum
mihi parvo Orbilium multa
dictare; sed emendata videri
pulchraque et exactis minimum distantia miror. Inter
quae verbum emicuit si
forte decorum, et si versus
paulo concinnior unus et
alter, iniuste totum ducit
venditque poema.

Subhead wants
space

Indignor quicquam repre-
hendi, non quia crasse compositum illepedeve putetur,
sed quia nuper, nec veniam
antiquis, sed honorem et
praemia posci. Recte necne
crocum floresque peram-
bulet Attae fabula si
dubitem, clament periisse
pudorem cuncti paene
patres, ea cum reprehen-
dere coner, quae gravis
Aesopus, quae doctus
Roscius egit; vel quia nil
recta, nisi quod placuit sibi,
ducunt, vel quia turpe
putant parere minoribus, et
quae imberbes didicere
senes.
    Quod si tam Graecis
novitas invisa fuisset quam
nobis, quid nunc esset
vetus? Aut quid haberet
quod legeret tereretque vir-

Subheads break up long columns of type.

Both these samples show *space before* the head set at p10 (10 points) and *space after* set at p4 (4 points).

To set *space before* or *space after*, choose **Style→Formats**.

Subheads with rule above.

C

Subhead plays second fiddle

Headline gets
top spot

Si meliora dies, ut vina, poemata reddit, scire velim, chartis pretium quotus arroget
annus. scriptor abhinc annos
centum qui decidit, inter perfectos veteresque referri debet
an inter vilis atque novos?
Excludat iurgia finis, "Est
vetus atque probus, centum
qui perficit annos." Quid, qui
deperiit minor uno mense vel
anno, inter quos referendus
erit? Veteresne poetas, an quos
et praesens et postera resuat
aetas?

"Iste quidem veteres inter
ponetur honeste, qui vel mense
brevi vel toto est iunior anno."
Utor permisso, caudaeque pilos
ut equinae paulatim vello
unum, demo etiam unum, dum
cadat elusus ratione ruentis
acervi, qui redit in fastos et
virtutem aestimat annis
miraturque nihil nisi quod
Libitina sacravit.
    Ennius et sapines et fortis
et alter Homerus, ut critici
dicunt, leviter curare videtur,
quo promissa cadant et somnia

Jailed for
copybreaking

Si meliora dies, ut vina, poemata reddit, scire velim, chartis pretium quotus arroget
annus. scriptor abhinc annos
centum qui decidit, inter perfectos veteresque referri debet
an inter vilis atque novos?
Excludat iurgia finis, "Est
vetus atque probus, centum
qui perficit annos." Quid, qui
deperiit minor uno mense vel
anno, inter quos referendus
erit? Veteresne poetas, an quos
et praesens et postera resuat
aetas?
"Iste quidem veteres inter
ponetur honeste, qui vel mense

brevi vel toto est iunior anno."
Utor permisso, caudaeque pilos
ut equinae paulatim vello
unum, demo etiam unum, dum
cadat elusus ratione ruentis
acervi, qui redit in fastos et
virtutem aestimat annis
miraturque nihil nisi quod
Libitina sacravit.
    Ennius et sapines et fortis et
alter Homerus, ut critici
dicunt, leviter curare videtur,
quo promissa cadant et somnia
Pythagorea. Naevius in
manibus non est et mentibus
haeret paene recens? Adeo
sanctum est vetus omne

Subhead wants
space

Si meliora dies, ut vina, poemata reddit, scire velim, chartis pretium quotus arroget
annus. scriptor abhinc annos
centum qui decidit, inter perfectos veteresque referri debet
an inter vilis atque novos?
Excludat iurgia finis, "Est
vetus atque probus, centum

qui perficit annos." Quid, qui
deperiit minor uno mense vel
anno, inter quos referendus
erit? Veteresne poetas, an quos
et praesens et postera resuat
aetas?
"Iste quidem veteres inter
ponetur honeste, qui vel mense
brevi vel toto est iunior anno."

Sidesaddle subheads attract attention and allow for lots of *white space.*

Figure 5-4.
Subhead choices.

Overline, catchline and sideline are just position names for a title used with a caption. A lead-in is similar, but it is found closer to the caption.

Captions

The 3-minute reader (see Chapter 8) might take the time to read the *captions*, explanations for photos or art. Make every word count. Someone should be able to read the caption to a picture and get the message without reading the text. Write captions next to, above, below, or inside the photo. Experiment with various styles of captions. Use a contrasting type to the body copy or perhaps the same type but smaller and in italics. Always give credit to the photographer or artist (*credit line*).

Figure 5-5.

sans serif

justified

lead-in is

bold caps

TODAY'S ANGELS – Who would have guessed that just yesterday Emily (left) decorated her bedroom walls with crayons and washed her body with butter? Her older sister, Sarah, can wear her wings proudly.
Photo by C. Cuddy

Figure 5-6.

sans serif

justified

catchline set in large type on the photo

Who would have guessed that just yesterday Emily (left) decorated her bedroom walls with crayons and washed her body with butter? Her older sister, Sarah, can wear her wings proudly.
Photo by C. Cuddy

Who would have guessed that just yesterday Emily (left) decorated her bedroom walls with crayons and washed her body with butter? Her older sister, Sarah, can wear her wings proudly.

(Photo by C. Cuddy)

Figure 5-7.
Serif, italic type. Right aligned type, but SET to the left side of the photo (called sidesaddle left).

Who would have guessed that just yesterday Emily (left) decorated her bedroom walls with crayons and washed her body with butter? Her older sister, Sarah, can wear her wings proudly.

(Photo by C. Cuddy)

Figure 5-8.
Serif, italic type. Left aligned type, but SET to the right side of the photo (called sidesaddle right).

Today's Angels

Who would have guessed that just yesterday Emily (left) decorated her bedroom walls with crayons and washed her body with butter? Her older sister, Sarah, can wear her wings proudly. (Photo by C. Cuddy)

Figure 5-9. Overline, photo and caption framed as a unit.

Who would have guessed that just yesterday Emily (left) decorated her bedroom walls with crayons and washed her body with butter? Her older sister, Sarah, can wear her wings proudly.
Photo by C. Cuddy

Figure 5-10. Photo and caption framed as a unit. Type for caption is left aligned.

Who woulda thought? *Just yesterday Emily (left) decorated her bedroom walls with crayons and washed her body with butter? Her older sister, Sarah, can wear her wings proudly.*
Photo by C. Cuddy

Figure 5-11. Sideline (right aligned bold type), butts against caption that is left aligned.

Headers and footers

Headers and *footers* include information such as the title of the publication, page number, chapter number and chapter title. You can have a header or a footer or both. The header is found at the *top of every page*, while the footer is found across the *bottom of every page*. A header or footer can be a rule (line) without words.

You may be familiar with these from your word processing programs. In QuarkXPress, you type them on a master page, and they appear on document pages.

In this book, the header contains the chapter number, chapter title and a rule below, while the footer contains a thin rule, the textbook title and page number.

Don't confuse headers with headlines. Standing heads that might repeat on several pages are not headers. The header is on EVERY page of the document.

Sidebars

A *sidebar* contains information that complements the story but is presented separately. The sidebar usually gives a local twist to the story. For example, if a newspaper article dealt with National Organ Donor Week, the sidebar might cover your university's Organ Donor Day. Or if the article dealt with car theft, the sidebar would give suggestions on safeguarding your car from theft. Magazines use sidebars with most articles to attract readers who are browsing through.

Figure 5-12. Sidebars localize a story or make the story more relevant to the reader. They are always set off in some way, usually in a framed box or a shaded box.

By any other name...

A pullquote called by any other name is still a pullquote.... They are called highlights, blurbs, pullouts, breakouts, liftouts, readouts, blowquotes...

But they are NOT called *callouts*. A callout is a word or phrase used to identify an element in an illustration — usually linked to the element by a straight line or an arrow.

Figure 5-3 (pages 68 and 69) is loaded with callouts.

Pullquotes

A *pullquote* is a sentence or phrase taken out of the body copy, set in larger, bolder type. Its purpose is to pique interest. Some people thumb through a publication, reading only pullquotes (this person is called the 3-minute reader – see page 116). Set a pullquote in a shaded box within the body copy, set it across the columns, put rules above and below or set it alongside the copy. Be sure to put sufficient white space around a pullquote. Use quotation marks for a graphic effect (example C). Try not to hyphenate any of the words, and stay away from justified alignment.

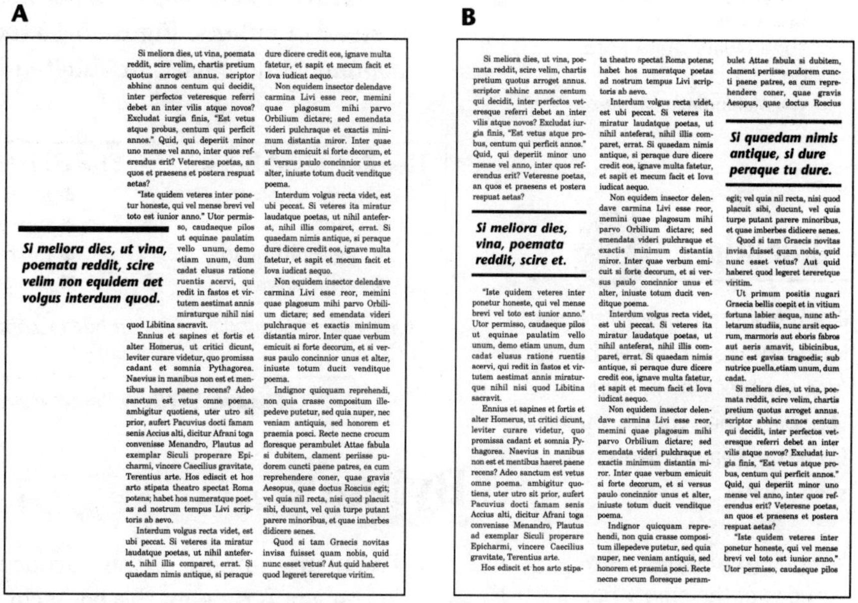

A

B

C

D

E

Figure 5-13. Varieties of pullquotes.

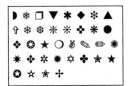

Figure 5-14. Symbols made from the Zapf Dingbat font.

The Quark Quick Card shows you how to make these symbols plus others. For a Quark Quick Card, go to **www.claudiacuddy.com.**

Quicktip

If you want to make a little box for registration forms and such, type the box ("n" in Zapf Dingbat). Then choose Outline from the measurements bar style choices. ■ = □

Wingdings font has a few versions of the empty box.

Bulleted lists

People love lists because they are easy to read. Use *bullets* or numbers to designate the items. The asterisk and dash are outdated. A typical bullet is the circle (•). A few bullets are built into your computer system, but others come from fonts that consist of symbols and icons, such as Wingdings and Zapf Dingbats (Figure 5-14). Depending on which bullet you choose, you may have to make it a bit smaller than the type size. You usually "hang" copy in a *bulleted list* so all copy lines up under itself. This will be covered in the flier chapter (page 144).

Figure 5-12A (page 72) shows a sidebar with a list using numbers instead of bullets. Figure 5-15 (below) shows examples of three popular bullets used in bulleted lists.

Reader Grabbers	The Skeleton	Design Principles
◆ large photos	■ grids	• repetition
◆ color	■ margins	• alignment
◆ big, bold heads	■ gutters	• proximity
◆ pullquotes	■ columns	• dominance
		• contrast
made in Zapf Dingbats with "u"	*made in Zapf Dingbats with "n"*	*any font, option 8*

Figure 5-15. Bulleted lists using three common bullets.

Bylines

The printed name of the author is the *byline*. Bylines are often set in the same type as the body copy but perhaps smaller, in italics, or in bold — or a combination of those. Sometimes a rule might be above or below the byline. Choose a style and be consistent in using it. Many times you'll find the byline at the end of the article.

Quark King visits room 30

by Craig Stratton

It's not every day that a king visits a classroom. But last Thursday, students in room 30 got to meet...

Quark King visits room 30

by Craig Stratton

It's not every day that a king visits a classroom. But last Thursday, students in room 30 got to meet...

Quark King visits room 30

Craig Stratton

It's not every day that a king visits a classroom. But last Thursday, students in room 30 got to meet...

Quark King visits room 30

CRAIG STRATTON

It's not every day that a king visits a classroom. But last Thursday, students in room 30 got to meet...

Figure 5-16. Examples of bylines.

Jumplines

The *jumpline* tells you to go to the page where the article is continued. When you get to that page, the *continuation line* tells you where the article came from (Figure 5-17). In both elements, include a keyword from the headline and the page numbers. When the continuation line contains a shortened version of the original head, it is referred to as a *jumphead* — common in newspaper layout.

Choose the style you want for jumplines and then be consistent. If you choose to use the abbreviated form for "continued," check your dictionary. The most common two forms are "contd" and "cont" — neither is listed with a period. You can also write out "continued" or use the style shown below.

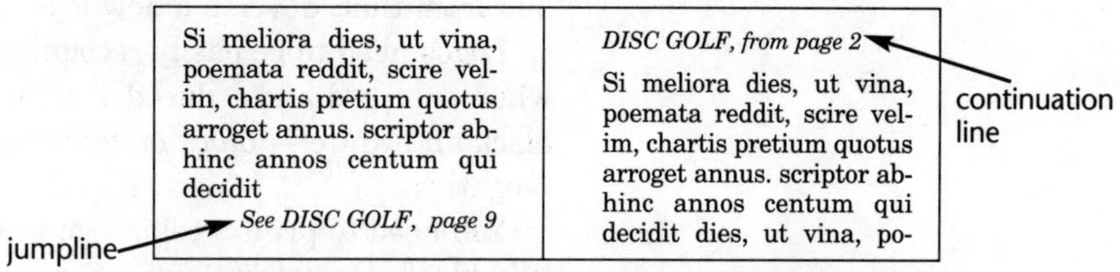

> Si meliora dies, ut vina, poemata reddit, scire velim, chartis pretium quotus arroget annus. scriptor abhinc annos centum qui decidit
> *See DISC GOLF, page 9*

> *DISC GOLF, from page 2*
> Si meliora dies, ut vina, poemata reddit, scire velim, chartis pretium quotus arroget annus. scriptor abhinc annos centum qui decidit dies, ut vina, po-

jumpline

continuation line

Figure 5-17. The jumpline tells you where to find the rest of the story, and the continuation line tells you where the article came from. Notice the bottom jumpline is right aligned, while the continuation line, or jumphead, is left aligned. Your eye would follow it that way as you read.

Design enhancers

Visuals of any kind (photos, clipart, graphs, charts) enhance page layout. Since Chapter 7 deals with photos and art, they are not covered in this chapter, although they certainly are essential page elements.

Most of the elements that make up the page were covered in this chapter, but it is important to mention a few additional layout and design enhancers:
- framed boxes (borders)
- shaded boxes
- rules (lines)
- *drop shadows* (shaded object behind an object)
- white space
- *sinks* (a band of white space at the top of each page — notice the first page of each chapter of this book)
- *bleeds* (solid color or image extending to edge of page — the cover of this book is done as a bleed)
- *drop caps* (large capital letters that drop down into copy) or large initial caps
- *end signs* or *dingbats*

Some people use "jumpline" for the jumpline AND the continuation line. Be sure to clarify your terminology with your co-workers.

Quicktip

In Quark, to make a jumpline and continuation line that change if you change layout:

Draw a small text box for the jumpline, touching the box it accompanies. Set runaround to "none." Type *Continued to page* ⌘**4**. For the continuation line, type *Continued from page* ⌘**2**.

The **4** and **2** will be translated into the actual page number of the copy and where it continues. This is very useful for newspaper layout because of so many story changes.

Quite magical. It's these things that will make you love QuarkXPress.

Logos

A *logo* provides immediate visual identification of a product, idea, company, institution, organization or even an event or occasion. It can be a word (Figure 5-18), a symbol (Figure 5-19) or a word and symbol combination (Figure 5-20).

Logos can be used anywhere: in the nameplate area of a newsletter, on a mailing panel, business cards, ads, posters, fliers, product labels and clothing items.

Much research goes into developing a logo to match the attitude and personality of the company or organization. Logos usually hold a "story" behind them — the symbols mean something. Focus groups or committees often evaluate the visual identity of the organization and from that, develop a new logo.

Logos need to be easily recognizable. They must maintain clarity when enlarged and reduced. A color logo needs to be reproducible in black and white — *black on white* (positive) as well as *white on black* (negative).

You need to print a color logo in its *exact* color — otherwise, print it in black. Do not use any other color. When an organization sends you its logo for publication, it sometimes sends an entire packet of information with instructions for using the logo and several variations of the logo. Always respect the guidelines.

Figure 5-18.
Words only. The letters themselves have an old look.

Laura's Antique Attic

Figure 5-19.
Logo only. This logo represents Society in Khaos, a clothing company. The three links represent three activities:
• surfboarding
• snowboarding
• skateboarding
(See their business cards on page 180.)

Figure 5-20.
Symbol and words.

Quick Quiz

Fill in the missing word.

1. Some people thumb through a magazine reading only the _____, which are salient points from the story.

2. The author's name is called the _____.

3. The more important the story, the bigger the _____ should be.

4. To break copy into bite-sized chunks, use _____.

5. A lead-in to a story or a one-sentence synopsis of the story, usually found after the headline, is called a _____.

6. Rather than reading a full paragraph, a reader often likes to read a _____ _____ to give them information quickly.

7. The _____ tells you where the story is continued.

8. Never run a picture without a _____.

9. A _____ localizes a story and gives it relevance to the reader.

10. What are three characteristics to remember when designing a logo?

    _____

    _____

    _____

Out of the Quandary

1. Page elements

   a. Find an example of each of the page elements listed below.

   b. Cut out each piece and paste or tape it to a piece of paper. You can put more than one on a page, or you can use one item per page, depending on the size of the item. Be neat.

   c. Label each item.

   d. Find these items:
   1. **headline or title**
   2. **subhead (breaks up copy)**
   3. **photo caption**
   4. **header OR footer**
   5. **pullquote**
   6. **sidebar**
   7. **bullet list**
   8. **summary deck**
   9. **byline**
   10. **jumpline/continuation line**

   e. Staple all the pages.

Hint: A newspaper or magazine contains all of these items.

2. Headlines

Find examples of six different headline styles. Cut them out and paste them on paper. Label them (all caps, left aligned, downstyle and so on).

3. Captions

Find examples of five different captions. Cut them out with their pictures. Paste them on paper. Describe their format.

4. Logos

Find a sample of each kind of logo: word only, symbol only, word and symbol together.

 # Quantum Leap

Find a newspaper or magazine page that contains all 10 page elements (*Out of the Quandary, question 1d*) on that one page. Label the elements.

6 Color

Color adds tremendous meaning to communication as it vitalizes the visual message, delivering an instantaneous impression that is, most often, universally understood. Color…crosses cultural boundaries….

Leatrice Eiseman
Pantone Guide to Communicating with Color

Quest Objectives

- Explain the difference between spot color and the four-color process.
- Correlate three colors with associated moods.
- List three ways to achieve an "illusion of color."
- List five elements on a page that could be set in color.

Quest Skills

- Duplicate a box.
- Step and repeat.
- Color a box.
- Shade a box.
- Frame a box.
- Make a blend.
- Center vertically.
- Color type.
- Shade type.
- Make a drop shadow.
- Make a reverse.
- Group and ungroup items.
- Isolate an item in a group.

Quest Terms

blend	registration
CMYK	RGB colors
color moods	second color
four-color process	shade
gray page	spot color
Pantone Matching System	two-color job/three-color job

Color is a major attention-getter and mood-setter. It can separate parts of a publication as well as unite them. Aim for consistency in your use of color. For example, set all the pullquotes in the same color, or use the same color for all lines in the publication. *Spot color* and *four-color process* are the two methods of printing color.

Spot color

The generic term *spot color* can be remembered if you think of a color being put in various spots on the page to draw attention. Switch gears and imagine using a color chart to pick paint for your bedroom. You examine numerous samples of various colors and shades. Then you pick the color, write down the number and give it to the sales clerk in the hardware store. The clerk then mixes various paints based on a formula to get the exact color you want.

In printing, we have a similar system, but it involves ink instead of paint. When you go to a professional printer, you tell the printer what ink color you have chosen. One of the popular systems of ink color, or spot color, is the *Pantone Matching System* (PMS), which has hundreds of ink color choices.

You can pick your color from the "swatch book" (Figure 6-1) and then designate it on the computer. Or you can bypass the swatch book and go right to the computer. On the next page you will see how to pick a color (Figure 6-2). After you pick a color, it is added to the color palette for that document.

If you are using a spot color plus black, then you have a two-color publication, referred to as a *two-color job* when you go to the printer's. You could add a third spot color and have a *three-color job*, but the expense might not be worth it. When you use a spot color and black, the spot color is called the *second color*. Black is usually assumed to be the first color.

Qool Fact

Color is the second most important layout element to attract a reader to a page (a large photo is first — and a large color photo is even better).

Most of your professional printing will be one-color or two-color jobs.

Figure 6-1. Pantone Matching System color swatch book.

Figure 6-2.
Create a new color.

1 Under the Edit menu, choose Colors.

2 Click on New.

3 Click on Model (default is RGB) and make a choice. We chose Pantone solid uncoated. ("Uncoated" refers to the paper.)

Also check "Spot color."

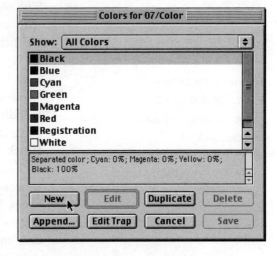

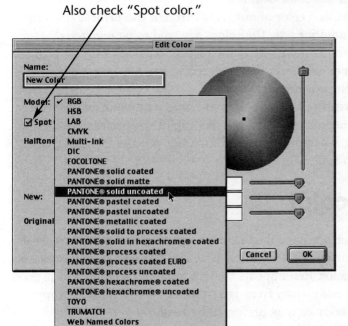

4 Scroll through the colors and click on your choice. Then click OK.

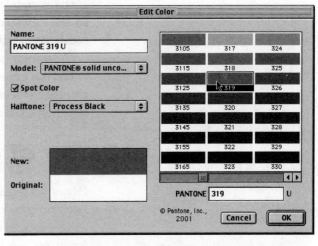

5 Save your document. The color will now be added to your color palette for this document. Compare this illustration to step 2.

Four-color process

The other method for printing colors is called the *four-color process.* This must be used when you have a color photograph in your publication.

Your decision between two-color and four-color process usually depends on your budget.

If you own a color inkjet printer, you have most likely bought ink cartridges. You buy two cartridges: one has black ink and one has three colors. The three-color cartridge contains cyan (blue), magenta (reddish-pink) and yellow. Put these four colors together and you have the four-color process, or *CMYK* (Cyan, Magenta, Yellow and Black — the K stands for black).

Four inks are used to produce full color. The professional printing process prints each color in a separate "pass" through the printing press. These colors print in tiny dots. If a yellow dot touches or covers a magenta dot, you get orange. If a yellow dot touches a blue dot, you get green. The more dots, the stronger the color. The fewer dots, the lighter the color (*shade*).

When the printed color of one pass through the printer lines up perfectly with another one, the colors are said to be *registered.* If the *registration* is not correct, the picture will look blurry. In the newspaper, now and then you might see a color photo or comic strip with poor registration.

Although printing in four colors at home with your inkjet printer is not too expensive, when you are dealing in the professional printing world, it's another story. Four-color process is much more expensive than spot color.

Power of color

Pages with color are described as more exciting and more powerful. According to various color studies, blue is a favorite among readers as the second color. Red appeals to both men and women and is good for direct mail. Stay away from red, pink or orange for body copy. Black type for body copy is preferred by readers.

Choose your second color based on the tone of the publication. You want the color to convey an appropriate emotional message. For example, never use red for a budget or money-related publication because someone might interpret the group to be "in the red." Green is a better choice in those publications.

Red and orange are warm colors. They provide strong contrast and attract attention. Don't overuse them. On the other hand, blue and green are cool colors, and more of those colors can be used in a publication. Be aware of *color moods,* which are the effects colors have on emotions.

Color moods

- Black – strong, formal, ominous
- Green – refreshing, peaceful, envious
- Yellow – cheerful, healthy
- Orange – happy, festive, energetic
- Red – passionate, active, exciting
- Purple – royal, wealthy
- Brown – masculine, nostalgic, old
- Blue – dignified   lighter blue: purity, cool
                                       darker blue: wealth, status

Using color

When the type is in color, make the type bold. If your layout includes photos, print your photos in black, not the second color. (You don't want red, green or blue people.) Repeat a second color for similar elements in a publication to achieve consistency throughout the publication. Don't overdo the color, but consider using color for some of the following elements: heads, lead-in text, drop caps, frames, lines, pullquotes and shaded text boxes.

Shades

A *shade* is a percentage of the color. We used to refer to shades as *screens* because the printer used actual screening material to filter the ink so 100% of the ink did not print. Perhaps only 20% printed — that would be a 20% screen, or *shade* as QuarkXPress calls it. Use shades to give contrast to a page or to emphasize an item.

Type in shaded boxes should be bigger and bold. More leading is also good. Make shades light. A black shade on coated paper might only need 8% to come out dark enough. Usually a shade of 10–20% is fairly safe when putting type on top of the shaded area. Shades vary from inkjet to laser printers, so be flexible and experiment. Figure 6-3 shows various gradations of shades.

Blends

A gradient fill, or *blend*, is a gradual transition from one color or shade to another. In QuarkXPress, make a blend in the modify box (⌘M). Choose **Box → Blend**. Pick a color for the box, then pick a color for the blend. Assign a percentage. Figure 6-4 shows four of the six choices of blends.

Quicktip

Use color for:
- heads
- lead-in text
- drop caps
- frames
- lines
- pullquotes
- shaded text boxes

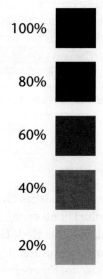

Figure 6-3.
Shades of black.

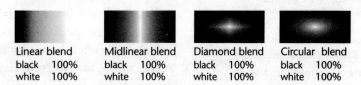

Figure 6-4. A few of the blends available.

Qool Fact

Gray space refers to all text on the page.

Black space refers to a photo or artwork.

White space is empty space. It's the part that doesn't print. It gives the page some breathing room.

Quicktip

Liven up a dull, gray page of type by using various copybreakers. This is said to give "color" to an otherwise drab page. Changing a 2-column format to 3-column format creates more white space.

Illusion of color

If you are using only black, adding copy-breaking devices brings "color" to a dull, *gray page* of type. Try some drop caps, lines, frames, pullquotes, photos, captions, subheads, reverses and shaded sidebars (Figures 6-5 and 6-6).

Another way to give people an *illusion of color* use is to use colored paper or colored ink — but stay with the tone of your publication. Black ink on yellow paper is a good choice, although black ink on white paper is still the best for legibility.

Figure 6-5. "Gray page."

Figure 6-6. Illusion of color.

RGB and Web colors

Figure 6-7. Color models supported by QuarkXPress.

for use on Web pages

Although QuarkXPress supports several color models, this chapter introduced you to CMYK and Pantone (spot color). The other significant color model to recognize is *RGB*, which stands for Red, Green and Blue. These are the colors used by monitors, scanners, TVs and projectors. If you are using pictures for the Web, for PowerPoint presentations, or to print to an inkjet printer, use RGB for your files. (If you are printing to a color laser printer, change the file to CMYK.)

QuarkXPress 5 has introduced two new models to use with Web design: *Web Named Colors* (chosen by number or swatch) and *Web Safe Colors* (chosen by name or swatch) (Figure 6-7). Individual colors can be picked from these Web choices. However, color photos should still be in RGB format. (In Photoshop, you designate CMYK and RGB from the menu: **Image → Model**.)

Quick Quiz

1. How do you use color to achieve consistency in a publication?

2. When do you use spot color and when do you use four-color process?

3. Choose three colors and describe what emotional messages are attached to each one.

4. How do you achieve the illusion of color on a gray page?

5. What does it mean if registration is incorrect?

6. What does it mean if I am taking a two-color job to the printer?

7. What are the different uses for RGB, CMYK, Pantone (spot color) and grayscale?

 Out of the Quandary

1. Add to the list of color moods associated with colors (list found earlier in this chapter).

2. Find a publication (ad, brochure, flier) with a second color used explicitly to evoke an emotion. In a sentence or two, explain why it achieves or doesn't achieve the purpose of the publication.

3. Find a black and white page that gives the illusion of color because of its contrasting copy-breaking devices.

4. Find a newspaper picture or comic strip with poor registration.

 Quantum Leap

1. Color separations

To check your consistency and accuracy in a two-color job, run the pages out in *color separations*. One page will print with all the elements that should be black, while the other page will print all the elements that should be in color.

How to run out a color separation:
1. Apply color to a document.
2. **Print** → Check the **Separations** box.
3. Then click Print.

2. Color palette

Under **View** → **Show colors**, or using the **F12** key, open the color palette. Experiment.

What are the hot colors right now? What about for the future?

"There are some definite trends for the future, the most notable being the Latin influence, which is coming from food, music and infusion of people from Latin cultures who are part of our society. As for mixtures, the most notable are the reds, mangoes, amber yellows accented by red-purples, and warm yellow-greens. It's exciting, alive and very sexy. The blues are evolving into turquoise and aquas, while greens are very *vegetal*."

Leatrice Eiseman
*Director of the
Pantone Color Institute*

From an EyeWire chat with Leatrice Eiseman; http://www.eyewire.com/magazine/profiles/colortalks/

Quark Quest

☐ 1. Create a folder on your disk called *Color*.

☐ 2. Open a new document 8½ x 11. Margins 6p, 1 column. Gutters don't matter because the page is 1 column.

☐ 3. Name it *colorexercise.qxd* and save into the Color folder.

☐ 4. Draw a small text box on the page.

Use this tool.

Duplicate a box

☐ 5. With item tool, click on the box to highlight it.

☐ 6. ⌘ **D** or **Item → Duplicate**. Do this 3 times.

☐ 7. Item tool: drag the boxes away from the other boxes.

Color a box

☐ 8. Highlight one of the boxes.

☐ 9. ⌘ **M** or **Item → Modify**.

☐ 10. Choose **Box → Color**. Pick a color. Hit **Return** (Mac) or **Enter** (Windows).

Shade a box

☐ 11. Highlight the box.

☐ 12. ⌘ **M**.

☐ 13. **Box → Color**. Choose a color.

☐ 14. **Shade → Choose a percentage**.

Make a blend

☐ 15. Color another box.

☐ 16. Highlight it (it is probably already activated).

☐ 17. ⌘ **M**.

☐ 18. **Box → Color**. Choose a color.

☐ 19. Below the color choice, see **Blend → Style → Solid**. Hold down the bar and choose a blend.

☐ 20. Choose a different color and a percentage. You can also use the same color with a percentage. Later, experiment with angles and various percentages.

Step and Repeat

☐ 21. Highlight one of your boxes on the page.

☐ 22. **Item → Step and repeat**.

☐ 23. Type in a number, perhaps 8. Hit **OK**. This is very cool, especially when you use various shades for the boxes.

Item tool

Used for:

• moving items

• grouping (then you can move the group without changing tools)

Mystery-solving jingle

For Mac users:

When you don't know what to do, Apple-M might work for you!

(apple is ⌘ — the command key)

For Windows users:

When you don't know what to do, Control-M might work for you!

(sounds like "control 'em")

Most of the answers to your dilemmas can be found in the **Modify** box, which is ⌘ **M** or **Item → Modify**.

Content tool

Used for:

- typing or adjusting type
- contents of a box (graphic)
- contents of a group (isolating and working on one of the pieces of a group)

3 Magic Keys

Mac Users

⌘ ⌥ ⇧   command, option, shift

Windows Users

⌘ ⌥ ⇧   control, alternate, shift

control
shift
alt

About every 5 minutes, save. Just hit ⌘ **S**.

Save jingle

For Mac users:

Apple-S will save you stress.

For Windows users:

Control-S will save you stress.

Color the type

☐ 24. With the content tool, click on one of the boxes. Type your name.

☐ 25. Center your name using the measurements bar.

☐ 26. Highlight type.

☐ 27. Make the type bold (use measurements bar).

☐ 28. From top menu bar: **Style → Color**.

☐ 29. Slide cursor to right and select a color.

Shade the type

☐ 30. Highlight type.

☐ 31. From top menu bar: **Style → Shade**.

☐ 32. Choose percentage of shade.

Drop shadow behind a reverse

☐ 33. Make a rectangular box 14 picas wide, 7 picas high. Use measurements bar to size it.

☐ 34. Duplicate the box.

☐ 35. With either tool, click on the back box. Then shade it.

☐ 36. Click on the front box. Frame it. ⌘ **M → Frame**. **Type in a width**. If you don't type in a number, you don't get a frame (0 is no frame).

☐ 37. Using content tool, type your name in the framed box.

☐ 38. Highlight your name. Make it Arial, bold, larger point size. Use the measurements bar or hold down those three magic keys and use the greater than sign: ⌘ ⌥ ⇧ >.

☐ 39. Center vertically (from top to bottom): ⌘ **M → Text → Vertical Alignment → Centered**.

☐ 40. Using content tool, highlight type and color it **white** (see #28 above).

☐ 41. Highlight box. Color the box (see #9 & #10). Your work should resemble this:

Jason

If you see a little red box with an X in the corner of the back box, don't worry about it. It doesn't print. It just means there is something being pushed away. In this case, a text box is pushing away another text box.

Sometimes it means there is more body copy, and the end of the box has cut if off. Sometimes it is just a paragraph return that is left over. To eliminate these extra paragraph returns: Windows users can use the Backspace; Mac users can use the special key in the group of nine: it is labeled *del* with an X in a polygon. On the laptop, hit Function, then Delete.

del

Grouping is one of the most valuable skills you will learn. You can use it for pictures and captions, heads and their stories and quadrillions of other things.

Grouping and ungrouping

Draw a few little boxes on the page.

Grouping – Method 1

☐ 1. Item tool.

☐ 2. Draw an invisible box — a marquee — touching all items you want to group. This will highlight each item. (See page 63 for explanation of marquee.)

☐ 3. ⌘ **G**. It is now grouped.

How to know it is grouped:

Use item tool. Put it on the group and move it. If all items move, it worked. If not, then ⌘ **Z** (undo) and group it again.

Ungroup items

☐ 4. Item tool.

☐ 5. Click on the group.

☐ 6. ⌘ **U**.

☐ 7. CLICK OFF THE BOX TO FINISH TASK.

How to know it is ungrouped:

Use item tool. Put it on the group and move an item. If that item moves, it worked. If the whole group moves, repeat task. Be sure to click off to complete the task.

Now that you have ungrouped, try method 2 (below) for grouping.

Grouping – Method 2

☐ 8. Item tool.

☐ 9. Hold down shift key.

☐ 10. Click on each item you want to group.

☐ 11. ⌘ **G**.

Quicktip

Isolating an item in a group

Use content tool. Click off the group, then on the item in the group. This isolates the item.

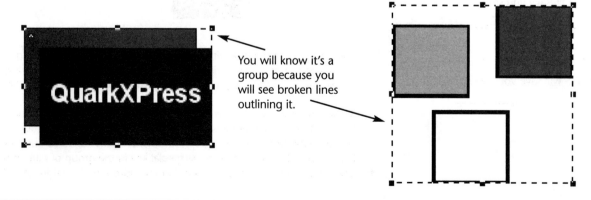

You will know it's a group because you will see broken lines outlining it.

Lines

The line, or rule, comes in several styles. From the toolbar, select the line you want. If you want a straight line, choose the cross. For diagonal, use the diagonal. For curved, use the squiggly. The pen tool is the Bézier — take it from point to point to create a line.

Use the measurements bar to make changes in the line or use the old standby, ⌘ **M**.

line tools

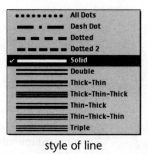

style of line

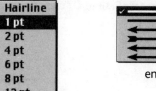

⌘ **M** for line

The vertical barrier lines on each page of this book are *hairlines*. A hairline is about .125 point wide.

width of line – you can also type in a value

endcaps of line

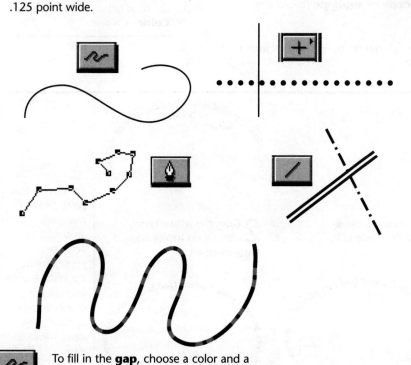

To fill in the **gap**, choose a color and a percentage in the modify box ⌘ **M.** This is a Bézier line with a gap color of 40% black.

Quicktip

Increase or decrease width of lines – pick one method:

• use measurements bar

• use modify box (⌘ **M**)

• hold down those 3 magic keys and hit > or <

---

3 Magic Keys

Mac Users

⌘ ⌥ ⇧ command, option, shift

Windows Users

⌘ ⌥ ⇧ control, alternate, shift

Typing on an arc

One of my requirements for students on the flier assignment is to type on a curved text path. Some students design their fliers with type on an arc — either oval or circular, and they want to know how to get it perfect. Here is one way to do this:

1 Draw a round or oval text box. Duplicate it and drag the duplicate away — just in case you want to do something else with it later. Forget about it for now.

2 Type in the text box.

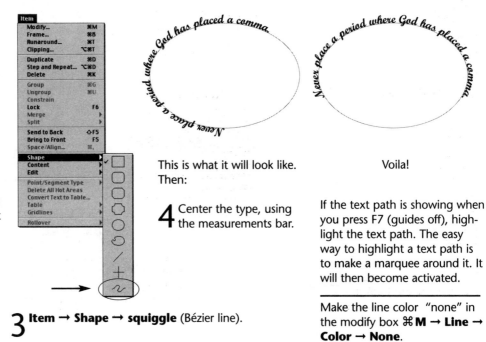

3 Item → Shape → squiggle (Bézier line).

This changes your oval or round text box into a Bézier text path.

This is what it will look like. Then:

4 Center the type, using the measurements bar.

Voila!

If the text path is showing when you press F7 (guides off), highlight the text path. The easy way to highlight a text path is to make a marquee around it. It will then become activated.

Make the line color "none" in the modify box ⌘ **M → Line → Color → None.**

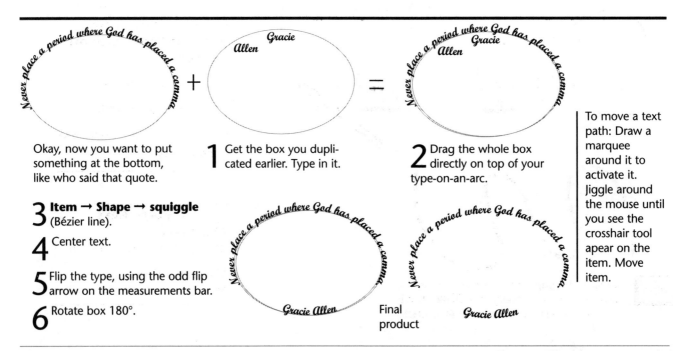

Okay, now you want to put something at the bottom, like who said that quote.

3 Item → Shape → squiggle (Bézier line).

4 Center text.

5 Flip the type, using the odd flip arrow on the measurements bar.

6 Rotate box 180°.

1 Get the box you duplicated earlier. Type in it.

2 Drag the whole box directly on top of your type-on-an-arc.

Final product

To move a text path: Draw a marquee around it to activate it. Jiggle around the mouse until you see the crosshair tool appear on the item. Move item.

7 Photos and Art

One picture is worth a thousand words, so you can figure that two pictures are worth 500 words apiece and four pictures are worth 250 words apiece. You may have so much good art that you want to run it all, but don't. A good visual editor knows what to leave out as well as what to put in.

Bill Noblitt
(Designer and Editor)

Quest Objectives

- List three kinds of photos that people like.
- Define cropping and sizing.
- Give five "dos and don'ts" for using photos.
- List five ways to present a photo.
- Discuss the ethics of using altered photos.

Quest Skills

- Get a picture.
- Fit a picture proportionately and unproportionately.
- Move the picture around box and to middle.
- Flip picture.
- Rotate picture; rotate box.
- Resize picture; picture and box.

- Color box.
- Color picture.
- Shade picture.
- Frame box.
- Kill a box.
- Group and frame items.

Quest Terms

caption	headshot
clipart	JPEG
cropping	photofiction
dpi	point of entry
EPS	principle of proximity
GIF	sizing
grayscale	TIFF
grip 'n' grin	

People love pictures! They attract attention as well as impart a bit of information to the hasty reader. Photos also bring a sense of reality to a publication. A large photo most likely becomes the point of entry on the page because the reader's eyes are drawn to the photo and then travel from there (Figure 7-1). Color pictures have even more appeal.

Figure 7-1. Notice the eye-catching appeal of the larger photo on the right.

Which photos to use

Relevance, relevance, relevance. The photo must relate to its story and to the needs and lives of your audience. If the photo stands alone with a *caption*, the caption should give a full explanation of the photo.

People like pictures of other people, especially when those in the picture are smiling and look friendly. Close-ups are appealing because people like to look at faces. Readers prefer people in the pictures, even if the main element of the photo is a building, scenery or another object. Unposed pictures are preferred to posed shots. Pictures with three or fewer people are preferable to large groups — some editors won't even print a photo with more than three people!

Increasing readership

Photos are powerful. Research has proven that more attitude changes occur with a story and an accompanying picture than with the story alone. Even a small photo of a columnist, called a *headshot*, increases readership of that column (Figures 7-2 and 7-3).

standing head ——→

head ——→

byline ——→

drop cap ——→

headshot ——→

caption ——→

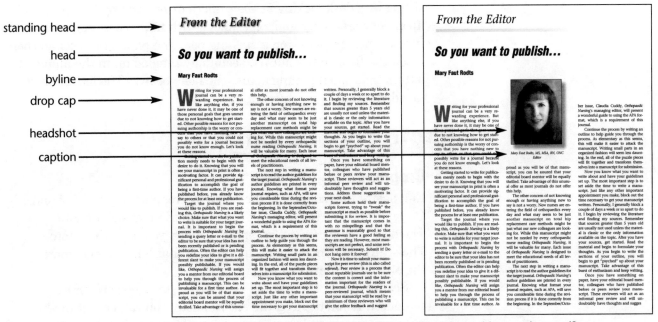

Figure 7-2. Which of the above editorials would you rather read? The headshot of the editor gives a personal touch.

standing head ——→

head ——→

headshot ——→

byline doubling as a caption ——→

Figure 7-3. Gary Baker's sports column runs each week in the university's newspaper. Those who enjoy his columns recognize them by his photo as they thumb through the six sports pages. Although they might not have met Gary, they feel as if they know him.

Photo clichés

Forget the typical *grip 'n' grin* photo, where two people are shaking hands and smiling. Other worn-out poses include someone holding a trophy or certificate, speakers with open mouths on platforms, a committee sitting around a table pretending to be working, an official sitting at a desk looking at the camera or pretending to write. Call upon your creativity and experiment with new poses. For example, two seventh graders won a spelling bee. The photographer had them lie on the floor in the library, seemingly tangled up in the alphabet letters that usually hung across the blackboard. (The letters were taped together.)

Photo "operations"

Cropping

Emphasize the message of the photo by cropping (Figures 7-4 and 7-5). *Cropping* means to get rid of the unwanted parts of a photo. The best time for initial cropping is when you scan the photo. The scanning window gives a marquee that lets you designate the area you want scanned.

Scanning just the wanted area saves storage space on the computer. If you do keep the entire photo, you can crop it in Quark by moving it around the picture box or by enlarging the photo. Quark remembers the entire photo, so printing can get slowed down.

Cropped

Figure 7-4.
Cropping out extraneous background emphasizes the focus of the photo: the people, in this case. No size was changed.

Cropped and enlarged

Figure 7-5.
Cropping takes away the unwanted portions of a photo. The photo on the right has been cropped AND made larger to zoom in on only three runners in that group.

This picture was taken with a digital camera at low resolution. For best quality in digital pictures, use the *high* or *super high* quality setting. Otherwise, when enlarged, the pictures become pixelated like this one.

Don't distort people. They won't find it humorous.

Sizing

Sizing means to make the picture larger or smaller if necessary (Figure 7-6). One way to do this is by using the measurements bar.

Figure 7-6. X and Y % scales.

Be careful to change BOTH the X% and Y% to the same value or you will get a stretched or widened picture.

If you know your desired finished size, it is always good to size the photo when you scan it. For example, if you know the photo will be about 75% of the original, then scan it at 75%. That way it takes less space on your disk and less time to process when it prints.

Figure 7-7. The picture box ☹ was made and framed. The photo was imported, then sized to fit the box *unproportionately* by accident. We forgot the option/alternate key. The picture stretches to fit the box. Not good.

Figure 7-8. A horizontally stretched ☹ photo. It is so easy to make this mistake.

Figure 7-10. Dragging in ☺ left and right sides of the box crop out unnecessary background. Now this picture of Jack and Koa can be sent to Grandma.

drag this top line down to fit the picture

drag this bottom line up to fit the picture

Figure 7-9. The picture box was made and framed. The photo was imported, then sized to fit the box *proportionately* (three magic keys and F). Now the frame needs to be adjusted to fit the picture (highlight the box and drag the bottom and top to the photo's bottom edge).

Dominant photo

It's better to have one large photo on the page than several small ones. The large photo often becomes the *point of entry* on the page — the point toward which your eye gravitates. Compare Figures 7-11 and 7-12.

Figure 7-11. Although the above arrangement of pictures allows many pictures to be used, a reader doesn't know which one to look at first.

Figure 7-12. A dominant photo leaves a stronger impression. One large photo is always a better choice than several little ones. In this large photo, you can see Michelle's expression as her dad shows her how to pick up a horseshoe crab. The two small photos add shape contrast. Eric joins his sister in the top right photo.

Quicktip

A large photo, especially in color, is the leading attention-getting device in page layout.

Ways to present a photo

A photo can be presented in several ways as shown below.

As is,
no frame

Framed

Framed with
white space
between photo
and frame

Framed
with
caption
enclosed

Sandy and John laugh at the
photographer making funny faces.

Silhouette

PR tip

At some time you might use an action shot of an "important person" — for instance, your company president swinging the golf club at the company's annual golf tournament. Always ask your resident expert on golf (or whatever activity it is) to see the picture first to be sure the president's golf swing isn't going to embarrass him and negate the value of the picture.

Figure 7-13.
Ways to present photos.

Dos and don'ts

Odd Shapes

Don't cut pictures into odd shapes.

Figure 7-14. Odd shape.

Orientation

Place photos squarely on the page *most of the time* (don't tilt them).

Figure 7-15. Tilted photos.

Story and photo

Place a related photo near its story (*principle of proximity*). Place a picture above the story to get more attention (rather than below the story) (Figures 7-16 and 7-17).

 ## 'Twas a good day fishing

Si meliora dies, ut vina, poemata reddit, scire velim, chartis pretium quotus arroget annus. scriptor abhinc annos centum qui decidit, inter perfectos veteresque referri debet an inter vilis atque novos? Excludat iurgia finis, qui deperiit minor uno mense vel anno, inter quos referendus erit? Veteresne poetas, an quos et praesens et postera respuat aetas?nihil nisi quod Libitina sacravit.

Mayor caught in net

Hos ediscit et hos arto stipata theatro spectat Roma potens; habet hos numeratque poetas ad nostrum tempus Livi scriptoris ab aevo.

    Interdum volgus rectum videt, est ubi peccat. Si veteres ita miratur laudatque

 Figure 7-16.

Photo falls below the story. The reader will tend to zoom in on the photo and then travel downward, ignoring the top story that relates to the photo.

 Figure 7-17.

Photo is found above its story. The photo will draw a reader in, and then the reader's eyes travel down to the related story.

'Twas a good day fishing

Si meliora dies, ut vina, poemata reddit, scire velim, chartis pretium quotus arroget annus. scriptor abhinc annos centum qui decidit, inter perfectos veteresque referri debet an inter vilis atque novos? Excludat iurgia finis, qui deperiit minor uno mense vel anno, inter quos referendus erit? Veteresne poetas, an quos et praesens et postera respuat aetas?nihil nisi quod Libitina sacravit.

Mayor caught in net

Hos ediscit et hos arto stipata theatro spectat Roma potens; habet hos numeratque poetas ad nostrum tempus Livi scriptoris ab aevo.

    Interdum volgus rectum videt, est ubi peccat. Si veteres ita miratur laudatque

Captions

Always include a *caption*. Captions should say something of substance about the photo that might not be found in the body copy. If a reader flips or skims through your publication, that reader should be able to capture the flavor of the stories or gain some information tidbits through the captions only. *See Chapter 5 (Page Anatomy) for variations on layout of captions.*

A photo on the cover of a magazine or book would not always have a caption, but then you might find the caption inside the front cover. Or the related story is mentioned on the cover, and that teaser line is enough to identify the photo.

Sometimes headshots are used with columns. If the byline is the same person as the photo, there is no need for a caption.

Time sequence

If more than one photo is used, put them in time order of events (Figures 7-18 and 7-19).

Si meliora dies, ut vina, poemata reddit, scire velim, chartis pretium quotus arroget annus. scriptor abhinc annos centum qui decidit, inter perfectos veteresque referri debet an inter vilis atque novos? Excludat iurgia finis, "Est vetus atque probus, centum qui perficit annos." Quid, qui deperiit minor uno mense vel anno, inter quos referendus erit? Veteresne poetas, an quos et praesens et postera resput aetas?

"Iste quidem veteres inter ponetur honeste, qui vel mense brevi vel toto est iunior anno." Utor permisso, caudaeque pilos ut equinae paulatim vello unum, demo etiam unum, dum cadat elusus ratione ruentis acervi, qui redit in fastos et virtutem aestimat annis miraturque nihil nisi quod Libitina sacravit.

Ennius et sapines et fortis et alter Homerus, ut

critici dicunt, leviter curare videtur, quo promissa cadant et somnia Pythagorea. Naevius in manibus non est et mentibus haeret paene recens?

Adeo sanctum est vetus omne poema. ambigitur quotiens, uter utro sit prior, aufert Pacuvius docti famam senis Accius alti, dicitur Afrani toga convenisse Menandro, Plautus ad exemplar Siculi properare Epicharmi, vincere

Caecilius gravitate, Terentius arte.

Hos ediscit et hos arto stipata theatro spectat Roma potens; habet hos numeratque poetas ad nostrum tempus Livi scriptoris ab aevo.

Interdum volgus rectum videt, est ubi peccat. Si veteres ita miratur laudatque poetas, ut nihil anteferat, nihil illis comparet, errat. Si quaedam nimis antique, si peraque dure dicere credit eos, ignave multa fatetur, et sapit et mecum facit et Iova iudicat aequo.

Non equidem insector delendave carmina Livi esse reor, memini quae plagosum mihi parvo Orbilium dictare; sed emendata videri pulchraque et exactis minimum distantia miror. Inter quae verbum emicuit si forte decorum, et si versus paulo concinnior unus et alter, iniuste totum ducit venditque poema.

Interdum volgus rectum videt, est ubi peccat. Si veteres ita miratur laudatque poetas, ut nihil anteferat, nihil illis comparet, errat. Si quaedam nimis antique, si peraque dure dicere credit eos, ignave multa fatetur, et sapit et mecum facit et Iova iudicat

Figure 7-18.
This page is out of time sequence. The first picture shows men fileting the fish, and then we see John holding up the fish. Then we see the fish after they had been caught and brought back in the cooler.

Si meliora dies, ut vina, poemata reddit, scire velim, chartis pretium quotus arro-

Abhinc annos centum qui decidit, inter perfectos veteresque referri debet an inter vilis atque novos? Excludat iurgia finis, "Est vetus atque probus, centum qui perficit annos." Quid, qui deperiit minor uno mense vel anno, inter quos referendus erit? Veteresne poetas, an quos et praesens et postera resput aetas?

"Iste quidem veteres inter ponetur honeste, qui vel mense brevi vel toto est iunior anno." Utor permisso, caudaeque pilos ut equinae paulatim vello unum, demo etiam unum, dum cadat elusus ratione ruentis acervi, qui redit in fastos et virtutem aestimat annis miraturque nihil nisi quod

Libitina sacravit.

Ennius et sapines et fortis et alter Homerus, ut critici dicunt, leviter curare videtur, quo promissa cadant et somnia Pythagorea. Naevius in manibus non est et mentibus haeret paene recens? Adeo sanctum est vetus omne poema. ambigitur quotiens, uter utro sit prior, aufert Pacuvius docti famam senis Accius alti, dicitur Afrani toga convenisse Menandro, Plautus ad exemplar Siculi properare Epicharmi, vincere Caecilius gravitate, Terentius arte.

Hos ediscit et hos arto stipata theatro spectat Roma potens; habet hos numeratque poetas ad nostrum tempus Livi scriptoris ab aevo.

Interdum volgus rectum videt, est ubi peccat. Si veteres ita miratur laudatque poetas, ut nihil ante-

ferat, nihil illis comparet, errat. Si quaedam nimis antique, si peraque dure dicere credit eos, ignave multa fatetur, et sapit et mecum facit et Iova iudicat aequo.

Non equidem insector delendave carmina Livi esse reor, memini quae plagosum mihi parvo Orbilium dictare; sed emendata videri pulchraque et exactis minimum distantia miror. Inter quae verbum emicuit si forte decorum, et si versus paulo concinnior unus et alter, iniuste totum ducit venditque poema.

Interdum volgus rectum videt, est ubi peccat. Si veteres ita miratur laudatque poetas, ut nihil anteferat, nihil illis comparet, errat. Si quaedam nimis antique, si peraque dure dicere credit eos, ignave multa fatetur, et sapit et mecum facit et Iova iudicat aequo.

Si meliora dies, ut vina, poemata reddit, scire velim, chartis pretium quotus arroget annus. scriptor

Figure 7-19.
Photos are readjusted to be in time sequence. The large photo was cropped to make the picture a better closeup. Also, it was flipped so the men face into the copy — the eye is not drawn off the page. Flipping people is not the best option (see page 101).

Face people toward center of page

Have people in photos facing toward the center of the page or toward the story rather than off the page. A reader's eyes will travel in the direction the person in the photo is facing.

Figures 7-20 to 7-23 show partials of pages 1 and 2 of a newsletter, while Figures 7-24, 7-25 and 7-26 show a headshot with a president's message.

Page 1

Figure 7-20.
Person in photo faces off the page, causing a reader to follow the direction of the photo, right off the page.

Figure 7-21.
Person faces toward the center of the page. This keeps the reader on the page.

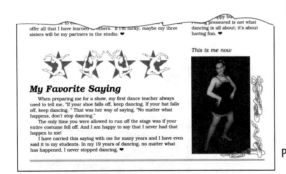

Page 2

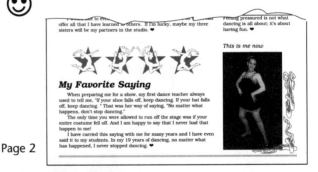

Figure 7-22.
Susan's face is looking toward the inside, but her body is facing off the page.

Figure 7-23.
In this one, she seems to be looking off the page, but her body now points toward the page.

Conclusion: Figures 7-22 and 7-23
Sometimes a person seems to be facing forward. Either photo works in this case. A class vote resulted in using the one on the right because they liked the foot pointing toward the corner of the page. Which do you prefer?

original photo

Implications of flipping

- words can be reversed

- truth is altered (e.g., a wedding ring would be on the right hand if picture is flipped; someone would be writing with the other hand)

Qool Fact

Knowing which way to face pictures is one of those caveats that will set you apart from a co-worker. Many students have reported that their bosses have been surprised when they have picked up that mistake on company publications. It seems like common sense, but many layout artists don't even think about it.

Figure 7-24.
The president's face looks off his message. If he's not interested in his own words, we certainly won't be!

Figure 7-25.
We flipped the photo to make him look inward. This can be done in a pinch, but usually you shouldn't flip people. Their sides change and then the photo isn't truthful anymore.

Figure 7-26.
Best solution. We moved the photo to the right side. Now he faces inward, and we maintained the integrity of the photo.

Welcome to the 23rd Toys 4 All National Exhibition

Why are we all here? To play with the toys, of course! This year our design team has come up with some fun — and educational — toys and games. Visit the life-sized human ant farm and create intricate tunnels of your own. Relive your childhood in a giant ball pit — cheese balls, that is. Test-drive our hover board room, complete with wall ramps and jumps. And have fun! What other job gives you the chance to play with toys all day?
Chris Lukach,
President, Toys 4 All

Welcome to the 23rd Toys 4 All National Exhibition

Why are we all here? To play with the toys, of course! This year our design team has come up with some fun — and educational — toys and games. Visit the life-sized human ant farm and create intricate tunnels of your own. Relive your childhood in a giant ball pit — cheese balls, that is. Test-drive our hover board room, complete with wall ramps and jumps. And have fun! What other job gives you the chance to play with toys all day?
Chris Lukach,
President, Toys 4 All

Welcome to the 23rd Toys 4 All National Exhibition

Why are we all here? To play with the toys, of course! This year our design team has come up with some fun — and educational — toys and games. Visit the life-sized human ant farm and create intricate tunnels of your own. Relive your childhood in a giant ball pit — cheese balls, that is. Test-drive our hover board room, complete with wall ramps and jumps. And have fun! What other job gives you the chance to play with toys all day?
Chris Lukach,
President, Toys 4 All

Digital photos

Your photo will originate from a digital camera or from a scan of an existing photo.

For the most clarity from a digital camera, set your camera on the highest resolution. Low resolution means there are not many pixels in the picture, and it doesn't go through the professional printing process very clearly.

For a scan of a photo for publication, a setting of 300 dpi (dots per inch) works well. When you scan a photo, you will choose *grayscale*, not line art or black and white. Save your file as a TIFF if you're using it for a publication (*filename.tif*).

A JPEG will also work, but reserve that choice for files you want to put on a Web page or send to other people via e-mail. Be sure to name them as filename.jpg. You can assign less dpi (dots per inch) for those files when you scan. Smaller files are easier to send than large ones.

Which graphic file?

Various graphic files are used for different purposes. The basis for their differences lies in the way the file was made. *TIFF files* are my preference for working in Quark. They can be converted easily in Photoshop from color to grayscale or bitmap (lineart). They can be reduced with little data lost.

Created by a drawing program such as Adobe Illustrator, *EPS files* are high quality but large files. A novice Quark user cannot easily convert them to grayscale or black and white lineart (bitmap).

JPEG files contain less data, leading to a smaller file. Thus they are good for Web design, but not for page layout for printing. Their colors are saved in RGB mode (rather than CMYK), which is what the Web calls for.

GIF files are very small files, also used for Web but never print.

PSD is a Photoshop file with layers, not readable by Quark. Convert it to a TIFF to use in a Quark document. In Photoshop, from the file menu, choose **Layer → Flatten Image**. Then you can save it as a TIFF file.

You have most likely already been downloading *PDF files* of documents from the Web. PDF files can be imported into Quark just like the other files. For print jobs, make them in CMYK, not RGB.

Using art from Web sites

Most art on Web sites is copyrighted. You are not allowed to use it in publications without permission. In addition, graphics from Web sites are very low in resolution and do not print clearly. Nevertheless, many students use Web art in their assignments. Use Web art only with permission from your instructor. To use a graphic from a Web site, convert it to a TIFF file. Follow the steps listed below.

☐ 1. Hold down mouse on the graphic for a few seconds. A menu pops up. Windows users: right click on the graphic.

☐ 2. Choose either "Save image as" or "Copy image."

☐ 3. Open Photoshop application. If you copied the image, **File → New document → "OK"** in the dialog box. PASTE into the new document. If you chose "save as," then **File → Open**. Navigate to find the newly saved file and open it.

☐ 4. Save as a **TIFF file** to a **Scans** folder on your disk. If it gives you only the *Photoshop* option, then go to (top menu) **Layer → Flatten Image**. Then you can save it as a TIFF file.

Now you have the picture or piece of artwork to use again. If you copy art from a Web site and paste it into your Quark document, you don't actually have the digital file. Running it through Photoshop makes an actual copy of the digital file.

Quicktip

If you want to use art from the Internet for a professional publication, seek permission from the source and then cite the permission. However, the best thing to do is to ask the company if they can send you a TIFF file or even a PDF.

In the first few pages of Chapter 16 (Newsletters), notice small pictures of the *Profiles and Perspectives* and *Design Tools* newsletters. These files were provided to me by their publishers as PDF files. They maintain clarity as they are shrunken and brought into a picture box.

Using clipart

Clipart is a term used to describe illustrations that you can buy on CD or from Web sites. If you own the art, you have the right to use it. Remember that many other people own the same clipart, so you might see the most popular pictures in other places. However, you can alter the clipart piece in Photoshop to make it different.

Some clipart is made in black and white.

Figure 7-27. Clipart in black and white.

Some clipart is in color. Although you can't see the color here, notice the shades.

Figure 7-28. Clipart in color.

Treat clipart as you would photos. You make a picture box and then "Get picture" under the file menu. When it comes into the box, size it to fit the box and then adjust it by percentages if desired. You will practice doing this in the Quark Quest at the end of this chapter.

You can crop, size and flip a piece of clipart. Unlike real photos, flipping clipart is usually acceptable.

Flipped horizontally.   Flipped vertically.

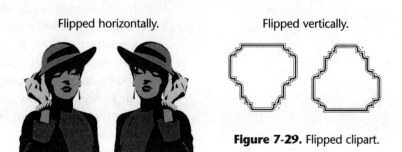

Figure 7-29. Flipped clipart.

All the clipart on this page was used from the Clipart file in Microsoft Word.

You can find clipart on the Web or you can buy CDs with clipart. One popular clipart collection is *Art Explosion* by Nova Development Corporation.

To flip a piece of art

Highlight the picture box with the art. Then click on the black arrows on the measurements bar to flip the art either horizontally or vertically (180°).

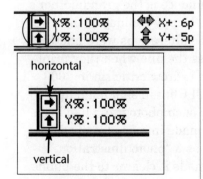

If you want to rotate — but not 180° — use the angle on the bar.

to rotate whole box   to rotate picture inside the box

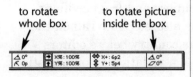

Ethics of photo use

Each Thanksgiving, a grandmother has a picture taken of herself and her grandchildren. She then sends out Christmas cards using the picture. This particular year, Brian (Figure 7-30) wasn't present, so his father stood in his place when the picture was taken (Figure 7-31). Brian's mother took a picture of Brian. Then a friend scanned both photos, and using Photoshop, he removed the father from the group. He then inserted Brian. In addition, he changed the background curtain to a "photographer's background" (Figure 7-32). He also brightened the photo to give it more contrast. (The first one is duller than the final one.) Examine the photos and then read on!

Brian

Figure 7-30. Brian, who was not in the group picture

Brian's dad, Bruce

Figure 7-31. Picture of grandmother and kids. Dad Bruce is "placeholding."

Figure 7-32. Final picture. It looks as if Brian had been there when the picture was taken.

Truth matters.

Was it unethical to alter the photo in this way? Consider the first questions to ask when doing a publication: "Who is the audience?" Then, "What is the message?" If the audience is the grandmother's friends and family, and the message is "Happy Holidays," then we would probably scoff at the idea that the alterations were unethical.

On the other hand, publications cross the line when they print altered photos. The *New York Daily News* drew criticism in 2000 when it printed a photo of President Bill Clinton shaking hands with Cuban President Fidel Castro. No such photograph had been taken that day. Two pictures had been made into one (composite) and although the newspaper labeled it as a "photo illustration," the paper later said they should have made it clearer to the public that the picture was not an actual photo.

Three years later, a photographer from the *Los Angeles Times* was fired during the war in Iraq after he used his computer to combine two photos of United States soldiers and Iraqi civilians into one to improve its composition. The altered photo ran on the front page and in newspapers across the country before editors discovered the photo had been altered — a violation of journalistic ethics. *Check it out:*

http://www.latimes.com/news/custom/showcase/la-ednote_blurb.blurb.

Credibility of photos

With photo editing programs like Photoshop, you can alter a photo any way you want. You can put people in photos or remove them. You can change a person's appearance or alter a crime scene. Technology has added a new dimension to the credibility of photos.

Using photos in publications requires responsibility and ethical standards. Photos must be authentic and reflect the truth. Any alterations should not alter facts or change anyone's appearance. If anything of substance is changed, the change must be disclosed in the caption. Adhering to those guidelines will continue your publication's credibility.

Photofiction

How about pictures that are obviously not true? Someone may question good taste or appropriateness, but not ethics. Tabloids and satirical publications have used this type of photo manipulation for years, even before Photoshop existed! People should automatically recognize that the photos have obviously been changed.

A silly example is found in Figure 7-33, where a student was given the task of isolating a person to crop out a headshot. After he did the serious work, he put her on a beach in Cancun. It should be obvious that the person wouldn't be in Cancun in a dressy suit. Therefore, it falls under the category of *photofiction*.

Effective graphics are:

- purposeful
- honest
- simple
- labeled
- placed near accompanying copy

Person isolated from a group picture.

Person placed on beach in Cancun.

Figure 7-33. An example of photofiction.

(picture side
would NOT
be showing)

front of scanner

Many scanners require the picture to be put in with the head to the front of the scanner. You would not see the picture, of course. The picture faces the glass.

Figure 7-34.

Scanning

If you can photocopy something, you can learn to scan something. The principle is the same. Below are listed some scanning directions for using the Agfa brand of scanner. Most scanners work similarly.

☐ 1. Put your photo or drawing on the scanner with the top toward the front of the scanner. Picture side is down on the glass. Turn on the scanner according to your instructor's directions: some scanners turn on when you open the application used with the scanner (Photoshop in many cases).

☐ 2. Insert your disk. Open your disk and create a folder called "Scans."

☐ 3. Under the **File** menu, choose **Import → Scanwise**. This will open the scanning plug-in. Yours may not be Scanwise. Check with the instructor.

☐ 4. **Original Type** (probably says Photo-glossy). That is correct if you are scanning a photo. If you are scanning something else, change the setting.

☐ 5. Crop your photo. Look at the moving dotted box around the photo (it's called a marquee). Move it around, drag sides in.

☐ 6. Click on **Destination**. Says **Photoshop 5.0**. Leave it.

☐ 7. Click on **Image Control – Grayscale** or **Lineart**. Choose *grayscale* for a photo, unless you want a color photo. Then you would choose *color*. *Lineart* is for black and white art.

☐ 8. **Dimension** – It says 100%. If you want to make it different, change it. 100% will probably work. You can also change the dpi (dots per inch). 300 works well for a photo; as high as possible for lineart.

☐ 9. Then click on **SCAN**.

☐ 10. To save: Name the document: **filename.tif**
Choose TIFF file.
Navigate to save the document in your Scans folder.

☐ 11. Open your disk and folder to be sure you saved it in the right place.

☐ 12. Eject your disk by **dragging it through trash can** (Mac) or **Eject** (Windows).

Adjusting your scanned photo

Go back to your own computer if the scanner was somewhere else. Open up the TIFF document, which will launch Adobe Photoshop.

In Photoshop, choose **Image → Adjust → Brightness/Contrast**. Drag the triangle to the left or right and watch the changes. When you have what you want, click OK. Then save again. Close Adobe Photoshop.

You now have a piece of art that you can pull into a picture box in your Quark documents. You *do not open* the TIFF document to use it. You draw a picture box in Quark, highlight it, and then **File → Get picture** or ⌘**E.**

Quick Quiz

1. What are three kinds of photos that people like?
2. Define cropping and sizing.
3. What are two "dos" and two "don'ts" for using photos?
4. What are five ways to "present a photo"?
5. What are three guidelines to follow when using photos in publications?

Out of the Quandary

Scans in picture boxes

1. Scan two or more pictures.
2. Make five picture boxes of different shapes and sizes.
3. Bring your scans into the picture boxes. (You will repeat some of the scans if you scan only two pictures.)
4. Crop and size them in the different boxes.
5. Frame the boxes.
6. Rotate all the boxes (not just the contents) using the angle on the left side of the measurements bar.
7. Put your name in reverse on top of one of the photos — use "none" for color of the text box. Remember, reverse means to make the type white. It does NOT mean to reverse the letters!

Quantum Leap

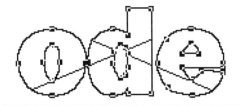

Put a picture behind type

1. Type a word in a very bold font. Enlarge it. The sample is 92-point Franklin Gothic Heavy.

2. Highlight the word.

3. From top menu, choose **Style → Text to box**. The letters are now open boxes.

4. **File → Get picture**. Size the picture if desired.

5. Move the picture around with the content tool (hand) until you get it where you want it. The picture is one big picture behind the entire word.

You can separate the letters, and the picture in its entirety will be behind each letter! This is amazing!

Outside paths

Go to **Item → Split**. Choose **Outside paths**. Each letter now acts as a separate picture box. The picture will duplicate itself three times. (Notice Morgan in each letter.) Using content tool, move around the photo. Using the item tool, move the letters or rotate them. These are rotated 5° and -5°. Move the picture around until you get what you want.

All paths

Go to **Item → Split**. Choose **All paths**. This even separates the counter space (inside of the "o"). Again, each letter and counter acts as a separate picture box. Move around the pictures. You can even resize the photo in each section by itself.

This is the picture used in the exercise.

Morgan, Kamali and Cristin.

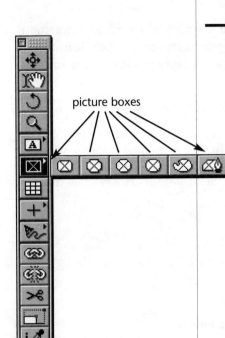

picture boxes

Figure 7-35.
Toolbar showing
picture box tools.
They have an "X"
in them.

Quark Quest

Get a picture

☐ 1. Draw a picture box using the rectangular picture box tool
(Figure 7-35). The right half of the measurements bar changes
to look like this:

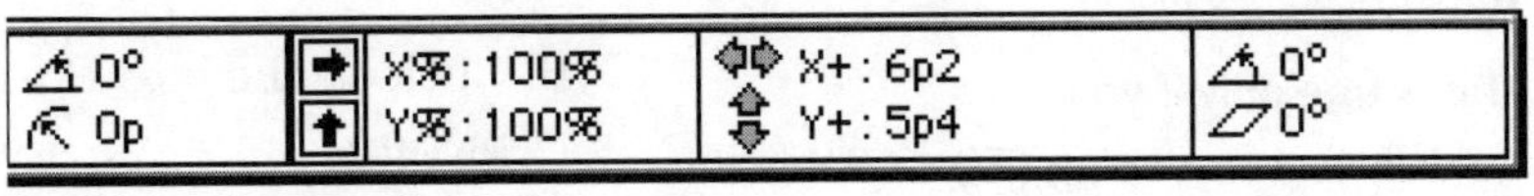

△ 0°	→ X%:100%	X+: 6p2	△ 0°
⊼ 0p	↑ Y%:100%	Y+: 5p4	⟋ 0°

Figure 7-36. The right side of the measurements bar looks like this when
a picture box is highlighted.

☐ 2. Highlight the box.

☐ 3. **File → Get picture** or use the key command ⌘ **E**.

☐ 4. Navigate to the picture or clipart folders on the CD (Figure 7-37).
Microsoft Office also has a clipart folder. Keep clicking through
folders until you get the piece of clipart you want. A preview
picture will come up on the left box so you can see the choices.

Click twice and the picture will come into your picture box
(or press **Open**).

The picture or clipart will now come into the box, but sometimes
it looks as if nothing is there. If the "X" disappeared, then the art
is in there, but it is too big. As a starting point, follow direction #5
on the next page.

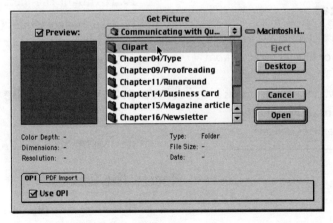

Figure 7-37. The "Get picture" dialog box. Navigate the
computer and/or disks until you find clipart files to select.

How do you know it's a picture box?

It has an "X" in it — until you put a picture in it. If the "X" disappears when you "get picture," but you still don't see the picture, follow step 5 and your picture will appear.

This is true only if your guidelines are showing (F7).

Symbol Refresher

Mac Users
⌘ = command (⌘)
⌥ = option
⇧ = shift

Windows Users
⌘ = control
⌥ = alternate
⇧ = shift

Make the character dance!

Draw a picture box and get an animal or funny character from clipart. Then flip it several times with the black arrows on the measurements bar. The character dances!

Fit the picture proportionately

☐ 5. Click on the picture box. Hold down the three magic keys and F (**F** for **F**it) — ⌘⌥⇧**F**. That will fit the art **proportionately** in the box. Or from the menu, choose **Style → Fit picture to box (proportionately)**.

The picture may not be the exact size you want, but it's a starting point.

Fit the picture unproportionately

☐ 6. Click on the box. Press ⌘⇧**F** (no ⌥ key). This stretches the picture.

Move picture in the box

☐ 7. Use the content tool. It becomes a hand in a picture box. Move around the picture.

Make picture larger or smaller (two ways):

☐ 8. Use percentages in the measurements bar. Change both X% and Y% to the same number (Figure 7-38).

or

☐ 9. ⌘⥠⇧**>** (larger by 5% increments)
⌘⥠⇧**<** (smaller by 5% increments)

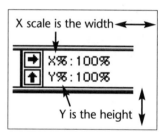

Figure 7-38. X and Y scales.

Flip picture

☐ 10. Highlight the picture box.

☐ 11. Use measurements bar. Click on the black horizontal or vertical arrow (Figure 7-39).

Move picture to middle of box

☐ 12. Highlight box.

☐ 13. ⇧⌘**M** Your picture will move into the middle of the box.

Figure 7-39. Flip arrows.

Resize the box only

☐ 14. Symmetrically: Drag from the bottom right corner toward the top left corner (to reduce size). Drag out on diagonal to increase size.

☐ 15. Shorter/taller or narrower/wider: Drag the handle on the side — NOT THE CORNER — in the direction you want.

Resize the box and the picture at the same time

☐ 16. Hold down those three magic keys (⌘ ⌥ ⇧) and drag the **corner** of the box, either downward or upward.

Rotate the whole box

☐ 17. Click on the box with either tool.

☐ 18. On the left of the measurements bar, there is an angle (Figure 7-40A). Highlight the current number. Type in the desired measurement. The entire box will rotate with its picture.

A Rotate box

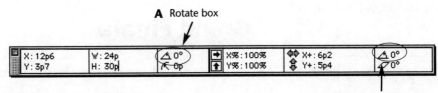

Figure 7-40. Rotation angles.

B Rotate the picture, NOT the box.

Rotate the picture WITHIN a box

☐ 19. Use the content tool because you are dealing with the CONTENT of the box, not the box itself.

☐ 20. Use the angle on the right of the measurements bar (Figure 7-40B). Type in the desired measurement. Just the innards of the box will rotate!

Color the box

☐ 21. Click on the box. ⌘ **M → Box → Color**.

Color the picture

☐ 22. Click on the box. ⌘ **M → Picture → Color**.
This doesn't always work. It depends on how the clipart was made or the kind of file used for a photo.

Shade the picture

☐ 23. Click on the box. ⌘ **M → Picture → Shade**.
This doesn't always work. Fix the art in Photoshop or run out a copy of it in black. Scan it and then you can manipulate it as you want.

Quicktip

Zap it back!

When you make a mistake, you can *undo*. Immediately lift your hands up from the keyboard as if the keys were burning your fingers. Then take a deep breath and think: "Okay…Undo. Zap it back!"

⌘ **Z** is the easiest, but you can also use the menu: **Edit → Undo**.

How to remember this:

"**Z**" is the LAST letter of the alphabet, and you want to undo the LAST thing you just did. Zap it back the other way.

(Wouldn't it be nice to have a ⌘ **Z** for things you say or do?)

Remember:
When you don't know what to do, Apple-M might work for you!

(Control-M for Windows users)

Frame a box

☐ 24. Click on the box to highlight it.

☐ 25. ⌘**M** → **Frame**.

☐ 26. Type in a width.

☐ 27. Choose a style, color, shade.

☐ 28. Click **OK**.

Kill a box

☐ 29. Click on the box. Then ⌘**K**.

Grand Finale

Figure 7-41 exemplifies the final product.

☐ 1. Make a picture box and import a picture: photo or clipart.

☐ 2. Size the picture to fit proportionately in box. Adjust as necessary.

☐ 3. Under the box, draw a text box and type a short caption in it.

Frame the entire unit

☐ 4. Draw a picture box to enclose both the picture box and the caption. It will completely cover the other two boxes. Don't worry.

☐ 5. Frame the box 2 points.

☐ 6. Send the framed box to the back of the other two boxes. On menu: **Item** → **Send to back**.

☐ 7. Adjust sides of framed box to fit well.

Group the entire unit

☐ 8. Group the three items. *See Chapter 6 (Color) – Quark Quest for instructions on grouping.*

☐ 9. Use item tool. Duplicate entire unit (⌘ **D**). Move new unit away from the other one by putting item tool on one of the pieces and dragging.

Resize whole group

☐ 10. Use **item tool**. Click on grouping. Hold down those three magic keys (⌘ ⌥ ⇧) and drag a corner to make larger or smaller. You did this in direction #14 for a box with its contents.

Print the document

☐ 11. Type your name somewhere on the page.

☐ 12. To print, ⌘**P** or **File** → **Print**. Choose a printer according to your teacher's instructions and the accessibility of your system. Usually you use the **Setup** folder to make some decisions.

For a laugh

1. Make a few boxes on the page.

2. Click on a box.

3. Hold down the three magic keys and K. A little guy will come out and blow up the box.

4. Repeat this action a few times, and another guy will come out and shoot at the first guy.

When things go wrong and you need a lift, try it!

We call this woman the "flaky shopper."

Figure 7-41.
Grand Finale project.

8 Communication Concepts

*Think like a wise man, but communicate
in the language of the people.*

William Butler Yeats

Quest Objectives

- Draw a communication model with its six parts.
- Give several examples of graphic noise.
- Explain the 30–3–30 rule of readership.
- Perform the dollar bill test.
- Differentiate legibility and readability.
- Identify trends in the publishing field.

Quest Terms

channel	legibility
comfort level	message
communication model	noise
dollar bill test	readability
feedback	receiver
graphic noise	sender
Gunning Fog Index	30–3–30 rule of readership

Communication model

The foundation of all communication can be explained by the *communication model* (Figures 8-1 and 8-2). Theory textbooks may present this model in more detailed fashion, but for our use as desktop publishers, the following six items will help us form the necessary mindset:

Sender	person/group/organization who has a message to send
Receiver	person/group/organization who is supposed to receive the message
Message	what is to be communicated
Channel	medium through which the message is to be sent
Feedback	resulting behavior of receiver that lets the sender know the message was received
Noise	interference with the message

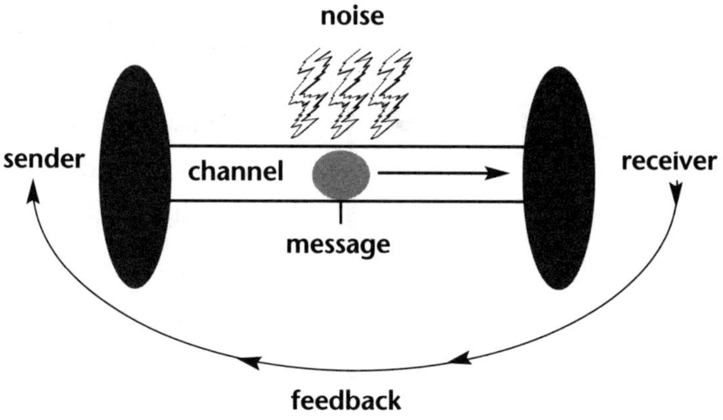

Figure 8-1. Generic communication model.

Figure 8-2. Communication model applied to a "noisy" publication. In this case, it's a letter from a professor to students.

Dear Student,
I'm happy to see that you are in my Publications
Layout class this coming semester. We will be doing
desktop publishing from the communication perspective. You don't have to be an artist to do a good page
layout, but you do have to know certain techniques
and guidelines (which style and size of type communicates best, how to use clipart and photos, and so
forth). We will work with the QuarkXPress program
on the Macintosh G3. If you are used to a PC and
familiar with Windows, you'll adapt quickly to the
Macintosh. Our first few projects will include:
- A FLIER
- LETTERHEAD
- BUSINESS CARD
- SMALL BLACK AND WHITE AD (FROM NEWSPAPERS OR BACK PAGES OF MAGAZINES — SIZE OF AD WOULD BE ABOUT 1/4 OF A MAGAZINE PAGE).

If you can collect any samples of those items in the
next few days, you will be a step ahead. Feel free to
e-mail me with any questions: editorcuddy@mac.com.
Professor Cuddy

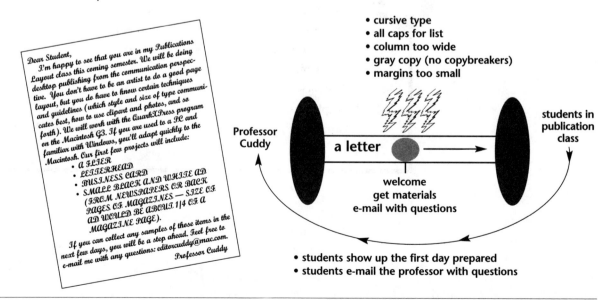

Graphic noise

Noise is anything that interferes with the message. It can be physical (static on radio), psychological (emotional state of receiver at the time of the message) or semantic (words don't mean the same thing to sender and receiver). Stretching the physical sense of noise as applied to publications, let's propose a fourth type of noise: *graphic noise*.

Although an editor pays attention to semantic and psychological noise, layout professionals are more concerned with graphic noise. Graphic noise can be divided into *type* problems and *layout and production* problems.

Noise created by type

- illegible type
- too many fonts
- unsuitable font choice
- font size too small or too big for audience
- all caps for body copy
- tracking too tight or too loose
- leading too tight or too loose
- long lines of type (columns too wide)
- columns too narrow
- reverse with serif type (should be sans serif)
- red, pink, orange or yellow ink for body copy
- text in a shape (like a heart or circle) (Figure 8-3)
- type with graphic behind it (Figure 8-4)

Noise created by layout and production

- no restraint! too many pictures, fonts, boxes
- gray page (no copybreakers/fails dollar bill test – *see page 117*)
- competition with other items — no dominance
- pictures of people printed in red, green or blue ink
- graphic not relevant to publication
- poor photo quality
- dark paper
- ink too light (poor print job)
- not enough white space
- too much white space
- shade too dark

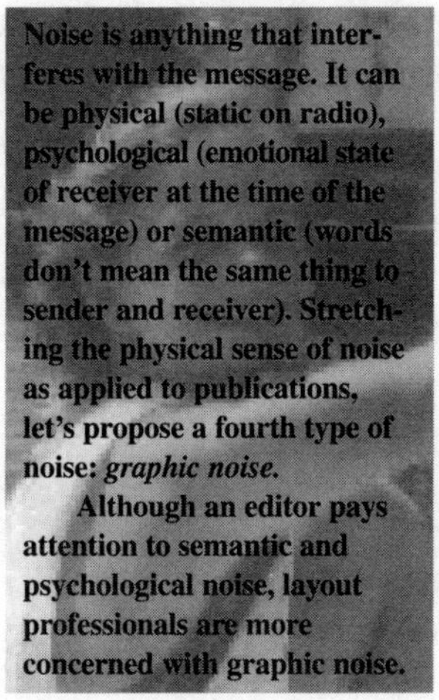

Noise is anything that interferes with the message. It can be physical (static on radio), psychological (emotional state of receiver at the time of the message), or semantic (words don't mean the same thing to sender and receiver). Stretching the physical sense of noise as applied to publications, let's propose a fourth type of noise: *graphic noise*. Divide that into type problems and layout/ production problems.

Figure 8-3. Type in shapes makes reading very difficult.

Noise is anything that interferes with the message. It can be physical (static on radio), psychological (emotional state of receiver at the time of the message) or semantic (words don't mean the same thing to sender and receiver). Stretching the physical sense of noise as applied to publications, let's propose a fourth type of noise: *graphic noise*.

Although an editor pays attention to semantic and psychological noise, layout professionals are more concerned with graphic noise.

Figure 8-4. Competition of type and picture! Type on a graphic is frustrating. It's hard to see the picture, and it's hard to read the type. If you MUST do this, do it with a short headline or label, and make the letters big and bold.

30–3–30 rule of readership

The *30–3–30 rule of readership* divides the readers of your publication into three groups:
• 30-second readers – page flippers
• 3-minute readers – skimmers
• 30-minute readers – in-depth readers

To follow the rule, you must design your layout to reach each of these groups. Your goal is to communicate your message, or at the least, leave an impression of your publication. To do either, you need to use a variety of layout elements.

30-second readers (page flippers)

These are low-interest readers who will pick up a publication and flip its pages. They might be attracted to photos, bold heads and pullquotes. Color also helps attract their attention. Did we succeed in giving them an impression of our publication? Did we get their attention to move them to the next level of readership? Will they read more now or come back to the publication later?

3-minute readers (skimmers)

These are potential converts to our publication who, similar to the flippers, are drawn in by photos, color, pullquotes and bold, punchy heads. In addition, they might read summary decks, subheads, photo captions, bulleted lists and sidebars. They are looking for something to pique their interest. Some readers have said they often read through an entire magazine "pullquote by pullquote" (Figure 8-5). This puts a heavy responsibility on the editor to select pullquotes that represent the essence of the message.

30-minute readers (in-depth readers)

You love this group of readers! This group has the most interest in the content. Copybreakers and design are not very important to them. However, interesting, informative, substantive content counts. Keep in mind short sentences, familiar words, active verbs, clarity, accuracy and sensitivity. Edit well for this interested reader.

Apply the 30-3-30 rule to your publications to reach as many people as possible.

Compare the 30-second audience to a biker. A biker zooms right along, hardly noticing anything.

Compare the 3-minute audience to a jogger. A jogger goes at a medium speed but notices some things along the way.

Compare the 30-minute audience to a walker. A walker takes time to smell the flowers!

Quicktip

Placing pullquotes, boxes or photos on the top outside of pages helps catch the eye of the page flipper or skimmer.

Figure 8-5. Pullquotes set to outside of pages.

Dollar bill test

How do you know if you have too much text on a page? The *dollar bill test* is a simple, creative way to check. Lay a dollar bill in various places on your page. It should touch a copybreaker. If it does NOT touch a copybreaker, then you have too much text and you failed the dollar bill test. Examine Figures 8-6, 8-7 and 8-8.

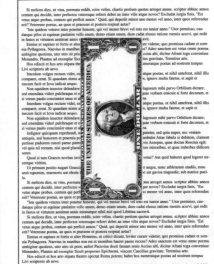

Figure 8-6. The dollar bill touches no copybreakers whatsoever. This page fails the dollar bill test. The page needs to be improved.

Figure 8-7. Even though the text is now made into three columns, gutters are weak copybreakers in the dollar bill test. The page needs more work. This page gets a D- on the test.

Figure 8-8. The page now has subheads and a pullquote. Wherever you lay the dollar bill, it touches a copybreaker. This page passes the dollar bill test!

Legibility vs. readability

Legibility – what you see

Legibility has to do with the look, or the *clarity* of the physical aspect of the publication. How well can you distinguish the type? Are the ascenders too short? Is the counter space (space in the o, e, a) big enough? Is the x-height of letters large enough to make letters easily seen? Is there too much bold or italic type? Is the type too light? (Some fonts appear very light.) Are lines of type too close (i.e., leading too tight)? Are the columns too wide? Is the print job sloppy? Are the photos blurry or dull?

If you answered yes to one or more of those questions, legibility needs improvement.

Readability – what you get

Readability, on the other hand, is the ability of the publication to be read and understood by the intended audience. Readability depends foremost on legibility — if legibility is poor, the message is hindered.

If legibility is good, then examine the other factors that contribute to readability. An 8-point font might be very legible, but is it readable for an older adult? All caps might be legible, but they hinder readability. A gray page (one that fails the dollar bill test) might physically be legible, but it doesn't rank high in readability for an audience with little interest in the topic. Adding copybreaking devices like subheads, pullquotes and photos improves the readability. Further, consider your audience's interest in the topic, knowledge of the topic and educational level — write at your readership's level. The easier it is for someone to read, the more likely they are to read it. (The next section deals with measuring readability level.)

To sum it up, legibility aids readability. You can have legibility without good readability, but you can't have good readability without legibility. Ponder that.

You can have legibility without good readability, but you can't have good readability without legibility.

Quicktip

For better readability

Writing

Use:
- short, familiar words
- short sentences
- short paragraphs
- short distance between subject and verb
- active verbs
- no unnecessary words (e.g., redundancies, wordiness)

Layout

Use:
- columns
- legible type
- appropriate type size for audience
- contrast
- copybreakers, copybreakers, copybreakers! (see page 117)

Qool Fact

In 1992, the National Center for Education Statistics assessed the literary skills of people 16 years and older and found that half of the U.S. adults read at levels between first and eighth grades. Nearly one-quarter of U.S. adults read below fourth grade level. As of spring 2003, the Center is conducting an updated survey. (Check their Web site to get the latest information: **http://nces.ed.gov.** Then go to the survey and program areas.)

Measuring readability

As one of the popular readability formulas to test writing difficulty, Robert Gunning's "fog index" approximates the grade level at which a person must read to understand the material.

1. **Select a sample** of 100 words, ending with a period. You may go slightly over 100, but be sure to end with a period.

2. **Count the total number of sentences** in the sample.

3. **Calculate average sentence length.** Divide the total number of words in the sample by the number of sentences to get the average sentence length of the sample. Round off to the nearest tenth.

4. **Count the number of "hard" words** in the sample. These are words containing 3 syllables or more. Do not count:
   - proper nouns
   - 3-syllable verbs ending in -ed or -es
   - 3-syllable compound words made of easy words such as *schoolteacher, masterpiece, postmaster, heartbroken*
   - words that sound like two syllables such as *business, every*

5. **Find the percentage of hard words.** Divide the total of long words by the number of words in the sample to get the percentage of long words. (For example, if your answer is .12, that translates to 12%, so you will use 12 in the next step.)

6. **Add the average sentence length and the percentage of long words.**

7. **Multiply this sum by 0.4.** This gives you the reading level of the passage. The numbers correlate to the grade level of the passage.

8. Do at least three random samples and average them.

Most readers feel more comfortable reading at one or two levels below their actual level — this is called the *comfort level*. Knowing your audience will help you write at their comfort level.

Run the *Gunning Fog Index* on some of your current materials to test their readability. Choose three random samples from the same publication. Find the readability level of each one and find the average of the three. This process is informative as well as fun.

What can you do to lower the fog index?

- Use many five-letter words. Use words with one syllable and two syllables. Choose familiar words rather than unfamiliar words.
- Keep sentences to an average length of 17 words. Vary sentences to avoid a monotonous rhythm, but keep "short" in mind.
- Prefer simple sentences to compound or complex.
- Prefer active voice to passive.

See sidebar on page 118 for more tips.

Fog is "dense," just as your writing is dense when it is too complex for your audience.

Qool Fact

What are the readability levels of some current publications?

Harper's Magazine	12
Reader's Digest	10
Newsweek	11
Time	11
Ladies Home Journal	8
comic books	6

Aiming at the seventh to eighth grade levels in many cases is fairly safe.

Quicktip

Microsoft Word runs an automatic readability check based on a method devised by Rudolph Flesch. It is similar to the Gunning Fog index.

Trends

Indents

The indent at the beginning of a paragraph signals the start of a new paragraph. In addition, the indent is white space that creates a rest for the reader's eye between blocks of type. However, a subhead breaking up the body copy signifies a new paragraph will follow. Therefore, after a subhead, an indent is not needed. (*See "Alignment of subheads in a magazine article" on page 15.*)

Sans serif vs. serif

Every one of the readability studies I have found in the past 30 years supports the theory that serif type is more readable than sans serif in large blocks of text — in the United States. American children learn to read from primers with serif type. On the other hand, sans serif type is found in many European children's early reading materials. Therefore, you will see sans serif type used more frequently in European publications.

Nevertheless, I have noticed a trend toward the use of sans serif in various American publications. For instance, a very recent copyediting textbook uses sans serif in its entire book.

For now, stick with serif for body copy. But stay tuned!

Captions set on photos

At one time, American journalism frowned on captions set on a photo. However, newspapers are taking liberty to do that now. Sometimes the caption is set in reverse in a dark part of the photo. Other times, it just floats in a light area.

Two surprise visitors show up at a summer picnic.

This man feels as if he's up against a wall.

Figure 8-9. Captions set on photos are acceptable.

One space after period at end of sentence

Professional typesetting has always used one space after a period at the end of a sentence. Type produced on a typewriter needed two spaces because of the monospacing of the letters (see page 52). One space crowded the type too much. However, computer typing (typesetting mode) calls for only one space after a period, especially if you are using justified type. Otherwise, you get "rivers" of space. Typing two spaces is a very hard habit to break, but when you have mastered the "one-space-after-a-period" practice, you will never go back!

Color

People are seeing an increased use of color in nonprofessional and professional publications. With inexpensive inkjet printers available, nonprofessionals easily and often print in color. In addition to more frequent use, color printing is reflecting more quality than it did in the past. Therefore, people are getting used to color on everything, and thus producers of professional publications must meet the color expectations of the public. Even newspapers, traditionally only black and white, include many four-color pages. While four-color printing remains expensive, it may become commonplace in the future.

Quality

Though color is an exception, it appears that people are beginning to accept a poorer quality in publications, especially regarding photos, type and printing. Unfortunately, this negative trend is also happening in layout — people are not as concerned with proper layout.

This trend, I propose, is a result of the rising popularity in home publishing programs. These programs allow amateurs to create "professional-looking" publications. However, most amateurs are not familiar with layout theories, and thus many "rules" are broken. For example, people use low-resolution digital photos instead of quality, high-resolution photos, and thus readers' eyes are, unfortunately, becoming accustomed to lower quality photos. Center-aligned type is also a common sight as are large amounts of copy in reverse in these "professional-looking" publications.

Of course, I don't see this trend as a positive one in professional publishing. I believe we must continue to uphold our publishing standards: quality should be a priority.

One last thought

We live in a moment of history where change is so speeded up that we begin to see the present only when it is already disappearing.

R.D. Laing, *The Politics of Experience*

> Never mistake legibility for communication.
>
> David Carson
> (Graphic designer)

Quick Quiz

1. What elements do you need to provide in a publication to attract or keep the interest of all three types of readers described in the 30-3-30 rule?

2. What are the six parts of the communication model?

3. What are some examples of graphic noise?

4. What is the significance of the dollar bill test?

5. How do legibility and readability relate?

6. What are three publishing trends?

 # Out of the Quandary

1. Communication Model

Find a "noisy" publication, which you will use to do the following:

• On a separate piece of paper, draw the communication model and label its six parts (see page 114). Your publication will be the *channel*. Label the other parts specific to your publication.

• List graphic noise factors (related to type and layout — not psychological, semantic or physical).

• Attach the publication to the paper.

2. 30-3-30 Review

1. Go through a magazine and pick out the elements that would appeal to each of the reader groups.

2. For what publication(s) or book(s) are you a 30-second reader? a 3-minute reader? a 30-minute reader?

 # Quantum Leap

Contribute to the trends section of this chapter for the next edition. E-mail the author with a trend you have discovered in the publishing field. Go to **www.claudiacuddy.com**.

9 Proofreading

Ode to the Typographical Error

The typographical error is a slippery thing and sly;
You can hunt till you are dizzy, but it somehow will get by.
Till the forms are on the press, it is strange how still it keeps.
It shrinks down in a corner, and it never stirs or peeps.
That typographical error, too small for human eyes —
Till the ink is on the paper, then it grows to mountain size.
The boss, she stares with horror, then she grabs her hair and groans;
The copyreader drops his head upon his hands and moans.
The remainder of the issue may be clean as clean can be,
But the typographical error is the only thing you see.

Anonymous

Quest Objectives

- Differentiate between editing and proofreading.
- Give three tips for better proofreading.
- Describe the relationship of a stylebook and "its" dictionary.
- Apply proofreader's marks to a publication.
- Interpret proofreader's marks made by someone else.
- Adjust copy and layout to fit the proofreader's marks.

Quest Skills

- Use the QuarkXPress spell check utility.

Quest Terms

copyediting
editing
page proofs/page proof stage
proofreader's marks

proofreading
spell check
stylebook

Proofreading is used in all venues — from something as simple as a parent's note to a child's teacher to something as complex as a 500-page book. A careful writer is a careful proofreader.

Qool Fact

Computerized editing has replaced much of the traditional "editing with a pencil." In news-rooms and publishing houses, reporters enter their stories and articles into the network. Editors access those stories from the network onto their own computers. They do their editing right on the electronic file, instead of marking up a hard copy. However, at a later stage, proofreading marks are used on the typeset copy (page proofs).

Proofreading? In a desktop publishing book? Proofreading is crucial in the publishing process — as well as in the rest of your writing activities. Basic proofreader's marks are recognized nationwide, so you should be familiar with them.

For many years I assumed students knew proofreader's marks by the time they had an upper level class. However, I discovered that despite their varied backgrounds and years of schooling, many students were unfamiliar with the marks. That discovery prompted me to include a brief overview of proofreading and proofreader's marks in this book. For some, the topic will be review — for others, it will be new.

Proofreader's marks (also called *copyediting marks*) aren't used only for editorial work. Many of these symbols can be used on layouts to designate space, deletions and alignments, as well as copy corrections.

Everyone makes mistakes

The best way to find your mistake in a publication is to print 10,000 copies! Many stories have been told about staffs who did numerous proofreadings, and then upon publishing, discovered one major, obvious mistake. What is worse, of course, is when that obvious mistake is discovered only after distributing the publication.

How many times have you thought your piece was perfect (after you proofed it a few times), and then a friend looked at it and found some mistakes? You wondered, "How in the world could that have gotten by me?" It happens to all of us. Never fear — you can improve your work. First of all, there is life after the spell checker. Use it as a first quick check, but don't rely on its accuracy. It doesn't know if you meant "soul" or "sole," or "roll" or "role."

A project takes a little more time if you proofread thoroughly. But the additional time you spend proofreading will result in a higher quality publication and a better professional reputation.

For Fun

Read the following sentence:

FINISHED FILES ARE THE RE-
SULT OF YEARS OF SCIENTIF-
IC STUDY COMBINED WITH
THE EXPERIENCE OF YEARS.

Now count the F's in that sentence. Count them ONLY ONCE: Do not go back and count them again.

Answer on page 132

Figure 9-1.
Find the F's.

Edit or proofread in style

Clarify whether you are supposed to edit or proofread the copy. *Editing* is usually done on works in progress, while *proofreading* is done on almost-finished works. A very important proofreading is done at the *page proof* stage of a publication, one of the final stages before printing.

Keep a dictionary, grammar handbook and *stylebook* at your working area, and remember to use the dictionary that is the "official dictionary" of your particular stylebook (see Qool Fact sidebar on page 127).

Preferred styles

Keep a style sheet for each client. Record preferences. For example, if a client (an association perhaps) likes to capitalize officers' positions, write that down. If another association likes having no periods in their credentials, write that down. And so on.

Some editors use a sheet of paper (or more than one) for each client or job. On the paper, they divide the page into boxes, putting alphabet letters in the boxes. Decisions on word usage are written in the box. For example, if you decided to use the word *pullquote* as one word instead of two, write the word *pullquote* in the "P" box. Put these papers into a notebook for future reference.

Tips for proofing

Proofread your publication at least three times — at different sittings with time between for more objective viewpoints. Or better yet, have someone else proof it for you as well. Reading aloud can help you catch mistakes, especially in numbers. To check spelling, read backward. Pay special attention to all names, numbers, phone numbers and Web site addresses. Go to the Web sites to be sure they are current.

Since it is easier to proofread double-spaced copy, double space the copy (or increase the leading) for proofing purposes. After you have made the corrections on the computer file, return the copy to its original spacing or leading settings.

Proofreading from a computer screen

One of the best ways to proof on the computer screen is to enlarge the view. Mistakes are more easily seen when they are big! As in proofing hard copy, double space the type on the screen — or increase leading if the type is in Quark. Revert to your original settings after you have finished proofreading.

Put the original hard copy of the document in front of you as you proof the formatted copy on the screen. If you have used proofreading marks for corrections, be sure you have fixed everything.

Use a clean hard copy for your final proofing.

There are only two types of typographic errors. The one you catch prior to printing and the one that pops out while being printed.

Len Cockman
The Wit and Wisdom
of PR Success

Paris
in the
the Spring

Birds
of a
a feather

A
bird
in the
the hand

Figure 9-2.
Eye Examination.

Read the copy in the triangles. Notice anything odd?

See page 132.

This is an unusual paragraph. I'm curious how quickly you can find out what is so unusual about it. It looks so plain you would think nothing was wrong with it. In fact, nothing *is* wrong with it! It is unusual though. Study it, and think about it, but you still may not find anything odd. But if you work at it a bit, you might find out. Try to do so without any coaching!

Answer on page 132

Figure 9-3.
Unusual paragraph.

Proofreader's marks

print in boldface	Rowan University
print in italics	The Whit
close up space	Ame͜rican
delete and close up space	Amerᵉrican
change the order of words	change the order⟨words⟩of
insert	a⋀day *sunny*
delete; remove something	Here today, gone ~~gone~~ tomorrow.
indent	]Attitude counts.
begin a new paragraph	¶Attitude counts. Aptitude is second.
no paragraph	NO ¶ Attitude counts.
spell out or check spelling	(lbs) (thier)
make the letter(s) upper case	≡american
make the letter(s) lower case	Ǿctopus
align left	‖To: Susan
	‖ From: John
align centered	]Title of Paper[
let it stand (you made a correction and then decided it was right the original way)	STET
put space between words	Columbus│Day #
put space here	#
move to next line	United States⌐of America

When in doubt, write out the correction!

Quicktip Get out that pencil when you proofread! Actually, you can use a red, green, purple or blue pen. Just don't use black. Black is too hard to see on black type. Be emphatic with your marks — the gentle touch doesn't work. Notations are too easy to miss.

Proofing the layout

Overall copy

☐ Widows and orphans are eliminated whenever possible.

☐ Tracking is consistent (not positive): no huge white gaps of space are creating rivers down the page.

☐ One space after periods at the ends of sentences (pages 121 & 201).

☐ Leading is consistent.

☐ En and em dashes are used correctly (page 248).

☐ Straight quote marks and straight apostrophes are replaced by "real" quote marks and apostrophes (page 250).

☐ All stories have bylines (if bylines are used in the publication).

☐ Copy in framed or shaded boxes is vertically centered.

☐ Copy in framed or shaded boxes has text inset applied.

Photos

☐ Photos face toward their stories or the center of the page.

☐ All photos have captions and credit lines.

☐ Captions have no misspellings.

☐ All people in photos are identified.

Heads

☐ Heads are in correct font and style.

☐ Heads contain no typos.

☐ Subjects and verbs agree.

☐ Heads are well placed — more space above than below.

Page design

☐ Items are aligned along an imaginary line.

☐ Contrast is evident.

☐ Proximity issues: chunks of information are found together.

☐ Color is used consistently. Check color usage by running out color-separated pages.

Additional checkpoints for multipage documents

☐ Pages are in the correct sequence.

☐ Page numbers in table of contents match articles and chapters in the publication.

☐ Headers and footers carry correct information.

☐ Top or bottom borders and rules are consistent for alignment across spreads.

☐ Jumplines and continuation lines have correct page numbers.

☐ On page 1 or on the masthead: correct date, edition, volume.

☐ Overall consistency of pages in a multipage document.

Qool Fact

Check the dictionary — but WHICH ONE?

Organizations and publishing houses adopt a particular stylebook as their guide to achieve uniformity and consistency in manuscript preparation as well as in usage and writing. A stylebook, in turn, recommends a certain dictionary.

Below are a few of the stylebook and first-choice dictionary combinations.

The Associated Press Stylebook (AP)
Webster's New World College Dictionary

Publication Manual of the American Psychological Association (APA)
Merriam-Webster's Collegiate Dictionary

MLA Style Manual (The Modern Language Association of America)
Merriam-Webster's Collegiate Dictionary

American Medical Association Manual of Style (AMA)
The American Heritage Dictionary

Chicago Manual of Style
Webster's Third New International Dictionary

Check the author's Web site for more information on stylebooks and dictionaries: **www.claudiacuddy.com**

Quick Quiz

1. What errors on the layout are designated with proofreading marks?

2. What are some things you can do to better proofread your copy?

3. What is the difference between editing and proofreading?

4. What is a stylebook and what is its connection to a dictionary?

Out of the Quandary

PDF files for these exercises can be found on the CD (Assignments: Chap9.Proofreading), or you can photocopy them from this book.

Body copy

1. Apply proofreading marks (Exercise 9-1).

2. Interpret proofreading marks (Exercise 9-2).

Layout

3. Find layout mistakes on a newsletter page (Exercise 9-3).

4. Interpret layout corrections on a small ad (Exercise 9-4).

Spell Check

5. Use the Quark document on the CD (Exercise 9-5) to check spelling. See page 132 for instructions on using spell check.

Quantum Leap

1. Purchase the latest AP stylebook, *The Associated Press Stylebook and Briefing on Media Law.*

2. Purchase AP's preferred dictionary, *Webster's New World College Dictionary.*

3. Begin your own notebook of style choices. Label each page with a letter. While editing, when you make a decision on a word or phrase, write it on that page. It seems that an editor checks the same words continually, and you'd be surprised that you can't remember what choice you made. Use a brightly colored 5 x 7 notebook that won't get lost among your papers.

Perils of Editing

This is a real e-mail I received from a student.

Oh! I have to tell you about an embarrassing copyediting experience I had this summer. The professor invited a speaker to our class, Organizational PR and Management. We were all e-mailed a copy of the speaker's resume ahead of time. I, of course, doodled on my copy by circling the typos and making changes as if it were my resume. I brought it with me to class. As the professor was introducing him, the speaker ducked off to the side and asked me for the copy of his resume so he could check some facts. He saw all of the typos I had circled! I was mortified! I never thought I would have an embarrassing copyediting moment!

– Cristin

Exercise 9-1. Apply proofreading marks to the passage below.

Using standard proofreading marks, correct the copy. Choose a sensible place to break the selection into two paragraphs. Style preferences: AP style, all paragraphs indented, no hyphenated words, newsletter's name is *PRomo*. Just for this exercise — to practice proofreading marks — make any person's name bold. Use pencil or red, green or blue ink — no black.
Disclaimer: These articles were written without any errors. I purposely imposed all the errors.

While public rel ations practitioners strive ot relay messages, educate audiences and change attitudes, messages, education and at titudes are nothing without action. Christi black, managing director of Ogilvy Public Relations Worldwide, explains, "You cancreate a campaign to educate, but ultimutely you want audience your to do something." To moove your audience to action, you must first create a clear

goal. What are you trying accomplish? what doyou want youR audience to *know*? what do do you want your audience to *do*? "Onee of the biggest mistakes wE make is Developing messages that relate To us, to our clients and to Our committtees," says Black. "We are not the audience".

REprinted from "Moving Your Audience to Action,"

Melissa Juhas, PRomo, December 2002

Exercise 9-2. Interpret proofreading marks.

Retype the passage according to the proofreading marks.

James Earl Jones suggested that the best way to understand culture is through an onion and its layers. the outer layer of culture makes up the covering of the onion — clothes, custjoms and traditions. the middle layer determines what is right right and what is Wrong. finally, the core of culture encompasses the philosuphy of life. The key is learning to incorporate as many positive aspects from other cultures into your own. by doing this, one fuses the ability to work with a variety of people from deverse backgrounds. In words other — communicate better. And isn't that what we want — to train ourselves to become the best communicators possible?

REprinted from "While You're Changing Culture, You're Changed, Too!,"

Courtney Eitel, PRomo, December 2002

Exercise 9-3. Find layout mistakes on a newsletter page.

Assume a copyeditor read the body copy for errors. Your job is to find layout errors. Use proofreading marks or, if a mark does not apply, circle and write out the necessary change. Use a pencil or red, green or blue ink. Heads should be Arial bold, left aligned, upstyle (page 66). First paragraphs use drop caps. Refer to the Checklist on page 127. You should find at least 20 layout errors. To see a good copy of this page, see page 224.

Quark quandary

| Fall 2005 | A Newsletter of Quark Quintessence | Vol. 1 No. 1 |

On the Quark Quest

When a photo faces off the page, flip it if possible.

Avoid teh Quark quagmire,

QuarkXPress 5.0 is made up of five major items: picture box, text box, Bézier text path, line and table. Everything we do is made of these five elements or variations of them.

While working in Quark, we need to show invisibles (⌘I) and show guides (F7). These are also found under the View menu. Occasionally, turn them off to look at your beautiful work! Remember — F7 takes you to heaven.

Sometimes it seems that Quark won't let us do an operation. In this

We need to hit apple-s every five minutes.

case, the first thing to ask yourself is if you're on the correct tool. The second thing to check is that the selected text or picture box is really selected. Can you see the little black handles? Or does your text need to be highlighted?

One of our best friends in Quark is apple-S. (PC users call this control-S.) We should hit this key every five minutes. Our other best friend is apple-Z (control-Z), which undoes something we just did that we don't like. If we make a mistake, we can also "revert to saved," assuming we keep saving

See QUAGMIRE, page 2

The Invisible box

Here's a Quark trick that you will just love. You can put copy on an image (like a name on a person's shirt) by drawing the text box on a picture and typing copy in it. With the item tool, move the box where you want it. Make your text box background invisible ("none" in background color in the apple-m dialog box).

Create a Reverse

If the image is dark enough, reverse the type and you've created a different effect. To create a reverse, highlight your type. From the Style menu, choose color – white. Click off your text box, in some white space somewhere. Voila! ⌘

Hang ThatIndent

When we use a list, bullets emphasize our points. Use dots, squares, diamonds or other shapes from the Zapf Dingbats or Wingdings font. Asterisks and hyphens are rather old-fashioned.

To look professional, set a hanging indent so all copy lines up under the letter, not the bullet. Type all lines of copy first. Format with "space before." Go back and type the dingbat in front of each item. Then space

once, or to be more professional, type a "thin" space (opt-shift-space) [alt-shift-space] after the dingbat. (This doesn't work in all fonts.) Then hit command \ [control \]. Subsequent lines of type in that unit will "hang" right under the first line of type. Continue with all other lines of type.

This is a simple detail that marks the difference between the professional and the amateur and gives your document a crisper appearance. ⌘

⌘ Quark Quicktip ⌘

For Mac users only: To make the apple logo, type option-shift-k. Then choose Chicago font.

What's In This ISSUE?	
Avoid the Quark Quagmire	To Group or Not to Group
Hang That Indent	Professional or Amateur?
The Invisible Box	Quark Quips
Personality Profile	Quark Quote of the Week

Exercise 9-4.
Interpret proofreading marks to correct a small ad.

Interpret the corrections needed on this ad, correlating with the numbers. Refer to the correct form of the ad below.

1._____

2._____

3._____

4._____

5._____

6._____

7._____

8._____

9._____

10._____

11._____

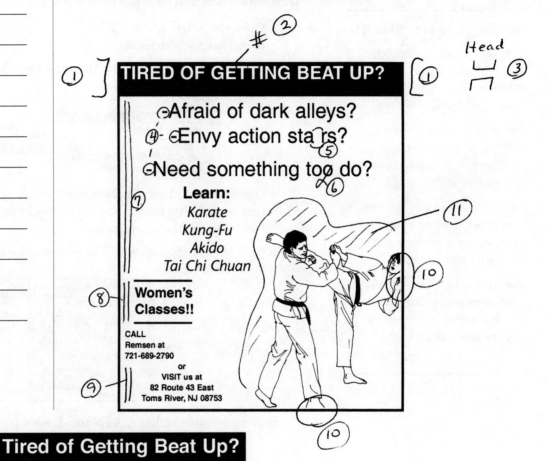

Remsen's small ad emphasized a large line art picture and a reverse head with strong contrast. All copy is left aligned, head is centered, both horizontally and vertically.

I made the mistakes on the ad above on purpose — Remsen's ad is this one!

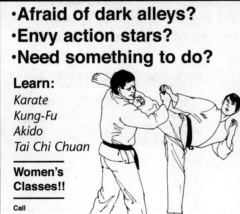

Exercise 9-5. Use spell check.

Run spell check on Exercise 9-5, the Quark file found on the CD.

Quark Quest

Use spell check. Use Exercise 9-5 found on the CD.

☐ 1. Open the exercise. *Note:* If it's your own document, **Save** before doing any spell checking.

☐ 2. From the menu, choose **Utilities → Check Spelling**.

☐ 3. Choose **Word**, **Story** or **Document**. *Story* refers to a particular text box with its linked boxes. You would have to click on that box to choose the *Story* option.

☐ 4. A dialog box pops up with the word count. Click **OK**.

Quark "suspects" these words are spelled wrong.

Total words in document.

Actual words without any repeats ("the" counted as one, "and" counted as one, and so forth).

☐ 5. Then decide whether to **Replace**, **Look up** or **Skip.**
At this point, the *spell check* works similarly to other programs.

The example below chooses to **Replace** the misspelled word with the suggestion given by QuarkXPress. If the suggestion isn't correct, type in the word you want. Click **OK** to finish.

Quark's suggestion. If it's not what you want, type in your word.

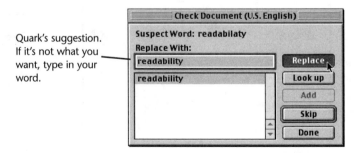

☐ 6. Save your document.

If you use certain words repeatedly in your publications, and they always come up in *spell check*, you can add them to the dictionary. Use one of the in-depth QuarkXPress handbooks for instructions.

Spelling Chequer Blue It!

Eye halve a spelling chequer,
It came with my pea sea.
It plainly marques four my revue
Miss steaks eye kin knot sea.

Eye strike a key and type a word
And weight four it two say
Weather eye am wrong oar write,
It shows me strait a weigh.

As soon as a mist ache is maid,
It nose bee fore two long,
And eye can put the error rite,
Its rare lea ever wrong.

Eye have run this poem threw it,
I am shore your pleased two no.
Its letter perfect awl the weigh,
My chequer tolled me sew.

Sauce Unknown

Answers

Figure 9-1. There are six F's in the paragraph. You often don't "see" the F in "of" because it sounds like a "V."

Figure 9-2. Double "the" and double "a" in the triangles. You usually read it the way you think it will be. Many mistakes are made in simple situations like this one. You tend to check difficult words but miss little words.

Figure 9-3. The paragraph contains no E's.

---

10 Flier

Publicity is the life of this culture — insofar as without publicity capitalism could not survive — and at the same time publicity is its dream.

John Berger
Ways of Seeing

Quest Objectives

- List the two main goals of a flier.
- Describe various uses of a flier.
- Identify components of a flier.
- Perform the visual magnetism index.
- Use QuarkXPress skills you have learned so far to create a flier that incorporates principles of design.

Quest Skills

- Frame a box.
- Adjust art to fit.
- Make a drop shadow.
- Type on a curved text path.
- Reverse copy.
- Draw a line.
- Use text inset.

- Vertically center copy.
- Use hanging indent.
- Type bulleted list.
- Manipulate type.
- Move items.
- Collect for output.

Quest Terms

bulleted list
doorhanger
flier
handbill
hanging indent

mailer
poster
10-foot rule
text inset
visual magnetism index

Your flier needs to follow the *10-foot rule*: If it isn't interesting or identifiable from 10 feet away, then the dominant graphic or headline is not bold or large enough.

Quicktip

Remember, the main goals of a flier are to attract attention and quickly impart a message.

Qool Fact

Is it flier or flyer?

Dictionaries present both as correct. However, the *Associated Press Stylebook* prefers **flier** for a handbill or an aviator!

From the communications viewpoint, it is important to use terms consistent with the stylebook of your field.

A *flier* is typically a one-sided publication that presents a single message. Its orientation can be either portrait (8½ x 11) or landscape (11 x 8½). Although letter-size paper is the most common, a flier can be other sizes. If it is distributed by hand, it is called a *handbill*.

If it is posted on bulletin boards, it is called a *poster*. If it is posted on a bulletin board, keep in mind that it needs to catch a person's attention and deliver its message from about 10 feet away. Also, a flier can be mailed (*mailer*), and other times it is put on windshields! A neighborhood canvassing campaign sometimes uses a *doorhanger*, another form of flier.

The principles you learned earlier are important for fliers. For instance, the principle of dominance plays a major role in a flier's design because one item needs to attract attention. Contrast is important so that certain items jump out. Alignment governs overall placement of items on the page. Proximity is represented as all related information is chunked together for easy reader absorption, such as in bulleted lists.

A flier usually contains:
• a relevant graphic
• a large headline
• a few points made in a few words, perhaps as bullet points
• contact information

Before you design the flier, be sure to identify the audience and the message. Choose an element to be dominant. Will it be the art or the headline? How will your flier stand out from others on a crowded bulletin board?

Stick with one or two fonts. Use lots of white space. Make type large enough to be seen from 10 feet away.

Differentiating fliers

The handbill and the mailed flier usually have more copy than the other types. Take into account folding if the flier is mailed. The windshield flier needs to impart an immediate benefit to the recipient or it will be trashed before it is read. The poster flier should be simple with large elements so that it can be read from 10 feet away.

Standing out in the crowd

What can you do to make your poster flier noticed on that crowded bulletin board?
1. Use a distinguishable paper color, like fluorescent yellow.
2. Make your dominant element relevant to your target audience as well as relevant to the message.
3. Incorporate consistency (repetition) in your flier or poster if the format will be more than a one-time use. You want people to look

at it and instantly know it is one of "yours." This can be achieved by use of a logo or distinctive graphic element, use of a certain color or use of the same layout each time.

Using the same look

If you always use the same color paper, change the layout enough each time so people quickly realize it's a different promotion or announcement. If you choose the same layout from one flier to the next, you probably want to change the color of the paper. When the flier is printed in color, change the colors of some of the items. Without significant changes, people glance at a flier and think, "I've already seen that."

Your first Quark project

Your first Quark assignment will be to make a flier (see *Out of the Quandary*). You must include six items that will start building your skills. You also must explain how you used any of the design principles.

Required elements:
1. a curved text path with words on it
2. a framed box
3. drop shadow (shaded box behind the other box)
4. copy in reverse
5. a rule (line) at least 1 point, any style
6. scanned picture, digital picture or clipart

The next four pages show fliers made by students who had never worked in QuarkXPress before — except for two. Can you guess which ones they are? Can you pick out the six elements on each of the fliers?

Visual Magnetism Index In her book *Public Relations Publications,* Linda Morton presents the *visual magnetism index* to test the effectiveness of a flier.

1. Select 10 people with characteristics similar to those of your target public.

2. Tell them to rate the *look of the page* rather than the content.

3. Hold the publication up from a distance of 10 feet.

4. Have subjects note what they see first, second and third.

5. Assign points to items as follows:
   Noticed first = 3 points
   Noticed second = 2 points
   Noticed third = 1 point

6. Add the points. The items with the highest sums attracted the most attention. If the items you intended to emphasize did not score highest, make adjustments and retest.

Figure 10-1. Visual magnetism index.

Both fliers announce sports events — one to watch and one to participate in. Michele (Figure 10-2) used the drop shadow under the picture, while John (Figure 10-3) used it behind the names of the teams.

Compare the two versions of Michele's flier. In the second one, she has eliminated the box around the graphic and used her drop shadow at the top. The graphic becomes more dominant.

Notice John's interesting use of the lines in an "L" shape. All the other items align down the center.

Figure 10-2.

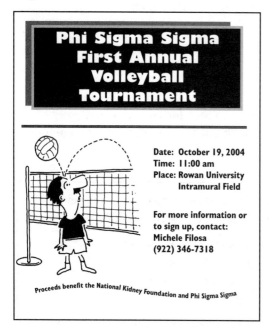

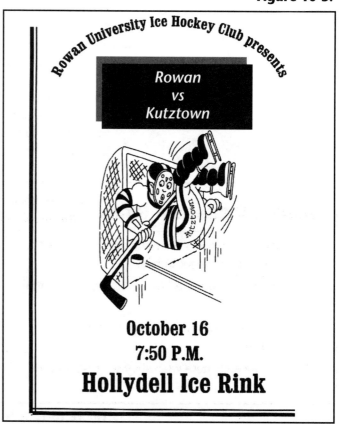

Figure 10-3.

Kevin chose a gray background with a reverse banner across the top. His photo is in an oval with the drop shadow applied to it. Notice the font (Steamer) he used for the "Wanted" and the reward amount: it has a homemade, western appeal. His lines create a frame effect. Although all caps are not usually allowed, in this case they fit the theme.

Figure 10-4.

Figure 10-5.

Jodie also chose to make her drop shadow under the circle. Her curved text is the word "bake" at the top. Once again you see all caps, but they are two short words, so readability is not an issue. Her dotted lines and stars add repetition to the page.

Figure 10-6.

Janeen used the Bézier picture box tool to create the curved gray area. For her drop shadow, she used white letters under the "For Sale" black letters. To make the white letters under the black, she first made a text box over the gray. She typed "For Sale" in black. She duplicated that text box, highlighted the letters and made them white. She used **⌘M → Runaround → None** for each of those two boxes. Then she clicked on the first box (with the black letters) and chose **Item → Bring to Front**. She moved the boxes into position (**Item tool**) to produce the white shadow.

Figure 10-7.

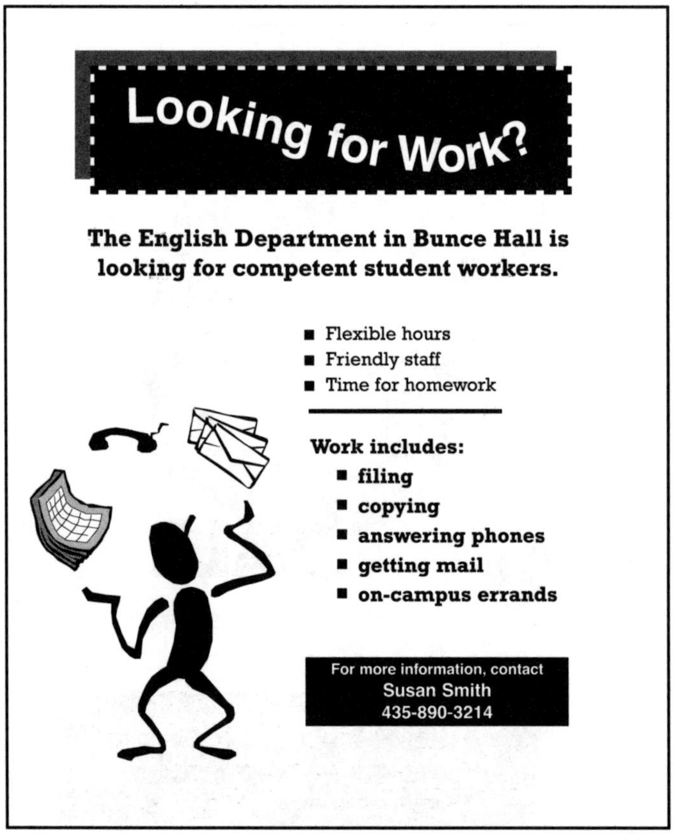

Jill chose clipart from Microsoft Office to create a whimsical effect to contrast the serious topic. In addition, the two reverses plus the solid black character create contrast. The two black boxes align on the right.

Alex started with two circles, one black and one gray. To get the half-circle effect, Alex moved the circles so that half of the circle was on the page, and half was off the page. He then covered those circles (off the page) with a white picture box. He repeats the circle theme with a round frame for the cow. For his curved text paths, he made one that he liked and then duplicated it three more times and moved them into the positions he wanted.

Figure 10-8.

Figure 10-9. Taking apart the flier.

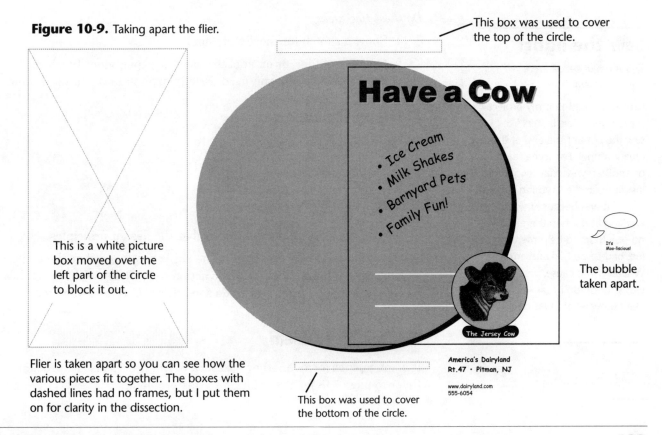

This box was used to cover the top of the circle.

This is a white picture box moved over the left part of the circle to block it out.

The bubble taken apart.

Flier is taken apart so you can see how the various pieces fit together. The boxes with dashed lines had no frames, but I put them on for clarity in the dissection.

This box was used to cover the bottom of the circle.

Design principles

repetition
alignment
proximity
contrast
dominance

Other considerations

eye direction
simplicity
balance

Saw the light!

This is a real e-mail I received from a student.

I am so excited that my project turned out so well. I feel like I saw the light at the end of the Quark tunnel. For some reason or another, yesterday a lightbulb just lit up and everything clicked. I think it was because I was working at it when there was no one there to help me, so I just had to do trial and error. Whatever the cause, yesterday was a lot of fun because I felt like I knew what I was doing!

– Robert

Quick Quiz

1. What are the four components of a flier?
2. What are five uses of a flier?
3. What is the purpose of the Visual Magnetism Index?
4. What are two things you can do to make your flier stand out on a crowded bulletin board?

Out of the Quandary

Design a flier in QuarkXPress.

Use the following six items on your flier (they can be combined):

☐ 1. a Bézier curved text path with words on it   *p. 63*

☐ 2. a framed box   *p. 112*

☐ 3. drop shadow (shaded box behind the other box)   *p. 87*

☐ 4. copy in reverse (on a picture or in a solid box)   *p. 87*

☐ 5. a rule (line) at least 1 point (can be larger),
     any style (dashes, arrow, etc.), curved or straight   *p. 89*

☐ 6. scanned picture, digital picture or clipart   *p. 109*

Do these two tasks:

☐ 1. Show a sketch (or more than one).

☐ 2. On back of flier, or on another piece of paper, identify which design principle(s) you used. Briefly explain how you used them.

Planning the flier

☐ Decide on your message.

☐ Write the copy.

☐ Write a catchy headline.

☐ Choose a graphic.

☐ Sketch out a rough layout. Remember the design principles.

☐ Open QuarkXPress and begin. The skills you learned at the end of Chapters 4, 6 and 7 are put into action here. Refer to those chapters if you forget how to do something. Use the index, too.

A potential problem

If a box pushes away another box, lack of *Runaround* is the problem. Refer to page 148 for the solution to this problem.

Quantum Leap

1. Perform the visual magnetism index with a few people to test a flier.

2. Using the same basic information, make variations on a flier to fit all four venues: handbill, poster, windshield, mailer. You can add copy if you need to.

Quark Quest

Create a flier

☐ 1. Make a folder on your disk called *Flier*.

☐ 2. Create a new document, letter size with 3p margins.

☐ 3. Name the document with your last name and flier.qxd. (For example: *Jonesflier.qxd*.)

☐ 4. Save it to your disk in your Flier folder.

☐ 5. Use your sketch as your guide. Include all the required items. Remember the design principles.

☐ 6. Save every few minutes.

☐ 7. Collect the artwork and fonts in the same folder as the document. **File → Collect for Output** (page 146).

☐ 8. Print. Make corrections. Use a buddy as a checkpoint.

☐ 9. Final printing: Print out as per your instructor. Two copies produce one for grading and one for your own portfolio).

The flier will most likely be done in black and white unless your instructor tells you otherwise.

Quicktip

Check these:

• vertical centering if text is in box or frame

• text inset if copy is in box or frame — may not be necessary if vertical centering took care of it

• lists have bullets and hanging indents

• one or two fonts used

• all six required elements

Quarkphobia

OK, you are staring at the new document. Blank page paralysis takes over. Shake it off. Try the following things to unleash your creativity and confidence:

1. Draw a big picture box on the page.

2. Draw a text box and type your headline. Make it big and bold. If your head is going to be on the curved text path, draw the curved text path and type the head on that.

3. In a separate box, type your bullet points or other copy.

4. Start moving things around. Enlarge, shrink.

5. When you have a first copy, run out a proof to see it. Make changes until you are pleased with your results.

New skills on your quest

Vertical centering • Text inset • Bulleted list and hanging indents

Vertical Centering

When text is at the top of a *framed* or *colored* box, move it to the center both horizontally (use measurements bar) and vertically (Figure 10-11).

Box framed. | Centered horizontally and vertically.

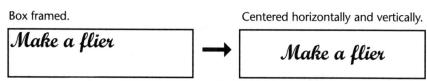

Make a flier → *Make a flier*

Figure 10-10. Desired result after centering both ways.

- ☐ 1. Click in text box.
- ☐ 2. ⌘ **M** (modify).
- ☐ 3. Choose the **text** folder (Figure 10-11).
- ☐ 4. Click **centered** under **Vertical Alignment**.
- ☐ 5. Click **OK**.

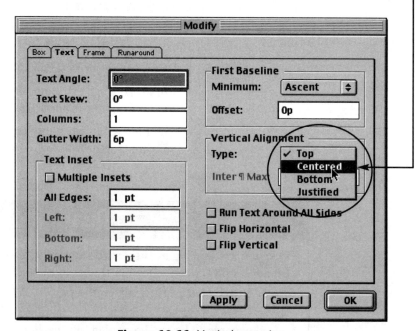

Figure 10-11. Vertical centering.

Don't miss this!

When the text box is NOT framed, shaded or colored, DO NOT use *vertical centering*. Just leave the setting at the default, which is the top. "Top" is good because you can adjust the box as needed.

Quicktip

Sometimes copy won't center vertically. Why not?

1. You might have an extra paragraph return in the beginning or end of the typed copy. Take out the return and your problem should be solved.

2. The text box might not be a rectangle. If you choose anything other than a rectangle, vertical centering won't work.

3. The type might be filling almost all of the box (e.g., a head in large letters). If you make the box's height larger, the copy should center. Or make the type smaller.

4. Another box is pushing away the text, thus inhibiting vertical centering. To solve this, assign "none" for runaround on the other box (⌘ **M** → **Runaround** → **Type: None**).

Text inset

When text touches the edges of a framed or colored box, you need to move the text away from the edges of the box. This is called *text inset*.

Figure 10-12. From no text inset to 4 points text inset.

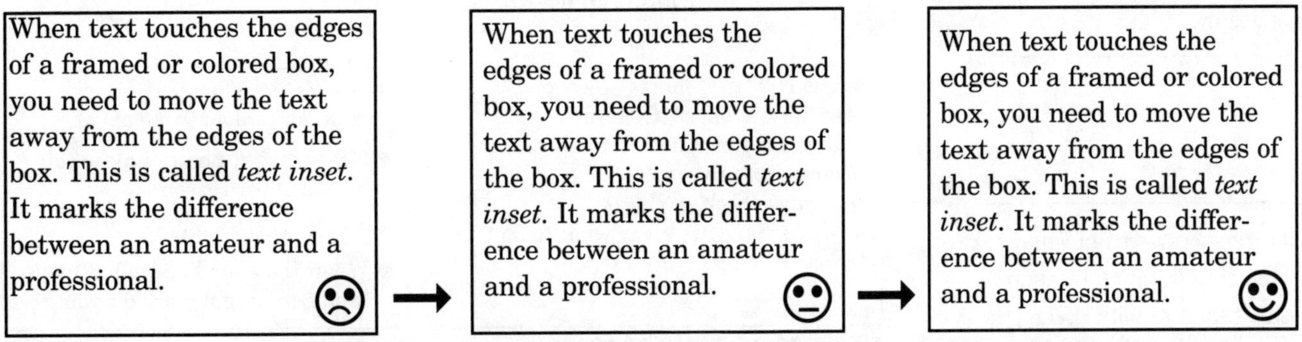

When text touches the edges of a framed or colored box, you need to move the text away from the edges of the box. This is called *text inset*. It marks the difference between an amateur and a professional.

Box framed.

When text touches the edges of a framed or colored box, you need to move the text away from the edges of the box. This is called *text inset*. It marks the difference between an amateur and a professional.

Text inset is set at 4 points on all sides. Notice there is more space at the bottom than the top. To solve this, center vertically. See next box.

When text touches the edges of a framed or colored box, you need to move the text away from the edges of the box. This is called *text inset*. It marks the difference between an amateur and a professional.

Copy is now centered vertically. This is the way it should look.

Warning!

Use text inset only in framed or colored boxes.

- [ ] 1. Click in text box.
- [ ] 2. ⌘ **M** (modify).
- [ ] 3. Choose the **text** folder (Figure 10-13).
- [ ] 4. **All edges:** type in the value for inset. 4 or 5 are good choices.
- [ ] 5. Click **OK**.

Sometimes you want different insets for top, bottom, left or right. In that case, click on **multiple insets** and type in the values. See the partial modify box in Figure 10-14.

Quark 4 doesn't give you the individual options under the **multiple insets** option.

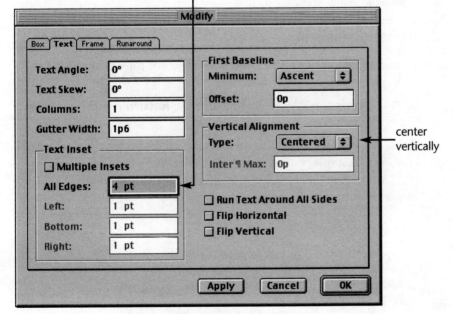

Figure 10-13. Text inset.

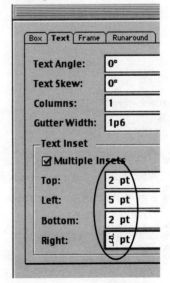

Figure 10-14. Multiple insets.

Bulleted lists

For a *bulleted list* you will do three new activities:
- create a bullet
- set a *hanging indent*
- set additional space above each item

Refer to page 74 to refresh your memory about bulleted lists as an element of page anatomy.

Proximity governs bulleted lists: chunks of information stay together with space before each chunk.

> ◆ Use NO "city" fonts (Chicago, New York, Monaco, Geneva).
> ◆ Never distort photos unless you have a super reason.
> ◆ Always check spelling.
> ◆ When you don't know what to do, "apple-m" might work for you!

Figure 10-15. Bulleted lists with no extra space between items and no hanging indents.

> ◆ Use NO "city" fonts (Chicago, New York, Monaco, Geneva).
>
> ◆ Never distort photos unless you have a super reason.
>
> ◆ Always check spelling.
>
> ◆ When you don't know what to do, "apple-m" might work for you!

Figure 10-16. Bulleted lists with p4 (4 points) added between items and hanging indents set.

1. Create a bullet

☐ 1. Type the copy first.

☐ 2. Then go back to the first item and make the bullet. Type the keyboard character and then apply the font you need to make the dingbat — usually Wingding or Zapf Dingbat.

☐ 3. Space once between the dingbat and the typed copy. Setting a tab works well here, too, but a space will suffice for now.

☐ 4. Then copy that dingbat and paste it down the list. Or make the dingbat each time.

2. Set hanging indent

☐ 1. Insert cursor before the letter that all other copy is supposed to "hang" under.

☐ 2. ⌘ \. (That's the BACK slash, above the **Return** key (Mac), **Enter** key (Windows).

Subsequent lines of this copy will "hang" right under the first line of type. For example, in Figure 10-17, the cursor would have gone right before the "U" in "Use." Notice the dotted line where the "hang" is supposed to occur.

Quicktip

\ is the back slash. This is the slash you use for hanging indents.

/ is the forward slash.

Put cursor before the U. Then ⌘ \.

> ◆ Use NO "city" fonts (Chicago, New York, Monaco, Geneva).¶
> ◆ Never distort photos unless you have a super reason.¶
> ◆ Always check spelling.¶
> ◆ When you don't know what to do, "apple-m" might work for you!

Figure 10-17. Screen shot to show the hanging indents. Notice, also the little dots between words. These are called "invisibles." Work with them showing.

3. Create "space before" – it's actually space above

Look at Figure 10-16 on the previous page and you will notice how much easier it is to read the items with space above them. To get this look, we go into the **Formats** dialog box.

- ☐ 1. Highlight the paragraph you want to work on. (Remember that a paragraph could be even one word — it's whatever text exists before a paragraph return.)

- ☐ 2. Choose from the top menu **Style → Formats → Space Before** (Figure 10-18).

- ☐ 3. Designate in points how much space you want. **Apply** to see how it looks. Then say **OK**.

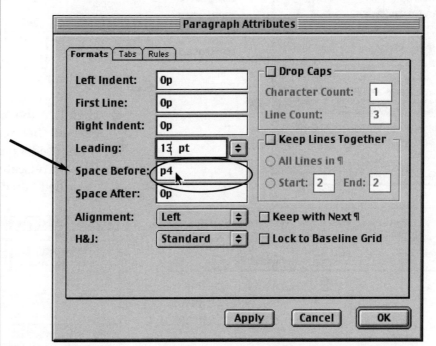

Figure 10-18. Space before.

Notice toward the top of the dialog box a *left indent*, *first line* and *right indent*. You can set these to indent both sides of text, like in a quoted paragraph for a research paper. You can use first line indent to make a paragraph indent. Later you will make up style sheets, typing number values in for *first line*. When you click on the style sheets, the paragraph will automatically indent. This is very cool.

Collect for output

If you are in the classroom making a flier, for example, and you decide to take it to some other lab or a quick-print store to run it out, you will have left the original artwork behind on the classroom computers! What you have on the screen is simply a representation of the actual artwork. You need to "collect" the original artwork. The computer will make duplicates of all the art files you used and put them in the folder you designate. *For Quark 5 or higher:* You can also collect fonts used in that document.

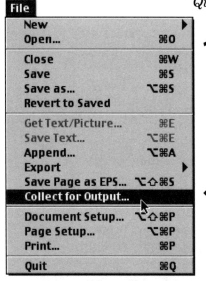

1 Save first. Then with the document open, go to **File → Collect for Output**.

Steps 2 and 3 might not happen to you.

2 A dialog box will tell you if any pictures are missing. Click on **List pictures**.

3 Highlight the missing picture in the dialog box and then navigate to find it. For example, if you used a picture from a CD, insert the CD and relocate it. Sometimes is just says "modified." Just click **Update** in that case.

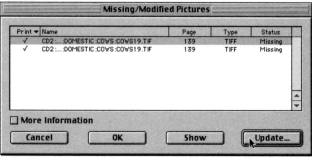

4 A dialog box will ask you if it's okay to save. Click **OK**.

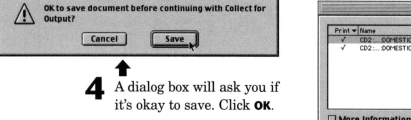

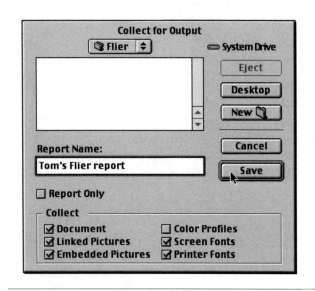

5 Then it will ask you where to save it. Create a new folder or put it in your working folder. In Quark 5, you also have to check what items you want collected (see checkmarks on figure). Save and then watch the computer collect everything.

6 Now your artwork and fonts are in the same folder as your document. Your file is complete.

11 Runaround

You've got to think about big things while you're doing small things, so that the small things go in the right direction.

Alvin Toffler
(Futurist)

Quest Objectives

- Describe the three main kinds of runaround and their uses.

Quest Skills

- Set up a document with multiple columns.
- Use the grids from the ruler for guidelines.
- Copy and paste text from one document to another.
- Link text boxes.
- Apply runaround to art.
- Clean up widows and orphans.
- Collect for output.

Quest Terms

auto image runaround	outset
clean up widows	overlapped text boxes
full to empty	runaround
item runaround	watermark
linking	widow
orphan	

Runaround controls how type wraps around a graphic or a box. Sometimes one box pushes away another box, and the text in the first box disappears. This is a runaround issue. Notice in the *overlapped text boxes* below that one box is actually over the other box (Figure 11-1).

Figure 11-1. Overlapping text boxes. The examples on the right show the outline of the text boxes.

Take a look at how one of these examples was made (Figure 11-2).

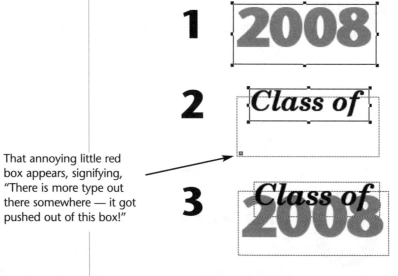

One text box is drawn and typed in. Type is shaded 40% in this.

The second box is drawn, typed in and moved over the first one. The text in the first one disappears.

That annoying little red box appears, signifying, "There is more type out there somewhere — it got pushed out of this box!"

Runaround of **none** is applied, and both boxes overlap with no loss of text. To be safe, apply **none** to both boxes.

Figure 11-2. The layered look unraveled.

⌘ **M → Runaround folder → Type: None**

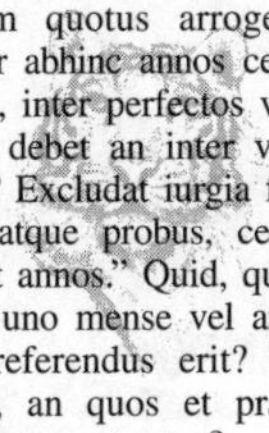

Runaround choices

None

Choosing **none** makes the box transparent. The copy flows right beneath the selected box, and you can't read the copy. (This is not usually a good thing!) However, the **none** setting is very useful when one box is pushing around another box of text. We can get a picture or text very close to the copy without the copy disappearing.

When you choose **none**, the box color immediately changes to **none** as well. However, you can make the box white again if you want to.

Item

Use **Item** when you want the text to go around the *box* itself, not around the shape of the image inside the box. Item runaround is usually used for a framed box, but sometimes you use it without the frame (Figure 11-4A).

Auto Image

Auto Image makes the text flow around the actual piece of art. The box becomes transparent (see next page). This is really cool!

More options

There are more options for runaround available, but this is enough information for you now. Experiment with the other choices, but save your document first.

Pullquotes

"Item" runaround is used for a pullquote.

ata reddit, scire velim, chartis pretium quotus arroget annus. scriptor abhinc annos centum qui decidit, inter perfectos veteresque referri debet an inter vilis atque novos? Excludat iurgia finis, "Est vetus atque probus, centum qui perficit annos." Quid, qui deperiit minor uno mense vel anno, inter quos referendus erit? Veteresne poetas, an quos et praesens et postera respuat aetas?

Figure 11-3.
Applying **none** to a picture box results in the picture over the text.

In Quark Quest, you will apply **none** to a picture box, but then you will shade the picture and send it to the back of the text. This creates the *watermark* effect.

ata reddit, scire velim, chartis pretium quotus arroget annus. scriptor abhinc annos centum qui decidit, inter perfectos veteresque referri debet an inter vilis atque novos? Excludat iurgia finis, "Est vetus atque probus, centum qui perficit annos." Quid, qui deperiit minor uno mense vel anno, inter quos referendus erit? Veteresne poetas, an quos et praesens et postera respuat aetas?

Figure 11-4.
Item runaround is used for pullquotes to retain the rectangular shape.

Interdum volgus rectum videt, est ubi peccat. Si veteres ita miratur laudatque poetas, ut nihil anteferat, nihil illis comparet, errat. Si quaedam nimis antique, si peraque dure dicere credit eos, ignave multa fatetur, et sapit et mecum facit et Iova iudicat aequo. Non equidem insector delendave carmina Livi esse reor, memini quae plagosum mihi *Use "item" for pullquotes. Experiment with left and right number values to get the best look.* parvo Orbilium dictare; sed emendata videri pulchraque et exactis minimum distantia miror. Inter quae verbum emicuit si forte decorum, et si versus paulo concinnior unus et alter, iniuste totum ducit venditque poema.Indignor

quicquam reprehendi, non quia crasse compositum illepedeve putetur, sed quia nuper, nec veniam antiquis, interdum volgus rectum videt, est ubi peccat. Si veteres ita miratur laudatque poetas, ut nihil anteferat, nihil illis comparet, errat. Si quaedam nimis antique, si peraque dure dicere credit eos, ignave multa fatetur, et sapit et mecum facit et Iova iudicat aequo. Non equidem insector delendave carmina Livi esse reor, memini quae plagosum mihi parvo Orbilium dictare; sed emendata videri pulchraque et exactis minimum distantia

A. Item runaround is applied to pullquote. Notice the white space shaped in a rectangle, especially on the right side.

Interdum volgus rectum videt, est ubi peccat. Si veteres ita miratur laudatque poetas, ut nihil anteferat, nihil illis comparet, errat. Si quaedam nimis antique, si peraque dure dicere credit eos, ignave multa fatetur, et sapit et mecum facit et Iova iudicat aequo. Non equidem insector delendave carmina Livi esse reor, memini quae plagosum mihi parvo Orbilium dictare; sed emendata videri pulchraque et exactis minimum distantia miror. Inter quae verbum emicuit si forte decorum, et si versus paulo concinnior unus et alter, iniuste totum ducit venditque *Use "item" for pullquotes. Experiment with left and right number values to get the best look.*

poema.Indignor quicquam reprehendi, non quia crasse compositum illepedeve putetur, sed quia nuper, nec veniam antiquis, interdum volgus rectum videt, est ubi peccat. Si veteres ita miratur laudatque poetas, ut nihil anteferat, nihil illis comparet, errat. Si quaedam nimis antique, si peraque dure dicere credit eos, ignave multa fatetur, et sapit et mecum facit et Iova iudicat aequo. Non equidem insector delendave carmina Livi esse reor, memini quae plagosum mihi parvo Orbilium dictare; sed emendata videri pul-

B. This pullquote is framed and shaded. Itern runaround is applied. Both left and right examples are treated the same.

In addition to allowing overlapped text boxes, runaround helps text flow around an illustration or the whole box. Take a look at the following examples and see their corresponding dialog boxes on the opposite page.

Quicktip

#1 Mistake

Choosing type of runaround but forgetting to assign a number value to it. The default is 1 point, which isn't enough to make a difference.

Si meliora dies, ut vina, poemata reddit, scire velim, chartis pretium quotus arroget annus. scriptor abhinc annos centum qui decidit, inter perfectos veteresque referri debet an inter vilis atque novos? Excludat iurgia finis, "

Est vetus atque probus, centum qui perficit annos." Quid, qui deperiit

minor uno mense vel anno, inter quos referendus erit? Veteresne poetas, an quos et praesens et postera respuat aetas?

"Iste quidem veteres inter ponetur honeste, qui vel mense brevi vel toto est iunior anno." Utor permisso, caudaeque pilos ut equinae paulatim vello unum, demo etiam

Figure 11-5.

Item Runaround

Use **Item** runaround when you want the text to go around the whole FRAMED box. Runaround goes around the ITEM, which is a picture box or text box.

Si meliora dies, ut vina, poemata reddit, scire velim, chartis pretium quotus arroget annus. scriptor abhinc annos centum qui decidit, inter perfectos veteresque referri debet an inter vilis atque novos? Excludat iurgia finis, "

Est vetus atque probus, centum qui perficit annos." Quid, qui deperiit

minor uno mense vel anno, inter quos referendus erit? Veteresne poetas, an quos et praesens et postera respuat aetas?

"Iste quidem veteres inter ponetur honeste, qui vel mense brevi vel toto est iunior anno." Utor permisso, caudaeque pilos ut equinae paulatim vello unum, demo etiam

Figure 11-6.

There would be no point in setting **Item** runaround on this one without a frame around the picture. Notice the rectangle of white space.

Auto Image Runaround

Si meliora dies, ut vina, poemata reddit, scire velim, chartis pretium quotus arroget annus. scriptor abhinc annos centum qui decidit, inter perfectos veteresque referri debet an inter vilis atque novos? Excludat iurgia finis, "

Est vetus atque probus, centum qui perficit annos." Quid, qui deperiit minor uno mense vel anno, inter quos referendus

erit? Veteresne poetas, an quos et praesens et postera respuat aetas?

"Iste quidem veteres inter ponetur honeste, qui vel mense brevi vel toto est iunior anno." Utor permisso, caudaeque pilos ut equinae paulatim vello unum, demo etiam unum, dum cadat elusus ratione ruentis acervi, qui redit in fastos et virtutem aestimat annis miraturque nihil nisi quod

Figure 11-7.

Use **Auto Image** runaround so the text goes around the actual piece of art. The effect is more interesting and appealing than a rectangle of white space.

Do not frame the box when using **Auto Image** runaround.

Compare the runaround on the owl picture (11-6) to the runaround on the pullquote (11-8). It is okay to show the square area for the pullquote even though there is not a frame around the quote. But it is not okay to leave the square area on the owl. Either use **Auto Image** to go around the owl or put a frame on the box and then use **Item** runaround.

Interdum volgus rectum videt, est ubi peccat. Si veteres ita miratur laudatque poetas, ut nihil anteferat, nihil illis comparet, errat. Si quaedam nimis antique, si peraque dure dicere credit eos, ignave multa fatetur, et sapit et mecum facit et Iova iudicat aequo. Non equidem insector delendave carmina Livi esse reor, memini quae plagosum mihi parvo Orbilium dictare; sed emendata videri pulchraque et exactis minimum distantia miror. Inter quae verbum emicuit si forte decorum, et si versus paulo concinnior unus et alter, iniuste totum ducit venditque poema.Indignor

Use "item" for pullquotes. Experiment with left and right number values to get the best look.

quicquam reprehendi, non quia crasse compositum illepedeve putetur, sed quia nuper, nec veniam antiquis, interdum volgus rectum videt, est ubi peccat. Si veteres ita miratur laudatque poetas, ut nihil anteferat, nihil illis comparet, errat. Si quaedam nimis antique, si peraque dure dicere credit eos, ignave multa fatetur, et sapit et mecum facit et Iova iudicat aequo.Non equidem insector delendave carmina Livi esse reor, memini quae plagosum mihi parvo Orbilium dictare; sed emendata videri pulchraque et exactis minimum distantia miror. Inter quae verbum

Figure 11-8.

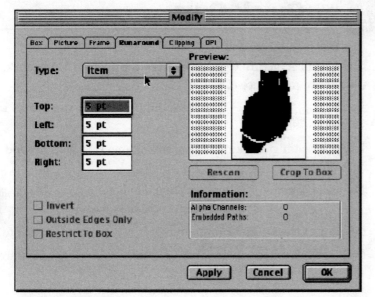

Figure 11-9.

Item Runaround

Notice there are four numbers to type: top, left, bottom and right. Sometimes you want more or less on one side than the other.

For example, in left aligned type, the right side of the type is ragged. Runaround on an item looks as if it has more on that side. Look at Figure 11-10.

Figure 11-10.

Si meliora dies, ut vina, poemata reddit, scire velim, chartis pretium quotus arroget annus. scriptor abhinc annos centum qui decidit, inter perfectos veteresque referri debet an inter vilis atque novos? Excludat iurgia finis, "Est vetus atque probus, centum qui per-

ficit annos." Quid, qui deperiit minor uno mense vel anno, inter quos referendus erit? Veteresne poetas, an quos et praesens et postera respuat aetas? "Iste quidem veteres inter ponetur honeste, qui vel mense brevi vel toto est iunior anno." Utor permisso, caudaeque pilos ut equinae paulatim vello

There is more space here. Set less space on left side for runaround.

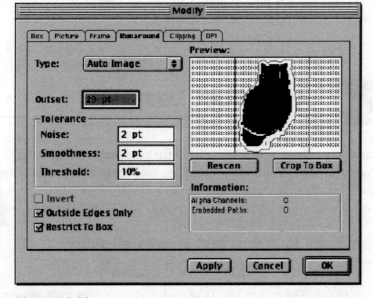

Figure 11-11.

Auto Image Runaround

There is only one number choice: **Outset**. *Outset* is the outside edge(s) of the object.

Always save the document before experimenting with numbers.

When the box is a rectangle, you have four choices of runaround numbers, one per side.

Figure 11-12.

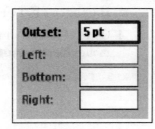

When the box is an oval, rounded corner box, Bézier box or polygon, you have only one number to type in. Quark recognizes there are not actually four equal sides to the figure, so it sets runaround equally around the item.

Quick Quiz

1. If you want a picture to go behind the copy, like a watermark, use the runaround choice of _____.

2. Apply _____ runaround if you want the text to wrap around the shape.

3. To get a rectangular kind of runaround, one that goes around the box, choose _____.

4. The most common mistake people make is forgetting to _____ after choosing a type of runaround.

5. Before you choose any runaround, _____ your document.

6. Pullquotes used as copybreakers require _____ runaround.

 ## Out of the Quandary

Read *Applying Art and Applying Runaround* on page 153. Be ready to work on the runaround project in class.

 ## Quantum Leap

Runaround deals with highlighting the item and then applying space around it. This works when items are positioned between columns (across gutters) or on the sides of the page. However, sometimes you want the item to be placed in the middle of a wide column of text.

Directions for "Run text around all sides"

☐ 1. Highlight the TEXT box, not the picture box.

☐ 2. Go to ⌘M and in the **Text** folder, choose **Run text around all sides**.

   then

☐ 3. Highlight PICTURE box.

☐ 4. Go to ⌘M and in the Runaround folder, choose your runaround mode: **Item** or **Auto Image**.

Interdum volgus rectum videt, est ubi peccat. Si veteres ita miratur laudatque poetas, ut nihil anteferat, nihil illis com-   paret, errat. Si quaedam nimis   antique, si peraque   dure dicere credit eos,   ignave multa fate-   tur, et sapit et mecum   facit et Iova iudicat aequo. Non equidem insector delendave carmina Livi esse reor, memini quae plagosum mihi parvo Orbilium dictare; sed emendata videri pulchraque et exactis minimum distantia miror. Inter quae verbum emicuit si forte decorum, et si versus paulo concinnior unus et alter, iniuste totum ducit venditque poema.Indignor quicquam reprehendi, non quia crasse compositum illepedeve putetur, sed quia nuper, nec veniam antiquis. sed honorem et praemia posci. Recte   necne crocum   floresque peram-   bulet Attae fabula si   dubitem, clament   periisse pudorem   cuncti paene patres, ea cum reprehendere coner, quae gravis Aesopus, quae doctus Roscius egit; vel quia nil rectum, nisi quod placuit sibi, ducunt, vel quia turpe putant

Figure 11-13. Picture inserted into one-column text.

Read this page to pick up some pointers. This is the copy you will use for your runaround exercise. It is found on the CD: Assignments: Chap11.Runaround: runaround.qxd. Your project will look similar to this, but your pictures will be different.

Adding Art and Applying Runaround

To place artwork in the text or anywhere else on a page, you need a picture box. The box tool with an X on it is a rectangular picture box. Other boxes are rounded corner, oval, polygon and Bezier.

Make a picture box. Select the picture box tool for the shape that you want to use. Remember, a picture box contains a big X across it; a text box doesn't. Move the cursor to the upper left corner of where you want the picture box to start. Depress the mouse button, and drag down to the lower right corner of the picture box and release the mouse button. You can frame the box or leave it unframed.

Put the picture in the box. Choose the content tool. Highlight the picture box (handles will show). Move the cursor to the File menu. Click the mouse, go to "Get Picture…" and release the mouse. Or just use Command E (Control E). From the menu that appears, navigate until you can select the file name of the picture that you want to place within the picture box. When the image appears in the box, click on it twice or click "open." Using the three magic keys — Command-Option-Shift-F (Control-Alternate-Shift-F), fit the picture to the box. Move the picture within the box with your content tool, which now has become a hand!

Resize the image. If the image is too big or too small for the picture box, either make the box bigger or smaller or make the image larger or smaller.
To change the size of the box, click in the picture box until eight black handles or squares appear

around the perimeter, then grab a handle on a side and drag until the box changes to the size you need for the image. The corner handles make the box proportionally larger or smaller while the middle handles simply make the box wider or taller. Exact dimensions are shown in the measurement bar across the bottom of the screen.

To change the image size, you have four choices:

(1) The first is to fit it *proportionately* in the box. Hold down those three magic keys and F on the keyboard.

(2) The second is to *fit unproportionately* (not usually the best choice). Hold down Command-Shift-F (Control-Shift-F).

(3) The third is to fit it by using the percentages in the measurements palette. Change both the same so the picture remains proportionate (unless you want a distortion).

(4) The fourth way is to depress those three magic keys again and then hit the < or > key. Each time you hit a < or > key, your picture will resize by 5%.

After changing the size of a picture or the box you may have to use the hand (the content tool) to reposition the illustration within the picture box.

Resize the box AND the picture at the same time. You have the picture situated inside the box and you like what you have. Later you decide you want the whole thing bigger or smaller. Hold down those three magic keys and drag the corner of the box. The picture reduces or enlarges along with the box. Amazing!

Move the entire picture box if necessary. If the picture box is the right size and shape, but you simply want to move this item to a new location within the

publication, click on the item tool. Using the item tool, click **inside** the picture box to be moved and drag it to the new location. You can also cut and paste the box. The artwork should not change position, size or shape during the move.

Apply runaround. We now have several choices of applying runarounds to our artwork. First, SAVE the document.

(1) The first choice is "**None**." This makes the picture box transparent, and the copy might flow right beneath the picture; the copy might actually go out of sight. (This is not usually a good thing!) However, the "None" setting is very useful when one box is pushing another box of text around. We can get a picture very close to the copy without the copy disappearing.

(2) Another choice is "**Item**." Frame the box. Then choose how many points runaround you want. This makes the picture box white, and the runaround goes around the entire item — the picture box itself.

(3) A third way is to say "**Auto Image**." This makes the text flow around the actual piece of art. The box becomes transparent.

(4) More options are available, but this is enough information for you now.

Readjust your type. Reduce your type size and leading if your copy runs off the page. You can also increase the box size by pulling down the handle on the bottom of the text box.

To clean up widows. A widow is a word or short phrase that sits all by itself at the end of a paragraph or at the top of a column. Highlight the entire paragraph and then change tracking. Your range will be from 0 to -5. If it doesn't work, leave the widow there.

Quark Quest

Halt!

Did you read the copy
on page 153? Read it
before you lay it out.

Apply runaround

☐ 1. Create a new folder called *Runaround*.

☐ 2. Open a new document:

    8½ x 11
    3p margins all sides
    3 columns
    1p6 width gutters.

☐ 3. Name it *Name runaround.qxd*. (Type in your name.)

☐ 4. Save it to your Runaround folder.

☐ 5. From the ruler, bring down a guideline to 6 picas (grab a grid – page 36).

☐ 6. Draw three separate text boxes in the three columns, starting at the top of box at the green grid line (6 picas down). OR draw one and duplicate it twice. Drag to the other columns.

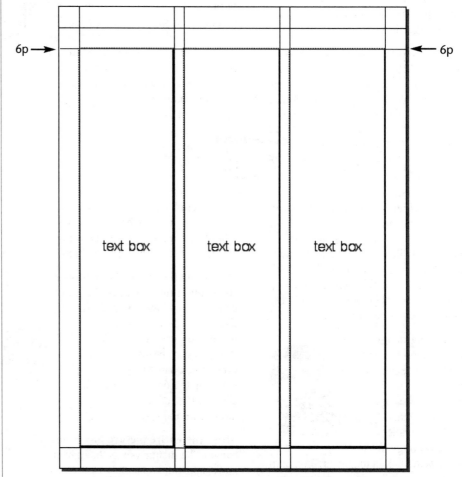

Figure 11-14. Three text boxes drawn on the page.

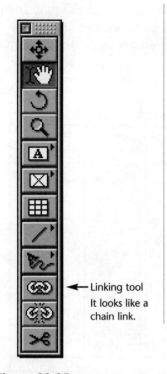

←Linking tool
It looks like a
chain link.

Figure 11-15.

☐ 7. From the CD, open the Quark document called
   Runaround exercise.qxd (Assignments folder: Chap9).

☐ 8. Click in the text box. **Select all** the text (⌘ **A**). Copy it (⌘ **C**).

☐ 9. Paste the text into the first column of your new document with
   three columns. SAVE.

☐ 10. Close the *Runaround exercise.qxd* document. Close any other
   windows so you just have your document open on the desktop.

Link text boxes

☐ 11. *Link* the three columns. First read this:

   You're driving around with a full tank, and all of a sudden it's
   EMPTY. How quickly it goes from FULL to EMPTY is the point.

   ☐ Click on the linking tool from the toolbar.

   ☐ Click on the FULL box of type and then click on the EMPTY
   box — where you want the type to go. Think: *Full to empty.*

   ☐ Get the linking tool again from the toolbar and click on the
   most recent FULL box, then click on the next empty box.

   If you totally mess up, just **Revert to Saved** under File menu.

Figure 11-16. Linking the text boxes.

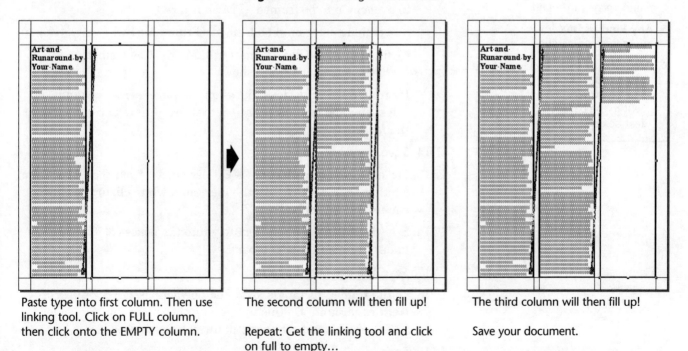

Paste type into first column. Then use
linking tool. Click on FULL column,
then click onto the EMPTY column.

The second column will then fill up!

Repeat: Get the linking tool and click
on full to empty...

The third column will then fill up!

Save your document.

The six boxes for your runaround task

1. Rectangle
Framed
Item runaround

2. Oval/circle
Framed
Item runaround

3. Irregular polygon
Framed
Item runaround

4. Any kind of box
Auto image runaround

5. Any kind of box
Auto image runaround

6. Any kind of box
None – runaround
Shaded 20%
Sent to the back
Text box color – None

☐ 12. Draw a box for the title from left margin to right margin from the 3-pica top margin to the 6-pica guideline you drew. Copy the title from the text into this box. Eliminate any extra paragraph returns (Figure 11-17).

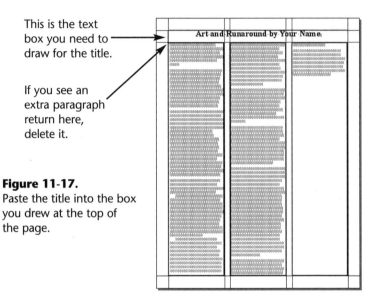

This is the text box you need to draw for the title.

If you see an extra paragraph return here, delete it.

Figure 11-17.
Paste the title into the box you drew at the top of the page.

☐ 13. Make six picture boxes:

1) rectangle to be framed. (Frame it now.)

2) oval/circle to be framed. (Frame it now.)

3) irregular polygon to be framed. (Frame it now.)

4), 5), 6) box type doesn't matter; they won't be framed, so the box shape won't show.

Position them in various places on the page: across columns, on sides, etc. The best places are across the gutters of columns or at the far left or far right.

☐ 14. **Save**.

☐ 15. For each box, **get picture** (⌘E). Use clipart from the CD or from another source. Stay with the black and white clipart because runaround works better.

☐ 16. Size the art to fit proportionately into the boxes (⌘⌥⇧F or under **Style** on the menu bar).

☐ 17. **Save** the document again.

☐ 18. To the framed rectangle, oval and polygon: assign **5 points** of **Item** runaround. Do this by opening the runaround file folder (⌘M). You should see text pull away from the box.

☐ 19. **Save**.

☐ 20. For two of the other boxes, assign 5–20 points of **Auto Image** runaround. Your text should wrap around the object. No frame.

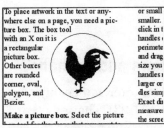

Figure 11-18. Placement of picture causes trapped white space. That is white space that doesn't flow off the page — it's within body copy. Just move around the picture and find a better placement for it. ☹

Figure 11-19. Item runaround was chosen, but the default 0 wasn't changed. Frame too close to copy. ☹

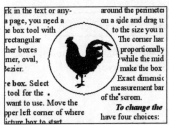

Figure 11-20. Item runaround of 4 points works fine. ☺

Figure 11-21. Click on the feather to unlink boxes.

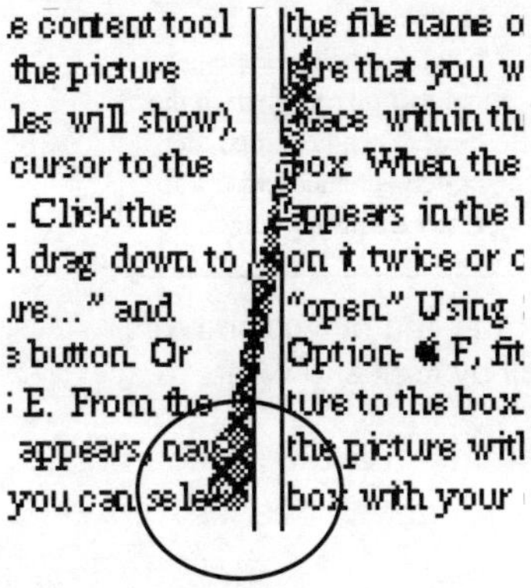

☐ 21. For the last box (see giraffe on the sample exercise):

    ☐ Draw picture box and get art. Size it. This one can be large.

    ☐ Shade the art to 20%.

    ☐ Assign runaround **None**. The picture covers some text.

    ☐ Send the art to the back: Click on picture box. **Item → Send to back**.

    ☐ Make the TEXT box color **None**: Click on box, then **⌘M → Box → Color → None**.

IMPORTANT: Drag one of the handles of the picture box beyond your text boxes so you can grab it when you need it. The picture box can hang over the edge of the margin. If the box is between columns, you will be able to grab it in the gutter.

The shaded art will now be seen through the text! **Save!**

There's still more…

☐ 22. Now move around the boxes to make them look the best on your page. Start moving from top left and continue in reading direction. Resize boxes if necessary. The copy should reach close to the end of the third column. Don't worry if you lose type at the bottom or have a little space. It's okay for this exercise.

☐ 23. **Save**.

☐ 24. *Clean up widows and orphans.* To eliminate a widow, highlight entire paragraph and tighten tracking. Your range will be from 0 to -5. If it doesn't work, leave the widow there. To eliminate an orphan, grab the handle on the bottom of the text box and drag it up a little bit until the line moves into the next column.

☐ 25. **Save**.

☐ 26. Collect for output (see page 146).

☐ 27. Print a hard copy and check for:

    ☐ too much trapped white space (Figure 11-18). Move around the pictures to correct.

    ☐ lack of runaround (you applied runaround but didn't change the number from 1 point – the default – so the copy is too close to the art) (Figure 11-19).

    ☐ widows and orphans (see next page).

☐ 28. Print a final hard copy.

How to unlink text boxes

Click on unlinking tool. Click on the text box and the arrows with feathers will appear (Figure 11-21). Click on the FEATHER of the arrow to break the chain. Enlarge the screen if you have trouble with this (click with magnifying tool or change left bottom corner percentage).

Quicktip

Clean up widows

Highlight entire paragraph and then change tracking. Your range should be from 0 to -5. If that doesn't work, leave the widow there.

No positive tracking!

If you are the editor of the publication, you can add or subtract words to fix widows.

Keyboard shortcut

Tighten tracking by one point: ⌘ ⌥ ⇧ [

Loosen tracking by one point: ⌘ ⌥ ⇧]

Symbol Refresher

Windows Users   **Mac Users**

⌘ = control   ⌘ = command (⌘)
⌥ = alternate   ⌥ = option
⇧ = shift   ⇧ = shift

Continuation of story from Figure 11-22

He brought her closer and asked her to feel the carrots. She did and noted that they were soft. He then asked her to take an egg and break it. After pulling off the shell, she observed the hard-boiled egg. Finally, he asked her to sip the coffee. The daughter smiled as she tasted its rich aroma.

The daughter then asked. "What does it mean, father?"

Her father explained that each of these objects had faced the same adversity — boiling water — but each reacted differently. The carrot went in strong, hard and unrelenting. However, after being subjected to the boiling water, it softened and became weak. The egg had been fragile. Its thin outer shell had protected its liquid interior. But, after sitting through the boiling water, its inside became hardened. The ground coffee beans were unique, however. After they were in the boiling water, they had changed the water.

"Which are you?" he asked his daughter. "When adversity knocks on your door, how do you respond? Are you a carrot, an egg, or a coffee bean?"

Widows and orphans

What's the difference between widows and orphans?

Some people use the terms *widow* and *orphan* interchangeably, while others differentiate (Figures 11-22 and 11-23). They say that an orphan (first line of a paragraph) is placed on purpose at the end of a column or page to attract readers to continue reading, forcing them to go to the next column or page. However, widows (less than one line of type at the end of a paragraph or column) happen by accident. Therefore, we don't want them. Widows can be found at the bottom OR the top.

widow

A certain daughter complained to her father about her life and how things have been so hard for her. She did not know how she was going to make it and she wanted to give up. She was tired of fighting and struggling. It seemed that just as one problem was solved another **widow →** arose.

Her father, a chef, took her to the kitchen, filled three pots with water and placed the fire on high. Soon the three pots came to a boil. In one he placed carrots, in the other he placed eggs, and in the last he placed ground coffee beans. He let them sit and boil, without saying a word

The daughter waited impatiently, wondering what he was trying to do. She had problems, and he was making this strange concoction. In half an hour he walked over to the oven and turned down the fire. He pulled the carrots out and placed them in the bowl. He pulled the eggs out and placed them in the bowl. Then he ladled the coffee out and placed it in a bowl. Turning to her, he asked. "Darling what do you see?" Smartly, she replied. "Carrots, eggs, and coffee." **← widow**

See sidebar for the rest of the story!

Figure 11-22. Widow – a word or short phrase that sits all by itself at the **END** of a paragraph or at the top of a column. Less than half the line of type would make it qualify as a widow.

A certain daughter complained to her father about her life and how things have been so hard for her. She did not know how she was going to make it and she wanted to give up. She was tired of fighting and struggling. It seemed that just as one **widow →** problem was solved another arose.

orphan → Her father, a chef, took

her to the kitchen, filled three pots with water and placed the fire on high. Soon the three pots came to a boil. In one he placed carrots, in the other he placed eggs, and in the last he placed ground coffee beans. He let them sit and boil, without saying a word **← widow**

The daughter waited impatiently, wondering

what he was trying to do. She had problems, and he was making this strange concoction. In half an hour he walked over to the oven and turned down the fire. He pulled the carrots out and placed them in the bowl. He pulled the eggs out and placed them in the bowl. Then he ladled the coffee out and placed it in a bowl. Turning to her, he

Figure 11-23. Orphan – one line of type at the end of a column or page that **BEGINS** the next paragraph. It is all by itself and wants to join its family at the top of the next column!

12 Small Ad

*Just because your ad looks good is no insurance
that it will get looked at. How many people do you
know who are impeccably groomed...but dull?*

William Bernbach
(Legendary copywriter, Founder of DDB Needham)

Quest Objectives

- Explain the four main components of a small ad.

- Defend the importance of the head in a small ad.

- List some layout and design guidelines for making
  the small ad.

- Write brief ad copy.

- Put the proper components in a small ad and use layout
  principles to make the ad an effective one.

Quest Skills

- Draw a text box with specific measurements.

- Find the center of the page.

- Position a box in the middle of the page using black handles
  and grid lines.

- Lock an item.

- Arrange items to produce an effective ad.

Quest Terms

filler	space ad
house ad	visual
response area	yellow pages
small ad	

A ds are designed to attract attention and give a message in a limited amount of space. Although you'd think a full-page ad would draw more attention than smaller ads, sometimes it's easier to miss or ignore an entire page. People pass by the page. On the other hand, if someone is reading something on a page with a small ad, it will be hard to overlook the ad, especially if it is designed well.

Because of budget or time constraints, small ad design isn't always done by a graphics department. Sometimes the editor or the editorial support staff creates the ad. Therefore, knowing some basic information is important.

Small ad design

Small ads are sometimes referred to as *space ads* because they are printed in purchased space in a publication. Common sizes of these ads are ½, ⅓, ¼, ⅙ or ⅛ of a page. Exact measurements depend on the page size of the publication.

The small ad is designed so that it:
- can be placed anywhere on a page (top, bottom, left, right)
- will be separate from the other elements on the page
- acts as an attention-grabber

Before designing the ad, look at the publication in which it will be placed. How can you make yours stand out? The most common way to separate the ad from the other elements is to use a border. A 2-point border works well — the larger the ad, the thicker the border. Also, a shaded background or item of strong contrast helps grab attention — for example, a solid band of black across the top or bottom with reverse type (Figure 12-12 on page 167).

Elements of a small ad

A strong, prominent *headline* carries the most weight in a small ad. The *visual* could be a related photo or piece of clipart. *Copy* can vary from a few words to 75 words or so, depending on your product. The last element, the *response area,* includes the contact information (address, phone number, Web site, e-mail and perhaps a logo).

Other considerations

If the ad is to be placed in a newspaper or the *yellow pages,* avoid solid black areas. They don't print well on newsprint, the kind of paper used for those two publications. Reverse type tends to disappear into the black ink. Shaded art and shaded boxes also don't reproduce well on certain kinds of newsprint.

Although white space is always desirable, small ads sometimes sacrifice the space in favor of more information. Whatever you do, always remember the K.I.S.S. principle (page 25).

If an ad requires lots of body copy, use tighter leading and a font that squeezes the most into a small space. For serif, Times New Roman works well, and for sans serif, Helvetica Condensed works well. The type can be smaller than usual, even 8 point. However, remember that someone needs to be attracted to the ad before they will read that small print. Therefore, make your headline big, bold and enticing. Keep in mind: *What is the benefit to the reader?*

Where it goes

How does the publication expect to receive the ad? On disk? E-mail? Hard copy? Always ask for specifications before you start. And always check deadlines — they are often much earlier than the actual publication date. Be sure you have a contact name.

Apropos: being both relevant and opportune

Apropos letter from a student

It is wonderful to hear from past students. This e-mail came from a public relations major named Michelle.

The position I interviewed for is working with…get this… small ads!!! Can you believe it?! If I got this job, I would be in charge of the small ads and the classified ads in the newspaper. Most of the ads look like some students did in class.

And ready for this? They made me take a layout test!! They set me up at a computer and explained that sometimes we'll just get an ad from the client over the fax and it's not camera ready so I would have to re-create the ad to the best of my ability.

So they gave me a sample ad and said, "Okay, go to work." Thank heavens, I brought my Quark Quick Card with me!!! The ad had symbols and bullets and accent marks, all of which I had forgotten how to do. I think I did a pretty good job.

I haven't worked in Quark in so long that it took me five minutes to get reacquainted. They work on Macs, which is good because that's what I'm most familiar with.

Your first instinct is to put the e-mail "letter" from Michelle in italics. Somehow it just seems right. But the reading difficulty increases, and you lose readers. Sometimes you have to give up the "look" for the sake of better readability.

The second part of the test was to look at a classified ad page and duplicate it in Quark. They had everything set up, so I didn't have to type anything. But I had to put everything in the right spot, lining everything up exactly how it was in the newspaper. I did really well with that. I checked it eight million times to make sure all the items were all lined up. (Did we call this alignment?)

How funny is it that I might be working with small ads! When they said that I almost laughed…what a coincidence. (Feel free to share this with your students when you get to that project.)

Michelle got the job, and after a year, she still can't believe she goes to the workplace every day to create ads in QuarkXPress.

The next six pages show a variety of small ads done by students. Each ad has unique features for you to examine. Eight of the 12 students had never worked in Quark before this.

Figure 12-1.

Alex continues his "have a cow" theme for this project. However, instead of the large shaded circle on his flier (page 139), he uses a shaded ice cream cone scan in the background. The powerful head is Arial Black. All boxes on the ad have **none** set for runaround. The subtitle is Arial bold, and body copy is Times bold. He used bold for everything because type is set over a shade. The Z pattern works here. He originally used bright orange for the headline and the cow logo.

Fonts and cow logo are consistent in his flier, small ad, letterhead and business card.

The second box is activated, ready to move on top of the shaded one

Make one box the way you want it.

Duplicate it.

Lighten or darken the type in the new box.

Set both to **none** in runaround.

Move one box on top of the other.

This is the large background graphic, brought into the main picture box.

John chose the Constitution for the dominant item on the ad. His headline type is Old English Text (ironic!). Body copy is Bauhaus Medium. Body copy and the reverse black box are left aligned. "ACLU" is centered in the black box. Ad is horizontal rather than vertical.

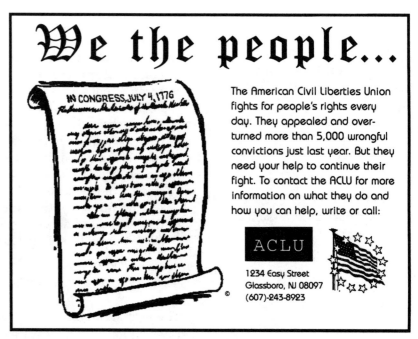

Figure 12-2.

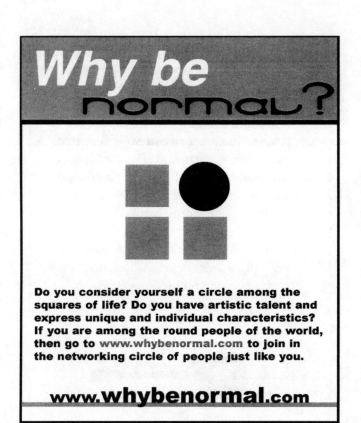

Figure 12-3.

Kari produced this ad in three colors: black, orange and blue-green. One of the considerations of small ad design is that you should be able to convert it into black and white and still be effective. Shading replaced color, and it works. Kari makes good use of white space as well. Fonts are a few variations of Helvetica as well as Apogee for the word "normal." The unusual font sets the tone for the head.

Picking out the just the right font, art and colors is quite time-consuming.

Using a "tall sandwich" clipart, Ami portrays contrast in shape. Brush Script is used for the lead-in and the title of the deli. Broadview is the serif type, while Helvetica is the sans serif. Left alignment is used with the first groupings of type, and then right alignment governs the bottom groupings of type. The 2-point rule separates the menu from the location information. Ami met the challenge of arranging several chunks of copy.

Figure 12-4.

Figure 12-5.

Chris cropped the clipart to show part of the guitar (see below). Using them at the top and the bottom and flipping them gave the ad balance, contrast and an interesting border effect. The reverse head is eye-catching, and the backward-6 pattern works well. Fonts are modern: Kabel Bold for body copy and Rockwell for the rest. Notice the slight shaded words behind the copy. The Rutstuck text box was set in Standard font, outlined, shaded 15% and rotated -30 degrees. The Records text box holds Stone Sans Bold, shaded 15%.

Full guitar

James didn't want to limit the appeal of the ad by using a specific graphic — which one would he choose — music? art? dance? Instead, he used contrast of shape (rectangle and oval) and color (black, white and gray) to make the ad stand out. The background box is shaded 40%. First he tried centering the type, but it was too much type to center (center no more than three lines). He solved the problem by aligning the type left in a text box, but then moving the text box to make it appear as if the type is centered.

This ad is called a *house ad*. Editors keep house ads on their computers ready to use as a *filler* when they have extra space on their pages.

Figure 12-6.

Figure 12-7.

Regina chose an interesting approach with arrows to lead the reader through the ad. Originally in color, this ad works well in black and white as well. Moderne (head) and Impact are the fonts. Notice the effective use of white space.

Coupons present a challenge to the ad designer. In the right ad, Marianna put the coupons on the outer right. If the ad runs on the top right of a page, the coupons tear off the page easily without disturbing the rest of the page. The redesign below calls for a bottom-of-the-page positioning. Where is the ad going? If it's the weekly shopper-type of news magazine or the daily newspaper, a person will cut into the page anyway to use the coupon. But if it's a tear-off coupon in a magazine, someone is less likely to rip the page if the coupons are not on an outer edge.

Contrast works well in this ad.

Figure 12-8.

Figure 12-9.

Erin probably should win a prize for detail work on this one! Although someone could alter the art in Photoshop, Erin stayed in Quark and drew an irregular polygon to "black out" some of the cup. Then she made a text box and reversed the type over the black (the dissection shows this in black type). The Z pattern is effective (discussed in Chapter 2). Contrast works through color, size and shape.

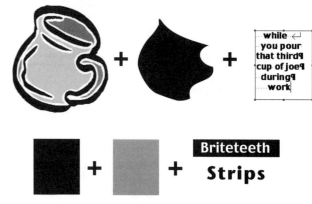

These "dissections" show the order in which the pieces were assembled.

Kristen used a beautiful color photo as the background — blue sky and silver plane (made grayscale for this book). Although in an earlier chapter I said NOT to put type over a photo, in this case the type doesn't conflict with anything. For easier reading, Kristen made the type bold. She used her own photo for this ad.

Kristen did not include a head, which is unusual. Most small ads depend on the strength of their headline.

Figure 12-10.

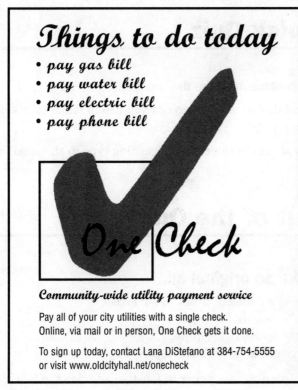

Figure 12-11.

Jerry chose dominance as his governing design principle. Notice the left alignment of items as well as contrast in size and color (large shaded checkmark). He used a script type (Script MT Bold) to simulate handwriting. Very simple, eye-catching ad. He chose "none" in runaround for all boxes in the ad.

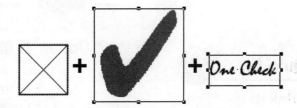

This "dissection" shows the order in which the pieces were assembled.

Crystal experimented with the half-and-half contrast. She created an eye-catching layout with center alignment and good balance. Her ad does not have the required body copy in it, but it was approved by the instructor.

See page 90 for instructions for making a perfect arc of type.

Figure 12-12.

Quick Quiz

1. What four components make up the small ad?

2. What layout and design techniques can you use to make your small ad stand out on a page?

3. What are a few things to remember regarding type in the small ad?

 # Out of the Quandary

Option 1. Make an original ad.

☐ Choose a product, idea or event to advertise.
  • Write 30–75 words of copy.
  • Construct a catchy headline.
  • Find a visual to go with the copy.

☐ Sketch your plan. Fold a paper in fourths, and use the four sections to design different sketch ideas.

☐ Follow the steps to making the ad on page 169.

☐ Use the ad checklist on page 170.

Option 2. Copy another ad.

Copy or redesign an existing small ad. Hand in the original ad with your version.

 # Quantum Leap

☐ Make two more variations of your small ad. In real life, you will often submit a few variations to be used as space permits, especially if the ad is a free one or used as a house ad.

☐ To do this, add two new pages to your document (**Page menu → Insert**).

☐ Group all the items in your ad.

☐ Copy and paste the ad onto the new pages.

☐ Redo one ad to fit into a much smaller box, about 2 inches wide x 3 inches long (see sidebar for shrinking).

☐ Make the other ad fit into a larger and *longer* box, about 3 inches wide x 9 inches long. This may mean some change in the elements to make them fit.

 ## Quicktip

Shrink it!

1. Group all items.

2. Hold down the three magic keys: ⌘ ⌥ ⇧

3. Put the mouse at the bottom right corner of the grouping. The mouse becomes a pointing finger.

4. From the corner of the grouping, drag with the mouse toward the other corner.

5. All the elements should shrink proportionately.

Use the same process to enlarge the grouping.

These are the green grids that you
pulled to find the center of the box.

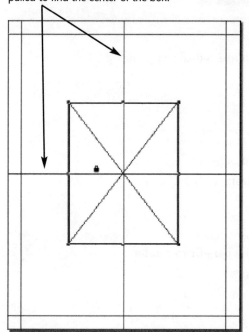

Figure 12-13.
Divide the page into fourths (to find center).
Then lock the picture box. The little black lock
shows up when you try to move the box.

Quark Quest

Create a small ad

☐ 1. Make a folder on your disk called *Small Ad*.

☐ 2. Open a new document:
    8½" x 11" – letter size
    one column
    margins of any width

☐ 3. Mark the middle of your page with green guidelines (grids) from the ruler. (See instructions in shaded box below.)

Find the middle of the page or a box

Find the middle of a page: Draw a large picture box over the entire page. From the ruler, grab a grid and drag to the middle handles of the box, both vertically and horizontally. Then **kill the box**. The middle of the page is where the green grids intersect.

Find the middle of a box: Highlight the box. Grab a grid and pull to the handles on the middle of the box — both vertically and horizontally. Again, the intersection of the grids is the center. If it's a picture box, the center of the X is the middle as well.

☐ 4. Make a 4" x 5" PICTURE box on the page. Use the measurements bar and type in 4" for the width (W) and 5" for the height (H).

☐ 5. Move the picture box into center position by using the arrows on your keyboard. Move the box until the handles on the box line up with the green guidelines (Figure 12-13).

☐ 6. Frame the box with a 2-point frame.

Lock a box

☐ 7. Lock the box in place by choosing **Lock** under the **Item** menu (Figure 12-14). This will prevent the box from moving.

☐ 8. Build your small ad using pieces (text boxes for headline, copy and response area; picture box for visual).
    Remember to use Runaround **None** when one box bothers another one.

☐ 9. Put your artwork in your Small Ad folder. If you used clipart from the hard drive, "collect for output" into your Small Ad folder (**File → Collect for Output**). Instructions for this are on page 146.

☐ 10. Print the document. Proofread and print again if necessary.

Figure 12-14.
Lock the ad on the page
by using this menu.

Checklist – Small ad

Sketch

☐ of ad — or original ad if you are redesigning one

Headline

☐ big, bold, punchy

Visual

☐ totally relevant to message of ad

☐ clear scan or line art – not from Web

Copy

☐ 30–75 words of copy

☐ convincing, succinct, contains benefit to reader

☐ no grammar or spelling errors

☐ no hyphenated word at the end of a line

☐ no widows

☐ no more than three lines centered

Response area

☐ necessary buying and contact information:
address, phone numbers, Web address, e-mail, business hours

☐ logo, if applicable

Design

☐ 4" x 5" (or 5" x 4")

☐ border

☐ uses one font or two *contrasting* fonts

☐ has dominant item

☐ uses some design principles (list them here):
_____

☐ designed so that it can be placed in any position on any page

Details

☐ font personality is relevant to topic

☐ type is not all caps

☐ leading and tracking appropriate

☐ size of type appropriate

☐ text inset — only if copy is in a box

☐ vertical centering — only if copy is in a box

☐ alignment of type consistent

☐ alignment of items consistent

☐ hanging indents if bulleted list

Quicktip

It will save you time if you type the copy at home or in your dorm and send it to your network folder or save it on a zip disk or other storage device. In class you can access it, open it in Microsoft Word, copy it and paste it into Quark.

13 Letterhead

Forgive me for writing such a long letter;
I didn't have time to write a short one.

Mark Twain

Quest Objectives

- Identify the nine main elements of the letterhead.
- Explain the importance of consistency in letterheads, envelopes and business cards.

Quest Skills

- Arrange items to design an effective letterhead.

Quest Terms

letterhead
message area
stationery package

*L*etterhead refers to the piece of paper stationery on which someone types or writes a letter. It is part of the business stationery package, along with the envelope and business card. Consistency among all three of those items helps people identify your company or organization.

Your letterhead portrays something about the nature and tone (formal or informal) of your company or organization. Don't let the design get in the way of clear communication. For example, using a large piece of shaded art on the body part of the letter, behind the words, can distract the reader.

The paper adds to the image as well. White paper is the most common choice, but don't be afraid to try other light colors. Office supply stores carry paper in a wide array of colors, textures and weights, along with matching envelopes and business cards.

Letterheads, business cards and envelopes make up the *stationery package.*

Elements of the letterhead

The letterhead would typically contain the following items:

1. Company or organization's name
2. Address (street, PO box, city, state, zip code)
3. Telephone number (include area code)
4. Fax number
5. E-mail address and Web address
6. Logo
7. Business motto if applicable
8. Officers or board members (optional)
9. Message area

It is acceptable to use the full name of a state (Alabama), the abbreviated version with periods (Ala.) or the postal abbreviation (AL). For phone numbers, choose a style and be consistent. Associated Press style is (987) 654-3210. Notice the space after the parenthesis. Other versions include 987-654-3210 (hyphens), 987.654.3210 (periods), 987 654 3210 (just spaces) and 987/654-3210 (forward slash after area code).

Message area

The message is the most important part of a letter. Be sure when you design a letterhead, the *message area* provides sufficient space for the letter. Since reading is more difficult over shading, don't place a large, shaded logo behind the message area.

Address information

The address information can be run as a single line or stacked with dingbats like diamonds or circles dividing sections of an address. Figure 13-1 shows address info stacked in twos.

Layout styles

Examine the slight differences in the letterhead examples. Figures 13-2 and 13-3 switch contact information and motto, while figures 13-4 and 13-5 use the "down the side" design. This works well when you need to run a list of officers on the letterhead.

13-6 uses the boxed look, with contact information outside the box (at the bottom), while 13-7 stacks contact information below the logo and uses a partial rule down the side and across to connect the motto. These two examples portray a strong sense of unity.

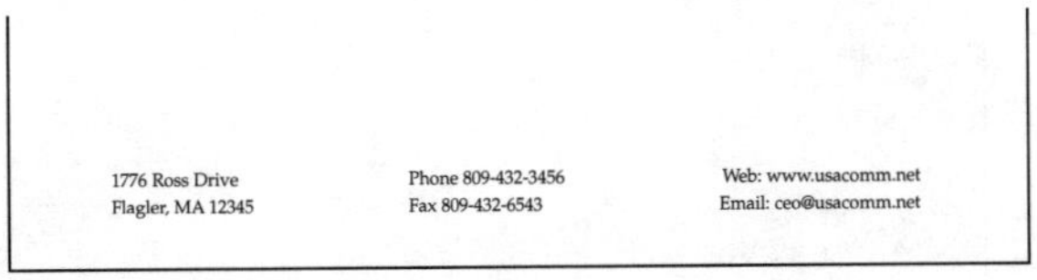

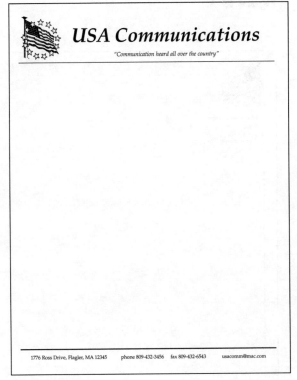

1776 Ross Drive
Flagler, MA 12345
Phone 809-432-3456
Fax 809-432-6543
Web: www.usacomm.net
Email: ceo@usacomm.net

Figure 13-1. Stacked contact information

USA Communications
"Communication heard all over the country"
1776 Ross Drive, Flagler, MA 12345
phone 809-432-3456
fax 809-432-6543
usacomm@mac.com

Figure 13-2.

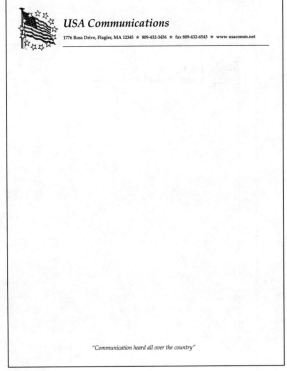

USA Communications
1776 Ross Drive, Flagler, MA 12345 ★ 809-432-3456 ★ fax 809-432-6543 ★ www usacomm.net
"Communication heard all over the country"

Figure 13-3.

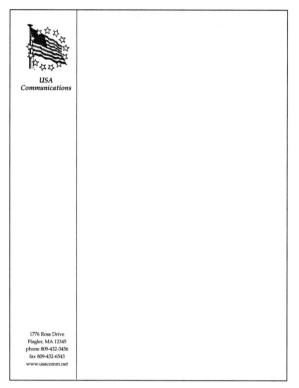

Figure 13-4.

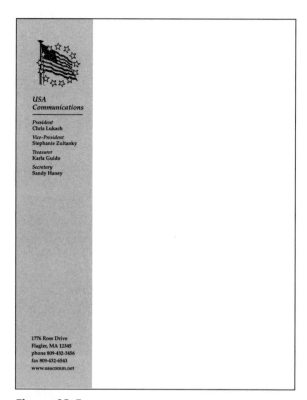

Figure 13-5.

Figure 13-6.

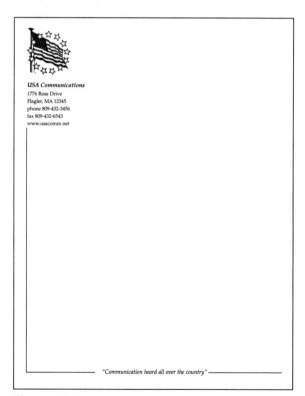

Figure 13-7.

Quick Quiz

1. What are the nine elements of the letterhead?
2. What is the purpose of the message area?
3. What three publications make up the stationery package?

Out of the Quandary

1. Find a few samples of letterheads and identify their elements. Which designs do you like and why? Which ones are weak?
2. Design a letterhead.

Quantum Leap

1. Design an envelope to match your letterhead.
2. *Redesign* a letterhead. Try a few layouts. Organize them in order of most effective to least.

Quark Quest

Create a letterhead

☐ 1. Create a new folder on your disk called *Letterhead*.

☐ 2. Open a new document. Use margins of 2 picas.

☐ 3. Name it *Yournameletterhead.qxd* and save it to your Letterhead folder. (Use your name.)

☐ 4. Use text and picture boxes to design your letterhead. Include these elements of a letterhead:

    ☐ Name of company or organization

    ☐ Logo

    ☐ Motto or statement of business philosophy

    ☐ Street address and mailing address (if different)

    ☐ Telephone number(s)

    ☐ Fax number

    ☐ E-mail address and Web address if applicable

    Use grids as guides. Don't eyeball alignment. Be exact.

☐ 5. Collect for output.

☐ 6. Print.

Envelope design

Envelope design should match the letterhead, but only logo, name and address are required on the envelope.

Check out your local office supply store for its letterhead paper selection. It comes with designs and backgrounds — in various colors and textures of paper. You can usually buy these by the sheet or package.

Review of the measurements bar

Text box is active – content tool is selected

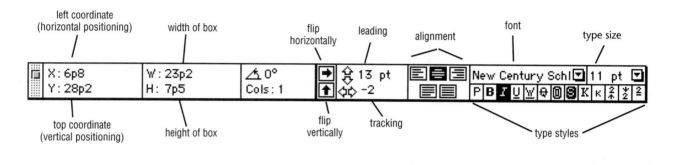

Picture box is active – content or item tool is selected

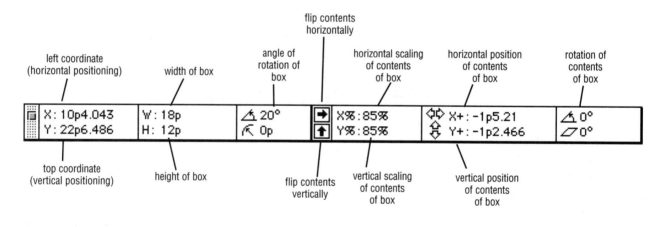

Line (rule) is active – content or item tool is selected

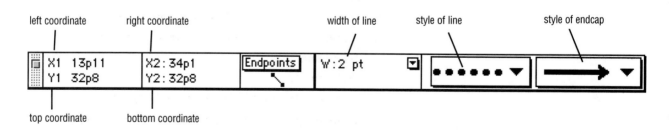

14 Business Card

Business cards grease the wheels of commerce and have become a cultural ritual in American society.

Michael Nolan
QuarkXPress Design Techniques

Quest Objectives

- Identify the elements that make up a business card.
- Describe the thumb test.
- Explain why the quadrant format is not effective.

Quest Skills

- Work within grids.
- Use step and repeat.
- Move groupings.
- Enlarge and decrease screen size.
- Feed paper into the printer through the manual tray.

Quest Terms

access information
bleed
business cards
calling cards

quadrant format
stationery package
thumb test

In the early 1700s, tradesmen used small cards to advertise their products. Later, in the 1800s, members of high society used little cards called *calling cards* to announce a desired visit with someone: a servant delivered the card to the residence and then waited for a reply. Or, if someone stopped by a residence and no one was home, the visitor would leave a calling card. By the 1900s, these cards developed into what we now call *business cards*.

Many people use business cards, including students. Some people even have more than one for their various activities. In essence, the business card gives someone your *access information*: your name, position, name of company, address, phone number, fax number, e-mail address and Web address.

Business cards often parallel the corporate identity of the firm or organization by using the same logo, ink color and typestyle as the firm's other publications. The business card is usually consistent with the letterhead and its envelope — all three items together make up the *stationery package*. Cards for all the employees often look the same, with the name and contact information changed.

Measuring 2" x 3½", most business cards are printed horizontally. However, vertical is acceptable. Using the back of the card allows you to provide additional information. Some designers choose a card that folds into the 2" x 3½" size — the side might fold over a little bit or the top might fold down. Whatever you do, stick with the standard size so your card will fit into wallets and business card holders without getting ruined.

Thumb test

Hold a business card and notice that your thumb covers a little part of the card. A card passes the *thumb test* when a thumb can hold the card and NOT touch copy or a graphic. In other words, all business cards should have an area of white space the size of a thumb — where the thumb can hold the card (Figure 14-1).

Figure 14-1. Examples of two different areas where the thumb would grasp the card. These two cards pass the thumb test.

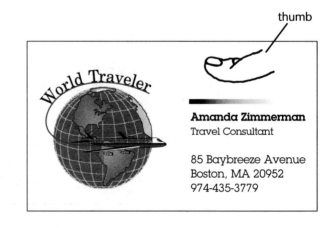

Purchase or make them yourself

Many printing companies offer good deals on business cards, and almost all local printers print them or send them out to be printed. In addition, many people buy cards from Web-based companies.

However, you might want to make them yourself. In that case, buy laser or inkjet business card paper. It is set up with 10 to the sheet and perforated. Many paper designs and colors are available, as varied as plain white, geometric patterns and cloud backgrounds.

A QuarkXPress template using guidelines is found on the CD. Stay within the green guidelines and you should have no trouble with copy overlapping another card when you perforate the cards. You can also make cards with bleeds, but this is a bit more difficult (see page 186 for instructions).

Quicktip

A *bleed* is ink that goes to the edge of the paper. The document needs to be printed on paper larger than the actual final size of the piece, and then it is trimmed to the final size.

Design principles and the card

Proximity governs placement of items in the business card. All contact information is found together rather than scattered in all four corners. A violation of proximity is the *quadrant format,* an outdated format that puts name and position in the center, while all four corners hold the other information. As a result, a reader's eye jumps all over the place (Figure 14-2).

Alignment is an important design principle on business cards. You can improve a card simply by changing the alignment. Notice varieties of alignments on the sample cards in this chapter (Figures 14-3, 14-4, 14-5 and 14-6).

Dominance might be represented by your name as the most prominent element or by a logo or graphic attracting attention.

Contrast will set apart certain elements. For example, your name and position can be contrasted: the size of the two items will be different, and your name could be in bold and the position in plain.

Repetition may not be applicable to such a small project, but consistency across various publications is important: same logo, ink color and typestyle.

The next few pages show several business card examples. See if you can identify the design principles. Do any of these cards make a strong impression?

Figure 14-2. Don't use the quadrant technique. It violates all the design principles, especially proximity. See the next page for improved variations on this same card.

Variations on the same theme

Building Memories
family photography

195 South Street
Chicago, IL 06253
1-800-555-GRIN
fax: 603-268-9578
www.saycheese.com

Leah Herring
President/General Manager

A

Building Memories
family photography

195 South Street
Chicago, IL 06253
1-800-555-GRIN
fax: 603-268-9578
www.saycheese.com

Leah Herring
President/General Manager

B

Building Memories

family photography

Leah Herring
President/General Manager

195 South Street
Chicago, IL 06253
1-800-555-GRIN
fax: 603-268-9578
www.saycheese.com

C

Figure 14-3.
A & B. Layouts are nearly the same. Contact information is grouped together on the right side of the card. The actual copy inside the text box in A is left aligned while the copy in B is right aligned. The company's name becomes the dominant item.

C. The camera becomes the dominant item. Copy is on right side of card, but left aligned with the left edge of the rule above.

(The same card is shown in Figure 14-2, but that version uses the outdated quadrant technique.)

A

B

C

Figure 14-4.
Jason and Brian began a company that sells clothing to surfers, snowboarders and skateboarders. All their class projects focused on the company. (Check out their Web site.)

All three business cards use heavy contrast. Slight variations resulted in three quite different looks. All the cards bleed off the edges — later in the chapter you will see how to set up a bleed on perforated business card stock.

Examples using dominant elements

KAREN D. DUNNINGTON*
Cat Walking Services, P.C.

203 Mantua Way
Pennington, VA 70324
702.945.7210 days
702.945.3496 eves
karendunnington@mac.com

*Member since 1989 Cat Walkers, Inc.

A

Jill Karatz
Director
117 Brookside Dr.
Brick, NJ 70943

B

Megan Goode
Co-President

Rowan University
Advertising Club

goode@yahoo.com
(245) 398-0975

C

Rob O. Miles

CEO, Moneychangers, Inc.

456 North Peach St. • Media, PA 22543 • miles@money.com
Ph 902-277-1234 • Fx 902-277-14321

D

Bagel Garden

Andrew Abel
Director of Public Relations

1021 Bagel Circle
Bagelville, CA 20322
Phone: (505) 563-4446
Fax: (505) 563-3496
E-mail: abel@mac.com

E

PEPPERS

WE'LL MAKE YOU SWEAT

2131 SCOVILLE ROAD
DALLAS, TEXAS 19780
PHONE: 1.800.PEPPERS
WWW.PEPPERS.COM
MEGAN J. RADICH

F

Figure 14-5. All of the above cards have a dorninant element on the left side. However, notice the differences in type alignment and font choices. Which ones also exhibit strong contrast?

Contrast in color, size and shape

janeen talarico
graphic artist

3587 myrtle avenue
pennsauken, nj 09562
janeentalarico@yahoo.com
cell. 906.302.8562

"think outside the box"

A

Heidi Bock
Writer and Proprietor

53 Tuckerville Rd.
P.O. Box 85
Manor Park, N.J.
06542
(536) 342-5840
chickscratch@aol.com

Chicken Scratch, Inc.
Freelance Writers

B

Mary Betina
Graphic Artist

marybetina@comcast.net
(203) 553-7647 ▪ (203) 621-7580

C

Buy the Inch

Jerrold Staas Haught
Freelance Writer

765-312-3396
jstaashaught@writers.com

D

Figure 14-6. A & B show contrast in color. In **C & D**, contrast is achieved by type — both in size and in shape (i.e., different fonts). All of them also display shape contrast with their various graphics.

Redesign

 Original

Redesign

 Commercial & Residential
Carpet & Upholstery Cleaning

METRO CARPET CLEANING
Client Satisfaction through
workmanship from an era long ago!

Visit us on the web · www.metrocarpetcleaning.com
Toll Free 1-800-638-7647
856-467-5717
Pager: 856-277-0774
E-mail: mcc5717@bellatlantic.net
Sherry Jones
Office/Marketing Manager

 Commercial & Residential
Carpet & Upholstery Cleaning

Metro Carpet Cleaning

www.metrocarpetcleaning.com
Toll Free 1-800-638-7647
Local 856-467-5717
Pager 856-277-0774
Sherry Jones, Office Mgr.

Figure 14-7. Sherry redesigned her cluttered business card (left). Changing the card into a simpler look, she uses right alignment of type.

How were they created?

Figure 14-8. Janeen made the "person" out of shapes. She started with a large black rectangle and put a white one on that. Then she put black ovals on the white rectangle to carve out the space. Last, the little white oval made the head.

Figure 14-9. Amanda used a world and a jet in picture boxes with "none" in runaround and color. She put the jet on top of the world (bring to front) and grouped the two items. Then she drew a curved text path starting from the jet. She used the space bar to move the "W" to the place she wanted it. Then she grouped all three items. Her copy was done in a separate box.

Quick Quiz

1. What is the quadrant format and why is it ineffective?
2. How is each of the design principles put to use in business card design?
3. What is the thumb test?
4. What elements need to be included on a business card?

 ## Out of the Quandary

1. Design a business card for yourself or a client.
2. Start collecting business cards for future reference.
3. Evaluate a few business cards for their effectiveness. How does each one use design principles? Which cards leave a lasting impression? Why?

 ## Quantum Leap

Design three or four variations of the same card.

 ## Quark Quest

Design a business card

☐ 1. Create a folder on your disk called *Business Card*.

☐ 2. Open the business card template (*businesscard.qxt*) from the CD (Figure 14-10). Name it *Yournamecard.qxd*. (Use your own name, of course.) **Save** it to your Business Card folder.

☐ 3. Work within the green grids of one of the boxes on the template. Enlarge your window to work more easily by using the magnifier tool.

☐ 4. Build your card with individual boxes of type and graphics (Figure 14-11). Move the boxes around until you like the placement. Don't use a text path unless it's for a special effect.

(If a box pushes away another box, apply **none** for runaround. That will solve most of your problems.)

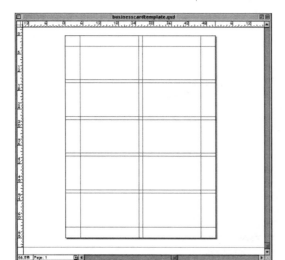
Figure 14-10. Business card template with grids.

Communicating With QuarkXPress

Use the magnifing tool to blow up the page on the screen. Click on the tool, then click on the page. Every click makes the page bigger.

To make the page get smaller, hold down the option key and click the magnifer.

☐ 5. Be sure one of your text or picture boxes has a border to line up with the template grids. You can pull out your graphic box to meet the corner of the business card area. This will help when you duplicate the cards and move them to other nine boxes.

☐ 6. **Save** your document.

☐ 7. Print the document from the CD called *practicepaper.pdf*. Feed that paper again through the printer and print your designed card. Does your card fit in one of the boxes?

If the answer is *no*: Adjust it.

If the answer is *yes*:

☐ 8. Group all the items in that first box. **Save.**

☐ 9. **Step and repeat** (under Item menu) 9 more times and move them to the other boxes, using your one border line or corner as your placement guide. (You can't eyeball this and get it right.) **Save.**

☐ 10. Examine the document. Do all the cards fit within the grids? If not, adjust.

☐ 11. **Save** document.

☐ 12. **Collect for Output** (file menu) into your Business Card folder.

☐ 13. Feed cardstock into the manual feed tray on the printer.

☐ 14. **Print** on the cardstock.

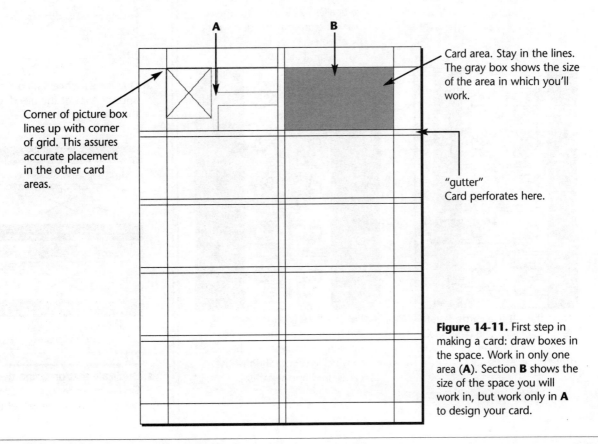

Corner of picture box lines up with corner of grid. This assures accurate placement in the other card areas.

Card area. Stay in the lines. The gray box shows the size of the area in which you'll work.

"gutter"
Card perforates here.

Figure 14-11. First step in making a card: draw boxes in the space. Work in only one area (**A**). Section **B** shows the size of the space you will work in, but work only in **A** to design your card.

To print cards with a bleed

Because a bleed runs off the side of the paper, it runs into the next business card if you use the perforated pages with 10 cards to a page. To solve this: first of all, **make your solid color in a picture box and put your text in a text box over it**. Make text box **none** in runaround. You will be dragging handles of the picture boxes, not the text boxes.

For a side bleed

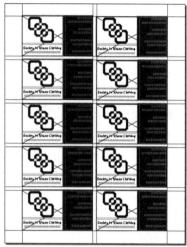

1. Duplicate all the cards as usual.

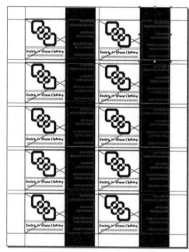

2. Pull bleeds into each other vertically. You are pulling the black picture box, so text won't be affected.

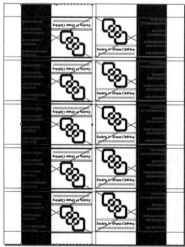

3. Group the left five cards. Rotate the group 180°. The bleeds for all cards are now on the outside of the page.

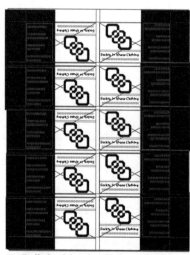

4. Pull the bleeds off the sides of the page. The edges can be uneven, as seen above, because they will get cut off. Print the cards, fold and separate!

For a top bleed

1. Position your first card the way you want it.

2. Duplicate it once. Pull out the sides and the tops of the bleed. Group those two cards.

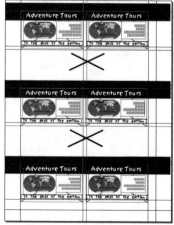

3. Duplicate that grouping two times. Skip every other card to allow the bleed to run off the top of the card.

15 Magazine Article

Today, almost every company and organization publishes at least one newsletter or magazine, and some have as many as a dozen aimed at various internal and external audiences.

James E. Grunig & Todd T. Hunt
Managing Public Relations

Quest Objectives

- Explain the five C's of the magazine milieu: cover, content, consistency, collaboration and calendar.
- Describe the editorial/advertising ratio.
- Define the elements of a magazine article layout.
- Differentiate a journal from a magazine.

Quest Skills

- Explain the use of a template and be able to use one for a magazine article.
- Use a document's existing library. Create a library.
- Explain the purpose of a master page.
- Apply style sheets to unformatted copy to produce a two-page article.
- Tighten up paragraphs to eliminate widows and orphans.
- Use a discretionary hyphen to tighten up a "loose" line of type.

Quest Terms

abstract	5 C's	perfect binding
article	folio	periodical
blueline	halftone	pipeline
book	imposition	pithy pullquote
break of book	library	saddle stitch
contents page	linking	saddle wire
cover	logo	self-cover
discretionary hyphen	manuscript	signature
dummy	master page	soft return
editorial matter	masthead	style sheet
editorial/advertising ratio or mix	milieu	template
	pagination	

lthough you will most likely need more experience to work in page layout of magazines in the real world, you will get a little taste of it in this chapter as you lay out two short articles. This chapter provides a brief overview of magazines — just enough to give you a new experience. We will use the word *magazine*, but all of the following applies to journals as well (see sidebar).

Five C's of the magazine milieu*

1. Cover

The magazine's *cover* gives an identity to the magazine and attracts the attention of the target audience. Setting the tone or mood of the contents, the cover lures the reader inside. Or conversely, the cover repels the reader.

2. Content

Content equates to the essence of the magazine. If you remember the ice cream sundae analogy on page 3, you can apply it to a magazine as well. The content is the ice cream while the cover is the syrup and whipped cream. Content includes articles, departments, columns and advertising. For the magazine to keep readership, content must meet the needs of the magazine's audience. Also, good editing is essential. Readability level must accommodate the audience.

3. Consistency of design

Consistency flourishes from issue to issue as well as from page to page — and the two can overlap. For issue-to-issue consistency, use the same:

- cover design
- masthead
- placement of regular features, departments, etc.

For page-to-page consistency, use the same:

- folio line format; headers and footers
- treatment of photos, captions, pullquotes, color
- font for titles; font for subheads; font for body copy
- margins, gutters and columns
- jumps (continuing article to another page)

Consistency supports the identity of the publication.

4. Collaboration

Collaboration in the publishing industry is important to the success of the individual publications as well as to the success of the publishing house.

Collaboration with workers involves defining who does what for each stage of the magazine and supporting each other when

*milieu – an environment or setting

Journal or magazine?

The words are used interchangeably in this chapter, but a difference does exist. Most consumer magazines inform and entertain. They are geared to segments within the general public. The editorial staff accepts or rejects manuscripts.

Journals contain research and authoritative articles by professionals. Journal articles are usually peer reviewed to decide acceptance or rejection. A journal's target audience is usually high interest — many journals are subscribed to or received as part of association dues. Therefore you will see more consistency and more formal layouts than in magazines.

The word *journal* creates a connotation of *scholarly*.

Qool Fact

How much advertising goes into a magazine or journal?

It is expressed as the *editorial/advertising ratio.* If the ratio were 60/40, it would mean 60% of the content is editorial, while 40% of the content is advertising. Other examples include 50/50, 70/30, two-thirds/one-third (that one is expressed in words, not in numbers).

How is this ratio decided?

1. Under postal regulations, the periodical can't contain more than 50% advertising (average for the year) to be mailed second class. Therefore, if postal preference is important, keep the advertising space under 50% of the book.

2. The ratio could be directed by policy of the organization that owns the publication. Some groups insist on a certain amount of editorial copy in each issue of their journal.

The ratio might also be referred to as the editorial/advertising mix.

Most important feature of calendar = meeting each deadline.

duties cross over. Tasks fall under editorial, art, sales, circulation and printing.

Collaboration with authors involves developing a good relationship. A satisfied author may become a repeat author, and that is usually a good thing. Many professional journals need articles and often hope to get enough copy to make it from one issue to the next. As one nurse editor said in workshops for future authors, "My garage is NOT filled with manuscripts as you all think. Please write for us!"

Questions to answer regarding your work with authors include:
- Does the author see the edited manuscript and/or page proofs?
- How many days do you allow for turnaround on corrections? (How much time do you give the author to return the corrected manuscript or page proofs?)
- How long is the manuscript in the pipeline? In other words, when can an author expect the article to be published?
- What are the deadlines?
- Does the author get paid?
- Who is the final authority?

Collaboration with the audience emerges as the foremost activity in publishing. Remember the first two questions you need to ask when starting a publication: *Who is my audience?* and *What is my message?* Adjust editorial content and graphic design to meet the needs of your target audience. Occasionally survey your audience to be sure you are providing what they want and how they want it.

5. Calendar

The last "C" word is *calendar,* to help you remember the schedule of the production process, or the timeline. The process of magazine production (or book production) is called "going through the pipeline." Meeting deadlines is essential in the magazine industry. If you miss your appointment (your slot) on the press, you may have to wait out the printing of a few other magazines before another open slot is available for you.

Steps of the calendar or stops along the pipeline include:
1. editing of manuscript
2. layout of article (note name change at this point from manuscript to article — see page 190 for description)
3. proofreading of page proofs of article by author and editor
4. correcting page proofs
5. imposition of magazine, incorporating corrected articles, ads, other material (see page 190 for description)
6. imposition (dummy) proofread by editor
7. imposition sent to printer with disk (layout, art, fonts) or by PDFs
8. proof made by printer, sent to editor for final look. This stage used to be called the *blueline,* but many printers now send back a set of clean laser pages, often printed in color (see page 190).
9. printer corrects proof, prints books and mails them

Words in the magazine milieu

The magazine and book industries speak a jargon unfamiliar to the general public. You saw a few of these words in previous chapters, but many of them are new.

Abstract – a short summary of the article.

Article – a complete piece of writing that is part of a magazine, book or newspaper. When it is sent to be published, it is called a *manuscript*. After the editorial work is done on an accepted manuscript, it goes to the art department for layout. After layout, it *officially* becomes an article.

Biosketch – a short summary (sketch) of the author's credentials; usually one or two sentences when used in a publication; can be longer if in a program book (e.g., keynote speaker's biosketch).

Blueline – final proof from printer that shows exact color breaks in varying shades of blue on white paper; this stage is being replaced by a final set of page proofs run in color. Many of us still call the final page proof stage a "blueline" even though it isn't blue anymore.

Book – slang for magazine.

Break of book – what goes where; the allocation of space for articles, features, departments and all material printed in the magazine.

Byline – printed name of the author at the end or start of an article.

Contents page – the page that lists articles, features and departments and their locations in the book.

Cover – the four pages that make up the outside wrap of the magazine; referred to as cover 1, cover 2, cover 3, cover 4 (or front cover, inside front cover, back cover and inside back cover).

Dummy – mockup simulating final product; there are various uses of the word *dummy*. One common type of dummy is the full template for the book. For example, you figure out the book will be 64 pages, so you build a document with 64 blank pages. Then you proceed to drag all the individual articles and ads onto that document. This is now your dummy. Some have replaced the word *dummy* with either *imposition* or *page proofs* — clarify your jargon with your co-workers.

Editorial matter – all copy, other than advertising, in a magazine or newspaper. Editorial matter includes photos and art as well as text. For example, a publisher might say, "We have 65% editorial and 35% advertising." This expression is known as the *editorial/advertising ratio* or the *editorial/advertising mix*.

Folio – page number, date and name of periodical on each page or spread.

Halftone – an image broken down into a series of dots (usually a photo scanned as grayscale).

Imposition – arrangement of pages so they will appear in proper sequence after press sheets are folded and bound. Imposition varies according to number of pages, sheet size, printing technique and binding method. Some people use the word *dummy* and *imposition* interchangeably — just speak the same jargon as your co-workers.

Figure 15-1.
The magazine cover.

Logo – symbol identifying the magazine; found on the cover, masthead and anywhere else.

Manuscript – typed copy before layout begins. The magazine (1) accepts, (2) accepts with revisions or (3) rejects a manuscript.

Masthead – the area that contains the staff listing, date of publication, contact information and other information about the publication or the organization.

Pagination – numbering the pages of a book, newspaper, or periodical. This can be confusing because in newspaper layout, *pagination* also refers to the actual layout of the paper.

Perfect binding – books bound by glue rather than having pages sewn in or stapled.

Periodical – publication issues on a regular schedule, such as every week or month. Magazines, newsletters and journals are periodicals. The term is not usually applied to newspapers or yearbooks, although each appear on a regular schedule and are technically periodicals.

Pipeline – the system through which the article goes from receipt of manuscript to publication of article in magazine.

Saddle stitch or saddle wire – binding in which staples are driven through the middle fold of the pages. (Pages are opened over a saddle-shaped support and stitched through the back.)

Self-cover – a cover printed on the same paper as the rest of the magazine.

Signature – printed sheet folded at least once, possibly many times, to become part of a book, magazine or other publication. Signatures always contain pages in increments of four, such as 8, 16 or 32 pages (Figure 15-2).

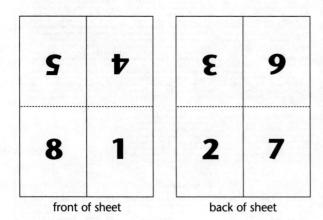

front of sheet   back of sheet

Each of these pages would measure the size of the finished publication.

Figure 15-2. An 8-page signature.

One large sheet of paper (e.g., larger than 17" x 22" to allow for trimmed edges) can print 4 pages on the front, 4 pages on the back. Fold it along the dotted line and then again vertically. Trim the top folded edge, and you get 8 pages.

Several of these signatures get folded and combined to make up the book. Signatures can run 4 pages, 8 pages, 16 pages and 32 pages (referred to as a 32-page signature).

You try it! Make a mini-book.

Fold a piece of paper in half from top to bottom, then in half again (French fold). Fold is at the top. Don't cut off the top folded edge yet.

Now number the pages from 1 to 8. Open up and you should see the numbers like the figure to the right. Refold and cut off the top folded edge. You have a little booklet. If you were actually producing an 8-page booket, this could serve as your *dummy*, a mockup of the page layout.

Anatomy of an article

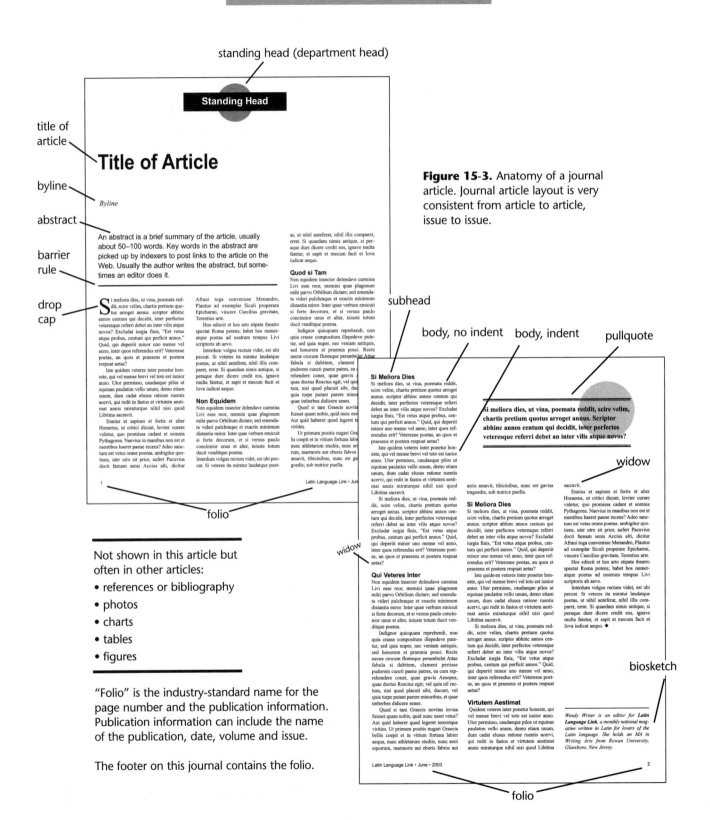

standing head (department head)

Standing Head

title of article

Title of Article

byline

Byline

abstract

An abstract is a brief summary of the article, usually about 50–100 words. Key words in the abstract are picked up by indexers to post links to the article on the Web. Usually the author writes the abstract, but sometimes an editor does it.

barrier rule

drop cap

Figure 15-3. Anatomy of a journal article. Journal article layout is very consistent from article to article, issue to issue.

subhead

body, no indent   body, indent   pullquote

widow

folio

biosketch

folio

Not shown in this article but often in other articles:

- references or bibliography
- photos
- charts
- tables
- figures

"Folio" is the industry-standard name for the page number and the publication information. Publication information can include the name of the publication, date, volume and issue.

The footer on this journal contains the folio.

Sample layout

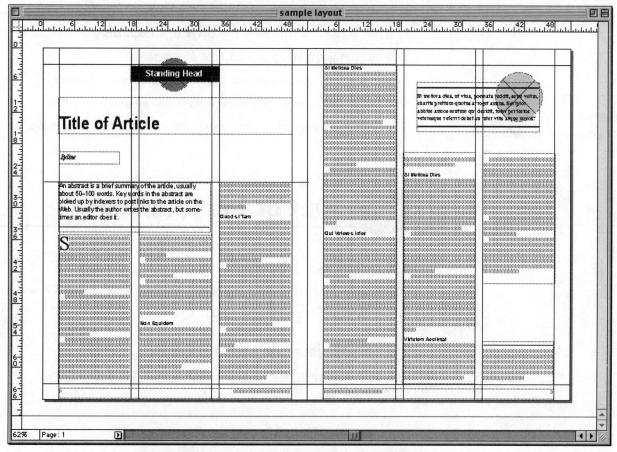

Figure 15-4. The computer window with a sample layout for this journal. Your article will look like this two-page spread.

A template has been called a:

- preformatted document
- pattern
- shell of a document
- basic structure
- boilerplate
- skeleton
- backbone

Template

A *template* is a pattern that can be used repeatedly. The QuarkXPress icon for a template looks faded compared to a document icon. When you open a template, the title changes from the template title to *Document 1* (or 2, 3, etc.). Name it and save it as a document. The template remains untouched.

To make a template, you merely save a document as a template. In the **Save as** dialog box, you would name the document and then for **Type**, select **Template**. (The default reads **Document**.) You will be making a template for your own newsletter.

Quick Quiz

1. How is a journal different from a magazine?

2. What is the importance of the cover of a magazine?

3. What items make up the content of a magazine?

4. How do you achieve consistency in a magazine or journal?

5. What issues need to be resolved with authors?

6. What does it mean to refer to the *editorial to advertising ratio*?

raw copy –
copy before it is formatted

 # Out of the Quandary

1. Lay out two articles
Lay out two journal articles in Quark. Use the template and raw copy provided on the CD.

2. Compare journals and magazines
Compare a few journals to a few magazines. Can you see the differences?

 # Quantum Leap

1. Redesign
Redesign the journal layout and then use your new version to lay out either article.

2. Flashy magazine article
Design a flashy magazine article layout for high school or college students. Use color and be creative.

3. Table of contents
Design an interesting table of contents for a magazine or journal.

Quark Quest

Lay out a magazine article (Article 1: I Punctuate; Therefore I Am)

☐ 1. Open QuarkXPress.

☐ 2. Find the *Magazine Article* folder on your CD. Drag the whole folder to your disk.

☐ 3. From that folder on your disk, open *articletemplate.qxt* and *maclibrary or windowslibrary.qxl*.

☐ 4. Save the template as *YourNameArticle1.qxd*. Be sure to save it into the Magazine Article folder.

☐ 5. View Menu: Show tools
        Show measurements
        Show style sheets
        Show invisibles

> *If the computer says fonts are missing, don't worry about it. Click OK and proceed for this assignment.*

Actually, when these are showing, the view menu will say "Hide ___"

☐ 6. Open RawcopyArticle1.qxd.

☐ 7. Use content tool to **Select all**. **Copy**.

☐ 8. Paste it into your article template, page one in the appropriate column (bottom left column). Now close the Raw copy document. **Save**.

☐ 9. Make your document very small on the screen so you can see both pages. (Use the percentage in the bottom left corner of the window.) Link the columns together so all the text flows. This is FULL to EMPTY. If you really mess up, "Revert to Saved" and begin again. (See sidebar for instructions on linking.) **Save**.

Use style sheets

☐ 10. Select all the copy. On the Style Sheets palette, click **No Style**. This neutralizes all copy to prepare it for stylizing. Your copy may already be in No Style format because it was prepared for you that way. However, normally, it wouldn't be.

☐ 11. From your pasted-in copy, cut out the article title and place it in the correct text box. Do the same thing with the byline, abstract and biosketch (at the end of the article). Apply style sheets to each of those text boxes. **Save**.

☐ 12. Remove any EXTRA paragraph returns in those boxes if you see any — this gets rid of those boxes with the red X. Check the very first line of your article — this commonly has a paragraph return above it.

How do you know if there is a paragraph return? Be sure you have **Show Invisibles** on, which is ⌘I, and you will see dots for spaces and paragraph marks for each return.

Quicktip

Linking

Click on the linking tool. Click in the column WITH the body copy (FULL box). You will see a moving marquee around the text box. Then click in the empty text box. The text will flow into that box.

Repeat.

Speed it up

When you get proficient, hold the option key down when you select the tool and it will stay on the linking tool. Then just click through the document. But for now, practice by doing it each time.

Applying a style sheet to text

1. **Menu → View → Show style sheets**

2. Click on the line or paragraph you want to change.

3. On the style sheet, click **No Style** at the top of the palette.

4. Then click on the style sheet you want.

5. Save your document.

Library – a palette that stores frequently used items or groups of items.

---

*pithy – forceful, brief, to the point and full of substance or meaning.

Soft return ▶

Do not vertically center or use text inset on this magazine article EXCEPT for pullquotes or in the box for article 2.

---

leading

```
┌─┬──────┬─┐
│→│⇧ 13 pt│▤│
│↑│⇔ -2  │▤│
└─┴──────┴─┘
```

tracking

Library palette (maclibrary or windowslibrary.qxl) (page 206)

☐ 13. From the library, use item tool and drag "Standing head" to the top of page one. Place it at Y coordinate 2p6, and center it horizontally. Use column gridlines to do that. **Save**.

☐ 14. Give the standing head a creative name. **Save**.

☐ 15. Now go through the rest of the article and apply style sheets to each paragraph. **Save** as you go.

Pullquotes

☐ 16. Choose a pithy* pullquote from the article. It does not have to be a direct quote said by someone.

☐ 17. To put a pullquote on a page: Drag down two columns on the page to make space. Use the black handle at the top of the column to drag down a column. Be generous with space.

☐ 18. Then drag the appropriate pullquote setup from the library (single or double column).

☐ 19. Highlight the type in the pullquote box and type your quote over the current type. It will keep the format as you type. Or, if you copy and paste the pullquote copy, apply the pullquote style sheet. It should be vertically centered. Remove any extra paragraph returns above or below the type if they impede centering.

☐ You may have to use a *soft return* (**shift-return**) to fix some of the ugly lines of the pullquote. Get rid of hyphenations — use no hyphenations in pullquotes.

☐ To move a pullquote around on the page: Use the item tool. The rules and the box move together that way. **Save**.

☐ To work on an individual item in the pullquote, use the content tool. Remember you have to click on the content tool, click off the text box in empty space and then click on the group (the three-click switch – see page 64).

Finishing touches

☐ 20. Type the information in the folio (the footer). Make up a name/date. **Save**.

☐ 21. At this point, run out a copy. Now look it over and circle all the things you want to change.

☐ 22. Clean up widows.

Select that whole paragraph (4 clicks). Try one of two methods to tighten the paragraph's tracking.

Measurements bar method:

Tighten tracking by using the measurements bar. You can go -1, -2, -3, -4 or -5. No more than that. If it doesn't work, then edit it or live with it!

REMEMBER: A correction often makes another change later in the document.

Keyboard method:

You can also tighten by selecting the paragraph and holding down the three magic keys and the [(bracket). Each tap of the [key gives you one more point of tighter tracking.

☐ 23. Fix extra full lines: orphans (full line at bottom that starts a paragraph) or full-line widows at the top of the column.

To get rid of an entire line, play with the heights of the partial columns near the pullquote. Lengthen or shorten them, using the handles on the top — not the corners.

☐ 24. Check for wide spaces between words in a line of type. To get rid of an ugly one, try this: Look at the line of type BELOW your "ugly" line. Look at the first word on that line below. Can you hyphenate that word? If yes, use the *discretionary hyphen*. That's "⌘-hyphen."

Discretionary hyphen ▶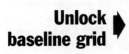

Reason for the discretionary hyphen: If you edit later, and the word pieces want to rejoin, they will go back together without the hyphen. You've probably seen examples of this done poorly, where the hyphen has been left in a word.

Wide spaces might also be corrected by changing the tracking. No more than -5.

Editor's notes or other extra information

Unlock baseline grid ▶

If there is no style sheet for various bits of information such as an editor's note, format it yourself in the same fonts of the rest of the journal. Possibly italicize special notes. If you do this, take the checkmark out of the "Lock to baseline grids" box. Go to **Style → Formats → Lock to baseline grid**. Uncheck the box.

Locking to baseline grids forces the copy to a preset leading. This causes lines of type to line up horizontally. See it under **View → Show baseline grid.** Body copy you are using for the magazine articles were made using a baseline grid style sheet. Highlight a few words in your magazine layout and try changing leading. You will see the type jump to the next gridline. Fix by: **Style → Formats → Lock to baseline grid – Uncheck**.

Printing on both sides

It's a good idea to type your name somewhere on the article. When the whole class is printing the articles, all the documents will look alike.

To print on both sides:
⌘ **P** gives you the printing dialog box. Then:

Printer
↓
General
↓
Layout
↓
Print on both sides

> *Note:*
> This process may vary according to the brand of printer you are using. Check with your instructor.

I Punctuate; Therefore, I Am ←——Title

By Lorie Boucher ←——Byline

←——Abstract

In the following article, Boucher makes a case for a person's use of punctuation as the measure of his or her personality. Although written tongue-in-cheek, the article might strike similarities to people you know. As you read it, discover which punctuation defines you!

First paragraph of the article (drop cap style sheet)

More than the words we write, the way we write them is considered by some to be a reliable indicator of personality. Perfect, oversized script? Drippy, sugary, kindergarten teachers who sing the alphabet and scold in rhyme. Bubble letters and hearts dotting i's? Bubblegum-smacking, hair-twirling teens squealing boy band gossip. Tight, jagged, EKG-monitor scribbles? Angry, no-one-understands-me artists.

But really, how can the involuntary metacarpal twitchings of handwriting have anything to do with the way we act, react, and interact? My own tiny, messy handwriting would suggest years of medical school and a shy, academic timidity. Yet the screams of laughter at that prospect from those who know me would deafen you, dear reader.

No, it is punctuation that mirrors our personality, punctuation that exposes our true spirits, punctuation that reveals the soul. The punctuation that saturates our writing, that is, the punctuation marks we choose to overuse, is the real ink blot test of personality.

Conveniently, the Punctuation Personality Indicator (PPI) slots all of the world's personalities into nine categories.

The Over-Exclaimer!!! ←—— Head

The more jovial first cousin of the screeching ALL-CAPSinator, the Over-Exclaimer (OE) is either perpetually surprised or very easily excited. Events are so astonishing and/or thrilling to the OE that a mere single exclamation point simply cannot convey the depth of the sentiment. And so the OE uses a series of exclamation points, their number directly proportional to the intensity of the statement that precedes them. "Ohmigod, that petunia pink cowl-neck twinset totally brings out your eyes!!!" exclaims the Over-Exclaimer, punctuated with an air-kiss hello.

Incidentally, scientific research indicates that this breed has multiplied exponentially with the incidence of e-mail. Holding down the shift and the #1 key for a few seconds requires far less effort than pushing lines and dots into paper. So we are at risk of living in an exhausting, over-demonstrative, super-exclamatory world. Ugh. Join me in exterminating the OE.

The Super-Interrogator???

The Super-Interrogator (SI) is eternally perplexed; a single question mark cannot communicate the profundity of the SI's confusion. So puzzling is the SI's query that it must be amplified with a series of question marks. "Why do people like cheese?" is a simple question of interest. "Why do people like cheese???" implies that the SI can't fathom, on this green earth, why anyone would put stinky, blue-molded milk curd into their mouth.

Many SIs find their way into the editing field, where they can indulge their penchant for multiple question marks at the first sign of even a mildly ambiguous phrase or turn of logic. They trounce the unsuspecting writer with a barrage of red question marks, implying that the reader could not possibly be expected to understand such a confounding, ill-worded sentence.

This overly critical subcategory of SI is manipulative — it is not that the SI is too slow to get the point, it is that the SI thinks the writer is too slow to make it properly. Resist the urge to counter the SI with multiple exclamation points. There is no excuse for being that annoying.

The Pedant;

So proud are Pedants of their ability to correctly apply the semicolon that the urge to display this capacity at every opportunity is irresistible. A highfalutin show-off, this breed is often born in first-year university classes, where the fledgling Pedant first attempts to stand on his knobby, tentative academic legs. In an effort to appropriate the rhythmic lull of scholarly diction and style, the Pedant inserts a semicolon between all related thoughts. Debating with the Pedant is a recommended cure for insomnia. Sleepless no more!

The Educator:

When the Educator can pry himself away from the Public Access channel long enough to write, the resulting text is riddled with colons. Whatever follows a colon is never offered hypothetically — it is a fact. The Educator makes only statements, never suggestions. Ask the

Educator, "What is the meaning of life?" and he will respond with the same certainty as when asked what's for dinner. Don't feel bad for hating the Educator. He has friends: Pedants.

The Drone.
The Drone is unimpressed with the fancy variety of punctuation marks and sticks to the good ol' meat-and-potatoes period. The Drone hasn't the time for inflection; he gets right to the point, as it were. Drones find employment as automated voice attendants and National Geographic narrators. Without the Drone, we would never know the car door is ajar.

(The Quipper)
The wise-cracking Quipper uses parentheses as a subversive device to slip asides into statements, like a jokey, visual elbow to the side. Parentheses create a certain intimacy with the reader, a "you-know-what-I'm saying" sort of kinship. "Jake asked me out the other day (as if), and I had to come up with a believable excuse right on the spot," explains the Quipper. "I told him I had to wash my hair (read: forever). Is that heinous?" The sassy, postmodern Quipper has no unwritten thoughts and watches too much Dennis Miller. But we love the Quipper (if tolerance is love).

The Rambler,
Why impose the authoritative finality of the period when the meandering comma can extend a sentence indefinitely? The Rambler is too insecure to make anything so assertive as a point, and so avoids it as long as possible, sending you on a grumbling, frustratingly fruitless hunt for the period. Ramblers are wandering, aimless window-shoppers who can never commit to buying anything. They insist on the importance of "the process, not the product," or "the path, not the destination." They are insufferable. In addition, there are also those Ramblers who overuse the comma as a method of clinging to the rhythm of speech, resisting the requirement to write things down at all. Hey, if you want to talk, use the phone. To all Ramblers: no one reads Faulkner for a reason.

The Cliff-Hanger...
The Cliff-Hanger must have suffered some period-related trauma as a child because he avoids it at all costs. While the Rambler meanders around endlessly in comma-land, he at least arrives at the period eventually. The Cliff-Hanger's psychosis is far more advanced. Nothing can force the Cliff-Hanger into asking a direct question or making a clear-cut statement. "I'm thinking of heading up to the cottage on the weekend... so if you know the directions..." What? Does he need directions? Does he want us to join him? It's all a big mystery. Tune in next week...

the hippie
Worse than the overuse of any punctuation mark is the total rejection of all punctuation. The absence of punctuation is often paired with the doubly irritating rejection of that other constricting imposition — capitalization. "punctuation is just The Man controlling self-expression right it's like totally confining my ideas i can't be jailed by your dictatorial punctuation regime man i'm all about the freedom the flow of emotion man yeah." The hippie treats every piece of communication like some stream-of-consciousness experiment. Ironically, the hippie turns every pacifist editor's thoughts to violence.

   Where would we be without the Over-Exclaimer, the Super-Interrogator, the Pedant, the Educator, the Drone, the Quipper, the Rambler, the Cliff-Hanger, and the hippie? Without them, editors would have little to bond over. We love to hate these overusers of punctuation, to peck at them mercilessly, like superior literary vultures. Without them, what would we do for fun?

*The masculine, singular pronoun is used throughout for simplicity and is not intended to imply that the display of freakish and annoying punctuation tendencies is a uniquely male trait.

Editor's Note: The personalities described above are purely fictional. Any resemblance to real people, alive or dead, is purely coincidental.

Lorie Boucher is a writer and editor in Ottawa, Ontario. Her essay, "I Punctuate; Therefore, I Am" originally appeared in the fall 2000 issue of *Writer's Block* (www.writersblock.ca), a quarterly online magazine for Canadians in the writing trade.

Visit the Writer's Block Web site:

www.writersblock.ca

Two comments that aren't always on articles

Biosketch

Checklist – Article 1

I Punctuate; Therefore, I Am

- ☐ Standing head is named (you name it!)
- ☐ Standing head is placed correctly at y = 2p6 and centered horizontally
- ☐ Title of article in correct format
- ☐ Drop cap used for the first paragraph
- ☐ First paragraph under each head is not indented
- ☐ All other body copy paragraphs are body, indent style
- ☐ Pullquotes: no typos
- ☐ Pullquotes: centered vertically and both rules show
- ☐ Pullquotes: no hyphenated words at the ends of lines
- ☐ Subheads formatted
- ☐ No widows (check page 158 for this info)
- ☐ No orphans (check page 158 for this info)
- ☐ No rivers of white space (fix by using a discretionary hyphen or tightening tracking)
- ☐ Folio on both pages is updated with name and date
- ☐ The asterisked information is formatted smaller
- ☐ The editor's note is treated differently typographically
- ☐ Biosketch aligns across the bottom with the other columns

You must always have at least two lines of type together. For example, if at the bottom of a column, you have a head, you must have at least two lines of copy under the head. Three is better, but two will do. Only one line under the head isn't good.

One line at the top of a column is a widow, but two lines makes it okay. Again, three is always better.

Directions for article 2: "Getting Your Notebook in the Door"

☐ 1. Repeat the layout steps for Article 1, but choose *RawcopyArticle2.qxd*. Then follow the directions below.

Find/Change ▶

See page 121 for the explanation of using one space after a period.

New skill:
Take out double spaces after periods at the ends of sentences (page 121).

☐ 2. Save document.

☐ 3. "Select all" the body copy in your new layout (that would include the subheads).

☐ 4. ⌘ **F**. Check: **Whole document**, **Ignore case**, **Ignore attributes**.

☐ 5. Click the space bar twice in the "Find What" box.

☐ 6. Click the space bar once in the "Change to" space.

☐ 7. Hit "Find next" to see one of them change. If that worked successfully, then do "Find next" and then "Change all."

☐ 8. Save your document.

Sidebar ▶

text inset
space before
bulleted list

New skill:
Set up the checklist as a sidebar (pages 142-145)

☐ 9. Draw a text box across one or two columns.

☐ 10. Select all checklist information. Cut it.

☐ 11. Paste it into your new box.

☐ 12. Set text inset of 5 points.

leading (left)   type size (right)

☐ 13. Select all. Set type to Arial 9/11 .That's 9-point type, 11-point leading.

☐ 14. Select all. Unlock baseline grid if it is locked. (**Style** → **Formats** → **Lock to baseline grid:** uncheck it)

☐ 15. Then set space before to p4 or more. (Menu bar: **Style** → **Formats** → **Space before**) Click **apply** to see if you like that distance. Then say **OK**.

☐ 16. Type a bullet before the lines. Use your Quark Quick Card to find a bullet you like in the Zapf Dingbat or Wingding font.

☐ 17. Then type a space.

☐ 18. Apply a hanging indent to those items that are two lines or more. See Quark Quick Card or Flier chapter for hanging indent.

☐ 19. Either frame the box (1 point) or shade the box (15%).

☐ 20. Title of boxed copy: Make it bold, larger, centered.

two pullquote versions

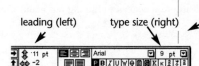

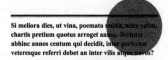

Figure out a good layout for the second page.

You may use either pullquote shape (sidebar). Watch for trapped white space (white space inside that doesn't "breathe" off the edge). You may also use a piece of clipart if it is relevant.

Article 2

The raw copy for this article is on your CD, labeled *Rawcopyarticle2.qxd.*

This copy is NOT in layout form. This is merely the typed version. If you were an editor, you would receive the manuscript typed in Microsoft Word, double spaced, one column wide (like your research papers).

Your job on this article is to format this manuscript in a Quark template for a particular journal. You will name the journal.

Read this article before you lay it out.

Getting Your Notebook in the Door ◄——Title

By June Moe Lim ◄——Byline

◄ Abstract

Registering for classes ranks with finding parking spaces: they both fill up before you get there! By the time it's your turn to register, there's nothing left. Your perfect schedule is now moot. This article presents a few different ways you can cope with the registration dilemma.

——— First paragraph of the article (drop cap style sheet)

Getting the classes you need is your ultimate goal when you register, but sometimes you run into trouble. How many of us have been in the following situation: you've drawn up your dream schedule for the semester, you try to register but find that one or more of your classes has been filled to capacity. Now you have to scrap your plans and scramble for open sections. You may even have to start from scratch if scheduling conflicts arise. Or do you? That's where this article you're reading comes in to help you out of your academic pinch.

Before you start anything, though, keep "safety" courses in mind. These are classes that you can get in without a hitch. Register for them. There's always the chance you won't get in the classes you need. If you receive financial aid, you may be penalized for not taking enough credits, so fill up your schedule with whatever courses you have to so that you stay on good terms with the Feds. You don't want to end up paying money back. After you have enough credits to keep you in good standing on paper, start your quest to get into the classes that you really want.

A Few Starting Steps ◄——Head

Consider taking the course you need with another professor. Some professors are more popular than others. That doesn't mean that the rest aren't any good. The change of pace and lack of familiarity can be refreshing. College is supposed to be about new experiences.

If you need a class to graduate or to complete a sequence for your major, then you may be able to convince a friend who may be in the class you need to drop the course. This is where you get to test your friendship. Be sure to have your paperwork ready so that you can be ready to register when you tell the professor that your friend will be dropping the course.

You can go straight to the registrar's office and find out if a class is really filled. Sometimes computer glitches give out contradictory information, and a half-empty class only seems to be filled. At the registrar's you can also find out if any new sections of a course have been added. Sometimes late additions to the semester's schedule don't make it into the book, and finding out about them becomes a hunt.

More Legwork

Sometimes, however, even jumping through the hoops of bureaucracy doesn't help. This is where you have to do a little more legwork.

Some students seek out the professor they need to talk to and ask to be signed into the course. Most schools have procedures for this and they tend to work.

Make No Assumptions

Don't think that it's enough to be put on a waiting list. Even being the first name on that list doesn't mean a thing if the professor is too busy to call you or you're not around when the green light comes. If you desperately need this course you should go that extra mile by going to see the professor. There's that old maxim that you can't say no to someone when you've put a name to a face. For insurance, put on a sad face.

Calling and regularly checking up on the availability of your course can backfire, too. Your persistence may end up irritating the professor you need on your side. The last thing you want is an angry professor holding your future in his or her hands.

What Professors Say

The general consensus among professors is that if a student needs to get into a class, he or she should go directly to see the professor. Oliver Arnold, a Princeton University English professor, recalls his own days at Berkeley when desperate students would camp out the night before at the registration site to get a jump on everyone else. Arnold notes that "[students] don't consider the possibility that just talking to the professor will help them get in."

Should a student just show up for a class he can't get into? Yes! Sound pushy? Well, it could be, but sometimes it's not enough to simply say that you're interested in a class. You have to demonstrate that you want to be in the class. Princeton English professor William Gleason says he likes to actually meet a student so that he can "gauge the student's interest on the spot." Gleason also adds, "If you really are interested, you need to show that interest."

Cornell University philosophy professor Fred Neuhouser agrees with Gleason and adds that if a student keeps coming to a class in the hopes that a spot will become available, then "the time investment made makes it difficult to turn the student down." Neuhouser also suggests that explaining any extenuating circumstances can be of great help to you. Just don't make up a sob story to worm your way in.

I needed to get into a course last semester called Publication Layout and Design at New Jersey's Rowan University. The section that I wanted got cancelled, and the remaining sections of the course were filled. I had to think fast. I went to the first class of one of the closed sections and spoke to the professor, Claudia Cuddy. She told me I was the low head on the totem pole. There was a waiting list eight people deep. I went out on a limb and asked if I could at least stay for the first class, just in case a space opened up. The gamble paid off for me. Cuddy later told me, "I'm glad you came to get signed in. If you had called on the phone, I would have probably said no, but I can't refuse a sad face." It helps that I'm also a pleasure to have in class.

The only thing that got me in was my "gumption," as Cuddy put it.

You're In!

Now that you've got your foot in the door remember that the first class is important. It gives you a feel for what you're getting yourself into and adds that much more to your credibility. You're not going to want to miss it. Other people will, though, and that's good. It makes your presence less of an inconvenience.

When you show up for class try to make a good impression from the get-go. That means not wearing your Grateful Dead tie-dye or your favorite pajama pants when you go in to see your professor. And rub the sleep from your eyes. Don't deck yourself out in your Sunday best, just dress presentably. After all, you're the one in need here and you're going to need everything running in your favor. You can dress down later in the semester when you've established yourself as worth the trouble the professor went to in getting you a seat in the class.

Remember, when you've impressed your way into your class, you're on your way to academic stardom. When it comes to not being able to get into a class, Princeton's Gleason says, "It's a matter of not accepting it as fate."

Sidebar

The Checklist

Load up on "safety" courses so that you have something to fall back on if you have to.

Put on a sad face.

Talk to friends (or make friends with people) already in the class you need. Someone may be willing to give up his or her spot in the class for you.

Keep checking with the registrar. Perhaps they made an error somewhere.

Take the class you need with another professor. There's no use in beating yourself senseless trying to take "the professor."

Keep going to class. In the event you get in, you don't want to be behind.

Dress presentably. You don't want your professor to notice a big stain sitting where a diligent student should be.

Keep your fingers crossed. Sometimes professors' hands are tied, and they can't help you even if they want to.

Be a pleasure to have in class. You don't want to become a burden or nuisance in class after your professor goes to all that trouble.

Biosketch

June Moe Lim, BA, graduated from Rowan University's public relations program. He was an A student; he received A's for his academic work as well as A's in attitude!

Use The Checklist *as a sidebar. Run it down one column or stretch it across two columns.*

Checklist – Article 2

Getting Your Notebook in the Door

☐ Standing head is named (you name it!)

☐ Standing head is placed correctly at y = 2p6 and centered horizontally

☐ Title of article in correct format and divided in the right place (use soft return)

☐ Drop cap used for the first paragraph

☐ First paragraph under each head is not indented

☐ All other body copy paragraphs are body, indent style

☐ Pullquotes: no typos

☐ Pullquotes: centered vertically and both rules show

☐ Pullquotes: no hyphenated words at the ends of lines

☐ Subheads formatted

☐ No widows (check page 158 for this info)

☐ No orphans (check page 158 for this info)

☐ No rivers of white space (fix by using a discretionary hyphen or tightening tracking)

☐ Folio on both pages is updated with name and date

These apply to the Checklist box:

☐ Text NOT locked to baseline grid (#14 in Article 2 instructions)

☐ Text inset is 5 points

☐ Box type is set to Arial 9/11

☐ Space before each unit is set to 4 points

☐ Box is framed or shaded or both

☐ Bullets have one space after them

☐ Hanging indents applied after the space

Overall:

☐ Double spaces removed and single spaces replace them (see Article 2 instructions, #2 through #8)

This article may not fill the second page. Arrange your layout to allow for a little filler announcement or a small house ad. This would mean moving up the biosketch so it does NOT align across the bottom of the page as it did in Article 1. However, keep items aligned wherever they fall on the page.

As an extra task, make an ad or an announcement and put it in the white space.

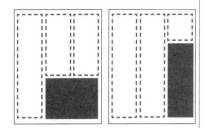

The gray boxes represent small ads or filler announcements. (They don't have to be shaded in the actual layout.) Of course your layout will have the sidebar checklist and a pullquote, which are not shown here.

The mighty master page

How to remember the purpose of the master page: "The master is the ruler." (The master page rules — or governs — other pages!)

The *master page* is a page that governs other pages in your document. Whatever you put on this page appears on other pages in the document. Every page added to the document shows those items. Page numbering is automatic: type ⌘**3** on the master page. This symbol appears: <#>. The symbol turns into an actual Arabic number on each page. The items on a master page for this book are header, footer, page number, text box and hairline along the text box.

Until you become more experienced, you won't use *multiple* master pages in one document. But you can easily use a single master page.

☐ 1. Open a new document: 8½ x 11, 3p margins, 1 column.

☐ 2. Show document layout under the **View** menu, or hit the **F10** key (Figure 15-5).

☐ 3. Click twice on **Master A**. A little lock at the top left corner designates it as a master page.

☐ 4. Type a header and/or a footer. Type ⌘**3** in the place you want a page number to appear. Type something in the middle of the page just for fun. Or put a picture in the middle of the page.

☐ 5. Now **click on page 1** on the document layout palette. Page 1 will appear on your screen. It should match your master page.

☐ 6. Add a few more pages to the document to test it (**File → Page → Insert**) or drag Master A page on the document layout to the palette space.

☐ 7. Another way to get to the master page is by clicking and holding down the little black arrow on the bottom scroll bar at the bottom of your screen (Figure 15-6).

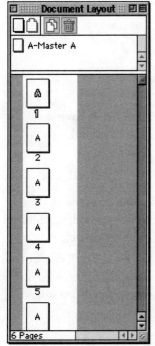

Figure 15-5. The document layout palette is one way to get to the master page as well as other pages. Add pages by dragging the master page down to the next space. Or insert a page between two pages.

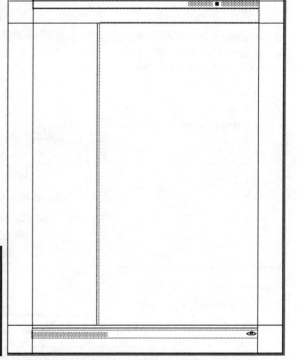

Figure 15-7. Here is the master page for this book. I built a text box on it as well, so I didn't have to draw it on each page in the document.

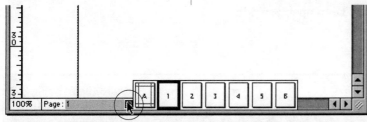

Figure 15-6. At the bottom of the screen, click on the little triangle (cursor is clicking on it in picture). A popup of the pages appears. The "A" page is the master page.

The amazing library

The QuarkXPress library stores frequently used items or groups of items. For example, if the newspaper runs a few weekly columns with headshots, store the headshots in the library. Keep logos and icons in the library for easy access.

This chapter introduced you to a library with the "standing head" logo in it (page 196). You used the item tool, clicked on the item in the library and dragged it onto the page. Take a look now at how to create a library and how to put an item in the library.

☐ 1. **File → New Library**. Click on **Create**.

☐ 2. Name the library. FYI: Libraries are not interchangeable between Macs and Windows.

☐ 3. Open the small ad you created a few classes ago. **Save As** *libraryad.qxd*. (Never experiment with your original.)

☐ 4. Ungroup all the items if they are grouped.

Put items in the library

☐ 5. With the item tool, drag the ad's items piece by piece to the library palette. Each piece will shrink. (When you drag the item back onto a page, it enlarges again — this is amazing.)

☐ 6. To name an item, click twice. A dialog box appears. Type in the name. Name all your library items. They don't have to be named to work, but naming them helps you become more organized.

Use items from the library

☐ 7. Now open a new document. Name it librarytest.qxd.

☐ 8. Drag the items one by one from the library onto the page to create a new ad. You don't have to design the ad — you just need to get the idea as to how the library works.

Delete an item from the library

☐ 9. Click on the item and hit **delete** on the keyboard. Or under the edit menu, choose **cut**. You can also hit ⌘ **X**.

Save the library

☐ 10. To save, close the library by clicking in the left corner (Macs) and right corner (Windows) of the library palette. This saves the library. Then open it again.

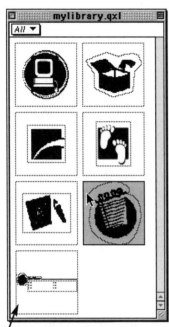

Figure 15-8. The library palette with some of the icons for this book.

This one is the *Quest Terms* used on the first page of each chapter. It's a group that comprises:
• icon
• text box with the head
• text box for the words
• line

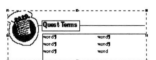

Look on page 93. For each of these documents, the standing head and headshot with caption are stored in a library and pulled over to construct the page for each issue of the publication.

Read this...

Library items are representations of the actual piece of art or original photo. The original art or photo must be on the hard drive or on your disk to be clearly read by the printer. It's the same principle as using a picture in a picture box — the actual scan or original clipart must be available.

16 Newsletter

*The beauty of regular publications is that
you can always do better next issue.*

Scott Albright
The Wit and Wisdom of PR Success

Quest Objectives

- List the characteristics that make a newsletter one
  of the most effective forms of communication.
- Describe six classifications of newsletters.
- Explain considerations for newsletter production.
- List the questions you must ask before starting the newsletter.
- Identify the elements of a newsletter.
- Defend layout decisions relating to overall design of newsletters.

Quest Skills

Produce Quark Quandary, a two-page newsletter.
- Make up style sheets.
- Set up a newsletter document using a three-column format.
- Modify one text box into multiple columns.
- Link text from page to page.
- Make bullets and hanging indents.
- Print on both sides of the paper.

Produce your own two-page newsletter.
- Create a template.
- Change style sheets.

Quest Terms

advocacy	dateline	nameplate
association	end signs	number pad
barrier rule	folio	sidebar
based on	footer	style sheets
body copy	header	subhead
byline	heads	subscription
caption	indicia	subtitle
consituency	in-house	summary deck
continuation line	kicker	table of contents
corporate external	mailing area	visual
corporate internal	masthead	
credit line	mission statement	

Anatomy of a newsletter

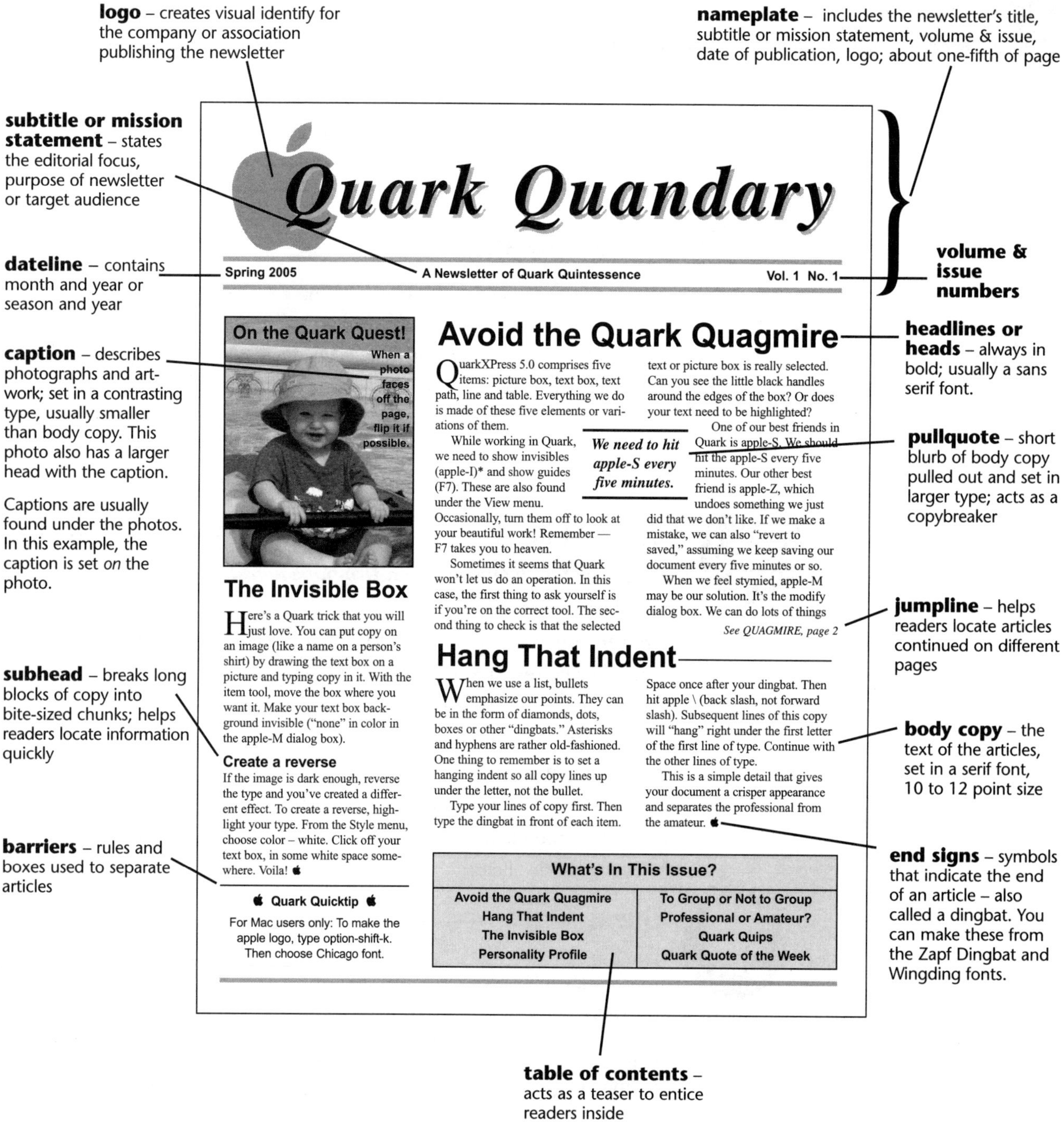

logo – creates visual identify for the company or association publishing the newsletter

nameplate – includes the newsletter's title, subtitle or mission statement, volume & issue, date of publication, logo; about one-fifth of page

subtitle or mission statement – states the editorial focus, purpose of newsletter or target audience

Quark Quandary

dateline – contains month and year or season and year

Spring 2005 — A Newsletter of Quark Quintessence — Vol. 1 No. 1

volume & issue numbers

caption – describes photographs and artwork; set in a contrasting type, usually smaller than body copy. This photo also has a larger head with the caption.

Captions are usually found under the photos. In this example, the caption is set *on* the photo.

On the Quark Quest!
When a photo faces off the page, flip it if possible.

Avoid the Quark Quagmire

QuarkXPress 5.0 comprises five items: picture box, text box, text path, line and table. Everything we do is made of these five elements or variations of them.

While working in Quark, we need to show invisibles (apple-I)* and show guides (F7). These are also found under the View menu. Occasionally, turn them off to look at your beautiful work! Remember — F7 takes you to heaven.

Sometimes it seems that Quark won't let us do an operation. In this case, the first thing to ask yourself is if you're on the correct tool. The second thing to check is that the selected

We need to hit apple-S every five minutes.

text or picture box is really selected. Can you see the little black handles around the edges of the box? Or does your text need to be highlighted?

One of our best friends in Quark is apple-S. We should hit the apple-S every five minutes. Our other best friend is apple-Z, which undoes something we just did that we don't like. If we make a mistake, we can also "revert to saved," assuming we keep saving our document every five minutes or so.

When we feel stymied, apple-M may be our solution. It's the modify dialog box. We can do lots of things

See QUAGMIRE, page 2

headlines or heads – always in bold; usually a sans serif font.

pullquote – short blurb of body copy pulled out and set in larger type; acts as a copybreaker

The Invisible Box

Here's a Quark trick that you will just love. You can put copy on an image (like a name on a person's shirt) by drawing the text box on a picture and typing copy in it. With the item tool, move the box where you want it. Make your text box background invisible ("none" in color in the apple-M dialog box).

Create a reverse

If the image is dark enough, reverse the type and you've created a different effect. To create a reverse, highlight your type. From the Style menu, choose color – white. Click off your text box, in some white space somewhere. Voila! ■

Hang That Indent

When we use a list, bullets emphasize our points. They can be in the form of diamonds, dots, boxes or other "dingbats." Asterisks and hyphens are rather old-fashioned. One thing to remember is to set a hanging indent so all copy lines up under the letter, not the bullet.

Type your lines of copy first. Then type the dingbat in front of each item.

Space once after your dingbat. Then hit apple \ (back slash, not forward slash). Subsequent lines of this copy will "hang" right under the first letter of the first line of type. Continue with the other lines of type.

This is a simple detail that gives your document a crisper appearance and separates the professional from the amateur. ■

jumpline – helps readers locate articles continued on different pages

body copy – the text of the articles, set in a serif font, 10 to 12 point size

subhead – breaks long blocks of copy into bite-sized chunks; helps readers locate information quickly

barriers – rules and boxes used to separate articles

■ **Quark Quicktip** ■
For Mac users only: To make the apple logo, type option-shift-k. Then choose Chicago font.

What's In This Issue?	
Avoid the Quark Quagmire	To Group or Not to Group
Hang That Indent	Professional or Amateur?
The Invisible Box	Quark Quips
Personality Profile	Quark Quote of the Week

end signs – symbols that indicate the end of an article – also called a dingbat. You can make these from the Zapf Dingbat and Wingding fonts.

table of contents – acts as a teaser to entice readers inside

Figure 16-1. Anatomy of a newsletter, page 1

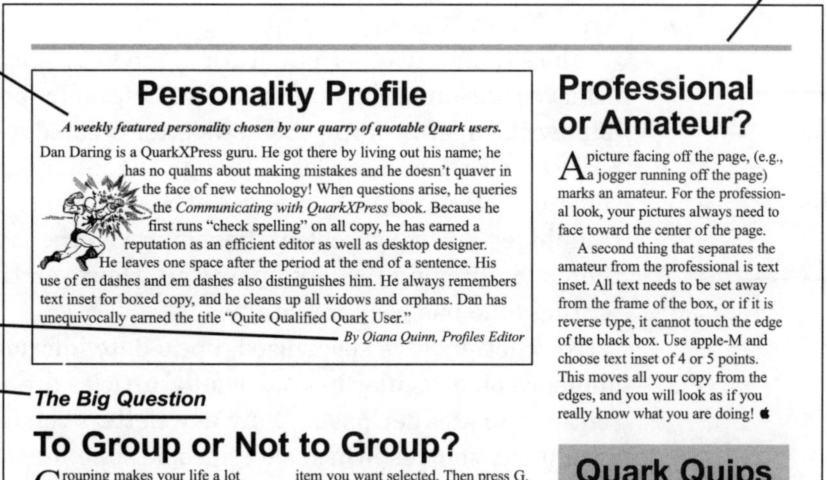

summary deck – a sentence that adds to the head and leads into the article; usually in italics or larger type than body copy

byline – identifies the author and can be placed at the start or end of an article

kicker – a small headline above the main headline; usually a rule (line) is under the kicker

continuation line – helps readers locate the continuation of an article from a previous page

visual – photo, clipart, graph, table, chart

This visual is a piece of clipart, duplicated and made in two sizes. One is flipped.

header – elements repeated at the top of each page. Can include the newsletter's title, date, page number, a rule or dingbat. (In this case, the header consists of only a rule.)

sidebar – related information that accompanies a bigger story. Often provides perspective or added detail to topics discussed in the articles. It is usually boxed or shaded.

This example is not actually a sidebar by definition, but it's the closest thing on these two pages that would look like a sidebar!

footer – information that runs across the bottom of all inside pages. Can include newsletter's title, page number, a rule or dingbat.

The first page often lacks a footer because the information is found in the name-plate.

Personality Profile

A weekly featured personality chosen by our quarry of quotable Quark users.

Dan Daring is a QuarkXPress guru. He got there by living out his name; he has no qualms about making mistakes and he doesn't quaver in the face of new technology! When questions arise, he queries the *Communicating with QuarkXPress* book. Because he first runs "check spelling" on all copy, he has earned a reputation as an efficient editor as well as desktop designer. He leaves one space after the period at the end of a sentence. His use of en dashes and em dashes also distinguishes him. He always remembers text inset for boxed copy, and he cleans up all widows and orphans. Dan has unequivocally earned the title "Quite Qualified Quark User."

By Qiana Quinn, Profiles Editor

The Big Question

To Group or Not to Group?

Grouping makes your life a lot easier. Highlight each item you want to group. You can do this in two ways. Select the item tool. Hold down the shift key and tap on each item you want. The little black handles showing means the item has been selected. Then press apple-G. Then click off somewhere outside the text box.

Or use the item tool and draw a box (actually it will be invisible — it's called a marquee) touching each item you want selected. Then press G. If you don't press apple-G, you get a temporary grouping.

To ungroup, use the item tool and tap on the grouping. It will show a dotted line around it. Then press apple-U and CLICK OFF. If you don't click off, it doesn't ungroup. ▲

QUAGMIRE, from page 1

to boxes. Some of the most common things we do with apple-M are to change background color, vertically align copy, make columns and gutters, and set text inset. ▲

* Windows users: Any time you see the word *apple* with a letter, translate it to *control*.

Quark Quote of the Week

If you can think it up, Quark can do it. You just have to find out how.

Professional or Amateur?

A picture facing off the page, (e.g., a jogger running off the page) marks an amateur. For the professional look, your pictures always need to face toward the center of the page.

A second thing that separates the amateur from the professional is text inset. All text needs to be set away from the frame of the box, or if it is reverse type, it cannot touch the edge of the black box. Use apple-M and choose text inset of 4 or 5 points. This moves all your copy from the edges, and you will look as if you really know what you are doing! ▲

Quark Quips

◆ Use NO "city" fonts (Chicago, New York, Monaco, Geneva).

◆ Never distort photos unless you have a super reason.

◆ Always check spelling.

◆ When you don't know what to do, "apple-M" might work for you!

◆ Save your document at least every five minutes.

◆ Use bold and italic type sparingly.

◆ Use serif for body copy; use sans serif for heads.

◆ Memorize the three magic keys.

◆ Use your Quark Quick Cards to help you learn shortcuts.

◆ Always make a backup copy.

Quark Quandary is published every semester by students in Publication Layout and Design classes at Rowan University in Glassboro, New Jersey.

Editor: Claudia M. Cuddy
Contact: editorcuddy@mac.com

2 ▲

masthead – usually includes the names of the editorial staff, the publisher's address, copyright information, subscription rates, phone and fax numbers, e-mail. This one is a bit limited in information. The masthead is often found on page 2 or on the back of the newsletter as part of the mailing area.

Figure 16-2. Anatomy of a newsletter, page 2

Examine Figures 16-1 and 16-2 on the previous two pages for the elements of a newsletter.

In early America, colonists often gathered in taverns or pubs to exchange news and gossip. The tavern owners collected items of interest from their patrons and wrote them in informal letter format, which they passed on to another tavern, possibly in another colony. These "letters of news" were eventually replaced by the newspaper, a more formal and larger system of publishing the news. Printers frequently kept the term "newsletter" in the title. In 1704, John Campbell printed the first regular newspaper, the *Boston News Letter*.

More than any other publication, the *newsletter* most effectively achieves one-on-one communication. Originally produced in handwritten letter form, the newsletter created a direct connection between writer and reader. Although the letter format is still used sometimes (Figure 16-3), the use of design principles, typographic techniques and copybreakers has improved the look of newsletters, thereby improving readership as well. However, the informal writing tone has been maintained.

Newsletters give specialized, up-to-date information to a target audience on a regular basis. Usually, articles are short and do not continue to another page. Many newsletters condense information from many sources, which saves people time. In addition, newsletters can be produced at low cost, which makes them a popular vehicle of information.

Bowties Inc.

From the heart of the President...

Dear Friend of Bowties, Inc.,

Si meliora dies, ut vina, poemata reddit, scire velim, chartis pretium quotus arroget annus. scriptor abhinc annos centum qui decidit, inter perfectos veteresque referri debet an inter vilis atque novos? Excludat iurgia finis, "Est vetus atque probus, centum qui perficit annos." Quid, qui deperiit minor uno mense vel anno, inter quos referendus erit? Veteresne poetas, an quos et praesens et postera respuat aetas?

Iste quidem veteres inter ponetur honeste, qui vel mense brevi vel toto est iunior anno." Utor permisso, caudaeque pilos ut equinae paulatim vello unum, demo etiam unum, dum cadat elusus ratione ruentis acervi, qui redit in fastos et virtutem aestimat annis miraturque nihil nisi quod Libitina sacravit.

Ennius et sapines et fortis et alter Homerus, ut critici dicunt, leviter curare videtur, quo promissa cadant et somnia Pythagorea. Naevius in manibus non est et mentibus haeret paene recens? Adeo sanctum est vetus omne poema. ambigitur quotiens, uter utro sit prior, aufert Pacuvius docti famam senis Accius alti, dicitur Afrani toga convenisse Menandro, Plautus ad exemplar Siculi properare Epicharmi, vincere Caecilius.

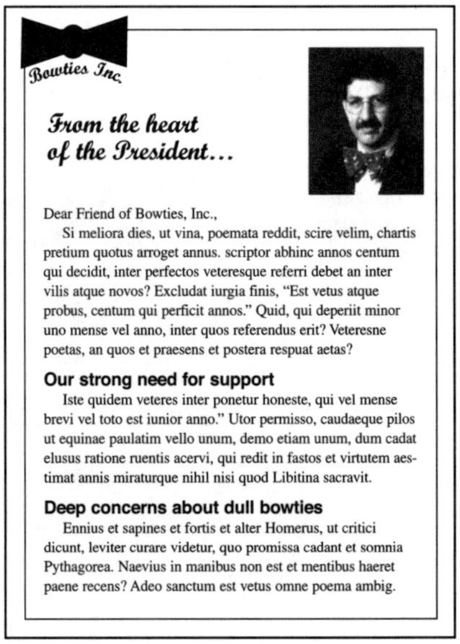
Bowties Inc.

From the heart of the President...

Dear Friend of Bowties, Inc.,

Si meliora dies, ut vina, poemata reddit, scire velim, chartis pretium quotus arroget annus. scriptor abhinc annos centum qui decidit, inter perfectos veteresque referri debet an inter vilis atque novos? Excludat iurgia finis, "Est vetus atque probus, centum qui perficit annos." Quid, qui deperiit minor uno mense vel anno, inter quos referendus erit? Veteresne poetas, an quos et praesens et postera respuat aetas?

Our strong need for support

Iste quidem veteres inter ponetur honeste, qui vel mense brevi vel toto est iunior anno." Utor permisso, caudaeque pilos ut equinae paulatim vello unum, demo etiam unum, dum cadat elusus ratione ruentis acervi, qui redit in fastos et virtutem aestimat annis miraturque nihil nisi quod Libitina sacravit.

Deep concerns about dull bowties

Ennius et sapines et fortis et alter Homerus, ut critici dicunt, leviter curare videtur, quo promissa cadant et somnia Pythagorea. Naevius in manibus non est et mentibus haeret paene recens? Adeo sanctum est vetus omne poema ambig.

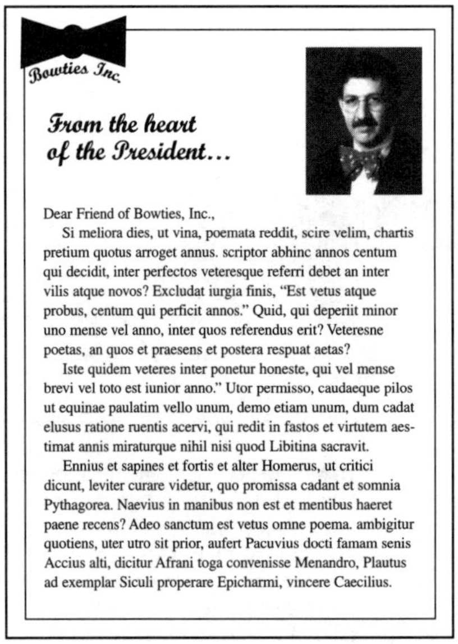

Figure 16-3. Typical "letter" style newsletter on left. The right example shows the same newsletter with subheads added. This one change increases readership.

Kinds of newsletters

Knowing something about the various newsletter categories helps you define the goals for your particular publication. Newsletters can be divided into six classifications: *corporate internal, corporate external, subscription, association, constituency* and *advocacy*.

1. Corporate internal

Newsletters circulated throughout the staff of a company, organization or faculty promote goodwill, teamwork and a sense of pride. News focuses on employees: their achievements, their goals and even their personal lives. Upcoming events in the company might be included. These newsletters are likely published *in-house* — everything is done in the company. This cuts down on expensive printing costs because newsletters are usually photocopied.

2. Corporate external

This kind of newsletter builds external support for the company or organization. It serves as a continual reminder to customers that the company's services are available. In addition, the newsletter promotes new products and new services. Articles meet the needs and interests of the target audience.

Figure 16-4. Corporate internal newsletters help employees connect with each other. College of Communication faculty at Rowan University receive this newsletter.

This newsletter from Anthony J. Jannetti, Inc. (Pitman, NJ) is sent out quarterly to clients. It contains updates on associations as well as tips for better management.

This newsletter follows the tradition of the original newsletters — it depicts an actual letter from the CEO, along with his headshot. Notice the eye-catching nameplate with reverse type down the side.

Figure 16-5. Corporate external newsletters keep the company's name out there and bring news to customers on products and services.

3. Subscription

This classification includes specialized information not found anywhere else. Subscribers pay to receive current information to stay educated and up-to-date in their specialty. Because these newsletters usually do not include advertising, the yearly subscription price tends to be higher than a journal or magazine. Therefore, subscribers expect quality information presented in easy-to-read articles that will save them time.

Figure 16-6. Subscription newsletters provide information to readers who want current, concise information on a particular subject. Note the simple three-column and four-column formats. *The Editorial Eye* uses a narrow left column as its table of contents and lots of white space. *Design Tools Monthly* adds thin rules between columns. Icons with heads create a lively effect. *Communication Briefings* uses the 1-2 pattern of columns with articles in modules, or chunks. Notice a similarity to the *Quark Quandary* (page 224). This layout was its model.

Subscription information for these newsletters on page 280.

4. Association

Association newsletters are published to maintain enthusiasm and communication among existing members and supporters. Members usually receive the newsletter as a benefit of membership — a portion of their dues supports the newsletter. Articles cover members' achievements, past and upcoming association events, related up-to-date discoveries or information germane to the specialty of the members. For example, a newsletter for orthopedic nurses might include an article reporting the results of a recent study on osteoporosis in men. Occasionally the association will mail sample newsletters to an additional list to solicit new members.

Figure 16-7. Association newsletters target members and supporters.

Figure 16-8. Constituency newsletters communicate with a common interest group.

5. Constituency

This kind of newsletter communicates with a common interest group to influence its readership and foster a sense of community. For example, a local hospital sends out a newsletter on a health topic, an elected official sends out updates to his voting constituency, a school sends its monthly newsletter or a university reaches out to alumni on a regular basis. The audience is a limited target audience. Sometimes requests are made for donations, time or money. In any case, the goal of the constituency newsletter is to create a sense of belonging and to be a continual reminder of the sender's existence.

6. Advocacy

Advocacy newsletters usually focus on a single topic and claim to be unapologetically biased. These newsletters might purport environmental concerns or the importance of not smoking. They are often put out by a corporation, an association or a politician. An advocacy newsletter differs from the others by its strong point of view.

Qool Fact

A single-topic newsletter might contain one long article with subheads. Use of copy-breakers becomes a necessity to keep the reader interested.

Qool Fact

The U.S. government is continually criticized for not being able to write in plain English. Therefore, hundreds of newsletters are published in our nation's capital to interpret policies, programs, decisions and projects to the public. Newsletter editors try to simplify government jargon so the "common folk" understand. As a result, Washington, D.C., is called the *cradle of newsletters*.

Figure 16-9. Advocacy newsletters originate from groups with specific purposes and agendas. NO D.I.C.E. (No Dumps in Clean Environments) was a local grassroots group mobilized to fight against a possible toxic waste dump. The NJPIRG (New Jersey Public Interest Research Group) champions a clean environment. This group has chapters nationwide.

Considerations for newsletter production

S-V-O Format

Active voice communicates more clearly and quickly than the passive voice. American brains think in the active format: **subject-verb-object** (S-V-O). When we hear or read something in the passive format, we have to first translate it to our comfortable mode, the S-V-O mode. Rather than making a reader go through that process each time with a passive verb, choose the active version instead — most of the time.

Passive voice
Many deadlines were missed by the feature writers.

Active voice
The feature writers missed many deadlines.

Writing

Although the writing in a newsletter can be informal and friendly, it should be accurate, concise and clear. Keep sentences short and to the point. Write most of your sentences in the active mode: subject–verb–object format (see sidebar). Make paragraphs short. Use lots of bullets and informative headlines. Prefer simple words to complex.

Consistency

Your readers should recognize your newsletter at first glance. Repetition of design elements creates consistency from issue to issue, leading to a sense of identity. Use the same paper, colors, nameplate, column headings, fonts and general layout every issue. Place the masthead in the same location each time, and if you run items such as a monthly calendar, keep them in a consistent spot.

Deadlines

The most difficult and most essential task in newsletter production is meeting deadlines. Because newsletters usually contain timely information, they need to meet their publication date. When working with newsletter contributors (who are often volunteers), be clear about the deadlines, and have a backup plan if one of the writers doesn't come through.

Distribution

If your newsletter is mailed, keep up with the ever-changing postal regulations. If applicable, be sure the *indicia* (postage stamp area) is correct. If your newsletter is a self-mailer, plan articles accordingly to fit above and below the folds for grabbing a potential reader while the newsletter is still folded. The fold should be at the bottom of the address panel so the newsletter runs through the sorting machines the most efficiently (Figure 16-10). Otherwise, you may have to pay a higher rate.

Figure 16-10. Mailing information at top of page, with fold at the halfway mark on the page. Folded in half, this newsletter becomes a self-mailer that can be run through postal machines efficiently. The top picture shows the newsletter in its full form, while the figure to the right shows the same newsletter folded.

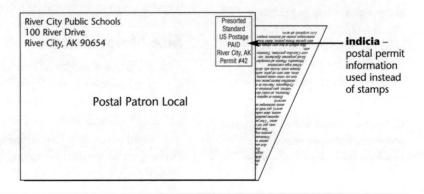

indicia – postal permit information used instead of stamps

Quicktip

Limit your newsletter to two fonts: a serif for body copy and a sans serif for heads.

If you use a serif for heads as well, use the same font as for body copy, but make heads larger and bold.

Qool Fact

One-page newsletters

In his recent venture, *Guerrilla Marketing & Design*, Roger Parker presents the *one-page newsletter*. He describes this as a monthly newsletter printed on both sides of a single sheet of paper, intended for both print and online distribution.

The one-page newsletter serves as a tremendous marketing tool because it:

• is economical in printing costs

• promises readers a "quick read"

• projects a professional image as it maintains your visibility

Roger Parker is one of the leading experts on writing and publishing effective publications. He has been my mentor through his books (see Chapter 19), Web sites, teleconferences and newsletters.

Check out Parker's site: **www.newentrepreneur.com**

Planning the newsletter

Several questions need to be answered before producing a newsletter. Some of the main questions include those listed below.

1. Who is the audience?
2. What is the message and purpose?
3. How does the newsletter reflect the company or organization? Will we use the same logo, colors, type?
4. What is the timeline for the project?
5. What is the budget? Is this black and white, spot color or four-color process?
6. What kind of paper will we use? Size of finished newsletter? How many copies?
7. Who will do the tasks involved? Am I chief writer, editor, layout person and proofreader? Do I have help? Who signs off on the final proof?
8. Will we use in-house printing or a commercial printer?

Layout decisions

Overall design

Design is governed by the level of interest of the audience. If the audience has a low level of interest, include large type and lots of white space. If the audience has a high level of interest, articles can be longer and more in-depth. *See Chapter 1 for more explanation on interest level and design.*

In most cases, the newsletter shouldn't look too expensive, but the design must be effective enough to attract readers or they will disregard the newsletter as junk mail. Remember to include elements to follow the 30–3–30 rule *(Chapter 8)*. Include photos, bold heads, sidebars and pullquotes to grab the reader.

Layout guidelines for type, color and art are the same as those described in the earlier chapters in this book. Two fonts work well: a serif font for body copy and a bold sans serif for contrasting heads. Type size ranges from 10-point to 12-point in most cases.

Size of newsletters

Typical page lengths of newsletters are four pages and eight pages, although some newsletters become almost like minimagazines because they contain 20 or more pages. A common page size is 11" x 17" folded once to become 8½" x 11". A six-page newsletter is also common. This would be an 11" x 25.5" folded twice into a three-panel format. Since most office laser printers do not take paper that large, you would need to go to a commercial printer.

Columns

Although a two-column grid is easy to handle, it tends to be dull. Beginners can produce a more professional-looking piece using three columns. Check *Chapter 3: Construct the Page* to examine the various column formats. You will work with a three-column format for the *Quark Quandary* assignment.

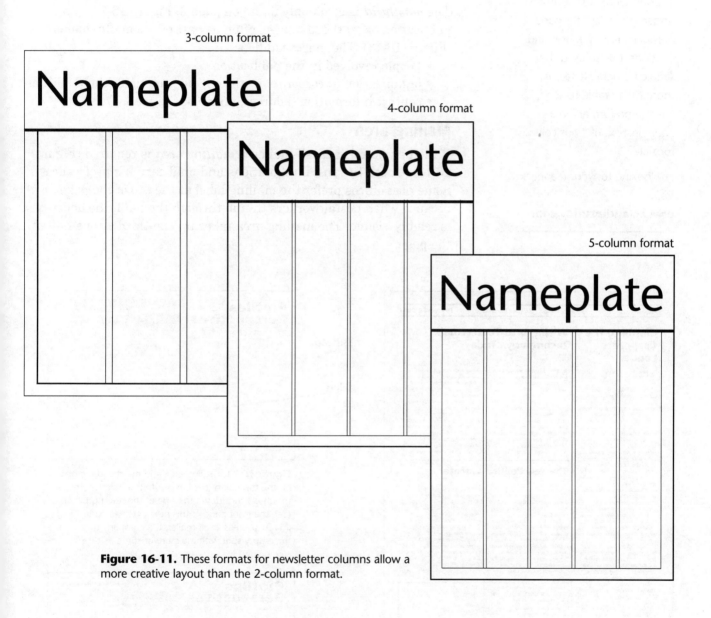

Figure 16-11. These formats for newsletter columns allow a more creative layout than the 2-column format.

Trio to remember

The masthead, mailing area and nameplate need special attention because of the important information found there. Careful layout decisions enhance the communication value of these areas.

Masthead

The *masthead* is commonly found on page 2 (Figure 16-12) of a publication or on the last page, often as part of the mailing label (Figure 16-13). The masthead lists:

- people involved in the publication
- organization or corporation officers and sometimes the publisher
- contact information (address, phone, fax, e-mail, Web site)

Mailing area

If the newsletter is a self-mailer, a *mailing area* is required (Figure 16-13). Check the postal regulations and mail carrier's preferences. Some post offices prefer the mailing label at the top of the page because when postal workers thumb through the mail, the address is readily visible. The mailing area takes up one-third or one-half of the page.

Figure 16-12. The masthead falls on page 2 every issue of this newsletter.

masthead

mailing area

Figure 16-13. Mailing area and masthead are placed on the top half of the back of this newsletter. The masthead runs down the side of the mailing panel. (See the front page of this newsletter on page 211.) If NOT used as a self-mailer, the company might fill the empty spot with a picture or some feature (see below).

Qool Fact

Volume and Number?

"Volume" indicates the year of publication. If a newsletter is in its fifth year, it would be Volume 5.

"Number" or "issue" denotes which issue of that volume year. If you produce four newsletters per year, the first one of that year would be Number 1 or Issue 1.

In the nameplate:

Volume 5 Number 1

or abbreviated:

Vol. 5 No. 1

Nameplate

The most important design element on the newsletter is the nameplate. This is also called a banner or a flag, but it is NOT the same as the masthead. The nameplate creates a visual identity for the newsletter and conveys the attitude of the newsletter. For example, it could be dignified, serious, humorous, corporate, fun, old-fashioned or contemporary depending on the audience.

Anatomy of the nameplate. The name of the publication needs to be as large as possible. Elements of the nameplate include name of newsletter, subtitle or mission statement (statement of purpose), date, volume number and issue number. The organization's name and logo can be included as well. Additional artwork enhances the logo and portrays the theme. Figure 16-14 shows a typical nameplate. Figures 16-15 through 16-20 show various examples.

Nameplates can be stretched across the top of the newsletter, taking up about one-fifth to one-fourth of the page. To create a different look, place it down the left side of the page. A *barrier rule* under the nameplate separates it from the heads and body copy.

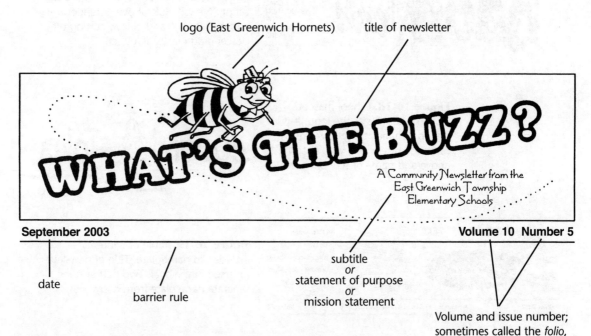

Figure 16-14. Typical nameplate of a newsletter. This one extends almost 2¼" (16 picas) from the top of the page, which equals one-quarter of the page. The reporter hornet* (logo) flies over the title, with the mission statement under and to the right. The flight pattern (dotted line) connects everything. Rules, with dateline and folio information in between, separate nameplate from body copy.

* The hornet has a reporter's pass in its visor and a pad and pencil in its "hands."

Nameplate examples

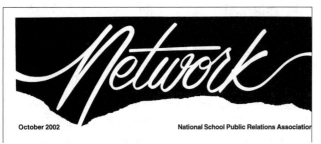

Figure 16-15. Solid teal green background with a torn-off effect. Simple script title reversed with dateline and name of organization below.

Figure 16-16. Shaded, staggered boxes create a modern look. (The original uses rust and blue.) Dateline and rule above. Good choice of font for the tone of the newsletter.

Figure 16-17. Embossed NAON (logotype of association) overlapped by script "News." Rule above, intentionally cutting off "N," and below, cutting off descending pieces of letters.

Figure 16-18. School mascot, leopard, doubles as the logo. It is placed between the title words. A rule stretches across, with dateline above and name of school below.

Figure 16-19. Table of contents included in nameplate. Title of newsletter reversed in the oval. Two barrier rules separate nameplate from copy.

Figure 16-20. Another version of the table of contents in the nameplate. Large page numbers with subject of article tease the reader.

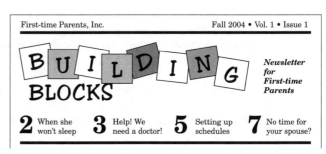

Quick Quiz

1. Why is the newsletter one of the most effective forms of communication?

2. What are the six kinds of newsletters?

3. Give six writing tips for effective newsletters.

4. Explain the importance of consistency in newsletter production.

5. What questions need to be answered before starting your newsletter?

6. What are some of the decisions to make regarding overall design, size of newsletters and columns?

7. Identify and define the elements that make up the "anatomy of a newsletter."

Out of the Quandary

1. Elements

Using a newsletter, label as many elements of its pages as you can.

2. Collection

Collect newsletter samples for your files. Find various column grids.

3. Redesign

Redesign a weak, outdated nameplate.

4. Evaluation

Evaluate the effectiveness of the layout of a newsletter given to you by the instructor. Make a list of the strong points and the weak points.

5. Quark Quandary

Refer to pages 223–245 for the capstone project of this book: *Quark Quandary*. This project incorporates almost every Quark skill you will need. You have already practiced most of the skills, and you will find extremely detailed instructions.

6. Your Own Newsletter

Refer to pages 246–251 for a follow-up newsletter project. This is a two-page newsletter patterned after the *Quark Quandary*, although you may deviate from the style. You will make a template, change style sheets and add a color to this project.

Your best newsletter reader survey instrument is the big wastebasket next to the mailboxes.

Dave Smoker
The Wit and Wisdom
of PR Success

Quantum Leap

Get the **apple.tif** from the CD:
Chapter 16/Newsletter:
Quark Quandary

Reproduce the nameplate below, using two picture boxes (apple and shaded box) and five text boxes. Apply **None** runaround to all the boxes. When necessary, use **Bring to front** and **Send to back** options found under the **Item** menu. The apple logo is found as a tiff file on the CD. New operation: horizontal and vertical scaling, found under the **Style** menu.

Registration
update
Fall 2004

Vol. 8
No. 4

For Graduate Students of Apple University

Clues: "update" is set with vertical scale 120%
"Fall 2004" is set with horizontal scale 105%
"For Graduate Students..." is horizontally scaled 105%
Fonts used: Arial, Arial Black, Times New Roman

Quark Quest

Quark Quest contains two newsletter projects that require many tasks.

pages 224-245

1 The first is the *Quark Quandary* newsletter. This two-page (front and back) newsletter encompasses almost every skill and operation you will need to use in QuarkXPress projects. Follow instructions carefully to reproduce the newsletter found on pages 224-225. The newsletter prototype is slightly smaller than the one you will do.

pages 246-251

2 The second project is your own newsletter, also a two-page project. This project is more flexible than *Quark Quandary*. It will be a topic of your choice. Layout is based on a template made from *Quark Quandary*. See page 249 for instructions.

Windows users: Whenever you see the word *apple* with a letter, translate it to *control*. For example, translate *apple-M* to *control-M*.

Raw copy for Quark Quandary

You'll find the copy below on the CD in the *Chapter16/Newsletter: Quark Quandary* folder — *rawcopy.qxd*. It is set in Arial. **Copy** and **paste** the copy below in a box on the pasteboard alongside your document. **Select all** and assign **No Style** from the style sheets.

Avoid the Quark Quagmire

QuarkXPress 5.0 comprises five items: picture box, text box, text path, line and table. Everything we do is made of these five elements or variations of them.

While working in Quark, we need to show invisibles (apple-I)* and show guides (F7). These are also found under the View menu. Occasionally, turn them off to look at your beautiful work! Remember — F7 takes you to heaven.

Sometimes it seems that Quark won't let us do an operation. In this case, the first thing to ask yourself is if you're on the correct tool. The second thing to check is that the selected text or picture box is really selected. Can you see the little black handles around the edges of the box? Or does your text need to be highlighted?

One of our best friends in Quark is apple-S. We should hit the apple-S every five minutes. Our other best friend is apple-Z, which undoes something we just did that we don't like. If we make a mistake, we can also "revert to saved," assuming we keep saving our document every five minutes or so.

When we feel stymied, apple-M may be our solution. It's the modify dialog box. We can do lots of things to boxes. Some of the most common things we do with apple-M are to change background color, vertically align copy, set text inset and make columns and gutters.

* Windows users: Any time you see the word *apple* with a letter, translate it to *control*.

The Invisible Box

Here's a Quark trick that you will just love. You can put copy on an image (like a name on a person's shirt) by drawing the text box on a picture and typing copy in it. With the item tool, move the box where you want it. Make your text box background invisible ("none" in color in the apple-M dialog box).

Create a reverse

If the image is dark enough, reverse the type and you've created a different effect. To create a reverse, highlight your type. From the Style menu, choose color – white. Click off your text box, in some white space somewhere. Voila!

Hang That Indent

When we use a list, bullets emphasize our points. They can be in the form of diamonds, dots, boxes or other "dingbats." Asterisks and hyphens are rather old-fashioned. One thing to remember is to set a hanging indent so all copy lines up under the letter, not the bullet.

Type your lines of copy first. Then type the dingbat in front of each item. Space once after your dingbat. Then hit apple \ (back slash, not forward slash). Subsequent lines of this copy will "hang" right under the first letter of the first line of type. Continue with the other lines of copy.

This is a simple detail that gives your document a crisper appearance and separates the professional from the amateur.

What's In This Issue?

Avoid the Quark Quagmire
Hang That Indent
The Invisible Box
Personality Profile
To Group or Not to Group
Professional or Amateur?
Quark Quips
Quark Quote of the Week

Quark Quicktip

For Mac users only: To make the apple logo, type option-shift-k. Then choose Chicago font.

Personality Profile

A weekly featured personality chosen by our quarry of quotable Quark users.

Dan Daring became a QuarkXPress guru by living out his name; he has no qualms about making mistakes, and he doesn't quaver in the face of new technology! When questions arise, he queries the Communicating with QuarkXPress book. Because he first runs "check spelling" on all copy, he has earned a reputation as an efficient editor as well as desktop designer. He leaves one space after the period at the end of a sentence. His use of en dashes and em dashes also distinguishes him. He always remembers text inset for boxed copy, and he cleans up all widows and orphans. Dan has unequivocally earned the title "Quite Qualified Quark User."

By Qiana Quinn, Profiles Editor

Professional or Amateur?

A picture facing off the page, (e.g., a jogger running off the page) marks an amateur. For the professional look, your pictures always need to face toward the center of the page.

A second thing that separates the amateur from the professional is text inset. All text needs to be set away from the frame of the box, or if it is reverse type, it cannot touch the edge of the black box. Use apple-M and choose text inset of 4 or 5 points. This moves all your copy from the edges, and you will look as if you really know what you are doing!

The Big Question
To Group or Not to Group?

Grouping makes your life a lot easier. Highlight each item you want to group. You can do this in two ways. Select the item tool. Hold down the shift key and tap on each item you want. The little black handles mean the item has been selected. Then press apple-G. Then click off somewhere outside the text box.

Or use the item tool and draw a box (actually it will be invisible — it's called a marquee) touching each item you want selected. Then press apple-G. If you don't press apple-G, you get a temporary grouping.

To ungroup, use the item tool and tap on the grouping. It will show a dotted line around it. Then press apple-U and CLICK OFF. If you don't click off, it doesn't ungroup.

Quark Quips

Use NO "city" fonts (Chicago, New York, Monaco, Geneva).
Never distort photos unless you have a super reason.
Always check spelling.
When you don't know what to do, "apple-M" might work for you!
Save your document at least every five minutes.
Use bold and italic type sparingly.
Use serif for body copy; use sans serif for heads.
Memorize the three magic keys.
Use your Quark Quick Cards to help you learn shortcuts.
Always make a backup copy.

Quark Quandary is published every semester by students in Publication Layout and Design classes at Your University in City, State.
Editor: Your name
Contact: Your e-mail or fake one

This is no

Quark Quandary

Fall 2005   A Newsletter of Quark Quintessence   Vol. 1 No. 1

On the Quark Quest!

When a photo faces off the page, flip it if possible.

Jack

The Invisible Box

Here's a Quark trick that you will just love. You can put copy on an image (like a name on a person's shirt) by drawing the text box on a picture and typing copy in it. With the item tool, move the box where you want it. Make your text box background invisible ("none" in color in the apple-M dialog box).

Create a reverse

If the image is dark enough, reverse the type and you've created a different effect. To create a reverse, highlight your type. From the Style menu, choose color – white. Click off your text box, in some white space somewhere. Voila!

■ Quark Quicktip ■

For Mac users only: To make the apple logo, type option-shift-k. Then choose Chicago font.

Avoid the Quark Quagmire

QuarkXPress 5.0 comprises five items: picture box, text box, text path, line and table. Everything we do is made of these five elements or variations of them.

While working in Quark, we need to show invisibles (apple-I)* and show guides (F7). These are also found under the View menu. Occasionally, turn them off to look at your beautiful work! Remember — F7 takes you to heaven.

Sometimes it seems that Quark won't let us do an operation. In this case, the first thing to ask yourself is if you're on the correct tool. The second thing to check is that the selected text or picture box is really selected. Can you see the little black handles around the edges of the box? Or does your text need to be highlighted?

We need to hit apple-S every five minutes.

One of our best friends in Quark is apple-S. We should hit the apple-S every five minutes. Our other best friend is apple-Z, which undoes something we just did that we don't like. If we make a mistake, we can also "revert to saved," assuming we keep saving our document every five minutes or so.

When we feel stymied, apple-M may be our solution. It's the modify dialog box. We can do lots of things

See QUAGMIRE, page 2

Hang That Indent

When we use a list, bullets emphasize our points. They can be in the form of diamonds, dots, boxes or other "dingbats." Asterisks and hyphens are rather old-fashioned. One thing to remember is to set a hanging indent so all copy lines up under the letter, not the bullet.

Type your lines of copy first. Then type the dingbat in front of each item.

Space once after your dingbat. Then hit apple \ (back slash, not forward slash). Subsequent lines of this copy will "hang" right under the first letter of the first line of type. Continue with the other lines of type.

This is a simple detail that gives your document a crisper appearance and separates the professional from the amateur.

What's In This Issue?

Avoid the Quark Quagmire	To Group or Not to Group
Hang That Indent	Professional or Amateur?
The Invisible Box	Quark Quips
Personality Profile	Quark Quote of the Week

Personality Profile

A weekly featured personality chosen by our quarry of quotable Quark users.

Dan Daring became a QuarkXPress guru by living out his name; he has no qualms about making mistakes, and he doesn't quaver in the face of new technology! When questions arise, he queries the *Communicating with QuarkXPress* book. Because he first runs "check spelling" on all copy, he has earned a reputation as an efficient editor as well as desktop designer. He leaves one space after the period at the end of a sentence. His use of en dashes and em dashes also distinguishes him. He always remembers text inset for boxed copy, and he cleans up all widows and orphans. Dan has unequivocally earned the title "Quite Qualified Quark User."

By Qiana Quinn, Profiles Editor

The Big Question

To Group or Not to Group?

Grouping makes your life a lot easier. Highlight each item you want to group. You can do this in two ways. Select the item tool. Hold down the shift key and tap on each item you want. The little black handles mean the item has been selected. Then press apple-G. Then click off somewhere outside the text box.

Or use the item tool and draw a box (actually it will be invisible — it's called a marquee) touching each item you want selected. Then press apple-G. If you don't press apple-G, you get a temporary grouping.

To ungroup, use the item tool and tap on the grouping. It will show a dotted line around it. Then press apple-U and CLICK OFF. If you don't click off, it doesn't ungroup. ⌘

QUAGMIRE, from page 1

to boxes. Some of the most common things we do with apple-M are to change background color, vertically align copy, set text inset and make columns and gutters. ⌘

* Windows users: Any time you see the word *apple* with a letter, translate it to *control*.

Quark Quote of the Week

If you can think it up, Quark can do it. You just have to find out how.

Professional or Amateur?

A picture facing off the page, (e.g., a jogger running off the page) marks an amateur. For the professional look, your pictures always need to face toward the center of the page.

A second thing that separates the amateur from the professional is text inset. All text needs to be set away from the frame of the box, or if it is reverse type, it cannot touch the edge of the black box. Use apple-M and choose text inset of 4 or 5 points. This moves all your copy from the edges, and you will look as if you really know what you are doing! ⌘

Quark Quips

◆ Use NO "city" fonts (Chicago, New York, Monaco, Geneva).

◆ Never distort photos unless you have a super reason.

◆ Always check spelling.

◆ When you don't know what to do, "apple-M" might work for you!

◆ Save your document at least every five minutes.

◆ Use bold and italic type sparingly.

◆ Use serif for body copy; use sans serif for heads.

◆ Memorize the three magic keys.

◆ Use your Quark Quick Cards to help you learn shortcuts.

◆ Always make a backup copy.

Quark Quandary is published every semester by students in Publication Layout and Design classes at Rowan University in Glassboro, New Jersey.

Editor: Claudia M. Cuddy
Contact: editorcuddy@mac.com

Quark Quest

Insert page ▶

Grids at   2p
               12p
               14p
               16p
Page 2:   4p6

F11 key shows style sheets.

Document Specs and First Steps

☐ 1. Copy the *Quark Quandary* folder from the CD onto your disk.

☐ 2. Open a new document. Document specifications:

    ☐ page – 8.5" x 11"

    ☐ margins – 3 picas

    ☐ columns – 3

    ☐ gutter – 1p6

    ☐ Auto text box – NO checkmark

    ☐ Facing pages – NO checkmark

☐ 3. **Save**: *YourNameQuandary.qxd* (type your name). Save it to your Quark Quandary folder on your disk.

☐ 4. Under the **Page** menu, **Insert** one page after page 1. Your document now has two pages.

5. Grids:
    ☐ **Page 1**. Pull down your green grid lines to the measurements **2p, 12p, 14p, 16p.** Use your measurements bar to see if you are at the right place. Sometimes you need to enlarge the screen to make it work better (use your magnifier).

    ☐ **Page 2**. Pull down a grid to **4p6**.

☐ 6. Draw a big text box on the pasteboard next to page 1.

☐ 7. Open the *rawcopy.qxd* document. **Select all** in the big box. **Copy**. **Paste** the text into the big text box next to page 1 of your document. It won't all fit. Don't worry about that. You will be cutting and pasting individual articles from this large text box to the smaller ones on your newsletter. Close the *rawcopy.qxd* document. You won't need this again unless you lose some copy.

☐ 8. **Save**.

☐ 9. Show style sheets palette (**F11**) or **View → Show style sheets**.

☐ 10. **Select all** (⌘ **A**) of the copy in your newly pasted text box. On the style sheets palette, click on the first one, **No Style**. This "cleanses" the copy, and it is now ready to stylize.

☐ 11. **Save**.

☐ 12. Make up style sheets with your teacher. The type specifications (specs) list appears on the next page. Detailed instructions to make the style sheets follow on several pages. If you understand what you are doing, move ahead. Pay attention to the details.

[Style Sheets palette: No Style, Normal; No Style, Normal]

Type Specs

Detailed instructions follow on the next few pages.
Start on page 228, and then refer to this page as needed.

Character style sheets

Bottom part of style palette

First one: **Call it "Dingbat"**
Zapf Dingbat font
10 point

Second one: **Call it "Wingding"**
Wingdings font
10 point

Third one: **Call it "Italics"**
Times New Roman italic
11 point

Fourth one: **Call it "Bold"**
Times New Roman bold
11 point

Fifth one: **(for Mac users only)***
Call it "Chicago apple"
Chicago font
10 point

---

* For some reason, the printers don't print the apple
logo in the Times font, but Chicago fonts works. So
just type the logo (option-apple-k), highlight it and
apply the Chicago character style sheet to it each time.
This works only on Macs.

Note:

If you don't have these fonts on your
computers, substitute fonts as per
your instructor.

Paragraph style sheets

Top part of style palette

1/Body, no indent
Keyboard equiv: ⌘ number pad 1
Edit: 11-point Times, plain, -2 tracking
Format: 13-point leading
Left alignment

2/Body, space before, no indent
Keyboard equiv: ⌘ number pad 2
Based on: 1/Body, no indent
New spec to set: Format: Space before: p5

3/Body, indent
Keyboard equiv: ⌘ number pad 3
Based on: 1/Body, no indent
New spec to set: Format: First line indent: 1p2

4/Drop cap
Keyboard equiv: ⌘ number pad 4
Based on: 1/Body, no indent
New spec to set: Format: Check the Drop Cap box:
1 character, 2 lines

5/Jumpline/byline
Keyboard equiv: ⌘ number pad 5
Based on: 1/Body, no indent
Edit: 10-point, Italic
Format: Right alignment

6/Heads
Keyboard equiv: ⌘ number pad 6
Based on: No style
Edit: 24-point Arial, bold, -2 tracking
Formats: 25-point leading
Space after: p4 (that's 4 points)
Left alignment

7/Subheads
Keyboard equiv: ⌘ number pad 7
Based on: No style
Edit: 13-point Arial, bold, -2 tracking
Formats: 15-point leading
Space before: p5 (that's 5 points)
Left alignment

"Number pad" refers
to the little square
set of numbered
keys on the right
of your keyboard.

Two kinds of style sheets

Paragraph style sheets allow you to change an entire paragraph. Click anywhere in the paragraph and then click on your style sheet selection. The whole paragraph changes.

What is a paragraph?

All the words before a paragraph return. It could be a few words, one line of type or many lines of type. Whenever the paragraph symbol (¶) appears, a paragraph has ended.

Character style sheets allow you to stylize specific parts of a paragraph, such as one word. For example, if you want to put the name of a newspaper in italics every time you use it, you can make up a character style sheet for italics. When you use the word, just highlight the word, click on the "Italics" character style sheet and watch your word turn into italics. The magic of this is that the rest of the paragraph remains untouched.

Making character style sheets

☐ 1. Open a Quark document. In this case, you are using the one you named *yournameQuandary.qxd*.

☐ 2. Show style sheets (**View → Show style sheets** or **F11** key).

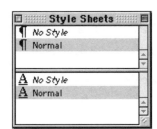

You will make up five character style sheets: *Zapf Dingbat*, *Wingding*, *Italics*, *Bold* and *Chicago apple*.

You are making up *Dingbat* and *Wingding* style sheets because it's easier to click on the style sheet palette than to scroll all the way down the font list.

The third character style is *Italics*. When you see a title of a book or want to emphasize a word, use the *Italics* style sheet to stylize the word(s). The same goes for the fourth character sheet, *Bold*.

☐ 3. Under **Edit** menu, select **Style sheets**.

To make a character style sheet

☐ 4. Choose **New**.

☐ 5. Select **Character**.

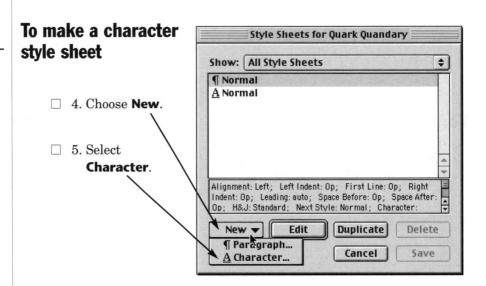

□ 6. Name the style sheet **Zapf Dingbat**.

□ 7. Font: **Zapf Dingbat**.

□ 8. Size: 10 point.

□ 9. Click **OK**.

Be sure "Plain" is checked under Type Style, as well as 100%, 0, and 0 in the three choices to the right.

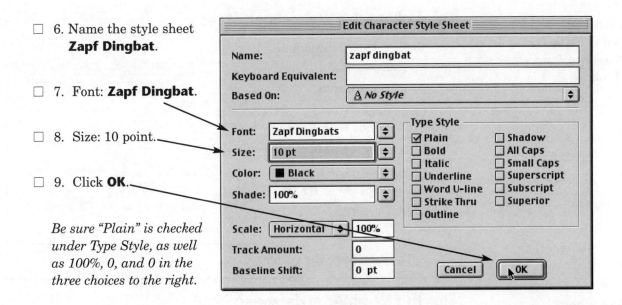

First one:

Call it "Dingbat"
Zapf Dingbat font
10 point

□ 10. Click on **Save**.

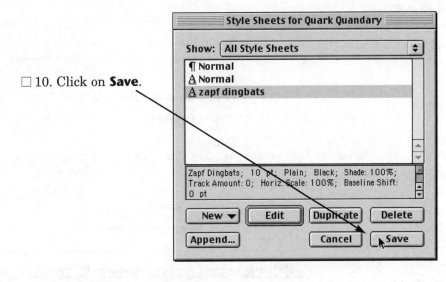

□ 11. Then **Save** the document.

Second one:

Call it "Wingding"
Wingdings font
10 point

Second character style sheet: Wingding

Repeat steps 3 through 5.

□ 6. Name the style sheet **Wingding**.

□ 7. Font: **Wingdings**.

□ 8. Size: **10 point**.

□ 9. Click **OK**.

□ 10. Click on **Save**.

□ 11. Then **Save** the document.

Third one:
Call it "Italics"
Times New Roman italic
11 point

Fourth one:
Call it "Bold"
Times New Roman bold
11 point

Fifth one:
(for Mac users only)*
Call it "Chicago apple"
Chicago font
10 point

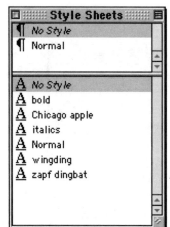

Third character style sheet: Italics

Repeat steps 3 through 5.

- ☐ 6. Name the style sheet **Italics**.
- ☐ 7. Font: **Times New Roman**.
- ☐ 8. Size: **11 point**.
- ☐ 9. *New direction:* Type Style: **Italics**.
- ☐ 10. Click **OK**.
- ☐ 11. Click on **Save**.
- ☐ 12. Then **Save** the document.

Fourth character style sheet: Bold

Repeat steps 3 through 5.

- ☐ 6. Name the style sheet **Bold**.
- ☐ 7. Font: **Times New Roman**.
- ☐ 8. Size: **11 point**.
- ☐ 9. *New direction:* Type Style: **Bold**.
- ☐ 10. Click **OK**.
- ☐ 11. Click on **Save**.
- ☐ 12. Then **Save** the document.

Fifth character style sheet: Chicago apple

Repeat steps 3 through 5.

- ☐ 6. Name the style sheet **Chicago apple**.
- ☐ 7. Font: **Chicago**.
- ☐ 8. Size: **10 point**.
- ☐ 9. Click **OK**.
- ☐ 10. Click on **Save**.
- ☐ 11. Then **Save** the document.

This is what your style sheets palette now looks like.

Making paragraph style sheets

Assumptions:

- Your *Quark Quandary* document is already open.
- Style sheets are showing (**View → Show style sheets** or **F11** key).

1/Body, no indent

1/Body, no indent

Keyboard equivalent:
⌘ number pad 1

Edit: 11-point Times, plain,
-2 tracking

Format: 13-point leading
Left alignment

☐ 1. Under **Edit** menu,
select **Style sheets**.

☐ 2. Choose **Paragraph**.

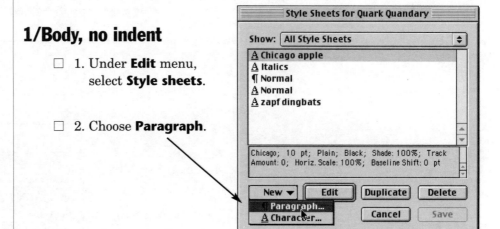

☐ 3. Name it
1/Body no indent.

☐ 4. Keyboard equivalent:
⌘ **number pad 1**.

What does *number pad* mean?

If you look to the right of your keyboard, you will see a group of keys in an arrangement like a calculator. This is in contrast to the keyboard numbers, which are found above the letters on the keyboard.

The number pad is also called the *numeric keypad,* or just *keypad.*

☐ 5. Click on **Edit**.
We are going to
choose a font
and choose its
attributes.

☐ 6. Font: **Times
New Roman**.

☐ 7. Size: **11 point**.

☐ 8. Tracking: **-2**.

☐ 9. Click **OK**.

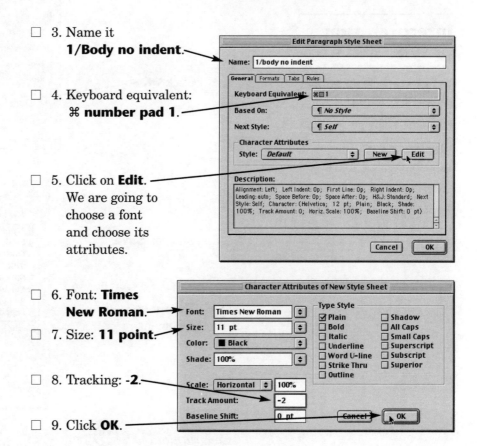

☐ 10. Choose the
  Formats tab.

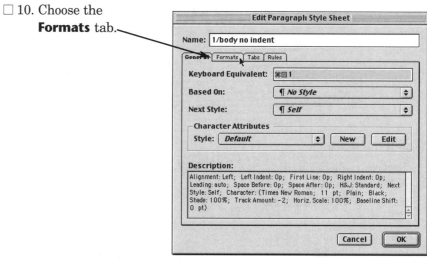

☐ 11. Leading: **13 point.**

☐ 12. Alignment: **Left.**

Interpretation of type specs

11/13 Times New Roman plain, -2 tracking

Font size: 11 point

Leading: 13 point

Font: Times New Roman

Style: Plain

Tracking: -2

☐ 13. Click **OK**.

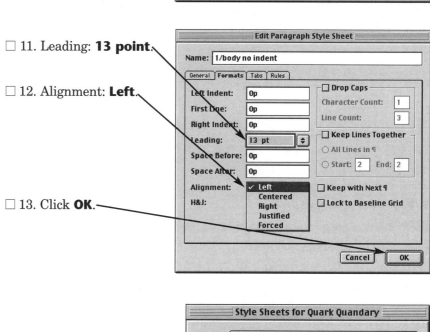

☐ 14. Click on **Save**.

☐ 15. Then **save** your
  document.

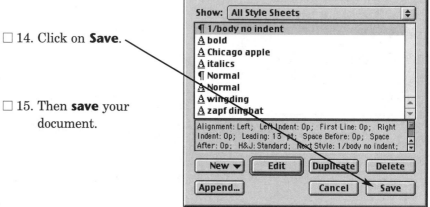

Congratulations!
You have just made your first paragraph style sheet!

"Based on"

The second style sheet introduces an essential direction: choosing "based on." This choice tells the style sheet to *base itself on* another style. It copies the other style. Then you would change the attributes you want to change.

Five of our style sheets will be based on the first one. If you decide to change fonts at any time, you just have to change **1/Body, no indent**. The other five automatically change accordingly.

2/Body, space before, no indent

2/Body, space before, no indent

Keyboard equivalent: ⌘ number pad 2

Based on: 1/Body, no indent

New spec to set:
Format: Space before: p5

Quicktip

To view the entire style sheet palette:

Use the bottom right corner to pull down the window and make it bigger (longer). Then put your cursor on the double line dividing the box, press down and pull down to see all the listings with the paragraph symbol next to them.

☐ 1. Under **Edit** menu, select **Style sheets**.

☐ 2. Choose **Paragraph**.

☐ 3. Name it **2/Body, space before, no indent**.

☐ 4. Keyboard equivalent: ⌘ **number pad 2**.

☐ 5. Based on: **1/Body, no indent**.

☐ 6. Click on **Edit** just to check it. It should say Times New Roman, 11 point, -2 tracking.

☐ 7. Click **Cancel** or **OK**.

☐ 8. Choose the **Formats** tab. The only thing you will change is **Space Before**. Make it p5. That puts 5 points above (before) a paragraph. (FYI: The paragraphs in these directions are set with 4 points before them.)

☐ 9. Click **OK**.

☐ 10. Click on **Save**.

☐ 11. Then **Save** your document.

For style sheets 3–7

Repeat the same procedure for the other style sheets, referring to page 227 for type specs. Make changes as called for.

When you are finished, your style sheet palette will look like this:

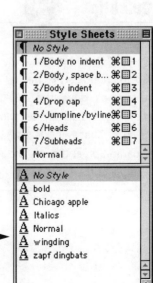

How to apply style sheets

First click on **No Style**. Then click on the style sheet you want.

You can also use the keyboard equivalent. For example, if you want to set a paragraph as **4/Drop cap**, click on the paragraph, then press the keys: ⌘ **number pad 4**.

Layout of Quark Quandary

Using pages 224-225 as your prototype, draw boxes (size and position estimated) on the two pages of your new *Quark Quandary* document. This gives you a very rough computer layout, but a good starting point.

Use the next pages for further instructions. Construct the newsletter piece by piece. It looks overwhelming, but conquer one element at a time, and you will succeed. Your goal is to produce an identical product to the one on pages 224-225 (except yours will fill an 8½" x 11" page — the prototype is smaller).

Copy *article by article* and paste each one *individually* into its appropriate box. Do not paste the entire "raw copy" document into one little text box on the page layout — the entire raw copy document gets pasted into a large text box next to the page, on the pasteboard (see page 39 for a picture of the pasteboard).

When you are finished, remember to put the dingbats at the end of each article. Mac users, make the little apples (see Quicktip on *Quark Quandary* for how to do it). Windows users, find a wingding you like and use it.

> ***Windows users:*** Any time you see the word *apple* with a letter, translate it to *control.* For example, *apple-M* would be *control-M.*

Quicktip

When you see a little *plus sign* next to the style sheet on the palette, that means it was tampered with. Perhaps you used a character style sheet in that paragraph. The plus sign isn't bad. However, sometimes you just can't get a style sheet to work because of it. Clicking "No Style" cleanses the paragraph and gets rid of the plus sign. Then click on the desired style sheet.

Quicktip

Rather than clicking first on "No style" each time you want to change style sheets, you can hold down the option key and select the style you want. That will "cleanse" the paragraph and apply the new style at the same time.

FYI	
13/15 Times bold centered italic **Translation:** 13-point type, 15-point leading, Times font, bold, centered, italic	24 point can be written as: 24' 24 pt. 24 point p24

Construct Quark Quandary piece by piece

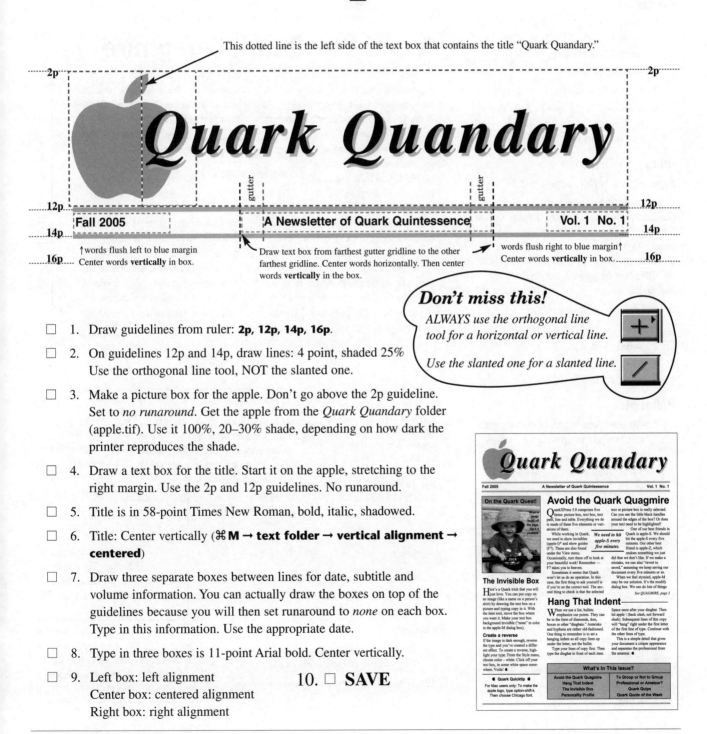

1

This dotted line is the left side of the text box that contains the title "Quark Quandary."

2p   2p

Quark Quandary

gutter   gutter

12p   12p

Fall 2005   **A Newsletter of Quark Quintessence**   **Vol. 1 No. 1**

14p   14p

↑words flush left to blue margin
Center words **vertically** in box.

Draw text box from farthest gutter gridline to the other farthest gridline. Center words horizontally. Then center words **vertically** in the box.

words flush right to blue margin↑
Center words **vertically** in box.

16p   16p

Don't miss this!

ALWAYS use the orthogonal line tool for a horizontal or vertical line.

Use the slanted one for a slanted line.

- ☐ 1. Draw guidelines from ruler: **2p, 12p, 14p, 16p**.

- ☐ 2. On guidelines 12p and 14p, draw lines: 4 point, shaded 25% Use the orthogonal line tool, NOT the slanted one.

- ☐ 3. Make a picture box for the apple. Don't go above the 2p guideline. Set to *no runaround*. Get the apple from the *Quark Quandary* folder (apple.tif). Use it 100%, 20–30% shade, depending on how dark the printer reproduces the shade.

- ☐ 4. Draw a text box for the title. Start it on the apple, stretching to the right margin. Use the 2p and 12p guidelines. No runaround.

- ☐ 5. Title is in 58-point Times New Roman, bold, italic, shadowed.

- ☐ 6. Title: Center vertically (⌘ **M → text folder → vertical alignment → centered**)

- ☐ 7. Draw three separate boxes between lines for date, subtitle and volume information. You can actually draw the boxes on top of the guidelines because you will then set runaround to *none* on each box. Type in this information. Use the appropriate date.

- ☐ 8. Type in three boxes is 11-point Arial bold. Center vertically.

- ☐ 9. Left box: left alignment
  Center box: centered alignment
  Right box: right alignment

10. ☐ **SAVE**

Head

☐ 1. Draw a text box across 2 columns, 3 picas high. Paste in title and assign head style sheet. Then make head larger until it fits the space (about 28'). DO NOT vertically center — only vertically center copy in framed or shaded boxes.

Article

☐ 1. Draw one text box across 2 columns, 20 picas high. Modify it (⌘ **M**) to make 2 columns, 1p6 gutter..

☐ 2. Paste in the article.

☐ 3. Format first paragraph *Drop cap*.

☐ 4. Make rest of paragraphs *Body indent*. It won't all fit. You will be linking the text to another box on page 2.

Jump

To jump the text from page 1 to 2.

Draw a little text box on page 2 (see *Quark Quandary* example). Use the linking tool on the large text box to link to the little box on page 2 so the text will flow from this box to that one. **Do not copy and paste text into the little box on page 2.** Let the linking tool do the work.

☐ 1. Choose the linking tool.

☐ 2. Click on the large text box.

☐ 3. Scroll to page 2.

☐ 4. Click on that box. Text should flow in automatically.

Pullquote

☐ 1. On your pasteboard, draw a separate text box, about 8p wide by 6p high.

☐ 2. Type in your quote, format it: **13/15 Times bold centered italics.**

☐ 3. Then center vertically as well.

☐ 4. Draw the 2-point rules above and below the type, but INSIDE the box.

☐ 5. When you get it the way you like it, group it.

☐ 6. Then drag the whole thing back to this article and place it.

☐ 7. To apply runaround to this grouping, use **content tool** and play with runaround numbers until you get the look you want. You may not need any on the left side. You might need it only on the right side.

☐ 8. **SAVE.**

2

Windows users: Any time you see the word *apple* with a letter, translate it to *control*. For example, apple-M would be control-M.

28 pt.

16p
16p

Avoid the Quark Quagmire

QuarkXPress 5.0 comprises five items: picture box, text box, text path, line and table. Everything we do is made of these five elements or variations of them.

While working in Quark, we need to show invisibles (apple-I)* and show guides (F7). These are also found under the View menu. Occasionally, turn them off to look at your beautiful work! Remember — F7 takes you to heaven.

Sometimes it seems that Quark won't let us do an operation. In this case, the first thing to ask yourself is if you're on the correct tool. The second thing to check is that the selected

We need to hit apple-s every five minutes.

text or picture box is really selected. Can you see the little black handles around the edges of the box? Or does your text need to be highlighted?

One of our best friends in Quark is apple-S. We should hit the apple-S every five minutes. Our other best friend is apple-Z, which undoes something we just did that we don't like. If we make a mistake, we can also "revert to saved," assuming we keep saving our document every five minutes or so.

When we feel stymied, apple-M may be our solution. It's the modify dialog box. We can do lots of things

Height of text box: 20 picas

Jumpline box

1 point rule

This is the continuation of the story from page one. You will use the linking tool to click on the box on page 1, then scroll to page 2 and click in this box. That will link the type to this box. DO NOT COPY AND PASTE TYPE HERE.

QUAGMIRE, from page 1

to boxes. Some of the most common things we do with apple-M are to change background color, vertically align copy, set text inset and make columns and gutters. ⬤

* Windows users: Any time you see the word *apple* with a letter, translate it to *control*.

Type continuation line in its own box. Use jumpline/byline style sheet, then **ALIGN LEFT** *by hand.*

Type in *Body, space before.* Then make it 10/11. Hang the indent under the W.

Mac users: Make the apple logo at the end of each story (option-shift-K, then apply Chicago style sheet or font.). *Windows users*: Choose a Wingding or Dingbat.

Jumpline

☐ 1. Draw a separate text box over the larger one — bottom right corner of it.

☐ 2. Format with jumpline/byline style sheet.

Hang That Indent

When we use a list, bullets emphasize our points. They can be in the form of diamonds, dots, boxes or other "dingbats." Asterisks and hyphens are rather old-fashioned. One thing to remember is to set a hanging indent so all copy lines up under the letter, not the bullet.

Type your lines of copy first. Then type the dingbat in front of each item.

Space once after your dingbat. Then hit apple \ (back slash, not forward slash). Subsequent lines of this copy will "hang" right under the first letter of the first line of type. Continue with the other lines of type.

This is a simple detail that gives your document a crisper appearance and separates the professional from the amateur.

Head

☐ 1. Draw a separate box above the article. Position box at 39p3 (Y scale).

☐ 2. Set type by heads style sheet (24'). Then enlarge it to about 26'.

Article

☐ 1. Draw one text box across the 2 columns. Modify it to make 2 columns with gutter width of 1p6 (⌘M → **text** → **2 columns**).

☐ 2. Paste in the copy for this article.

☐ 3. Use style sheet → *Drop cap* for first paragraph; *Body, indent* for others.

☐ 4. Last, draw a 1-point rule from head to right gridline. Center the rule vertically as well as you can. Use the arrows on the keyboard: each click moves 1 point; option-arrow moves it ¹⁄₁₀ of a point.

Table of Contents

This is made up of THREE boxes.

☐ 1. Draw a picture box 29p6 width, 8p2 height.

☐ 2. Shade the box 20%. Then frame it 1 point.

☐ 3. Make the headline box and one large text box. Make them both invisible (color = none). They're shaded here so you can see the different boxes.

☐ 4. Modify the large text box into two columns, 1 pica gutter.

☐ 5. Paste in type.
Set in Arial 11/16 bold. Center vertically *and* horizontally. The spacing will adjust itself. Copy will automatically flow to the second column.

☐ 6. Use the orthogonal tool +' to draw two 1-point rules — one horizontal and one vertical to make the subdivided look. To get the "T" juncture, blow up the screen to 800%. Keep clicking the magnifier tool.

To get back to a reasonable size, ⌘0 for "fit to window" or ⌘1 for 100%.

☐ 7. **SAVE.**

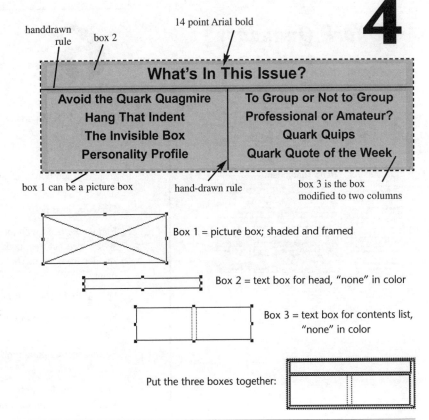

handdrawn rule   box 2   14 point Arial bold

What's In This Issue?

Avoid the Quark Quagmire	To Group or Not to Group
Hang That Indent	Professional or Amateur?
The Invisible Box	Quark Quips
Personality Profile	Quark Quote of the Week

box 1 can be a picture box   hand-drawn rule   box 3 is the box modified to two columns

Box 1 = picture box; shaded and framed

Box 2 = text box for head, "none" in color

Box 3 = text box for contents list, "none" in color

Put the three boxes together:

☐ 1. Make a picture box 14p wide, 17p5 high.

☐ 2. Frame it 1 point.

☐ 3. Import *babyonkayak.tif* from your Quark Quandary folder. Or you may use any photo of your own or one from the Clipart folder.

☐ 4. Size accordingly.

☐ 5. Draw a text box above the hat. Make the box "none" in color.

☐ 6. Make caption head in 15-point sans serif bold, centered. *

☐ 7. Don't let the words touch the top of the picture frame.

☐ 8. Make another text box on the side of the picture. Keep right edge away from edge of box.

☐ 9. Caption: 8/11 sans serif, bold, right aligned. Don't let the words touch the frame of the picture.

☐ 10. Text box on black handle. Make box "None" in color. Type something in box. Make a reverse: Arial, bold, white, about 11 point. Adjust placement of box to get the words in the middle of the handle.

---

* *AHA! Were you looking for a font called "sans serif"? Remember, that's a **class** of type, not a font name. See page 42 for suggestions.*

5

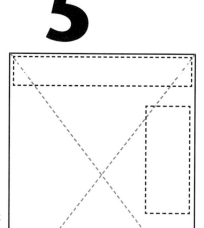

Leave a little space above the words

On the Quark Quest!

When a photo faces off the page, flip it if possible.

Jack

A word about flipping photos

Your first choice is NOT to flip a person. And sometimes you can't flip the picture because of rings, words on hats and so forth (see page 101). In this case, we did flip the picture. If I had used *kayakbaby.tif* (on CD – see right), the name of the kayak would prohibit flipping.

6

This is all one text box. You will be working on FOUR parts:

head

paragraph one

subhead

paragraph two

☐ 1. Draw one text box.

☐ 2. Format the head with the *Head* style sheet, but then make it smaller from there. This one is 20 point.

☐ 3. Format first paragraph *Drop cap.*

☐ 4. Format subhead by *Subhead* style sheet.

☐ 5. Format second paragraph *Body, no indent.*

☐ 6. Make the apple dingbat. (If in Windows, use another dingbat.)

The Invisible Box

Here's a Quark trick that you will just love. You can put copy on an image (like a name on a person's shirt) by drawing the text box on a picture and typing copy in it. With the item tool, move the box where you want it. Make your text box background invisible ("none" in color in the apple-M dialog box).

Create a reverse

If the image is dark enough, reverse the type and you've created a different effect. To create a reverse, highlight your type. From the Style menu, choose color – white. Click off your text box, in some white space somewhere. Voila!

☐ 1. Place a 1-point rule at 55p9 (Y scale).

☐ 2. Draw one text box.

☐ 3. Start by making all the copy *Body, space before*. Center the copy.

☐ 4. Make head Arial bold 15 point.

☐ 5. Make text 10.5/13 Arial centered.

☐ 6. Make apples 12-point Chicago. They might show up on the screen, but they will not print unless they are Chicago. (Windows users: Use another dingbat.)

☐ 7. Put a space on each side between the apple and the word.

7

this rule is at 55p9

🍎 Quark Quicktip 🍎

For Mac users only: To make the apple logo, type option-shift-k. Then choose Chicago font.

8

Footer on page 1: 4-point line shaded 25%. Set at 62p9 on Y scale.

62p9→

Page 2

Warning: Save every 5 minutes!

9

Header on page 2:

☐ 1. Draw a rule from margin to margin. Use the orthogonal line tool (+).

☐ 2. Position it 3 picas from top of page, which should be the blue margin grid.

☐ 3. Make it 4 points thick.

☐ 4. Shade it 25%.

☐ 5. Start the Personality Profile box at 4p6, where you should have a green gridline. (There must be space between the header line and beginning of the actual newsletter copy.)

☐ 6. **SAVE.**

Personality Profile
A weekly featured personality chosen by our quarry of quotable Quark users.

Dan Daring became a QuarkXPress guru by living out his name; he has no qualms about making mistakes, and he doesn't quaver in the face ...hnology! When questions arise, he queries the ...ting with Q... ...k. Because h~ first

Professional or Amateur?

A picture facing off the page, (e.g., a jogger running off the page) marks an amateur. For th~ ~~fession-

10

This is the grid pulled from the top ruler to 4p6.

Heads style sheet, then centered

Start with body, no indent. Then center, bold, italics, 10-point type, 13-point leading.

4p6

☐ 1. Draw a text box that stretches across two columns, 17p height.

☐ 2. Frame the box 1 point.

☐ 3. Apply *Heads* stylesheet to the head. Center it.

☐ 4. Format the summary deck (lead-in) as *Body, no indent.* **C**enter it, bold, italicize. Lower point size to 10 point.

☐ 5. Format the rest as *Body, space before.*

☐ 6. Set text inset of 5 (instructions in "Professional or Amateur" article).

☐ 7. Draw a picture box on left side.

☐ 8. "Get picture" — any piece of clipart.

☐ 9. **Save before using clipart.**.

☐ 10. Size picture as desired.

☐ 11. Apply auto runaround of about 8 points or more.

☐ 12. Byline = 10/13 Times italic, right aligned. You can use the jumpline/byline stylesheet, but then **align right.**

☐ 13. Italicize the name of the book in the paragraph.

☐ 14. Use soft returns to push unwanted hyphenated word parts to the next line.

Personality Profile

A weekly featured personality chosen by our panel of qualified Quark users.

Dan Daring became a QuarkXPress guru by living out his name; he has no qualms about making mistakes, and he doesn't quaver in the face of new technology! When questions arise, he queries the *Communicating with QuarkXPress* book. Because he first runs "check spelling" on all copy, he has earned a reputation as an efficient editor as well as desktop designer. He leaves one space after the period at the end of a sentence. His use of en dashes and em dashes also distinguishes him. He always remembers text inset for boxed copy, and he cleans up all widows and orphans. Dan has unequivocally earned the title "Quite Qualified Quark User."

By Wendy Writer, Profiles Editor

byline style sheet BUT aligned right

paragraph is **Body, space before.**

11

☐ 1. Draw one text box.

☐ 2. First paragraph: *Drop cap.*

☐ 3. Second paragraph: *Body indent.*

☐ 4. Head: *Heads* stylesheet.

☐ 5. **SAVE.**

Professional or Amateur?

A picture facing off the page, (e.g., a jogger running off the page) marks an amateur. For the professional look, your pictures always need to face toward the center of the page.

A second thing that separates the amateur from the professional is text inset. All text needs to be set away from the frame of the box, or if it is reverse type, it cannot touch the edge of the black box. Use apple-M and choose text inset of 4 or 5 points. This moves all your copy from the edges, and you will look as if you really know what you are doing!

12

This article is typed as FOUR separate boxes.

☐ 1. Kicker is set in 15-point Arial bold italic. 2-point rule.

☐ 2. The head has its own text box. Use *Head* style sheet.

☐ 3. Make two boxes for the type. Paste copy in the first box. Use the linking tool to connect them.

☐ 4. Make both boxes the same "Y" value. They will then line up with each other.

☐ 5. **SAVE.**

The Big Question

To Group or Not to Group?

Grouping makes your life a lot easier. Highlight each item you want to group. You can do this in two ways. Select the item tool. Hold down the shift key and tap on each item you want. The little black handles mean the item has been selected. Then press apple-G. Then click off somewhere outside the text box.

Or use the item tool and draw a box (actually it will be invisible — it's called a marquee) touching each

item you want selected. Then press apple-G. If you don't press apple-G, you get a temporary grouping.

To ungroup, use the item tool and tap on the grouping. It will show a dotted line around it. Then press apple-U and CLICK OFF. If you don't click off, it doesn't ungroup.

24′ = 24 point

13

☐ 1. Draw a text box 26p3 high and shade it 25%. No frame.

☐ 2. Head: *Heads* style sheet, then centered.

☐ 3. List: *Body, space before.*

There are no EXTRA paragraph returns between lines.

☐ 4. Set text inset = 5 points.

☐ 5. Center copy vertically.

☐ 6. Type the letter that will become a dingbat and then type a space. For example, the diamond bullet is made by typing a "u." Then apply the character style sheet (Zapf Dingbat) and it will become a diamond. Or use your Quark Quick Card to find a different dingbat you like.

☐ 7. Apply the hanging indent (see article in the *Quark Quandary* newsletter on that topic). Or refer to page 144.

☐ 8. Eliminate hyphens. Use a soft return (shift-return) before the hyphenated words to move them to the next line. This maintains the paragraph style sheet.

Quark Quips

◆ Use NO "city" fonts (Chicago, New York, Monaco, Geneva).

◆ Never distort photos unless you have a super reason.

◆ Always check spelling.

◆ When you don't know what to do, "apple-M" might work for you! } tighten tracking to -4

◆ Save your document at least every five minutes.

◆ Use bold and italic type sparingly. }

◆ Use serif for body copy; sans serif for heads. }

move words to the next line by using the soft return (shift-return)

◆ Memorize the three magic keys.

◆ Use your Quark Quick Cards to help you learn shortcuts.

◆ Always make a backup copy.

Personality Profile

A weekly featured personality chosen by our quarry of quotable Quark users.

Dan Daring became a QuarkXPress guru by living out his name; he has no qualms about making mistakes, and he doesn't quaver in the face of new technology! When questions arise, he queries the *Communicating with QuarkXPress* book. Because he first runs "check spelling" on all copy, he has earned a reputation as an efficient editor as well as desktop designer. He leaves one space after the period at the end of a sentence. His use of en dashes and em dashes also distinguishes him. He always remembers text inset for boxed copy, and he cleans up all widows and orphans. Dan has unequivocally earned the title "Quite Qualified Quark User."

By Quana Quinn, Profiles Editor

Professional or Amateur?

A picture facing off the page, (e.g., a jogger running off the page) marks as amateur. For the professional look, your pictures always need to face toward the center of the page.

A second thing that separates the amateur from the professional is text inset. All text needs to be set away from the frame of the box, or if it is reverse type, it cannot touch the edge of the black box. Use apple-M and choose text inset of 4 or 5 points. This moves all your copy from the edges, and you will look as if you really know what you are doing!

The Big Question

To Group or Not to Group?

Grouping makes your life a lot easier. Highlight each item you want to group. You can do this in two ways. Select the item tool. Hold down the shift key and tap on each item you want. The little black handles mean the item has been selected. Then press apple-G. Then click off somewhere outside the text box.

Or use the item tool and draw a box (actually it will be invisible — it's called a marquee) touching each

item you want selected. Then press apple-G. If you don't press apple-G, you get a temporary grouping.

To ungroup, use the item tool and tap on the grouping. It will show a dotted line around it. Then press apple-U and CLICK OFF. If you don't click off, it doesn't ungroup.

QUAGMIRE, from page 1

to boxes. Some of the most common things we do with apple-M are to change background color, vertically align copy, set text inset and make columns and gutters.

* Windows users: Any time you see the word apple with a letter, translate it to control.

Quark Quips

◆ Use NO "city" fonts (Chicago, New York, Monaco, Geneva).
◆ Never distort photos unless you have a super reason.
◆ Always check spelling.
◆ When you don't know what to do, "apple-M" might work for you!
◆ Save your document at least every five minutes.
◆ Use bold and italic type sparingly.
◆ Use serif for body copy; use sans serif for heads.
◆ Memorize the three magic keys.
◆ Use your Quark Quick Cards to help you learn shortcuts.
◆ Always make a backup copy.

Quark Quote of the Week

If you can't do it, Quark can do it. You just have to find out how.

Quark Quandary is published every semester by students in Publication Layout and Design classes at Rowan University in Glassboro, New Jersey.

Editor: Claudia M. Cuddy
Contact: editorcuddy@mac.com

2

Quark Quandary – Vol. 1 No. 1

14

1. Practice with the curved text paths before you put in the art.
2. Make two picture boxes, one larger than the other.
3. Fill them with the same black and white picture. Size the pictures so one is larger than the other.
4. Flip one of them so they face each other.
5. Shade pictures 30%.
6. Type your own *Quark Quote of the Week* or something on a curved text path.
7. If the pictures are on top of the words, send them to the back (**Item menu → Send to back**).

21′ Times Italic (but yours can be a different size)

Quark Quote of the Week

If you can think it up, Quark can do it. You just have to find out how.

This one is 17′ but yours can be different.

15

Quark Quandary is published every semester by students in Publication Layout & Design classes at Rowan University in Glassboro, New Jersey.

Editor: Claudia M. Cuddy
Contact: editorcuddy@mac.com

Use your name here.

masthead

1. Draw a text box one column wide, about 8 picas high.
2. Frame it 1 point.
3. Set text inset 5 points.
4. Change my name to yours with your e-mail.
5. Type is Times New Roman 10-point font with 12-point leading.
6. Format as in sample. Italicize *Quark Quandary*.

16 footer

4 point rule, shaded 25%

en-dash: option-hyphen

62p9

box is at 63p → 2

Quark Quandary – Vol. 1 No. 1

10′ ↑ en-dash↑ en-dash↑

To make the footer information:

1. Draw text box from margin to margin, Y = 63p . Make color of box *none*.
2. Type "2" then space, then make the apple. Then hit **option-tab (or alternate-tab)**. Type the rest of the footer info.
3. Format all of it in Arial 10 point bold.
4. Then apply the Chicago style sheet to the apple.

17

1. **Save** before printing.
2. Print on both sides. Ask your instructor for directions.
3. Use the checklist on the next three pages. Then correct your work and print a final copy.

Checklist – Quark Quandary

Page 1

Nameplate

- [ ] apple logo is shaded 20–30%
- [ ] name of newsletter is placed in middle of apple (vertically)
- [ ] name overlaps apple a little bit (horizontally)
- [ ] rules are shaded and not blocked out by the folio boxes
- [ ] rules are at 12p and 14p
- [ ] first of the copy begins at 16p
- [ ] publication information is in three separate boxes; Runaround = None
- [ ] publication information is placed left, center, and right
- [ ] publication information is typed in 11-point Arial bold
- [ ] publication information is aligned vertically between shaded lines
- [ ] tops of publication boxes line up or type lines up — use rulers or "Y" measurements to check

Avoid Quark Quagmire

- [ ] uses a separate text box for the headline
- [ ] head is enlarged to 28 point
- [ ] uses a text box modified into 2 columns for the copy
- [ ] headline close to article; shouldn't float (it's bad to have too much space after a head)
- [ ] first paragraph is made with *Body, drop cap*
- [ ] other paragraphs are *Body, indent*
- [ ] first jumpline is in its own box
- [ ] jumpline is in italics
- [ ] jumpline is RIGHT aligned

On page 2:

- [ ] continuation line in its own box
- [ ] continuation line formatted correctly and LEFT aligned
- [ ] continuation of text on page 2 is done by linking from page 1
- [ ] no *extra* paragraph returns in the article

Pullquote

- [ ] type is 13/15 Times New Roman bold italic
- [ ] tracking is less than 0 (-1, -2, -3). **No positive tracking**
- [ ] 2-point lines applied to pullquote
- [ ] lines are grouped with textbox
- [ ] pullquote placed well in article
- [ ] runaround good on all sides

Hang That Indent

- [ ] head is formatted with head style sheet; then enlarged to 26 point
- [ ] rule centered vertically off the "t"
- [ ] text box is modified into 2 columns
- [ ] first paragraph is made with *Body, drop cap*
- [ ] other paragraphs are *Body, indent*

Page 1

continued

What's in This Issue?

- ☐ one large box, shaded and framed
- ☐ headline box, not framed
- ☐ 1 copy box modified into 2 columns, not framed
- ☐ "T" rules meet well at edges, etc.
- ☐ type is Arial, bold 11/16, centered horizontally and vertically
- ☐ "What's In This Issue?" – Arial, bold 14'

Photo

- ☐ facing to inside of page
- ☐ larger title caption is 15 point, bold, centered
- ☐ small caption: 8/11, bold, right aligned
- ☐ letters do not touch edge of box, either on right or top
- ☐ letters on handle in bold, reverse (white), about 11 point

The Invisible Box

- ☐ one text box contains head and text
- ☐ head is made from head style sheet, then made 20 point
- ☐ drop cap for first paragraph
- ☐ subhead made from *Subhead* style sheet
- ☐ *Body copy, no indent* for second paragraph
- ☐ space above head (between picture and this article)

Quark Quicktip

- ☐ rule above it to separate from above article (55p9)
- ☐ apples show on either side of title, space between apples and words
- ☐ head set in 15-point Arial bold centered
- ☐ copy in Arial 10.5/13, centered and divided to match the master newsletter (use soft returns if necessary)

Footer Rule

- ☐ rule 4 point, 25% shaded, placed at 62p9

Page 2

Personality Profile

- ☐ all one text box, framed 1 point
- ☐ title centered, made with *Head* stylesheet
- ☐ summary deck is centered, Times, bold, italic, 10 point, 13-point leading
- ☐ text set as *Body, space before* to allow some space between summary deck and text
- ☐ text inset of 5 points
- ☐ sufficient auto runaround set on art (not 1)
- ☐ byline formatted by jumpline/byline style sheet (aligned right)

Professional or Amateur?

- ☐ one text box
- ☐ 24-point head, left aligned (*Head* stylesheet)
- ☐ first paragraph: *Drop cap*
- ☐ second paragraph: *Body copy, indent*
- ☐ no widows

Page 2

continued

To Group or Not to Group?

- ☐ separate text box for head
- ☐ decent space between that head and the Personality box
- ☐ kicker in 15 point with 2-point rule below it
- ☐ 2 text boxes linked
- ☐ both text boxes have same Y value
- ☐ *Drop cap* style sheet for first paragraph; *Body, indent* for rest
- ☐ rule at end of article to separate it from the jumped article

Quark Quote

- ☐ shaded art (light enough to see text over it)
- ☐ pictures are flipped to face each other; same pic used
- ☐ large on left, small on right
- ☐ smooth Bézier text paths
- ☐ any quote you want

Quark Quips

- ☐ shaded box (25%)
- ☐ 5-point text inset
- ☐ style sheet used: *Body, space before*
- ☐ dingbats used on each item
- ☐ space between dingbat and first letter
- ☐ hanging indent used
- ☐ lines end with no hyphens

Masthead

- ☐ box 8 picas high
- ☐ box framed 1 point
- ☐ copy 10/12
- ☐ inset 5 points
- ☐ your name and e-mail

Headers and footers on page 2

- ☐ header rule
- ☐ footer rule
- ☐ page number and apple logo
- ☐ folio information 10 point or less
- ☐ "en" dashes used instead of hyphens
- ☐ spaces on either side of the dashes

Overall items to check

- ☐ apples or other dingbats at ends of articles, plus wherever else used
- ☐ widows/orphans that can be corrected (some can't)
- ☐ gridlines are adhered to (Remember to stretch text boxes from grid to grid.)
- ☐ leading throughout 1 or 2 points more than type size
- ☐ tracking is consistently less than 0 (-1, -2, -3, -4)
- ☐ two-sided copy

Your Own Newsletter

Produce a newsletter based on the basic style of *Quark Quandary*. (You will make a template out of *Quark Quandary*.)

1. Type the copy for your newsletter outside of class time. Proofread the hard copy carefully, and make your corrections.

> How much copy do you need for a two-page newsletter? (two pages means a front and a back)
>
> If you type in 12-point, you will need about two pages of single-spaced copy to fill your newsletter. This copy should be divided into a few articles, ranging from 80 words to 250 words. *Quark Quandary* uses 1110 words in the entire newsletter. You will probably have photos that may take up more room, so you won't need as much copy. To get an idea of how many words fit into various sizes of spaces, see page 248.
>
> *Note*: When you hand in your copy, be sure you have it double spaced. Therefore, it will fill up about 4 pages.

2. **Make up your own topics** or pick from the suggestions.

3. **Devise creative heads.** Don't use the actual labels under the Ideas list. Try to make some interest-grabbing heads.

4. **Plan the layout.** The final layout must include:
   - one list of some kind with bullets
   - two pieces of art – one must be a new scan. The other is anything — a picture or clipart
   - a framed box
   - a shaded box — these can be the same box

Miscellany

- This newsletter will be composed of several short articles — not one long story.

- The reason "you" is suggested as the newsletter topic is so that you won't have to struggle with the writing and can focus on the layout. However, do not minimize the importance of succinct copy.

- If desired, you may do a newsletter for an organization or internship.

- You may not use copyrighted material for the newsletter. **Do not take your copy directly from the Internet**. That includes art as well.

- Write clearly and edit cleanly. The writing and typing always count in publications, so get a second reader/copyeditor for your copy.

If the instructor asks for the "hard copy" of your newsletter, provide about four pages of typed, double-spaced copy, broken into short articles.

Did you realize that miscellany is the noun while miscellaneous is the adjective?

Ideas for your newsletter articles

People (a person) who have (has) influenced my life

My best 10 traits

My best single trait and an example of it

What I like to do in my spare time

My favorites (as a list)

My favorite _____ (author, place, vacation, pastime)

My favorite expression/verse/saying

A funny thing that happened to me

What I would do if I won $1 million

A good memory

The movie or play that relates to my life the most

My college years

My sports life

My religious convictions/what I believe in

My political ambitions

Where I got my nickname

The meaning of my name

Haiku of my life

My family

My roots

My hometown

My best friends

My future plans

My hobbies, activities, work

Why someone should hire me for _____

And so on...

Ideas

_____

_____

_____

_____

_____

_____

_____

_____

_____

Word Counts

Below are examples of word counts for articles in *Quark Quandary*, set in 11-point Times, 13-point leading. You can write longer and fewer articles, but this will give you some idea as to how much copy will fit into two pages.

The hyphen, the en dash and the em dash

■ First, there is a **hyphen**. We won't explain that because you probably know how to use it.

■ Then comes the **en dash**, a slightly longer mark than the hyphen. It is about as wide as a capital N. Use the en dash for durations:

> 100–200 people
>
> 7:30 a.m.–6 p.m.

To make the en dash: type *option-hyphen*.

■ Then there's the **em dash**, a dash about the width of a capital M. The em dash takes the place of the two hyphens you type when you want to make a change of thought in a sentence. For example:

> I exercise every day — well, maybe not *every* day.
>
> You will find several em dashes used throughout this book — I like them.

To make the em dash: type *shift-option-hyphen*.

One additional thought:

AP style says to put a space before and after the dash. Most stylebooks say do *not* put spaces.

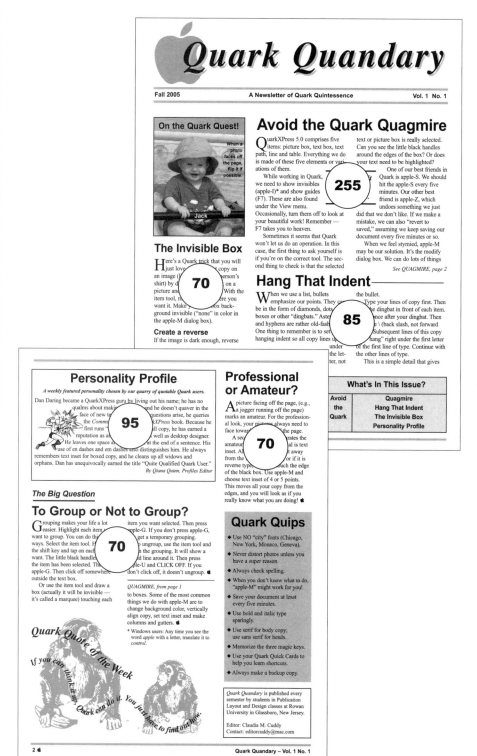

Directions for your own newsletter

☐ 1. Open your *Quark Quandary* folder. Click once on your closed *Quark Quandary* newsletter icon. *Mac users:* Hit ⌘ **D**. This will duplicate the icon and create a backup copy of your newsletter. The computer will name it with "copy" after the name. *Windows users:* Copy and paste the document. Do NOT hit ⌘ **D** — that deletes your file.

☐ 2. Make a new folder called *My Own Newsletter* on your disk. Put your newsletter typed copy into this folder.

☐ 3. Open the *Quark Quandary* **COPY** newsletter. If it doesn't open, delete the word "copy" in its label.

☐ 4. Wipe out all the copy on page 1. You can draw a marquee around all the items and delete. Or leave some items you want to keep for any other newsletters. For example, you might want to keep the shaded rules in the nameplate. Go to page 2. Do the same.

Save as "template" ───→ ☐ 5. **Save as** *NewsletterTemplate.qxd*. HOWEVER — instead of saving as a document, choose **template.** Save it to the folder you just named *My Own Newsletter*.

☐ 6. Close it. You have now made yourself a newsletter template that you can use over and over — complete with style sheets. If you look at the icon, it will be a slightly lighter icon than regular document icons.

☐ 7. Open the template. It will be called *Document 1* (it could be another number). If it is not, then you didn't correctly save it as a template. Ask for help.

If it does open as "Document 1," save it to your My Own Newsletter folder. Name it _____ *Newsletter.qxd*. (Fill in the blank with your name.)

☐ 8. Draw a big text box on the pasteboard next to page one. Copy and paste all your copy into that box. Select all and apply "No Style" to the new copy.

☐ 9. Close all other documents and windows. The only open window should be your newsletter.

☐ 10. Edit your style sheets. Change from Times New Roman to another serif font. You will need to change only the *1/Body, no indent* style to make this work. Change the heads from Arial to your choice of any sans serif or novelty type.

☐ 11. You must include the following items:*
    ☐ a list with bullets (dingbats) and hanging indents
    ☐ two pieces of art — one must be a personal scan that you haven't done yet. The other can be anything.
    ☐ a framed box
    ☐ a shaded box (can be the same box as above)
    ☐ variation of the nameplate (don't use the apple)
    ☐ use of a second Pantone color (you choose it)

You can leave the boxes and just wipe out the copy if you want to. Type "Title" over the *Quark Quandary* title.

Important Font Advice

If you choose a font with a larger x-height (see type chapter), increase leading OR decrease font size.
Be sure you have enough leading to maintain good readability.

* *Exception*: If you are doing a "real" newsletter for someone else, and all these elements simply don't work, talk to your instructor.

☐ 12. Stay within all grids and margins.

☐ 13. Make up creative heads.

☐ 14. Be risky about layout. Experiment. Check with the instructor.

☐ 15. Look at other newsletters to get some ideas.

To make a second color (see page 81)

☐ 1. Go to **Edit → Colors → New → Model: Pantone Uncoated**. When that opens, use your arrow keys to navigate around the Pantone colors box. You will have your choice of hundreds of Pantone colors. Choose one. Click on it. The program should name it with its corresponding number, but if it doesn't, you can name it. Then click **OK** and it reverts to the **Edit** box. Save.

☐ 2. Then **save** your document.

☐ 3. Your new color has now been added to your list of colors. Use your new color just as you used the standard list of colors. You can add more than one color if you want to.

☐ 4. How do you use your second color? You can use it for heads, shaded boxes, part of the nameplate, rules, dingbats and so forth. It's up to you. Have fun with it.

Finishing stages

☐ 1. When your newsletter is finished, **Collect for Output** into your *My Own Newsletter* folder. This command is found under the **File** menu.

☐ 2. Print on both sides.

☐ 3. Fill out the checklist for *Your Own Newsletter*.

Real quotation marks and real apostrophes

According to Robin Williams (*The Mac Is Not a Typewriter*), "Typewriter quotation marks are the single most visible sign of unprofessional type."

When you type in Quark, it's not usually a problem, especially if your preferences are set for "smart quotes." However, most text-heavy projects come from Word or another word-processing program. Quotation marks often revert to the generic ditto mark.

• straight quote marks (like ditto or inch marks)
  "Apple-s saves you stress."

• real quote marks, sometimes called *curly* or *smart* quotes
  "Apple-s saves you stress."

Sometimes they look slanted instead of curly because of the font. For example, in Stone Sans:
  "Apple-s saves you stress."

The three versions:

	straight	slanted	curly
quotes:	"	″	"
apostrophes	'	′	'

How do you change them if they come into Quark as straight quote marks? One way is to highlight the mark in Quark and retype it. That changes it.

The other way is to do a massive Find/Change (page 201). This is useful if you have several throughout the text.

The expression "curly quotes" refers to curly or slanted.

A note about straight quotes:
They are good for designating inch or foot marks.

Checklist – Your own newsletter

- ☐ Use of a new Pantone color
- ☐ Changed style sheets for body copy and heads
- ☐ Nameplate
    - ☐ title
    - ☐ logo/design
    - ☐ date, volume and number
    - ☐ subtitle (mission statement)
    - ☐ takes up about one-fifth of the page
- ☐ Grids and margins adhered to
    - ☐ vertical column guides
    - ☐ horizontal page depth guides (e.g., all copy below 16p)
    - ☐ margins and gutters respected
- ☐ List of some kind
    - ☐ dingbats on each item
    - ☐ hanging indents applied correctly
- ☐ Two pieces of art used
    - ☐ scanned photo is sized proportionately
    - ☐ runaround applied if necessary
    - ☐ caption with photo(s)
    - ☐ placed facing toward center of page, not off the page
- ☐ Framed article
    - ☐ text inset applied
    - ☐ vertical centering if applicable
- ☐ Shaded box
- ☐ Creative heads (how they're written)
- ☐ Consistent alignment of heads (all are centered or left aligned)
- ☐ More space ABOVE heads than below them
- ☐ Consistent type size used for body copy (you used the style sheets)
- ☐ Serif used for body copy
- ☐ Two or three fonts used on whole newsletter
- ☐ Leading 1 or 2 points more than type size
- ☐ Tracking is under 0 (-1, -2, -3, -4, -5)
- ☐ One space after a period instead of two (pages 121 & 201)
- ☐ Real quote marks and apostrophes — not ditto marks (page 250)
- ☐ En and em dashes used correctly (page 248)
- ☐ Contrast on page – lively appearance
- ☐ Sense of balance, proportion to pages
- ☐ Header and footer on page 2
- ☐ Dingbats at end of articles
- ☐ Tabs used instead of spaces
- ☐ Vertical centering only when copy is in a frame or colored box
- ☐ Spelling (Do a spell check. Proofread.)
- ☐ Grammar/sentence structure
- ☐ Two-sided copy
- ☐ Collected for output

Rebound Madness

Spring 2003   The Basketball Newsletter   Vol. 1 No. 2

Say It Ain't So, Mike

I guess the day had to come. Michael Jordan can't play forever, can he? I'm sure you know by now that Jordan, the most majestic athlete to ever play the game of basketball, has announced his retirement for the third and final time.

Michael Jordan laced up his sneakers before playing in front of a sold out crowd in Philadelphia for the last time on Sunday. It was scary to think Jordan's last game would be played in Philly. We've all heard the stories about out-of-control fans in that city. But much to my delight, the Philadelphia fans actually showed some class for

"Philadelphia fans actually showed some class."

once. The fans were well aware of what they were seeing.

The pregame was all about honoring the man who has amazed people of all different demographics for so many years. The crowd was in a frenzy, applauding the same guy who had hurt their dreams of a championship in the years past. But that didn't matter. Michael Jordan has respect for the game, and that respect is gratefully returned by fans spanning the globe. It didn't matter that his team lost the game, or even that Jordan played sub-par. The thing that matters is those fans were honored to see a legend play his

See MIKE, page 2

Leading NBA Scorers

- ✪ Tracy McGrady ...31.3ppg
- ✪ Kobe Bryant 30.0ppg
- ✪ Allen Iverson 27.6ppg
- ✪ Shaquille O'Neal ..27.5ppg
- ✪ Paul Pierce 25.9ppg
- ✪ Dirk Nowitzki 25.1ppg
- ✪ Tim Duncan 23.3ppg
- ✪ Chris Webber 23.0ppg
- ✪ Kevin Garnett 23.0ppg
- ✪ Ray Allen 22.5ppg
- ✪ Allan Houston 22.5ppg

Jerry West has been the NBA logo for over 20 years. With the exit of Jordan and the entering of James, who knows who the NBA will have on the logo in the future?

The Chosen One?

You've heard the hype. You've seen him in action. You know about the sneaker contracts worth millions. What does this all add up too? Lebron James should be one of the great ones in the years to come. But is all the praise necessary or even justified? Could anyone blame James if he somehow buckles under all the pressure? After all, he is just a senior in high school playing against others of the same age, with less than half the talent. You can't deny his ability though, dunking the ball with his chin above the rim, or the effortless passes that seem to make defenders look silly.

Lebron James has talent that has never before been seen in high school basketball. But is it possible to make the jump to the NBA and be effective in his rookie year? This all remains to be seen.

One thing is for sure, Lebron James will be a marked man. Players who have proven themselves year in and out never get this much exposure. Veterans will be jealous. It's going to be exciting to watch how Mr. James performs under all the pressure. ✪

For more information
log onto
www.bballmadness.com

Figure 16-21. Front page example.
Tom stayed with the 3-column format, but he changed several things. His sidebar sits at the top right corner, and his large graphic in the left bottom corner balances it well. He wrote the caption down the side of the graphic, which creates an interesting effect. Tom, a senior advertising major, had never worked in QuarkXPress before that semester.

17 Brochure

Customers buy for their reasons, not yours.
Orvel Ray Wilson
(Guerrilla Sales Expert)

Quest Objectives

- Identify the four different kinds of brochures.
- Describe ways to make the cover effective.
- List the elements of a brochure plan.
- Explain the elements of a typical brochure format.
- Demonstrate different methods of folding brochures.

Quest Skills

- Develop a timeline for production (brochure plan).
- Append style sheets.
- Create a three-panel brochure.
- Practice alignment.

Quest Terms

append style sheets
brochure
call to action
communication mix
French fold
life expectancy

panel
parallel fold
response panel
series of brochures
testimonials

Connotation of *brochure*

The word *brochure* sounds more prestigious than the word *folder* or *pamphlet*. The latter two sound less expensive.

Qool Fact

The word *brochure* is from a French word *brocher* that means "to stitch." You would think, then, that the binding of a brochure would be stitched or stapled (called *saddle-stitched*). But they often are not. Sometimes they are in the form of a booklet, but more often, they are simply folded.

The word *brochure* is used loosely to refer to various publications: fliers, pamphlets, tracts, folders, bulletins, little booklets and larger booklets. Whenever someone doesn't know what to call a certain publication, the word *brochure* is often applied. However, we will be using *brochure* to mean a single piece of paper folded for distribution or mailing.

Brochures usually focus on one theme or idea. They can be part of a mailing or they can be self-mailers (address is printed on one panel and no envelope is necessary). Each folded area is called a *panel*, and the three-panel brochure is the most common (Figure 17-1). People include brochures in media kits, sales presentations and other kinds of informational kits. They hand out brochures at events or put them on display racks for people to pick up.

Panel 1	Panel 2	Panel 3		Panel 4	Panel 5	Panel 6
Inside left	Inside center	Inside right		Inside flap	Back panel	Front panel

Figure 17-1. The plan for a typical three-panel brochure made from an 8½ x 11 page.

Kinds of brochures

Brochures can be categorized by their purposes:

1. to sell a product, service or idea
2. to explain, inform or teach
3. to announce an event, program or workshop
4. to promote membership and participation or encourage contributions

Sometimes it is hard to categorize brochures because intentions aren't always clear. A brochure about a new college major might be trying to promote the major while at the same time simply informing students of the program's requirements. A brochure about an annual fund drive for a library might be asking for contributions while at the same time explaining some of the library's benefits to the public. No matter how the purposes overlap, basic characteristics of all brochures are similar: simple, attention-grabbing, attractively laid out, well written, limited in space and easy to handle and store.

1. To sell a product, service or idea

A simple brochure can effectively advertise any product or service. One of the best techniques for this kind of brochure is using a dominant graphic on the cover or a bold, compelling headline — or both. The reader needs to immediately grasp personal benefits and then be further persuaded after opening the brochure. Testimonials are often used to provide validation from a satisfied consumer.

Buy this!

Examples of brochures with a product or service to sell:

- products such as air-cleaning system, newspapers, jewelry

- services such as financial planning, desktop publishing, guitar lessons, marriage counseling services, AIDS assistance

- place to spend time or attend such as vacation spots, apartment complexes, church

- educational institutions such as a college, nursery school, trade school, literacy institute

Figure 17-2. Jessica treated the inside three panels differently from the typical three-panel look. She encompassed all three columns under one big head. The original color for this was reflex blue to match the company's corporate identity. Textile font strengthens the heads with distinguished Palatino as body copy. Note also the repetition of "at home" in the cover copy, large head, subhead and even in the subhead for the Web information. This brochure is an example of a service to sell.

Panel 4 (inside flap)　　Panel 5　　Panel 6 (cover)

I was simply overwhelmed by all the decisions we had to make. Those other realtors talked down to us and never tried to understand what we needed. I knew we had to find someone we could trust.

"Dick Haviland took the time to understand what we were looking for and explained everything to us with real respect. He helped us find a wonderful home that is perfect for our family.

"If you are looking for a realtor, Dick Haviland is the only one to call."

– A Satisfied Home Buyer

At home on the web
Log onto *www.dickhaviland.com* where you can:
▼ View home listings
▼ Learn about mortgage and financing options
▼ Find tips on buying or selling a home
▼ Receive client updates
▼ Learn about Atlantic County communities
▼ Take a virtual tour of homes for sale
▼ and much more!

Dick Haviland
Atlantic Real Estate Sales
Office: 708-642-2300 ext 22
82 Black Horse Pike
Argonaut, NJ 08387
Home: 708-435-9875
Fax: 708-210-3296
Email: sales@dhaviland.com

Feel right at home

Dick Haviland, your trusted real estate expert for over 25 years

Feel right at home

Experience you can trust

Let's face it…real estate can be complicated. Buying or selling a home involves a dizzying array of options, from financing to property evaluation, mortgages, taxes, terms, conditions…the list goes on and on. Negotiating this process alone can be absolutely overwhelming.

But you don't have to do it alone. Your real estate transaction can be simple if you choose the right person to guide you through the process.

Dick Haviland has the knowledge, experience and integrity to help you achieve your goals and make your transaction as simple as possible.

Meeting your needs

Whether you are buying your first house or looking forward to retirement, planning a financial investment or upgrading to your dream home, looking for a home across town or across the country, Dick Haviland can make you feel right at home throughout your real estate transaction.

A South Jersey native, Dick Haviland knows the Atlantic County real estate market inside and out. He will help you find a home that's just right for you and your family.

As an industry veteran, Dick Haviland has the experience and credentials to simplify your transaction and satisfy your needs.

Dick Haviland has been a licensed realtor since 1973. For the past five years he has been a Broker and Associate with Re/Max, one of the most trusted names in real estate. Dick Haviland has earned many professional honors and awards, including the prestigious Re/Max 100% Club Award for outstanding service.

Satisfied clients speak for themselves…that's why 75% of Dick Haviland's business comes from repeat clients and referrals from satisfied buyers and sellers.

At home in Atlantic County

Business is booming in the popular Atlantic County real estate market. With the influx of new employment opportunities, beautiful array of homes available, and easy access to Philadelphia and New York, Atlantic County is a wonderful place

work, play, and live. If you like city life, suburban streets, country charm, or seaside serenity, you're sure to love to Atlantic County. Dick Haviland specializes in some of Atlantic County's most sought after areas, like Galloway Township, Port Republic, Smithville, Mullica Township and the Mullica, Bass and Wading River communities.

All you need to know

Dick Haviland gives you a local view of the communities you are interested in. You need to know about community safety, the quality of nearby schools and the history of the neighborhood, as well as lesser known details, such as the number of rental units on the same street. Dick Haviland will make sure you have all the information you need to make the best real estate decisions for you and your family.

Your real estate transaction can be simple if you choose the right person to guide you through the process.

Panel 1　　Panel 2　　Panel 3

Examples of educational and informational brochures:

- visitor guides

- welcome brochures (to an office, health clinic, program, dinner)

- sports schedules

- health issues such as diabetes, cholesterol, smoking

England and America are two countries separated by a common language.

George Bernard Shaw

2. To explain, inform or teach

A brochure provides a simple way to explain health issues such as osteoporosis, high blood pressure, cholesterol or back pain. Brochures are produced in educational arenas to teach parents about learning disabilities, techniques for helping their children do their homework and preparing for parent-teacher conferences. In the college setting, various departments produce specific brochures to describe each program of study. Sometimes a group wants to heighten the awareness of its community service projects and uses the brochure to educate the public.

Easy-to-read copy in short paragraphs must reach the needs of the targeted audience. Use copybreakers such as subheads as well as ample white space.

Panel 4 (inside flap) Panel 5 Panel 6

Some Dos and Don'ts

★ Always carry ID

★ Don't carry all your money at the same time

★ Bring as much film as you think you'll need; film is more expensive than here

★ Bring two pair of walking shoes and maybe one pair of dress shoes in case you want to go out

★ Don't assume locals will always understand you (see inside flap)

★ Throw a jacket in your suitcase; you never know when the weather will turn

★ Bring only essential items because you will be carrying your own luggage around

A reconstructed street of old York
York Castle Museum, York, UK

Entry gate at Warwick Castle
Warwick Castle, Warwick, UK

Carvings in the Charter House
York Minster, York, UK

ROWAN UNIVERSITY EF TOUR
England & Scotland 2001-2002

The England Experience

a travel publication for students embarking on a tour through England

King's Gallery
Palace Street, Canterbury

Famous Sites

In reality, **Big Ben** can be heard but not seen! Officially, the name refers not to the Parliament clocktower but to the 13-ton chime within.

The British monument of **Stonehenge** has generated centuries of intrigue. To this day, the precise heritage of these landmark monoliths remains a mystery. Through carbon dating, scientists have determined that Stonehenge was created in three distinct stages, first in approximately 2800 B.C., then in 2100 B.C., and again in 1500 B.C.

The **Tower of London** was begun in the reign of William the Conqueror (1066-1087) and remained unchanged for over a century. The Tower of London is a Norman and medieval site and also has an important Tudor and Victorian history.

Tea & Coffee

Tea in Britain tends to be served strong and milky; it might be accompanied by crumpets (buttered tea breads), scones, or another specialty such as Dundee cake. "Cream tea" comes with scones topped with butter, jam, and whipped cream. "Elevenses" designates a morning tea break; afternoon tea is served between 3 and 5 p.m., while the more substantial "high tea," an early supper, is usually served between 4:30 and 6:30 p.m. and comes with fancy little cucumber sandwiches and cookies.

"White coffee" is half coffee, half milk; to receive something different, ask for either "black coffee" (no cream) or "white coffee with just a little milk." If you just say "coffee," it will automatically be served with cream.

National Dishes

shepherd's pie: meat, mashed potatoes and gravy
Cornish pasty: a turnover filled with meat, potatoes and onion
bangers and mash: sausage and mashed potatoes
ploughman's lunch: bread, cheese, salad and pickles
cock-a-leekie: chicken and leek soup
roast beef and Yorkshire pudding
steak and kidney pie
fish and chips

Useful Phrases

British English		American English
Biscuits	→	Crackers or cookies
Call	→	To visit in person
Chemist	→	Pharmacy/drugstore
Coach	→	Tour/long distance bus
Crackers	→	Firecrackers or fire works
First floor	→	Second floor
Football	→	Soccer
Fortnight	→	Two weeks
Ground floor	→	First floor
Jumper	→	Sweater
Lift	→	Elevator
Lorry	→	Truck
Pants	→	Underwear
Petrol	→	Gasoline
Quay ("kee")	→	Pier
Queue ("cue")	→	Line
Ring up	→	Telephone
Scones	→	Biscuits
Subway	→	Underground walkway for pedestrians
Torch	→	Flashlight
Trunk call	→	Long-distance phone call
Tube Underground	→	Subway

Panel 1 Panel 2 Panel 3

Figure 17-3.

Jean immersed her enthusiasm for England in this project. She said she would have liked it if someone had given her this brochure before she went! This informational brochure is livened up by all the pictures. The font for heads is Chaucer (appropriate!), with Times for body copy and Stone Serif Bold for the photo captions. Jean made the cover deep-blue midlinear blend. To print it here, I changed it to a midlinear blend of 60% black.

3. To announce an event, program or workshop

An effective way to promote an event, program or workshop is a simple three-panel brochure mailed as a self-mailer. One panel becomes the response panel — to be torn off and mailed back. One panel contains the mailing address. That leaves four panels to promote the activity. Copy must be written succinctly to fit all the information into that small area.

However, some brochures for these purposes do not have a tear-off panel for response because, more than ever, people are being encouraged to register for an event online or to call.

Many conventions or bigger workshops promote their event using a large format: an 8½ x 11 format with several pages. Yet the booklet is often called an advance program *brochure* or a pre-conference *brochure*.

Attend this!

It is essential for the announcement brochure to clearly give all the information regarding the 5 W's and How:

Who should attend, Who is sponsoring

What is happening

When (date and time)

Where it's being held

Why it's important to attend

and

How to sign up or register (contact information)

Panel 4 (inside flap)   Panel 5   Panel 6 (cover)

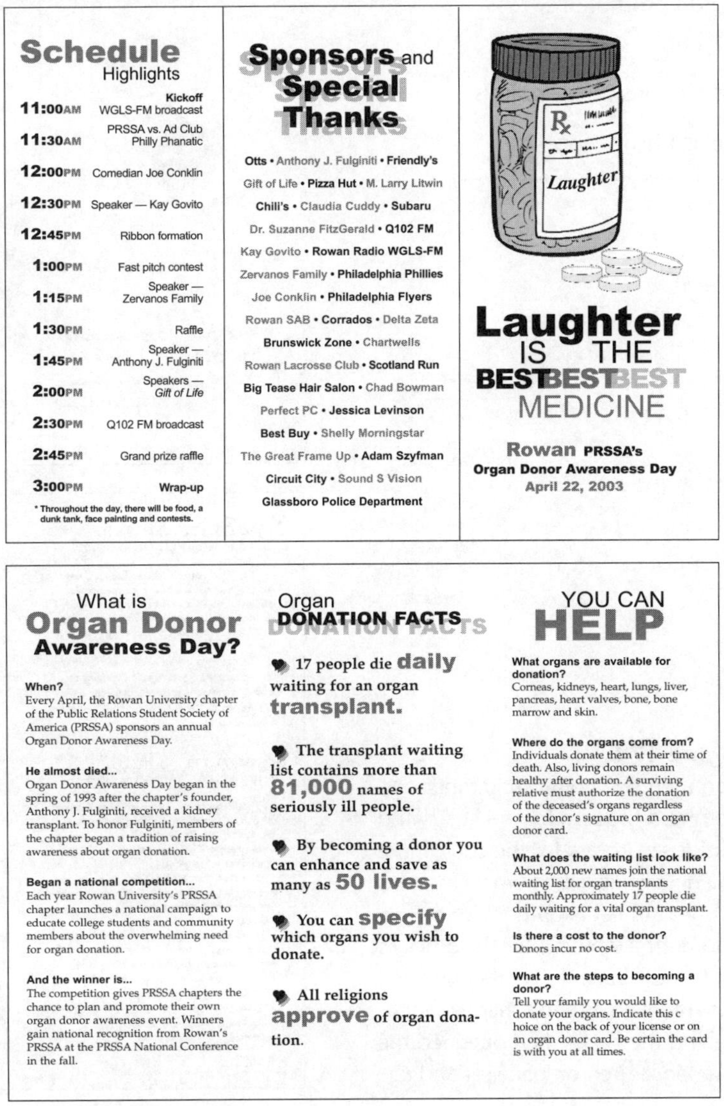

Schedule
Highlights

11:00AM	**Kickoff** WGLS-FM broadcast
11:30AM	PRSSA vs. Ad Club Philly Phanatic
12:00PM	Comedian Joe Conklin
12:30PM	Speaker — Kay Govito
12:45PM	Ribbon formation
1:00PM	Fast pitch contest
1:15PM	Speaker — Zervanos Family
1:30PM	Raffle
1:45PM	Speaker — Anthony J. Fulginiti
2:00PM	Speakers — *Gift of Life*
2:30PM	Q102 FM broadcast
2:45PM	Grand prize raffle
3:00PM	Wrap-up

* Throughout the day, there will be food, a dunk tank, face painting and contests.

Sponsors and Special Thanks

Otts • Anthony J. Fulginiti • **Friendly's**

Gift of Life • **Pizza Hut** • M. Larry Litwin

Chili's • Claudia Cuddy • **Subaru**

Dr. Suzanne FitzGerald • **Q102 FM**

Kay Govito • **Rowan Radio WGLS-FM**

Zervanos Family • **Philadelphia Phillies**

Joe Conklin • **Philadelphia Flyers**

Rowan SAB • **Corrados** • Delta Zeta

Brunswick Zone • Chartwells

Rowan Lacrosse Club • **Scotland Run**

Big Tease Hair Salon • Chad Bowman

Perfect PC • **Jessica Levinson**

Best Buy • Shelly Morningstar

The Great Frame Up • **Adam Szyfman**

Circuit City • Sound S Vision

Glassboro Police Department

Laughter IS THE BEST MEDICINE

Rowan PRSSA's
Organ Donor Awareness Day
April 22, 2003

What is
Organ Donor Awareness Day?

When?
Every April, the Rowan University chapter of the Public Relations Student Society of America (PRSSA) sponsors an annual Organ Donor Awareness Day.

He almost died...
Organ Donor Awareness Day began in the spring of 1993 after the chapter's founder, Anthony J. Fulginiti, received a kidney transplant. To honor Fulginiti, members of the chapter began a tradition of raising awareness about organ donation.

Began a national competition...
Each year Rowan University's PRSSA chapter launches a national campaign to educate college students and community members about the overwhelming need for organ donation.

And the winner is...
The competition gives PRSSA chapters the chance to plan and promote their own organ donor awareness event. Winners gain national recognition from Rowan's PRSSA at the PRSSA National Conference in the fall.

Organ
DONATION FACTS

❤ 17 people die **daily** waiting for an organ **transplant.**

❤ The transplant waiting list contains more than **81,000** names of seriously ill people.

❤ By becoming a donor you can enhance and save as many as **50 lives.**

❤ You can **specify** which organs you wish to donate.

❤ All religions **approve** of organ donation.

YOU CAN HELP

What organs are available for donation?
Corneas, kidneys, heart, lungs, liver, pancreas, heart valves, bone, bone marrow and skin.

Where do the organs come from?
Individuals donate them at their time of death. Also, living donors remain healthy after donation. A surviving relative must authorize the donation of the deceased's organs regardless of the donor's signature on an organ donor card.

What does the waiting list look like?
About 2,000 new names join the national waiting list for organ transplants monthly. Approximately 17 people die daily waiting for a vital organ transplant.

Is there a cost to the donor?
Donors incur no cost.

What are the steps to becoming a donor?
Tell your family you would like to donate your organs. Indicate this choice on the back of your license or on an organ donor card. Be certain the card is with you at all times.

Panel 1   Panel 2   Panel 3

Figure 17-4.
Steph and Jamie experimented with shaded type and layers of type for a lively effect. The bullets are triple hearts. The day's schedule is on the flap, easily torn off if someone wanted to. The "thank you to the sponsors" panel catches the eye.

Join us! Give us!

Examples of this kind of brochure would include:

- clubs and organizations that are providing information about their organizations, but they are hoping for you to join

- election promotions (go vote)

- subscriptions to periodicals

- scholarships to apply for

4. To promote membership and participation or encourage contributions

Volunteer organizations, clubs and unions use brochures to encourage membership or participation in their group or to ask for contributions. This type of brochure needs to present a strong argument to show the benefit to the audience and a clear call for action. Testimonials are a good way to identify with the reader, and bulleted lists would help as well. These brochures need to include such words as *join*, *donate* or *participate*.

Panel 4 (inside flap)   Panel 5   Panel 6 (cover)

"Wherever two or three are gathered in My name, there I am in their midst."
Matthew 18:20

Staff
Director
Father Mazz 856-881-5642
Assistant Director
Ann Polo 856-881-2554
Secretary
Lois Dark 856-881-3474

Center Hours
Monday-Thursday 9am-9pm
Feel free to call between these hours or leave a message at any time of the day.

The Newman Center
Rowan University
Route. 322 & Bowe Blvd. (Next to Wawa)
Glassboro, NJ 08028
www.Rowan.edu/clubs/Newman

The Newman Center
Catholic Campus Ministry

The Newman Center

N I C

Friendship
binds us.
Faith
guides us.

Figure 17-5.
Kari used two contrasting fonts: Bernhard Modern for the heads and Akzidenz Grotesk for the copy. Note the details regarding type. On panel 2, she uses left alignment for one list and right alignment for the other list, with lines drawn to create a box in the middle. Note the shaded type behind the heads. Kari designed the two logos used on panels 4 and 6.

Newman Center
What is the Newman Center ?

The Newman Center itself is a cozy building, set up like a house. It's the people inside that make it a home. With a number of service projects and social activities, the opportunity for involvement and meeting new friends seems endless.

The center provides a warm and friendly atmosphere that's just right for studying or hanging out. And is you are looking for a way to meet great new friends, join the Newman Club on campus.

Newman Club
What is the Newman Club ?

The Newman Club began to supplement campus life by providing a family atmosphere to gain further religious education and to meet the social needs of Catholics without excluding students of other religions.

The SGA-chartered club also strives to provide for religious and/or humanistic growth and development of the members of Rowan University.

Filled with college students, the Newman Club's relaxed environment welcomes everyone, no matter what religious background. And there are no registration fees.

The Newman Club meets every Wednesday at 5pm followed by a FREE home-cooked meal at 6 p.m. All students are welcomed.

Newman Club Activities

Social

BBQs
Dinners
Softball
Volleyball
Bowling
Skating
Day Trips
Retreats

Devotions
Bible Studies
Faith Sharing
Over-nighters
Coffee Houses
Guest Speakers
Service Projects
Spiritual Direction
Religious Education

Spiritual

St. Mary's Retreat House, Spring Retreat 2003

Newman Center
Mass Schedule

Sunday 7 p.m.
Mon-Thurs 12:30 p.m.

Confessions anytime.
Spritual Direction available on request.

R.C.I.A.
Rite of Christian Initiation of Adults

For those interested in becoming Catholic or entering more fully into the life of the church through the sacraments of Baptism, Communion, and Confirmation, classes are available through the Newman Center.

Please call the Newman Center for more information.

Visit us on the Web @
www.Rowan.edu/clubs/Newman

Panel 1   Panel 2   Panel 3

Series of brochures

Scenario: A brochure for a program or dinner is given out as you enter the program setting (informational brochure). It contains the agenda for the evening along with information about the keynote speaker and the association or organization. Three weeks earlier, you got a brochure announcing this dinner (event announcement). Weeks after the dinner, you will receive a follow-up brochure dealing with becoming a golden member of the group's scholarship foundation (contribution brochure).

How do you know these brochures come from the same organization? When a few brochures are involved, they must all be consistent in logo, type and color. They must be recognizable by the recipient (see section on corporate identity below).

Five characteristics of the brochure

Six-panel? Three-panel? Trifold?

Since each side of the paper contains three panels, there are six panels on the entire brochure. It might seem sensible to call it a six-panel brochure, but we usually don't. Many people call it a trifold, but that is even more inaccurate because there are two folds, not three! Three-panel seems to be the most widely used term.

1. Corporate identity

Brochures are often part of the whole promotional package or communication mix. Therefore, they need to be consistent with those items by employing the same logo, colors and type.

However, if the brochure stands alone, then the tie-in with the organization's image is even more important. The brochure needs to reflect the culture of the organization through its familiar logo, colors and type.

2. Life expectancy

Life expectancy of a brochure varies according to its purpose. If it announces an event, then its shelf life ends when the event occurs. However, if it is an educational vehicle, then its shelf life extends much longer. Five years is usually the the high end for life expectancy. One year is common for sales brochures.

Make your brochure worth keeping. Encourage the consumer to keep it handy. Creative formats will help in this area. Some examples include travel brochures that unfold into maps, yearly calendars of events or a piece that unfolds into a poster.

Date the brochure. It is useful to date the brochure somewhere, inconspicuously or by code, for future reference. Some people choose a certain corner and use 5 or 6 point type, hardly noticeable by the reader. Sometimes people even designate who printed it and how many they printed. A sample "code" might be GG90410000. This would stand for: Gateway Graphics (printer), September 2004, 10,000 copies printed. Dating the brochure lets you know which version people are using when they call you. Brochures are updated and reprinted frequently, and dating helps in record-keeping.

3. Limited space

Because of the brochure's limited space, clear, concise writing is of utmost importance. Use active verbs, descriptive adjectives, short sentences and lists. Heads need to be short and active.

4. Simplicity

If one word could describe a brochure, *simplicity* is it. (Remember, *keep it simple, student* [K.I.S.S.]). Brochures shouldn't appear too expensive unless you are promoting an upscale product or organization. Although sometimes a four-color brochure is necessary, a two-color brochure is usually ideal. The one-color brochure might look a little too homemade or low-scale.

5. Important information

Spotlight the important facts. A frequent criticism of brochures is that they do not give enough facts. If applicable, tell consumers what is included, the costs and the hours. Use graphics to help spotlight important information.

Five C's of brochure efficacy

1. Compelling cover

This is the most important part of the brochure because it determines whether someone opens the brochure. Use a dominant graphic rather than several small ones. Use a bold, compelling head in the form of a benefit-oriented title or statement. Tell the reader who you are, where you are and what you offer. The cover must clearly show what's inside.

2. Call to action

Specifically ask for the order or action if the brochure warrants it. What action do you want the reader to take? Write, call, e-mail, fax or send a check? Make the call to action clear and prominent.

3. Contact information

Repeat your telephone number, fax number or e-mail several times in the brochure. Don't make someone search for them. Place the logo near at least one of the contact information blurbs.

4. Captivating graphics

Photos are more realistic and more memorable than drawings, so choose creative and eye-catching photos when possible. Always put informative captions under photographs. (Readership of captions is almost double that of body copy.) Next to the cover, captions are probably the best-read element of any brochure.

5. Candid testimonials

Testimonials are statements from people who support your product, service or event. These are well read items, and if written well, they influence other consumers. Testimonials add a personal touch.

Typical format

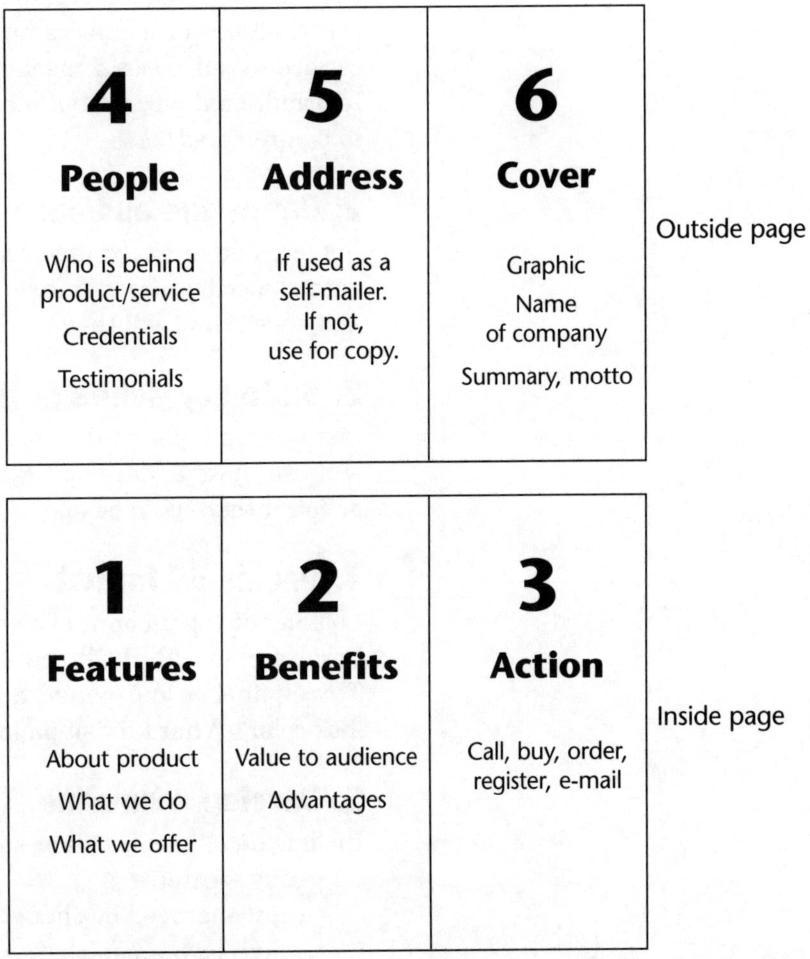

4	5	6	
People	**Address**	**Cover**	Outside page
Who is behind product/service	If used as a self-mailer. If not, use for copy.	Graphic	
Credentials		Name of company	
Testimonials		Summary, motto	

1	2	3	
Features	**Benefits**	**Action**	Inside page
About product	Value to audience	Call, buy, order, register, e-mail	
What we do	Advantages		
What we offer			

Figure 17-6.
A basic brochure plan. According to Elizabeth Adler (*Print that Works*), after the cover attracts you enough to open the brochure, you read panel 1 first, then 2, 3 and 4. Knowing the reading direction helps you effectively arrange your information. Adler suggests starting your "story" on panel 1.

Planning the brochure

Approach the brochure as you would any publication. Decide on the purpose, the audience, the key points of the message and benefits to the audience. Construct a timeline and find out what budget you have to work with. Choose the size and overall format based on the amount of copy and method of distribution. (See Figure 17-7, a sample brochure plan.)

1. State the purpose

In a few sentences, summarize the reason you need to produce this publication. Does the organization need to promote itself to gain contributions or memberships? Does someone have a product or service to sell? Does someone want to provide an educational, informational piece about a topic? Is there an event that needs to be promoted?

2. Define the audience and distribution

Is there one target group or a few? Brochures usually work best with a specific target audience. What is the reading level of the audience? How will they get this brochure?

3. State key points of the message (include benefits)

List the main points that need to be included in the brochure. You will use these to develop the more detailed copy. Include the call to action if there is to be one.

4. Decide on format

Looking at the amount of copy and the budget, decide on format. For example, will the brochure be one piece of paper or more? Three-panel or four-panel? 8½ x 11 or 8½ x 14? Two-color or four-color? What kind of paper?

5. Develop a timeline

Include deadlines for all or some of these activities:
- copy written
- copy approved by client
- rough layout sketch
- first computer draft
- computer draft approved by client
- final proof approved by client
- files sent to printer
- printer's proof approved by you (and client if requested)
- delivery or pickup of printed brochures

For class assignments, you won't have to include all the steps above. Refer to the sample plan (Figure 17-7).

In brochure writing, use:

- active verbs
- short sentences
- bulleted lists
- short, active heads

* Client refers to the person for whom you are doing the brochure. In this case, it was a committee of public relations students.

** Steps b and c are often done simultaneously, according to personal preference. Some people sketch the brochure even before the copy is written.

Laughter is the Best Medicine
Brochure for Organ Donor Awareness Day

I. Statement of purpose
The national PRSSA's (Public Relations Student Society of America) annual project promotes organ donations. Therefore, Rowan's chapter is holding a one-day event called "Organ Donor Awareness Day." Getting the word out to our college and local communities makes a difference in attendance at the event. This brochure will announce the day, present a schedule and inform people about organ donation.

II. Audience and distribution
The audience for this brochure will be Rowan University students and local community members. The brochure will be sent to all faculty through interoffice mail and placed in strategic locations on campus and in a few places in the community (post office, municipal building, Wawa).

III. Key points and benefits
a. What is Organ Donor Awareness Day?
b. Organ Donation Facts
c. What you can do to help
d. The day's schedule
e. List of sponsors and contributors

IV. Format
8½ x 11 three-panel brochure, white cardstock
Ink: black only

V. My Timeline
a. Plan submitted to client*	April 1
b. Copy written by me and approved by client	April 5
c. Rough sketch**	April 7
d. Computer draft approved by client	April 12
e. Completed brochure to duplicating center/printer	April 13
f. Ready to distribute	April 15

VI. Division of duties
a. Writing and layout – Jamie and Steph
b. Proofreading – Steph
c. Final approval – Melissa (president)
d. Pickup and distribution around campus – Jackie

Figure 17-7. Sample brochure plan.

Start to work

Write copy and do a rough sketch

After you have devised the overall brochure plan, get to work on writing the copy and making catchy heads. Some people like to write the copy and then do the rough draft, while others prefer to sketch out the rough draft and then write the copy.

Take a piece of paper the size of the final brochure and fold it the way the brochure will be folded. Label the panels (see Figure 17-6), and sketch the placement of your copy, graphics and heads on the correct panels.

There is a sample on the CD: *brochuredummy.pdf*. Print this. Fold it into thirds along the dotted lines. Fill it with your roughly sketched items and then keep it close while working on the computer.

How much copy? (see sidebar)

In most cases, don't put too much copy in a brochure. On the other hand, in some cases, don't be afraid of long copy. For example, if consumers have bothered to write for your brochure, or if they have picked it off a rack, they are hungry for information — especially if they are buying a big item such as a college education or a vacation. Consider the purpose of the brochure and the target audience.

The computer layout

After your sketch and copy are finished, start placing the pieces onto the brochure panels. Use the template provided on the CD: *brochuretemplate.qxt*. One panel is actually a bit larger than the other two so the fold works correctly.

Don't be afraid to have a graphic or copy run across two inside panels with an encompassing head across both panels. Hold the brochure as if you were the reader and see how your eyes work. Open the brochure the way you want a reader to open it.

Keep design principles in mind (repetition, alignment, proximity, contrast and dominance). Put a dominant item on the cover, and use alignment consistently on the three inside panels. Because the brochure is often just one piece of paper, repetition within the brochure isn't as important as repetition from brochure to letterhead to business card (consistency among the communication mix). Achieve contrast through the use of copybreakers and large heads. Let proximity govern the main points, benefits, call to action and contact information.

Make your brochure layout attractive and filled with attention-grabbing techniques such as pullquotes, initial caps, headings and shaded boxes. Use relevant graphics to enhance, with one dominant graphic on the cover. More text-intensive brochures are useful only when the audience has already taken the first step of accepting the product and is now deciding whether or not to buy.

To get inspired, look at samples of other brochures. You can collect them almost everywhere: doctors' offices, college offices, banks, businesses and so forth. Keep your eyes open for them.

Remember Cuddy's seesaw?

When interest is high, importance of design is low.

Brochure design usually calls for limited written copy, but in some cases, a text-intensive brochure is needed to cover the topic. People who are interested in a particular subject will read this brochure despite the amount of text because they are seeking content — they want information about the product or service.

text-intensive – a publication with lots of text.

Choose one or two fonts to fit the mood of your brochure. If the brochure is whimsical, choose Comic Sans or Jester for heads. If the brochure is stately or business-like, choose Arial or Helvetica for heads. (Refer to *Chapter 4: Type* for more information on font characteristics and personalities.)

For a text-intensive brochure, choose a readable serif font. However, if the body copy isn't too overwhelming, a sans serif font would be acceptable. Make heads strongly contrast the body copy — bigger and bolder.

Options for brochure folding

These folds can be applied to any size paper.

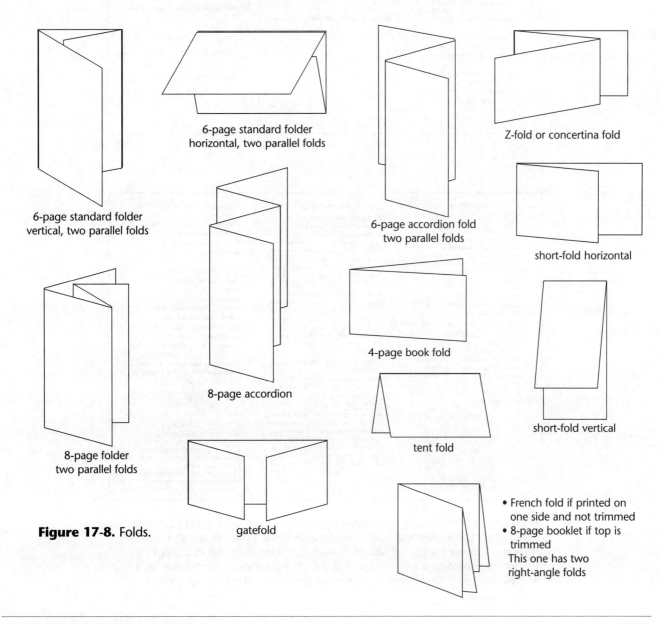

Figure 17-8. Folds.

Same topic, different twist

Rowan Radio
An award winning station

1997 College Station of the Year

★ *2000 Marconi Radio Awards:*
Excellence in Sportscasting –
The Profs Year in Review

★ *The Communicator Crystal*
Awards: Award of Distinction
(Education) – **The Rowan Radio**
Magic Hat Storytime

★ *Award of Distinction:*
(Documentary) – **The Internet-**
Birth of Dot Com Culture

★ *NJ Associated Press Broadcasters:*
First Place (Best College
Production) – **The Internet- Birth**
of Dot Com Culture

Rowan University
201 Mullica Hill Rd.
Glassboro, NJ 08028

Office: 856-863-WGLS
Fax: 856-256-4704

Email: wgls@rowan.edu

Listen to Rowan Radio
Live Online
http://wgls.rowan.edu

Do you want to
become a member of
Rowan Radio?

Find out what the
radio station is all
about and how you
can become involved.

About Rowan Radio
WGLS-FM is a noncommercial, educational radio station, licensed to the Rowan University Board of Trustees, for the purpose of broadcasting "in the public interest." Twenty-four hours-a-day staff of between 90 and 120 independent student volunteers broadcast a variety of entertainment, news, sports, public affairs and specialty programming.

The studios are located in the College of Communication on the campus of Rowan University in Glassboro, NJ.

Coverage
WGLS is a regional radio service with a potential audience of almost 1.3 million people. The broadcast signal covers South Jersey, parts of Philadelphia and Delaware. But if you are not within the broadcast signal then you can listen to Rowan Radio 89.7 WGLS-FM on the web at http://wgls.rowan.edu, any time and any place.

Frequently asked questions
➤ **How do I become a member?**
Any student interested must complete one of the station's training sessions. The sessions are held each semester and consist of lectures and demonstrations on radio station policies and procedures. At the end of the training session it is required that you pass a written test and a "hands-on" test demonstrating your skill in equipment operation.

➤ **Can I get on-the-air right away?**
Once you successfully complete the training program, you will be paired up with one of the daytime DJs who will help you learn the WGLS-FM format. You can then apply for your own daytime shift for the following semester. The demand for air shifts is high but we try to accommodate everyone.

➤ **Do I have to be a DJ to be a member of WGLS-FM?**
No. If you have an interest in working in other areas of station operations such as news, sports, engineering or public affairs, we welcome your participation.

➤ **What is expected of station members?**
All members are expected to represent Rowan University and the station in a positive and professional way. All members are also expected to attend station meetings, volunteer to help in various station departments, and participate in other station functions such as remote broadcasts, station promotions and much more.

Executive Staff 2001-2002

General Manager: Frank J. Hogan
Chief Engineer: Al Miller
Student Manger: Dan Reigel
Operations Manager: Jason Friedman
Bill Pavlou
Sports Director: Derek Jones
Traffic Director: Michelle Ulrich
News Director: Lance Feltman
Public Affairs Director: Mark Kasubinski
Daytime Director: Monica Newton
College Rock Director: Sue Smalley
Weekend Director: Bryan Nese
Urban Director: Natalie Neczypor
Promotions Directors: Bruce Hummer
Jake Nisenfeld
Underwriting Director: Sam Bonavita

Sports
Hear all the Profs sports action on Rowan Radio 89.7 WGLS-FM, including all playoff games for football, men's and women's soccer and basketball, baseball and softball.
* Tune in to the KC Keeler Show one hour before kickoff of the football games.

Figure 17-9. Michelle targeted students who might want to be part of the radio station staff. She is providing a lot of information in this brochure to lure potential students — notice the basketball with the sports information. She included a map to show the coverage area, which is large for a college station. She lists key people and awards (credibility affirmed). Contact information covers the back panel — easy to locate.

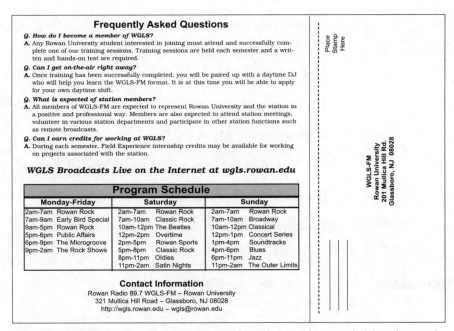

Figure 17-10. Example of an informational brochure with an underlying theme of "join us." Dan used one panel to make the brochure a self-mailer, and he used two other panels to create a return postcard. He added an incentive of a bumper sticker to entice returns. A mailing list can be compiled by the radio station from these returned postcards. Dan's brochure contains less copy than Michelle's, perhaps appealing to another audience.

Jumpstart

Get ideas for your own brochure!
Read through this list of brochure titles to get you going.

Make a big impact — Be a big brother or sister

Is Your child worth 42 cents? (Washington Township Public Schools)

Visit us at our new location and see what 47 years of community support has created! (East Greenwich Library's Annual Fund Drive)

Join the Women's Cross Country Team

Does my $50 really make a difference? (The Annual Fund Rowan University)

100 Years of Making a Difference (a sorority)

The Atlantic County Historical Society. We are preserving the past.

The Glassboro Fire Department welcomes volunteers!

So you want to be a residence hall director?

Welcome to our dental office

Concert ticket buyer's guide (courtesy of The Whit Entertainment Section)

All I ever wanted to know about SGA and was afraid to ask

You have a question. We have the answer. (support desk of university)

Commit to quit (about smoking)

The New York Yankees and Their 25 World Championships

Working with the Media

What would a dream job look like? (U.S. Navy)

The best way to have a good idea is to have lots of ideas.

Linus Pauling
Scientist and Peacemaker

Your ideas

Quick Quiz

1. What are the four kinds of brochures? Give an example of each.

2. How does a brochure differ from other publications? How is it similar?

3. What is the most important element of the brochure? Why?

4. What are five techniques that would make a brochure effective?

 Out of the Quandary

Pre-project: Prepare a simple brochure plan (see Figure 17-7). Then write your brochure copy and be sure you have it on your computer to use in the layout stage.

Choice 1

Produce an original three-panel brochure (8½ x 11).
Fold style: two-parallel fold or accordion fold.

• Use two PMS colors (black and another color).

• No Internet art. It is too blurry, and in most cases, it is copyrighted.

• Follow layout rules (2 or 3 fonts, serif for body copy, no automatic leading, etc.). If you deviate from the rules, get approval from your instructor beforehand.

Choice 2

Redesign an existing brochure. Improve on its font choices and overall layout.

 Quantum Leap

With permission of the instructor, design your brochure for the "Out of the Quandary" in a different format than the 8½ x 11 format.

Quark Quest

Make a three-panel brochure

☐ 1. Run out a copy of the brochure layout from the CD (*brochuredummy.pdf*). Fold the two pages together like a brochure. Panels are labeled on this — use it for your rough sketch so you don't get the panels mixed up.

☐ 2. Open the brochure template from the CD: *Chapter 17 / Brochure: brochuretemplate.qxt*.

☐ 3. Save as *Yournamebrochure.qxd* (use your name).

☐ 4. Append style sheets from your *Quark Quandary* newsletter to give you consistent styles. You don't have to use them all, and you may edit them. How to append style sheets is found at the end of these instructions (pages 273-274).

☐ 5. Use the folded example to remind yourself which panel is which.

☐ 6. Paste your copy into a text box on your pasteboard next to page 2 (that's where most of it will go). Select all and apply **No Style** to it. Then apply **Body, no indent** to it. This gives you a consistent base to build upon. Remember to change your **Body, no indent** style sheets if you prefer a different font or size.

☐ 7. Cut and paste your copy in sections. Use separate boxes for various topics. A few boxes give you flexibility of movement.

☐ 8. Format your copy in individual boxes by style sheets or by hand (or both).

☐ 9. Use rules, shaded boxes and art moderately.

☐ 10. Choose clipart or a picture for the front cover.

Other tips

☐ 1. Put spaces between paragraphs if you want to (rather than indenting paragraphs). Do NOT use a paragraph return — do it this way:

　• Highlight the paragraph(s)

　• Go to **Style → Format**.

　• Assign some value to **Space Before**. Good choice: p8

☐ 2. Choose related dingbats for lists. Experiment with drop caps or large numbers.

☐ 3. Use contrast. For example, if the copy is a question/answer format, your question might be in bold/italic, while your answer might be in plain.

☐ 4. You might want to use framed boxes or shaded boxes for contrast. Don't overdo anything.

Checklist – Brochure

☐ plan

☐ sketch

☐ cover has dominant element

☐ cover has compelling head

☐ benefits are clear

☐ all possible readers' questions are answered

☐ call for action is clear

☐ contact information is complete

☐ relevant graphics

☐ clear graphics – no Web art

☐ design principles adhered to

☐ simplicity heeded

☐ uses copybreakers (attention grabbers)

☐ one or two fonts (do they fit the tone of the brochure)

☐ leading is good

☐ copy is easy-to-read

☐ two colors

☐ lists have bullets, hanging indents and "space before"

☐ boxed or shaded copy has text inset

☐ no hyphenated words at ends of lines (unless copy is justified)

☐ no widows

☐ "check spelling" done

☐ mailing panel or response panel done correctly
   (if applicable)

☐ if coupon or return piece is on it, can it be detached easily?

Remember the design principles:

repetition

alignment

proximity

contrast

dominance

To make a brochure with a mailing panel and response panel

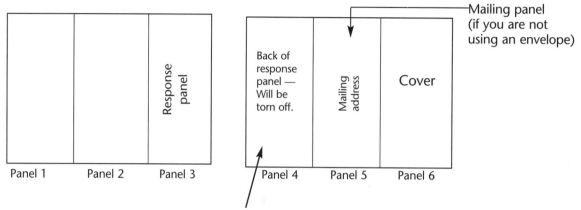

The left panel (panel 4) will be the flipside of the response panel (panel 3). The information on this should be less important and not something the reader needs to keep.

A panel is 17p4 width, 45p height. Therefore, for the mailing and address panels, you will make boxes that measure 45p width, 17p4 height. You will work in them horizontally and then rotate them 90°.

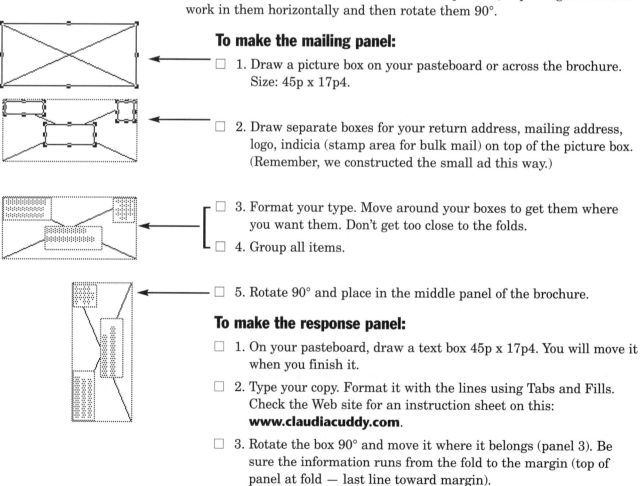

To make the mailing panel:

☐ 1. Draw a picture box on your pasteboard or across the brochure. Size: 45p x 17p4.

☐ 2. Draw separate boxes for your return address, mailing address, logo, indicia (stamp area for bulk mail) on top of the picture box. (Remember, we constructed the small ad this way.)

☐ 3. Format your type. Move around your boxes to get them where you want them. Don't get too close to the folds.

☐ 4. Group all items.

☐ 5. Rotate 90° and place in the middle panel of the brochure.

To make the response panel:

☐ 1. On your pasteboard, draw a text box 45p x 17p4. You will move it when you finish it.

☐ 2. Type your copy. Format it with the lines using Tabs and Fills. Check the Web site for an instruction sheet on this: **www.claudiacuddy.com**.

☐ 3. Rotate the box 90° and move it where it belongs (panel 3). Be sure the information runs from the fold to the margin (top of panel at fold — last line toward margin).

Append style sheets

If you open a new document and want to use the style sheets from another document, you can **append** any or all of the styles.

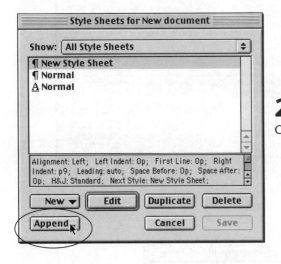

1

Edit → **Style sheets**.

2

Choose **Append**.

3

Navigate to find the file whose style sheets you want! Click on it twice or choose **Open**.

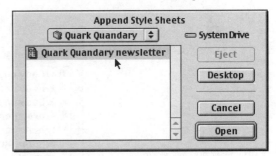

4

1. **Include all** (below, left). All style sheets will move to the right side of the window (below, right). Click **OK**.
   or
2. Select an individual style sheet. Then click the arrow. That single sheet will move to the right. Repeat. Finally, click **OK**.

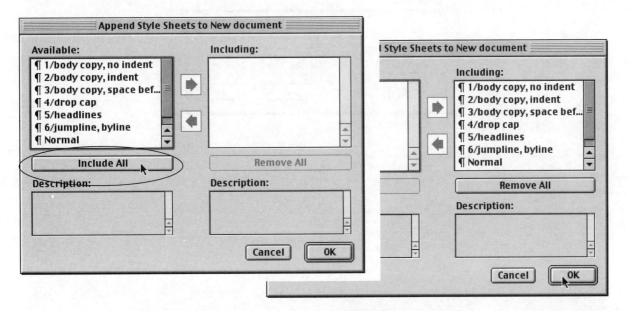

Turn the page...there's more...

5

If a style sheet has the same name as one in the new document, Quark will ask you if you want to rename the old one or use the new one. In most cases, I choose to use the new one — that's why I brought over these style sheets!

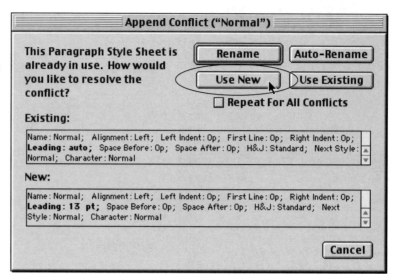

6

Save your new style sheets.

7

Then save your document.

18 Greeting Card

This project introduces a new skill: rotating a group. It's a quick, enjoyable project.

Do it at the end of the semester to thank someone who has influenced your life or meant something special to you. Be sure to mail it!

☐ 1. Find the greeting card template on your CD (*Templates folder: greetingcard.qxt*). Drag it to your disk.

☐ 2. Open greeting card template. Name the document *Yournamecard.qxd*. **Save** it to your disk.

☐ 3. Work in boxes:

    1 = cover – use clipart or photo.

    2 = left inside – can be blank.

    3 = right inside – your message.

    4 = back cover – your name, "company" and date if you want
        (e.g., Sandy's Sentiments © 2003)

Fold a piece of paper to mimic the card. Number the quadrants like below. You will better visualize your result.

quadrants   completed card

Fold here →

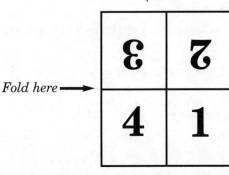

☐ 4. Work in the boxes and when you are finished, **group items** in block 3 and rotate the group 180°. If you put copy in box 2, rotate that copy 180° also.

☐ 5. The blue and green lines are grids. Staying in the green lines will allow you a little more space around the edges so the folds work better.

☐ 6. Print out and make corrections. Fix it until you are happy with it, and then run it out on colored paper or parchment to make a fancier greeting card.

You can buy envelopes for this size card at office supply stores. Look for "Invitation Envelopes" or No. 5½.

The number one error on this project is insufficient leading. So check the leading — the distance between lines of type. Be sure leading is at least 1 or 2 points more than the type size.

leading (left)   type size (right)

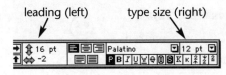

A few extra tips

Importing text from Microsoft Word documents

Click on a text box. Hit ⌘**E** or **File → Get text**. Navigate to find the Word document you want to bring into Quark. Click on it twice or click **Open**. The text will flow into the text box.

Find a layer

Sometimes you have boxes on top of boxes. How do you get to a box that is behind the others? Click on the box. Hold down the three magic keys (⌘ ⌥ ⇧). One layer will show its handles. Click again. Another layer shows its handles. And so on. Use the item or the content tool, depending on what you want to do.

The cursor has a little square attached to it!

The control key on a Mac is stuck. Jiggle the key to get it loose.

Qool Fact

Your feedback will make the second edition better!

E-mail the author through the Web site:

www.claudiacuddy.com

The Nays

No sans serif for body copy

No more than two or three fonts

No reverse copy in large hunks

No double spaces after the period at the end of a sentence

No widows or orphans

No centering more than three lines of type

No auto leading

No positive tracking for body copy

No floating heads

No "all caps"

No underlining using the styles on the measurements bar

No distorting photos

No complaining about computer problems

No quitting

The Yeas (or maybe that should be "Yays")

Read your book before class and be prepared.

Use the index to look up topics.

Be patient — the Quark Quest is methodical and gradual.

Keep a vision of success in your head: You will accomplish more than you ever thought possible.

Share your knowledge and skills with someone else.

19 For Your Bookshelf

Advertising

Fundamentals Of Copy & Layout: Everything You Need to Know to Prepare Better Ads (3rd ed.). Albert C. Book & C. Dennis Schick. McGraw Hill Trade, 1996.

Great Ad! Do-It-Yourself Advertising for Your Small Business. Carol Wilkie Wallace, TAB Books, Summit, PA, 1990.

Words That Sell: The Thesaurus to Help you Promote Your Products, Services, and Ideas. Richard Bayan. McGraw-Hill Trade, 1987.

More Words That Sell. Richard Bayan. McGraw-Hill/Contemporary Books, 2003.

Color

Color Harmony: A Guide to Creative Color Combinations. Hideaki Chijiiwa, Kaiko Nakamura (Translator), Geoffrey Mandel (Editor). Rockport Publishers, Rockport, MA, 1987.

Designing with Color: How the Language of Color Works and How to Manipulate It in Your Graphic Designs. Susan Berry & Judy Martin. North Light Books, Cincinnati, OH, 1991.

Eyes on the News. The Poynter Institute Color Research. Mario R. Garcia & Pegie Stark. (Ed Miller, Editor). The Poynter Institute, St. Petersburg, FL, 1991.

Pantone Guide to Communicating with Color. Leatrice Eiseman. North Light Books, Cincinnati, OH, 2000.

www.color. (It's a book title, not a Web site.) Roger Pring. Watson-Guptill, New York, 2000.

Copyright

Every Writer's Guide to Copyright and Publishing Law. Ellen Kozak. Owlet Books, New York, 1997.

101 Questions about Copyright Law, Revised edition. Andrew Alpern. Dove Publications.

Protecting Your Company's Intellectual Property: A Practical Guide to Trademarks, Copyrights, Patents and Trade Secrets. Deborah Bouchoux. AMACOM, 2001.

The Copyright Permission and Libel Handbook: A Step-by-Step Guide for Writers, Editors, and Publishers. Lloyd Jassin & Steven Schecter. John Wiley & Sons, Hoboken, NJ, 1998.

You can find all of these at Amazon.com. A few of the books are out of print but worth having — you can get them for a good price.

Design and Layout

Basics of Design: Layout and Typography for Beginners. Lisa Graham, Delmar – Thomson Learning, Albany, NY, 2002.

Design Companion for the Digital Artist (Against the Clock series). Valan Evers & Ericka Kendra. Prentice Hall, Upper Saddle River, NJ, 2002.

Design Principles for Desktop Publishers. Tom Lichty. Wadsworth Publishing, Belmont, CA, 1994.

Designing Visual Language: Strategies for Professional Communicators. Charles Rostelnick & David D. Roberts. Allyn & Bacon, Needham Heights, MA, 1998.

Desktop Publishing Style Guide. Sandra Lentz Devall. Delmar Publishers, Albany, NY, 1999.

Graphic Design Cookbook: Mix and Match Recipes for Faster, Better Layouts. Leonard Koren & R. Wippo Meckler. Chronicle Books, San Francisco, 2001.

Graphic Design for 21st Century Desktop Publishers. Marvin Jacobs & Linda I. Studer. Words & Pictures Publishing, North Olmsted, OH, 2002.

Graphic Design School. Alan Swann. John Wiley & Sons, Hoboken, NJ, 1999.

Graphics Master 7: Workbook of Reference Guides & Graphic Tools for the Design, Preparation & Production – Print and Internet Publishing. Dean Phillip Lem. Dean Lem Associates, Kihei, Maui, HI, 2000.

How to Understand and Use Design and Layout. Alan Swann. John Wiley & Sons, Hoboken, NJ, 2003.

How to Understand and Use Grids. Alan Swann. North Light Books, Cincinnati, OH, 1989.

Layout Index. Jim Krause. North Light Books, Cincinnati, OH, 2001.

Looking Good in Print. Roger C. Parker. Coriolis Group, Scottsdale, AZ, 1998.

The Makeover Book. Roger C. Parker. Ventana Press, Chapel Hill, NC, 1989.

The Non-Designer's Design Book. Robin Williams. Peachpit Press, Berkeley, CA, 1994.

Ready-to-use Layouts for Desktop Design. Davie Collier & Kay Floyd. North Light Books, Cincinnati, OH, 1989.

Robin Williams Design Workshop. Robin Wiliams and John Tollett. Peachpit Press, Berkeley, CA, 2001.

Roger C. Parker's One-Minute Designer. Roger C. Parker. MIS Press, New York, 1997.

Some books are to be tasted, others to be swallowed, and some few to be chewed and digested.

Francis Bacon
(Renaissance author)

Dictionaries

The American Heritage Dictionary

Merriam-Webster's Collegiate Dictionary

Webster's New World College Dictionary

Webster's Third New International Dictionary

Which dictionary accompanies which stylebook?
See page 127.

Editing

Creative Editing. Dorothy A. Bowles & Diane L. Borden. Wadsworth, Thomson Learning, Belmont, CA, 2000.

Editing for Clear Communication. Thom Lieb. McGraw-Hill Higher Education, New York, 2002.

Newsletter Design

Editing Your Newsletter – How to Produce an Effective Publication Using Traditional Tools and Computers. Mark Beach. Writer's Digest Books, Cincinnati, OH, 1995.

Newsletter Design: A Step-by-Step Guide to Creative Publications. Edward A. Hamilton. John Wiley & Sons, Hoboken, NJ, 1997.

Newsletters from the Desktop. Roger Parker. Ventana Press, Chapel Hill, NC, 1990.

Newspaper Design

The Newspaper Designer's Handbook, 5th edition. Tim Harrower. McGraw Hill, New York, 2002.

Newspaper Layout and Design: A Team Approach, 4th edition. Don Moen. Iowa State University Press, 2000.

Photos

Phototruth or Photofiction? Ethics and Media Imagery in the Digital Age. Thomas H. Wheeler. Erlbaum Associates, Mahwah, NJ, 2002.

Publications – Printing, Public Relations

Getting It Printed: How to Work With Printers and Graphic Imaging Services to Assure Quality, Stay on Schedule and Control Costs. Mark Beach & Eric Kenly. North Light Books, Cincinnati, OH, 1999.

Print Publishing: A Hayden Shop Manual (An on-the-job reference for graphic designers and prepress operators). Donnie O'Quinn. Hayden Books, Indianapolis, IN, 2000.

Print That Works: The First Step-by-Step Guide that Integrates Writing, Design, and Marketing. Elizabeth W. Adler. Bull Publishing Company, Palo Alto, CA, 1991.

The Public Relations Practitioner's Playbook (A Synergized Approach to Effective Two-way Communication). Larry Litwin. Kendall/Hunt, Dubuque, IA, 2003.

Public Relations Publications: Designing for Target Publics. Linda P. Morton. Sultan Communications Books – Colbert House, 1005 N. Flood, Suite 138, Norman, OK 73069, 2000.

QuarkXPress

Project QuarkXPress 5. Nat Gertler. Delmar – Thomson Learning, Clifton Park, NJ, 2003.

Real World QuarkXPress 5. David Blatner. Peachpit Press, Berkeley, CA, 2002.

QuarkXPress for Windows & Macintosh: Visual Quickstart Guide. Elaine Weinmnan & Peter Lourekas. Peachpit Press, Berkeley, CA, 2002.

QuarkXPress 4.0: A Step-by-Step Approach. Joanne R. Saliger. Morton Publishing Company, Englewood, CO, 2000.

QuarkXPress 5 Bible. Galen Guman & Barbara Assadi with Kelly Anton. Hungry Minds, New York, 2002.

QuarkXPress 5 for Dummies. Barbara Assadi & Galen Gruman. John Wiley & Sons, Hoboken, NJ, 2002.

Stylebooks

The Associated Press Stylebook (AP)

Chicago Manual of Style

Microsoft Manual of Style for Technical Publications

MLA Style Manual (The Modern Language Association of America)

Publication Manual of the American Psychological Association (APA)

Subscription Newsletters

Communication Briefings – ideas that work. Briefings Publishing Group, 1101 King Street, Suite 110, Alexandria, VA 22314, 800-722-9221 **www.combriefings.com**

Design Tools Monthly. (The Executive Summary of Graphic Design News) Jay Nelson, 400 Kiowa, Suite 100, Boulder, CO 80303, 303-543-8400 **www.design-tools.com**

The Editorial Eye (Focusing on publications standards, practices, and trends) EEI Press, 66 Canal Center Plaza, Suite 200, Alexandria, VA 22314-5507, 703-683-0683 **www.eeicommunications.com/eye/**

For information on related graphic and editing associations and Web sites, check out **www.claudiacuddy.com**.

Type

The Complete Manual of Typography. James Felici. Peachpit Press, Berkeley, CA, 2003.

Great Web Typography. Wendy Peck. Wiley Publishing, New York, 2003.

The Mac is Not a Typewriter. Robin Williams. Peachpit Press, Berkeley, CA, 2003.

Stop Stealing Sheep and Find Out How Type Works. Erik Spiekermann & E. M. Ginger. Adobe Press, Berkeley, CA, 2003.

Type & Layout: How Typography and Design Can Get Your Message Across—or Get in the Way. Colin Wheildon. Strathmoor Press, Berkeley, CA, 1995.

The TypEncyclopedia: A User's Guide to Better Typography. Frank J. Romano. R. R. Bowker Company, New York, 1984.

Typesense: Making Sense of Type on the Computer. Susan G. Wheeler & Gary S. Wheeler, Prentice Hall, Upper Saddle River, NJ, 2001.

Word Usage

The Careful Writer: A Modern Guide to English Usage. Theodore M. Bernstein. Free Press, 1995.

The Goof Proofer/How to Avoid the 41 Most Embarrassing Errors in your Speaking and Writing. Steven Manhard, 1999.

Grammar Gremlins. Don Ferguson & Patricia Hobbs. Glenbridge Pub. Ltd., 1995.

Lapsing into a Comma. Bill Walsh. Contemporary Books, Chicago, 2000.

A Treasury for Word Lovers. Morton S. Freeman. Philadelphia: ISI Press, 1983.

Word Court. Barbara Wallraff. Harcourt, Inc., New York, 2000.

The Wordwatcher's Guide to Good Writing and Grammar. Morton S. Freeman. Writer's Digest Books, Cincinnati, OH, 1990.

Writing Style and Instructional

The Art of Clear Thinking/The Art of Readable Writing/ How to Write Plain English/How to Write, Speak, and Think More Effectively. (All four by Rudolph Flesch).

Copywriting for the Electronic Media with Infotrac: A Practical Guide. Milan D. Meeske. Wadsworth, Belmont, CA, 2002.

The Elements of Style. William Strunk, Jr. & E. B. White. Allyn & Bacon, 2000.

How to Write for Magazines: Consumers, Trade and Web. Charles H. Harrison. Allyn and Bacon, Boston, MA, 2002.

On Writing Well: The Classic Guide to Writing Nonfiction. William K. Zinsser. Harper Resource, 2001.

How do you choose the right book?

Follow your instinct. Look through the book. If it appeals to you, it's for you. If you look at it and think, "Ugh. How boring," then you probably won't be using it much, and it will sit on your shelf.

You DO "judge a book by its cover" (and insides) with good reason: the graphic presentation needs to make the book easy for you to approach.

Painless, Perfect Grammar: Tips from the Grammar Hotline.
Michael Strumpf. & Auriel Douglas. Bandanna Books,
Santa Barbara, CA, 1997.

Rewrite Right! Your guide to perfect and polished prose. Jan Venolia &
Ellen Sasaki. Ten Speed Press, Berkeley, CA, 2000.

STET! Tricks of the Trade for Writers and Editors. Bruce O. Boston
(Editor). Editorial Experts, Inc., Alexandria, VA, 1986.

Style: Ten Lessons in Clarity and Grace. Joseph M. Williams. Longman,
New York, 2002.

Words into Type. Marjorie Skillin & Robert M. Gay. Prentice Hall,
Englewood Cliffs, NJ, 1974. *Word Court.* Barbara Wallraff. Harcourt,
Inc., Orlando, FL, 2000.

Write to the Point and Feel Better about Your Writing. Bill Stott.
Columbia University Press, New York, 1991.

Write to the Point! Letters, Memos, & Reports that Get Results. By
Rosemary T. Rruehling and N.B. Oldham. McGraw-Hill Book
Company, 1992.

Quest Terms

A

absolute leading – a set value for leading; leading remains consistent. Opposite of auto leading.

abstract – a short summary of the article.

access information – information provided on a business card. Includes your name, position, name of company, address, phone number, fax number, e-mail address and Web address.

advocacy – a type of newsletter that focuses on a single topic and claims to be unapologetically biased. Often published by a corporation, an association or a politician. Differs from other newsletters by its strong point of view.

alignment – position of the text in the text box, horizontally side-to-side or vertically top-to-bottom.

alignment of items – items match up along their top, bottom, left or right edges. Creates a visual connection between items, leading to unity on the page.

all caps – all capital letters. Words in all caps have no instant word recognition and must be deciphered letter by letter. Relates to a theory stating that people learn to read by combining uppercase and lowercase letters and recognizing the configurations as sight words.

append style sheets – to open a new document and use the style sheets from another document. You can append any or all of the styles.

article – typed copy after layout begins. An accepted manuscript that has been edited and sent to the art department for layout. Before it is called an article, it is referred to as a manuscript.

ascender – the part of a lowercase character that extends above the x-height.

association newsletter – a type of newsletter published to maintain enthusiasm and communication among existing members and supporters of an organization. Usually sent as a benefit of membership and funded by membership dues. Articles cover members' achievements, past and upcoming association events and related up-to-date discoveries or information germane to the specialty of the members.

auto image runaround – allows text around a picture box to flow directly around a piece of art, going along the shape of the art.

auto leading – the automatic leading setting in QuarkXPress. Automatically adjusts for the largest point size in a paragraph. Opposite of absolute leading.

B

background color – the color displayed behind an object or the main characters in a picture.

balance – items mirror each other, top to bottom or left to right (formal) or items on each side of an imaginary center line differ in weight, size or placement (informal).

barrier rule – a line used to separate items on a page. A common place for the barrier rule is under the nameplate of a newsletter to separate it from the heads and body copy.

based on – an essential direction that tells a style sheet to base itself on another style.

baseline – the imaginary line that the x-height part of the letters sit on.

biosketch – a short summary (sketch) of the author's credentials; usually one or two sentences when used in a publication; can be longer if in a program book (e.g., keynote speaker's biosketch).

bleed – solid color or image extending to the edge of the page.

blend – a gradient fill. The transition from one color or shade to another.

blueline – the final proof from the printer that shows exact color breaks in varying shades of blue on white paper. This stage is being replaced by a final set of page proofs run in color.

body copy – the main text. The text of the articles.

body type – the font used for the main text.

book – "shop talk" for magazine.

break of book – what goes where. The allocation of space for articles, features, departments and all materials printed in the magazine.

brochure – a simple publication, usually one sheet of paper and folded, used for distribution or mailing.

bullet – a varying size mark (usually an arrow or dot) used to highlight a list item. Is indented from the other copy.

bulleted list – a list that is organized by using a symbol, setting a hanging indent and setting additional space above each item.

business cards – provide access information. Often parallel the corporate identity of a firm or organization by using the same logo, ink color and typestyle as the firm's other publications.

byline – the printed name of the author at the start or end of an article.

call to action – one of the five elements of a brochure. To specifically ask for an order or action in your brochure. Should be clear and prominent.

calling cards – little cards once used by members of high society to announce a desired visit with someone. Developed into modern business cards by the 1900s.

callout – a word or phrase used to identify an element in an illustration, usually linked to the element by a straight line or arrow.

captions – the lines of text that explain a photograph or artwork. Usually found below or on the side of the picture and set in a contrasting type that is smaller than body copy.

channel – medium through which a message is to be sent.

chunking – breaking up long body copy.

chunks of information – copy presented in short segments.

city fonts – monospaced fonts created for use on early dot matrix printers, e.g., Chicago. These can look good on the screen but they are not good for print.

classes of type – general groups of fonts: serif, sans serif, script and novelty.

clean up widows – to remove widows highlight the entire paragraph and then change tracking. The range should be from 0 to –5.

clipart – illustrations, pictures and designs that can be bought on a CD or copied from Web sites.

constituency newsletter– a type of newsletter that communicates with a common interest group to influence its readership and foster a sense of community. i.e. a local hospital health care newsletter or a university alumni newsletter. Sent to a limited target audience and occasionally requests donations.

CMYK – the color-code used in a four-color printing process. Cyan (blue), magenta (reddish-pink), yellow and black are the four inks used to make all full color prints.

collect for output – the process of collecting art files and fonts used for a specific document. Everything for one file is in the same folder, and you can print your document from another location.

color mood – enables you to choose color based on the tone of your publication and convey the appropriate emotional message, e.g., green = refreshing, orange = happy, red = active, etc.

column – the vertical spaces on a page to place text boxes within.

comfort level – readers feel comfortable with material written two or three levels below their actual reading level.

communication mix – repetition and consistency in the publications; can include a company's letterhead, brochure, business card, newsletter, flier – whatever pieces they use for identity or for a specific campaign.

communication model – a theory that explains the foundation of all communication. Includes sender, receiver, message, channel, feedback and noise.

configuration – the shape of words based on the combination of uppercase and lowercase letters. When learning to read, people recognize words by their configurations – those words are called "sight" words.

contents page – the page that lists articles, features and departments and their locations in the book.

continuation line – helps readers locate the continuation of an article from a previous page.

contrast – using design aspects of different sizes, shades, colors and shapes in a publication to keep the reader's attention.

copy – typewritten information to be used within a publication or layout design.

copyediting – checking all grammar, spelling, punctuation, sentence structure and style within a publication. Can be heavy (some rewriting involved) or light (more on the side of proofreading).

copybreaker – the different elements that break copy on a page of text (subheads, rules, pullquotes, pictures, illustrations, captions, shaded boxes, sidebars, large initial caps, drop caps, etc.)

corporate internal newsletter – a type of newsletter circulated throughout the staff of a company, organization or faculty to promote goodwill, teamwork and a sense of pride. Focuses on the achievements, goals and even personal lives of employees. Often published in-house and photocopied.

corporate external – a type of newsletter that builds external support for a company or organization. Serves as a continual reminder to customers that a company's services are available and promotes new products and new services.

counter – the inside white space of a letter, e.g., the middle of an "o."

cover – the four pages that make up the outside wrap of the magazine. Referred to as cover 1, cover 2, cover 3 and cover 4.

credit line – appears with the explanation of a photo or illustration and gives credit to the photographer or artist.

cropping – getting rid of unwanted parts of a photo or image.

Cuddy's seesaw – the relationship between design and the interest of the reader. The design must be stronger if the reader's interest is low. If the reader's interest is high, the design of the publication has less impact on the reader.

cyan – the bluish color ink used in the four-color process (cyan, magenta, yellow and black).

D

dateline – contains the month and year or the season and year of a newsletter. Usually found in the nameplate of a newsletter.

descender – the part of a letter that descends below the baseline.

design – each aspect of the page complementing the others to present a clear message. These aspects include pictures, type size, font, headlines, graphics, alignment, etc.

dialog box – a small pop up box that has options to choose or blanks to fill in.

dingbat – a bullet or symbol used as an end sign.

discretionary hyphen – used to correct wide spaces between words in a line of type by hyphenating the first word in the next line of type. If you edit later, and the word pieces can rejoin, they will do so without the hyphen.

display type – type that is 16 points or larger and is mainly used for headlines. Attracts the attention of the reader.

dollar bill test – lay a dollar bill in various places on your page of text. It should touch a copybreaker in all cases.

dominance – an element on a page that catches the reader's eye and stands out from the other elements.

dominant photo – the largest photo on a page that attracts the reader's attention.

doorhanger – a flier distributed in a neighborhood canvassing campaign.

downstyle – a headline type where the first letter is capitalized and all others are lowercase.

dpi – dots per inch; a digital photo specification.

drop cap – a large initial capital that drops down a few lines into the text.

drop shadow – creates a three-dimensional effect through the placement of a shaded box offset below a text or picture box.

dummy – mockup simulating the final product.

E

editing – making changes to a work in progress to improve the quality of communication.

editorial matter – all copy, other than advertising, in a magazine or newspaper. Includes photos, art and text.

editorial/advertising ratio or mix – the distribution ratio of photos, art and text to advertising space in a magazine or newspaper, e.g., 65:35 denotes 65% editorial and 35% advertising.

emphasis – elements contrast to other elements on the page in greater or lesser degrees. *See* dominance.

endsign – a small symbol that marks the end of the copy or article.

EPS – encapsulated PostScript format; a high quality art file.

eye direction – the path that a reader's eye follows naturally over a page. This can be controlled and guided by the publication's design.

F

feedback – the resulting behavior of the receiver that lets the sender know the message was received.

filler – a house ad used to fill extra space on a page.

5 C's – the five components of the magazine environment include cover (identity), content (the essence of the magazine), consistency of design (supports the identity of the magazine), collaboration (with workers, author and audience) and calendar (schedule).

flier – a one-sided publication that presents a single message.

floating heads – headlines not attached to any other element.

flush left – when all copy lines up with the left margin on a page.

flush right – when all copy lines up with the right margin on a page.

folio – the page number. Can be expanded to include other elements near the page number.

font – choice of a typeface; a specific set of characters that have the same look and design. Font is used interchangeably with typeface.

footer – the type located at the very bottom of all inside pages. Can include chapter title, newsletter title, page number, a rule or a dingbat.

four-color process – printing a document in full color. Each color is printed separately on the paper: cyan, magenta, yellow and black.

frame – a specific marked area that surrounds text or an image; also called a border.

French fold – a type of greeting card fold.

free-floating boxes – text and picture boxes with edges not touching a vertical grid.

full to empty – the steps for linking text boxes. Paste the type into the first column, and then use the linking tool. Click on the full column, then click on the empty column.

G

graphic design – creating complementary type and visuals on a page to present a message or portray an image or an identity.

graphic noise – type problems (i.e. too many fonts) and layout and production problems (i.e., poor photo quality) that interfere with the message. Of special concern to layout professionals.

gray page – a publication that does not use copybreakers and will not catch the reader's attention. Page is text-intensive (a lot of text on page).

grayscale – a specification for a scanned photo. The photo is scanned in shades of gray and broken down into a series of dots.

grid – the lines that divide the page into segments.

grip 'n' grin – a photo in which two people are shaking hands and smiling; term is used generically to mean any of the standard posed photos taken of award winners, organization officers and so forth.

Gunning Fog Index – a readability formula created by Robert Gunning that approximates the grade level at which a person must read to understand the material in a publication.

gutter – the white space left between columns of type.

H

hairline – the thinnest line that can be made within a font.

halftone – image broken down into a series of dots; a photo scanned as grayscale.

handbill – a flier distributed by hand.

hanging indent – an indentation usually used to line up the first letter of text on bulleted lists.

headshot – a picture taken of a person's shoulders and above.

header – element or elements repeated at the top of each page. Can include chapter title, newsletter title, date, page number, a rule or a dingbat.

headlines (heads) –the titles of articles in a newspaper or newsletter. Usually in bold and often in a sans serif font.

house ad – an advertisement by the publication for the publication it appears in. Or by the organization who sponsors the publication. Can be made ahead of time and used as a filler for empty space in the publication.

I

illustration – an original drawing, done by hand or on the computer.

imposition – the arrangement of pages that will appear in proper sequence after press sheets are folded and bound. Varies according to number of pages, sheet size, printing technique and binding method.

indicia – the postage stamp area of a newsletter.

in-house – all publishing tasks are done in the company, e.g., a staff newsletter published and photocopied within the company to cut down on expensive printing costs.

inkjet printer – a printer that creates documents by placing tiny dots together on a page to form all characters, pictures, texts and images. (Compare to laser printer.)

item runaround – the text around a picture is set around the borders of the picture box.

J

JPEG (joint photographic experts group) – a digital photo format (appears as *filename.jpg*). To be used when saving files for use on the Web or to be sent by e-mail (smaller file size than tiff).

jumphead – a shortened version of the original head found on the continued page of an article.

jumpline – tells you where the rest of a story is continued when it can't fit on the page.

justified – horizontal alignment of copy from side to side.

K

kicker – a small headline above the main headline. A rule (line) is usually under the kicker.

K.I.S.S. – keep it simple, student. Use restraint. Blend contrast, alignment, proximity, repetition and dominance together. Have a purpose for each element you use.

L

laser printer – a printer that operates on an electrophotographic process. The image is created digitally by a laser beam. Compare to inkjet printer.

layout – the overall plan of a publication and how the publisher carries it out. Identifies the location of all elements on the page.

leading – the space between lines of type. For body copy, use 1–2 points of leading.

legibility – the clarity of the physical aspect of the publication.

letterhead – the paper stationery on which someone types, prints or writes a letter. Contains name, address, phone and fax numbers, e-mail, logo, business motto and message area. Sometimes, officer or board member listings.

library – a QuarkXPress palette that stores frequently used items or groups of items that are dragged from the library into the layout as you need them.

life expectancy – varies in a brochure according to purpose. Five years is the high end and one year is common for sales brochures.

linking – the linking tool looks like a chain link. Used for linking text boxes.

logo – provides immediate visual identification of a product. A symbol identifying a publication; found on the cover, masthead and anywhere else.

lowercase – words in all small letters; the small version of letters in the alphabet.

Macintosh™ (Mac) – a computer made by Apple™ that runs on an Apple operating system.

mailer – a flier distributed by mail.

mailing area – required on a self-mailer newsletter. Takes up one-third or one-half of the page. Post offices prefer the mailing label at the top of the page.

manuscript – typed copy before layout begins. The magazine accepts, accepts with revisions or rejects a manuscript. After editorial work is done on the accepted manuscript, it is sent to the art department for layout (it then becomes an article).

margin – the white space left on the outer edges of the page.

marquee – highlighted or activated items similar to a neon sign. A marquee in QuarkXPress is indicated by a dashed line that disappears when the mouse is unclicked.

master page – page that governs other pages in your document. Whatever you put on this page appears on other pages in the document. Saves you the time of adding borders, adjusting column placement and setting margins for each page. Allows you to use automatic page numbering.

masthead – includes the names of a magazine or newsletter's editorial staff, the publisher's address, copyright information, subscription rates, phone and fax numbers and e-mail. Often found on page 2 or on the back of the newsletter as part of the mailing area.

message – what is to be communicated.

message area – the most important part of a letter. Requires sufficient space.

milieu – an environment or setting.

mission statement (subtitle) – states the editorial focus, purpose of newsletter or target audience.

monospaced – each letter occupies the same lateral space, whether it's an "m" or an "i." Appears in city fonts such as New York, Chicago, etc., which look as if they were produced on a typewriter. Opposite of typesetting mode.

nameplate – includes the newsletter's title, subtitle or mission statement, volume and issue, date of publication, logo. Covers about one-fifth of the page. Can run at the top of the page or down the side.

newsletter – a publication used to give current information to a specific audience. Can be in various sizes (commonly in 8½ x 11), has a centerfold and is usually greater than one typed page. One-page newsletters have become a marketing tool as have Web newsletters.

noise – anything that interferes with the message. Can be too many pictures, many different types of fonts, etc.

novelty – a type of font that does not fit into the categories of serif, sans serif or script (cursive). Only use when it matches the tone of the publication.

number pad – a grouping of numbers that look like a calculator on the right side of a keyboard. The number pad contrasts to the keyboard numbers, which are found above the letters on the keyboard.

1-2-2 pattern – one type of a page grid. The page is split into five total columns. The left column stands alone. Typed copy stretches across 2 columns, then 2 columns again.

orphan – one line of type at the end of a column or page that begins the next paragraph.

outset – the outside edges of an object. When you choose auto image runaround, you need to type in a number for points of outset.

overlapped text boxes – text boxes overlap with no loss of text if a runaround of **none** is applied.

page layout – arranging the type and elements on a page.

page orientation – the arrangement of any rectangular page. Portrait pages are tall and narrow; landscape pages are short and wide.

page proof stage or page proofs – one of the final stages of correcting errors in a document before printing; very important proofreading is done at this stage. Used to be called blueline.

page setup – using the New Document dialog box in QuarkXPress to choose page size, orientation, margins, number of columns and gutter width.

pagination – the numbering of the pages of a book, newspaper or periodical. In newspaper layout, pagination refers to the actual layout of the pages. The person who does this work would be called a paginator.

panel – folded area of a brochure used to separate a theme or idea.

Pantone Matching System™ – a worldwide standard system of choosing a color from a swatch book to be matched by the printer. Will give the desired color on any print job.

parallel fold – fold parallel to the edge of the paper.

perfect binding – a book bound by glue rather than sewn in or stapled pages.

periodical – magazines, newsletters and journals. A publication with issues appearing on a regular schedule, i.e. every week or month. Not used for newspapers or yearbooks.

personal computer (PC) – a self-contained desktop computer with a Windows™ operating system. Can run applications compatible with MS-DOS and PC-DOS systems.

photofiction – a photo that is fabricated and has obviously been manipulated.

Photoshop ™ – production tool developed by Adobe™ that can allow the operator to create original artwork, retouch photos, etc.

picas – the basic unit of measurement in the graphics field. Six are equal to one inch. Used to measure parts of a document.

pithy pullquote – a pullquote that is forceful, brief, to the point and full of substance or meaning.

pipeline – the system through which the article goes from the receipt of the manuscript to the publication of the article in a magazine.

plan – the way you intend to set-up a publication. Must answer the seven questions (on page 5) to start a project. Focus on the audience the publication is trying to reach and the purpose of the publication.

point – the smallest unit of measurement in the graphics field. 12 points are equal to one pica, and 72 points equal one inch.

point of entry – the place in which a person's eye enters a page and begins looking at the elements of a page.

point size – the measurement to express type height. For example, 12-point type measures 12 points from the ascender to the descender.

poster – a flier posted on a bulletin board.

proofreader's marks – symbols indicating changes and corrections to be made on a final hard copy proof before printing, e.g., print in boldface, indent, align left, spell out or check spelling, move to next line.

proofreading – correcting an almost-finished work.

proximity – the distance between lines of type and things on a page. Keep related information close together.

publication – body of information distributed to others. Can take many forms such as flier, newsletter, brochure, etc.

pullquote – sentence or phrase taken out of the body copy and set in a larger, bolder type.

Q

qool fact – Cuddy's substitution for cool fact.

quadrant format – an outdated business card format that violates proximity by placing the name and position in the center and the other information in all four corners.

quandary – dilemma, uncertainty, perplexity.

quantum leap – significant advance in method, information or knowledge.

QuarkXPress™ – a computer program used to process type and design page layout. Allows the user to create high-quality publications. Often referred to as the "industry standard" for publishing.

quest – pursuit or search.

quintessential – being the most typical, the purest, of the essence.

Quarkomaniac – you, after completing this course and falling in love with QuarkXPress. This is a complimentary term!

R

readability – how easy it is for a reader to understand the message

reading Z – a theory of eye direction. The eye is drawn to the upper left quadrant and follows a Z pattern across the page.

receiver – a person, group or organization who is supposed to receive the message of the sender.

registration – occurs when the printed color of one pass through the printer lines up perfectly with another one. Incorrect registration causes blurriness.

relevance – all the items on a page must have a purpose and relationship to each other.

repetition – keeping the same elements consistent within a document and throughout the entire publication.

response area – the last element of a small ad. Includes the contact information (address, phone number, Web site, e-mail, logo, etc.)

response panel – one panel of a brochure to be torn off and mailed back to the sender. Some brochures lack a response panel to encourage readers to register for events online or to call.

reverse type – white type on a dark background.

RGB colors – a color model that stands for red, green and blue. Used by monitors, scanners, TVs and projectors.

rule of three – people connect things in groups of three. In publications, the rule of three applies to the three elements: head, graphic and copy.

rules – lines that break up copy and text.

runaround – the way that text is positioned around a picture. Some types of runaround are item, auto image, none, etc.

saddle stitch (saddle wire) – a binding in which staples are driven through the middle fold of the pages. Pages are opened over a saddle-shaped support and stitched through the back.

sans serif – a type of font that is clean and crisp. Letters do not have serifs (the short lines at the top and bottom of letters).

scanning – the process of capturing a physical image or picture as a whole.

script (cursive) – a type of font with individual letters that appear attached. Difficult to read in large blocks.

second color – the spot color in a two-color job (spot color plus black).

self-cover – a cover printed on the same paper as the rest of the magazine.

sender – a person, group or organization with a message to send.

series of brochures – several brochures, distributed in sequence, focusing on an organization, event, etc. Consistent in logo, type and color and must be recognizable by the recipient.

serif – a type of font that has small strokes on the top and bottom of each letter.

shade – (also called tint or screen) term used when you want to lighten the color used, e.g., 20% black is a light shade of gray.

Sherlock – the Find dialog box on Macs used to locate lost files.

sidebar – a story on the side of the page that complements and provides added detail or perspective to topics discussed in the feature articles, but is separate. Usually boxed or shaded.

signature – a printed sheet folded at least once, possible many times, to become part of a book, magazine or other publication. Always contains pages in increments of four, i.e. 4, 8, 12, 16, 24 or 32 pages.

sink – a band of white space appearing at the top of the page.

sizing – making a picture larger or smaller to suit the space.

sketch – a plan of where items will be placed on your page. A rough idea of the things you hope to include in a publication.

small ad (space ad) – advertisements printed in purchased space in a publication. Can be placed anywhere on the page and is separate from the other elements on the page. Sizes include $\frac{1}{2}$, $\frac{1}{3}$, $\frac{1}{4}$, $\frac{1}{6}$ or $\frac{1}{8}$ of the page.

soft return – used to replace hyphenations and fix ugly lines in a pullquote. Press **shift-return**. Keeps lines in the same paragraph for style sheet purposes.

space ad – *See* small ad.

space before/after – method in QuarkXPress of putting extra space above or below typed copy. Used for lists among other things. Found in the menu: Style → formats.

spell check (check spelling) – computer spelling checker that can ignore words misspelled in context, e.g., sea instead of see. If you use certain words repeatedly in your publications, and they appear in spell check, add them to spell check's dictionary.

spot color – extra color used on elements as highlights. Also a way of adding color to a publication.

standing head (department head) – the head used on a regular basis for a regular feature of a newsletter.

stationery package – a letterhead, business card and envelope.

style sheet – used to apply formatting to the copy.

stylebook – a particular guide used by organizations and publishing houses to achieve uniformity and consistency in manuscript preparation as well as usage and writing.

styles – many ways to manipulate a font, e.g., plain, bold, italic, capitals, underline, etc.

subheads – help to categorize and break up topics in the body copy. Usually bolder and two points larger than body copy.

subscription newsletter – a type of newsletter that includes specialized information not found anywhere else. Subscribers pay to receive current information in their specialty and quality information presented in easy-to-read articles. Does not include advertising and therefore sets higher subscription rates than journals or magazines.

subtitle – *See* mission statement.

summary deck – introduces a story, adds to the head and leads into the article. Located a line or two below the headline and usually set in italics or larger type than body copy.

T

table of contents – list of articles, features, departments, etc. in the publication. Acts as a teaser to entice readers inside a newsletter.

template – a document pattern that can be used repeatedly. The QuarkXPress template icon looks faded compared to a document icon.

10-foot rule – a guideline for fliers. If it is not interesting or identifiable from 10 feet away, then the dominant graphic or headline is not bold or large enough.

testimonials – statements from people who support a product, service or event.

text – all the type on a page.

text inset – moving the text away from the edges of a box.

30–3–30 rule of readership – three types of readers. The 30-second reader (a person who just flips pages), the 3-minute reader (a person who skims the pages) and the 30-minute reader (a person who reads in-depth).

three-color job – printer's reference to a publication using three spot colors. Usually black is one of the colors.

thumbnails – small sketches of a page.

thumb test – hold a business card and notice that your thumb covers a little part of the card; a card passes the test when your thumb (and finger underneath) can hold the card and not touch copy or a graphic.

TIFF (tagged image file format) – a digital photo format (*filename.tif*). To be used when saving art and scanned files for a publication.

tracking – the space between letters.

two-color job – printer's reference to a publication using two spot colors. Usually black is one of the colors.

2-2 pattern – one type of a page grid. The page is split into four total columns. Typed copy is formatted into single columns but the articles stretch across 2 columns. Heads stretch across 2 columns.

type specs (specifications) – describe the type in terms of font, size, leading, column width, alignment and any other type directions.

type styles – ways to stylize a font: plain, bold, italic, underline, strike-through, outline, shadow, capitals, small capitals, superscript, subscript and superior.

typeface (font) – a specific set of characters that have the same look and design.

typesetting mode – built-in kerning between pairs of letters that make the letters fit together in computer fonts.

U

upper third rule – a theory that states that the top third of a page (or layout area) carries the most weight in attracting the reader.

uppercase – words in all capital letters.

upstyle – headline type in which the first letter of each word is capitalized (except for prepositions and articles).

visual – a photo, clipart, graph, table or chart. A related photo or piece of clipart in a small ad.

visual connection – created by the alignment of items on the page.

Visual Magnetism Index – the test of flier effectiveness from Linda Morton's *Public Relations Publications*. Asks subjects to note what they notice first, second and third in a flier 10 feet away.

watermark – shaded art (usually shaded to 20%) that can be seen through the type.

widow – a single word or short phrase that sits alone at the end of a paragraph or at the top of a column.

Word™ – word processing and publishing program.

word spacing – the space between each word.

white space – empty space. Effective for layout.

x-height – the height of the letter "x" in a font; the height of any letter without ascenders and descenders. X is used because it has no ascenders or descenders and sits directly on the baseline.

yellow – one of the four colors in the four-color process. CMYK is cyan, magenta, yellow and black.

yellow pages – business directory in a phone book or on the Web where small ads appear.

zap it back! – expression used in this book to mean undo; key command is ⌘ **Z** (command-Z for Macs or control-Z for Windows).

Clipart Index

Larry's Clipart

Larry's sense of humor pervades these sketches. Because they are done in grayscale, you can lighten or darken them in Photoshop. You can even change them to bitmap if you prefer a smaller file.

Larry Gilbert is a 2003 graduate of Rowan University's public relations program. Many of his other illustrations have appeared in the university's **Venue** *magazine.*

2020monitor.tif

bearfoodtree.tif

bucketdesign.tif

citysketch.tif

clothrhino.tif

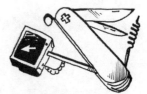

compknife.tif

cowboy.tif

crabtango.tif

dogopus.tif

dragon.tif

friendlycastle.tif

getinspired.tif

hypnoflamingo.tif

kittie.tif

Larry's Clipart

lizardzag.tif

metroparatrooper.tif

mooooon.tif

mouseantics.tif

nessie.tif

pipewhale.tif

plant.tif

redundantanteater.tif

snake.tif

stack.tif

surrealbowl.tif

utterlymeaningless.tif

veryhungrykitty.tif

webbedelephant.tif

worstcasescenario.tif

Regina's Clipart

Regina Marmon's artistic talent shows in her computer-generated art. Regina designed these pieces in Adobe Illustrator on her PC. (She is also proficient on the Mac). She graduated from Rowan University with a major in graphic design.

apple.tif

asparagus.tif

banana.tif

broccoli.tif

carrot.tif

celery.tif

cherry.tif

eggplant.tif

grapes.tif

lettuce.tif

orangeslice.tif

peach.tif

peas.tif

pepper.tif

Regina's Clipart

cucumber.tif

pineapple.tif

strawberry.tif

watermelon.tif

sandwich.tif

pizza.tif

pretzel.tif

What's your opinion?
Which direction should
the pretzel go?
Knobs up or knobs down?
www.claudiacuddy.com

nest.tif

daphnia.tif

eagle.tif

fish.tif

womansface.tif

plane.tif

computer.tif

Sonny's Clipart

Sonny Johnson is a college student with creative, artistic talent. We told Sonny, "Think random." And that's what he did! The next few pages contain random objects scanned as lineart.

alarmclock.tif

angel.tif

artistpalette.tif

baby.tif

barbecuegrill.tif

bike.tif

birdbath.tif

birdhouse.tif

bowl.tif

broom.tif

cake.tif

camera.tif

candycane1.tif

candycane2.tif

car1.tif

car2.tif

car3.tif

cat1.tif

cat2.tif

cat3.tif

chair.tif

cheese.tif

cowboyboot.tif

cowboyhat.tif

design1.tif

design2.tif

devil.tif

dinnerware.tif

dogandbone.tif

door.tif

easel.tif

elf.tif

eyeball.tif

face1.tif

Sonny's Clipart

face2.tif

face3.tif

face4.tif

face5.tif

flag.tif

flipflops.tif

flower1.tif

flower2.tif

flower3.tif

flower4.tif

flower5.tif

flower6.tif

flower7.tif

foot.tif

frame.tif

fruitapple.tif

fruitbananas.tif

fruitcherries.tif

fruitorange.tif

fruitstrawberries.tif

garage.tif

gaspump.tif

girl.tif

graduation1.tif

graduation2.tif

grandfatherclock.tif

grass.tif

guitar.tif

gun.tif

hand.tif

harmonica.tif

hotdog.tif

icecreamcone.tif

island.tif

jug.tif

lamp1.tif

Sonny's Clipart

lamp2.tif

leaf.tif

lightbulb.tif

manhappy.tif

maninahurry.tif

maninchair.tif

marker.tif

microwave.tif

music1.tif

music2.tif

necktie.tif

oven.tif

paint.tif

pants.tif

phone1.tif

phone2.tif

photoalbum.tif

photoframe.tif

picketfence.tif

pie.tif

piepiece.tif

pizza.tif

rabbit.tif

radio.tif

raincloud.tif

raindrops.tif

rocks.tif

rope.tif

saddle.tif

shedandmower.tif

snake.tif

snowman.tif

stopsign.tif

sun1.tif

sun2.tif

swingset.tif

Sonny's Clipart

table.tif

targetandarrow.tif

teapot.tif

television.tif

tennisracket.tif

tictactoe.tif

toilet.tif

tools1.tif

tools2.tif

tools3.tif

tools4.tif

tools5.tif

tools6.tif

toothbrushpaste.tif

trafficlight.tif

trashcan.tif

tree.tif

truck.tif

treehouse.tif

turtle.tif

vegcarrot.tif

vegpeppers.tif

vegtomato.tif

window.tif

windy.tif

wordbegin.tif

wordcool.tif

wordgo.tif

wordpow.tif

wordstop.tif

Communicating With QuarkXPress

Kari's Clipart

Kari Palmieri will graduate with a degree in graphic design in 2004. She created the icons used in the book and added some odds and ends, which you see here.

arrow.tif

baby.tif

hula.tif

parrot.tif

pet.tif

cathedral.tif

Photos

computerwreath

flakyshopper

Jackinthehat

kayakbaby

SanFran

santaandflamingos

These photos are in color and grayscale on the CD.

Skills Index

Topic Index

The formula for
success is a few
simple disciplines
practiced every day.

Jim Rohn
Business philosopher

CD Index

I hear and I forget.
I see and I remember.
I do and I understand.

Confucius